ALEXANDER
DOLGUN'S
STORY

ALEXANDER DOLGUN'S STORY

An American in the Gulag

by

ALEXANDER DOLGUN

with PATRICK WATSON

Alfred A. Knopf   New York   1975

Grateful acknowledgment is made to the following for
permission to reprint previously published song lyrics:

Barton Music Corp. and Edward Traubner & Co., Inc.: For three
lines of lyrics from "Saturday Night Is the Loneliest Night
of the Week" by Sammy Cahn and Jule Styne. Used by permission.

Drake Activities Corp., Al Hoffman Songs, Inc., Hallmark Music
Co., Inc., and Miller Music Co.: For nine lines of lyrics from
"Mairzy Doats" by Milton Drake, Al Hoffman, and
Jimmy Livingston. Copyright 1943 Miller Music Corp.
Renewed 1971. All rights reserved. Used by permission.

Leo Feist, Inc.: For four lines of lyrics from "Chattanooga Choo
Choo," words and music by Mack Gordon and Harry Warren.
Copyright © 1941, renewed 1969 by Twentieth Century Music
Corporation, New York, N.Y. Rights throughout the world
controlled by Leo Feist, Inc., New York, N.Y. Used by permission.

Shapiro, Bernstein & Co., Inc.: For three lines of lyrics from "As the
Caissons Go Rolling Along" by Edmund L. Gruber. Copyright
1921 by Philip Egner and Frederick C. Mayer. Copyright assigned
to Edmund L. Gruber, Copyright assigned to Shapiro, Bernstein
& Co., Inc. Copyright 1936 by Shapiro, Bernstein & Co., Inc.,
New York, N.Y. Copyright renewed. All rights reserved.
Used by permission. For seven lines of lyrics from "Beer Barrel
Polka" ("Roll Out the Barrel") by Lew Brown, Vladimir A. Timm,
Vasek Zeman, and Jaromir Vejvoda. "Skoda Lasky" (original
European title) Copyright 1936 by Jana Hoffmanna, vva. Assigned
to Shapiro, Bernstein & Co., Inc. Copyright renewed © 1961 and
assigned to Shapiro, Bernstein & Co., Inc. Copyright 1939 by
Shapiro, Bernstein & Co., Inc. Copyright renewed.
All rights reserved. Used by permission.

Warner Bros. Music and Chappell and Co. Ltd.: For eight lines of
lyrics from "Don't Fence Me In" by Cole Porter,
from the film *Hollywood Canteen*.
Copyright © 1944 by Harms, Inc. Copyright renewed.
All rights reserved. Used by permission.

TO THOSE STILL AT SEA

Acknowledgment

To Patricia Blake, my friend from the moment of my arrival in the United States, who has been my guiding star in writing this book

ALEXANDER DOLGUN'S STORY

CHAPTER

I

ONE DAY LATE IN 1948 A YOUNG AMERICAN OUT FOR AN INNOCENT WALK
in the streets of Moscow was accosted by an operative of the MGB, the
Soviet secret police. Had he been quick to run away through the crowded
streets to the American Embassy, only two blocks away, he would probably have been safe. Instead, he paused a moment to answer the agent
politely. It was a fateful pause. Within seconds, the young man was a
prisoner of the MGB. He would live under their shadow for the next
twenty-three years.

How it began was mundane enough. In the early thirties, when jobs
were scarce and pay was meager, a number of American technicians
accepted offers from the Soviet Union to work in Russia for a one-year
term. One of these men was Michael Dolgun, a Polish-born New Yorker
who went over in 1933 on contract to the Moscow Automotive Works. He
was well paid in dollars, but it was hard to be away from his wife and
two young children in New York, where he sent most of his pay. So when
his employers offered to help bring his family over if he would accept a
second one-year contract, Michael Dolgun accepted. Much as he disliked
Moscow, he thought he could stick it out one more year if his family was
with him. Besides, things were still pretty tough in America. But that one
year stretched into two, and then four, and then 1939 came and with it
came the prospect of war.

Michael Dolgun told the Soviet authorities he wanted to return home
with his family. His wife, Anna, and the two children had never been
happy in their drab little Moscow room anyway. But the Soviet authorities
stalled. Endless bureaucratic barriers to his repatriation appeared. Michael
was not politically sophisticated. If he even knew that there was an
American Embassy in Moscow by this time, it never occurred to him to go
there for help. After all, he had been dealing with the same officials of the
Soviet government for six years; *they* were his contact with the world
of passports and money and travel arrangements.

And before anything was done for him, war had come to Russia and
Michael Dolgun found that in the eyes of the Soviet government, and
without his having been consulted, advised, or asked to consent, he had
become a Soviet citizen, and he was drafted into the Red Army. For the
rest of the war his family saw little of him. They had a terrible time trying
to find food in the beleaguered city. Anna and the teen-age children, Stella

and Alexander, yearned to go home to New York, but of course there was no way to do that.

Alex was a Catholic boy. He had been taught plenty about hell. But the searing realities of the pit in which he spent most of his twenties would soon make all that pulpit hellfire seem insipid.

I know about all this because I am Alex Dolgun. Retracing my steps through the inferno in order to write this book has not been a joyful experience. It has been an act of catharsis and an offering to those still in the inferno.

Most of my story is what I actually remember, but some is what must have been. There are episodes and faces and words and sensations burned so deeply into my memory that no amount of time will wear them away. There are other times when I was so exhausted because they never let me sleep or so starved or beaten or burning with fever or drugged with cold that everything was blurred, and now I can only put together what must have happened by setting out to build a connection across these periods, a reconstruction between those points that are quite clear.

For instance, I know that in the spring of 1950 I was packed like a human sausage into one of the infamous Stolypin railway cars, to be shipped from the prisons of Moscow where I had been tortured and interrogated to the forced-labor camps of Kazakhstan. I was emaciated and feverish. After a year and a half of enforced sleeplessness I was mentally vague. I was the only American in the crowd of Russians and Ukrainians and Tatars and others on that train. I remember vividly some events from the transfer prisons along the way. I recall a wagon heaped with corpses outside the gates of the camp at Dzhezkazgan when we arrived at four o'clock in the morning. I know that I was too weak to walk without help at that point.

And yet the next thing I can recall is going to work in the stone quarry. There must have been a period of rest in between; I know there must have been the normal period of "quarantine" before I was given a work assignment. I know a number of things that happened during that period, because they happened to every arriving prisoner, and I can write about them with complete certainty that they happened to me. But I have absolutely no recall of that two-week period. It has been wiped out of my brain like an erased tape.

I have an extremely good memory. I can see now the faces of men who tortured me in Moscow prisons, in Lefortovo and Sukhanovka. I recall the number of every cell I was locked in, the number of days I spent in solitary hard punishment cells, the names of hundreds of fellow prisoners. As I worked on this book, faces and names and smells and sounds came to me after twenty years of being forgotten, and they came with complete clarity and vividness, just like opening a door and finding someone you know very well but have not seen for a long, long time.

To work on this book has sometimes been exciting because of the way in which my memory has responded to my probings. Not all the answers have been very palatable. I know that I suppressed some of the memories for twenty years because they were intolerable. But now, because the work of telling my story has become the foremost need of my life, and because I know that for the story to be credible it must have detail and texture and be very complete, even the pain of a terrible memory brings a certain reward from the simple, clear satisfaction of having been able to remember.

CHAPTER

2

ONE DAY LATE IN 1948 A YOUNG AMERICAN OUT FOR AN INNOCENT WALK in the streets of Moscow was accosted by an operative of the MGB. That is where the book begins, so I come back to that day—to the early hours of that day, between one and two in the morning, when I stood outside the apartment of my fiancée, Mary Catto, trying to say good night. I was in love with Mary Catto. She worked at the British Embassy. I worked at the American. Both of us were in junior positions, but we were a lively, outgoing couple and we had a lot of friends in the Moscow diplomatic community. As a result, we were invited to a lot of cocktail parties and theater outings and dinners that a twenty-two-year-old like me would not normally have been asked to, even though I was chief of the consular file room.

People knew Mary and I were in love. They made friendly fun of the difference in our accents and called us Mr. and Mrs. Haff-and-Hawff. I was out very late with Mary that night. We were very close and very loving, but we had not slept together; that would wait until we were married. It was one of those nights when saying good night is almost impossible. We stood in her doorway with our arms around each other, very happy, very dreamy, and completely innocent of what was going on around us.

I remember that I felt a kind of dramatic urge—I was really crazy about her and I had that need you get for expressing yourself with a lot of power—and so I said to her, "Darling, suppose something should happen to me and I should disappear for a few months." There was a look of genuine alarm on her face. I was enough of a kid, I'm afraid, to enjoy it: it meant I was really important to her. She must have thought I might be going on some embassy mission I couldn't talk about. That was the impression I tried to give. Mary didn't say anything. She just looked at me terribly seriously.

I said, "Would you wait for me?"

"I would wait forever, Al," she said. "I love you, and I would wait for you. Are you serious about this?"

I said, "Listen, forget it. We're going to the Bolshoi tomorrow night— no, God, it's tonight—and I've got to get some sleep. I just had to know how serious you are." She held me very tightly. It was probably half an hour more before I left her and walked back to the American Embassy residence with my head full of romance.

Now, I am not superstitious or mystical in the least, but that remark to Mary about disappearing for a while, and the dream I had later that same night, were both undeniably real and prophetic. . . .

I was on a bus, in Moscow, returning to the embassy from some errand, and I noticed that a man was watching me intently. In reality Ambassador Bedell Smith had warned us recently that there were indications of increasing harassment of American personnel. This was the time of the planning of NATO and the firm Western response to the Soviet takeover of Czechoslovakia, and I suppose it was felt that this might have some negative results for us Americans in Moscow. Anyway, we were used to being tailed by the MGB, and in my dream I recognized this as a tail, but it seemed more serious than usual. Then as we neared the embassy I realized there was more than one man watching me closely. I tried to act nonchalant, and as we came close to the embassy bus stop I stood up and pressed the button and waited by the side door of the bus. Three men got up and stood behind me. I leaped down from the bus and began to run toward the front door of the embassy. They ran after me. I was pulling away from them, but something was wrong with my knees. They felt weak and began to buckle. The three men began to gain on me. I stumbled and fell, forced myself up again and fell again, and they jumped on me. At that point I guess I woke up because that's all there was to the dream. It upset me a little but not immensely. I knew that there was always a danger in the city. Ambassador Smith had said never to go out alone at night and maybe I was reacting to having been out alone that night, I don't know.

It did stay with me, though. . . . It was vivid enough to remember and to tell to the girls in the file room when I went to work. One of them told me there had been another Russian woman at the embassy already that morning, asking for something. I say "another" because, not long before, a

poor desperate soul whose mind had snapped came in and claimed she was
the wife of Edward Stettinius (Roosevelt's last Secretary of State) and
that there was a warship waiting at Leningrad to take her home and why
weren't we looking after her. And just as she had been followed when she
left by one of the shadowy men who were always in Mokhovaya Street in
front of the embassy, so we watched as this second woman left the
embassy the morning of the thirteenth of December, and the Soviet duty
cop at the gate gave a slight nod to a man down the street who fell into
step behind her.

They would pick her up. We knew that. We had all been followed,
though never interfered with. I even had developed a considerable knack
for losing my shadows. I laughed and said to one of the girls that morning,
"Those MGB are everywhere, you know. For all you know, I'm one!"
And everybody laughed at that.

Before coming to work that morning I had picked up one of my guns.
I have always been crazy about guns, and at this time I had a collection of
three nice pistols—a Walther 9-mm.; a Japanese .22 revolver, small enough
to fit into the palm of your hand; and a really beautiful prewar Spanish
automatic, I think a .32-caliber gun, with a handsome brown bone handle
that had a little recess in it with a sliding marker to indicate how many of
your nine shots you had fired. This was the one I took to work that morning to oil with typewriter oil, because I had no decent gun oil at the
residence.

I also had a Luger-shaped air pistol that fired darts, and that gun
became an issue later on. It's a good thing I remembered to take the
Spanish gun out of my pocket and leave it locked in my desk at the
embassy when I went out for lunch, or there would have been a very big
issue over guns—I am sure of that.

Lunch was to be with Captain North, assistant military attaché at the
Australian Legation. Bert North was a friend of the special kind you get
only after you've had a fight with him. Before Mary and I started going
together, North used to take her out, and after she left him for me he was
jealous and aloof until one night at a cocktail party in the British Embassy
residence, about a year before this. He got terribly plastered and invited
me outside for a fight. As we started down the stairs, he lost his balance
and fell and cut his head. I half-carried him into a washroom and started to
wash the blood away, and he started to embrace me and said I was his
best friend and he never really meant to hurt me and a lot of drunken and
sentimental stuff like that. Afterwards we became quite good friends and
saw a lot of each other, and the rivalry over Mary was forgotten.

It is not easy to get good food in Moscow restaurants, but I was a
specialist by now, and so was North, and we had agreed to meet at the
Aragvi, a really fine Georgian restaurant on Gorky Street. It would be a

twenty-minute walk for me. I left the embassy a few minutes after one. I walked out of the drive at the front of the building, and when the duty cop looked at me, I winked at him. "Catch another spy this morning?" I asked. He gave me a stony look and turned away.

It was a bright, sunny day. The American Embassy was opposite the north wall of the Kremlin then, and as I crossed Gorky Street and looked to my right I could see the lines of people in front of the Lenin Mausoleum, and lots of strollers out in Red Square at lunchtime. There was no snow in the streets, although it was nearly Christmas. The colored domes of St. Basil's were brilliant in the sunshine.

I turned left along Gorky Street, threading my way through the crowds of people in front of the Council of Ministers building until I crossed the first street and started passing in front of the Diet Food Store, which is a high-class market. When I was just a young American kid scrounging the streets of Moscow during the war, a bomb fell near the Diet Store and people were lying all over this area, dead from the blast, with almost no visible injury—women, mostly, their string bags of cabbages and potatoes strewn about in the road. The woman cashier was sitting upright at the cash register, but her head was in the open cash-register drawer. I often thought of that grisly scene when I walked by the Diet Store, and I thought of it again that afternoon. But only for a moment, because shortly after I passed the store I heard someone call my name, loudly, from a short distance behind me.

I realized he had called me several times, and was half-running after me. But he called me Alexander Mikhailovich, a distinctly Russian form of address, and nobody ever called me that, so I hadn't paid much attention. Now he ran to catch me, and put his arms out as if to embrace me, and said in a much louder voice than made any sense for a guy two feet away, "*Kiryukha* [old buddy]! How wonderful to see you—it's been such a long time!"

I was completely mystified. I wondered if it was some nut. I had never seen this tall, grinning, good-looking man before. I was sure of it.

He kept talking loudly, and took me by the arm and pressed me toward the edge of the sidewalk, by the road.

"Such a surprise, such a surprise, how wonderful we should meet again. Let's just come over here out of the way of the people so we can talk!"

I wondered if he was mad, with this crazy grin and loud voice. I said, "Look, you're very much mistaken. I have never seen you before in my life." I was trying to free my arm without being rude. I still hadn't caught on. I said, "Please, you've got me mixed up with someone else."

By now we were at the edge of the road. He dropped his voice and said, "No, I don't think so. Your name is Alexander Doldzhin, isn't that right?"

Many Russians pronounced my name that way, as if it were *dole-gin*, like the drink, with the accent on the *gin*.

I said, "That's right, but who are you?" I was beginning to feel just a little uneasy. I don't know to this day why I didn't catch on faster and just start running. Especially after that dream.

The tall man reached in his pocket and pulled out an ID card in a blue and red folder. I opened it. His photograph was on it, and the name Kharitonov, S.I., Major, Operative Detachment, MGB—the Ministry of State Security.

I felt cold. But his manner was totally affable. He said, "Oh, don't worry, it's nothing important, we'd just like to talk to you for five minutes at the ministry."

I was going to get out of there. I pulled out my own ID card and said pretty brusquely, "Look, I am an employee of the United States Embassy. I am not allowed to talk to any Soviet officials without permission. I'm sorry." Kharitonov took the card. "You're the man," he said quietly. I held out my hand for my card. He just stared at me and slowly dropped his hand to his side without returning the card. That gesture turned me to stone. It was like a curtain going down. I hesitated one fatal moment, thinking, *I better get that card back*. Then I knew I couldn't and I tensed to run. I looked left for traffic on the street. I thought that he wouldn't dare shoot with all those people. And then before I could move, my elbows were seized from behind, firmly, by two pairs of hands. The men attached to those hands moved in close. I was trapped.

Kharitonov said in his broadcast voice again—for the benefit of the passers-by, I realized now—"Well! Here's luck! Here comes my friend with his car. We can take a drive and have a little chat."

A beige Pobeda pulled up right beside me, its back doors already open. The man on my right said in my ear, "Be quiet, now. Don't make any noise at all, please," and before I could even think, let alone react, I was squeezed in the back of the car between the two of them.

I looked wildly around me at the street. The scene photographed itself on my mind. The huge world clock on the Central Telegraph Office across the street said ten past one. Beside me, coming away from the Diet Food Store, I could see the lower part of a woman's body, and the string bag full of potatoes that she carried. These bags are called *avoski*. *Avoska* is derived from a word meaning "perhaps." In those days, and even now, most Russians carried an *avoska* because perhaps they would come across a food line where you could buy some bread or cabbage or potatoes. You never knew. *Perhaps.* As I think back, it is as if the woman were frozen, unmoving, although of course she was walking and I could see only her legs because of the roof of the car. A blue dress with white polka dots. The string bag was full of potatoes and a pair of women's shoes, with the toes sticking out. For some reason or other this struck me as funny, and as we drove off I giggled.

But at the same time I had an abrupt sensation of the termination of life.

Kharitonov rode in the front seat and looked back at me. He spoke in a very soothing voice. He said we were just going to the ministry for a little talk. "Don't worry," he kept saying. "Five minutes, that's all."

He was really smooth. For a moment I stopped worrying. I thought, Oh, for Christ's sake, they're going to make a pitch to me. Money, women, all that. They want me to be an agent. This is a recruiting job. That was the only thing that made sense.

"Here we are," announced Kharitonov. "Do you know what this is?"

We had left Kuznetsky Most, cruised along Pushechnaya, turned into Dzerzhinsky Square, and out of it again at the southeast corner. I looked out the window of the Pobeda as we drew up by a huge, gray stone building. It was the Lubyanka prison, headquarters of the MGB.

I said, "Sure I know. It's the Government Terror. The place where you lose your mind."

Kharitonov laughed a dismissing, easy sort of laugh.

Before the Revolution the prison was the Government Insurance Hotel. It was called *Gos Strakh*, for short. *Strakhkassa* means "insurance office." But *strakh* also means "fear" or "fright," so for a while the prison was called *Gos Strakh*, the Government Fright. Then, after the purges, when it was constantly swallowing people who never reappeared, people began to call it *Gos Uzhas*: the Government Terror. It is an imposing building. It fills one whole side of Dzerzhinsky Square. I had been by it often. It is only minutes from the embassy. The great steel doors had always been shut. But now as we slowed down they began to slide open. It was like a movie. I thought, Wait till I tell the boys about this!

The doors were on rails and slid sideways into the wall with a grinding sound. Then they closed behind us and the doors of the car opened and we were in a big central courtyard, deserted except for us, with Kharitonov very politely saying, "Look, don't worry, this will just take a few minutes, please come this way," in that soothing, reassuring voice of his. The smooth bastard. At the door, he stood aside politely for me to enter first, and then skipped in front of me to lead me along the hall. There was no one in sight and the other two guys had disappeared. My mind was running pretty fast now. I thought, If he's trying something dirty he's being damn polite about it. And then I thought, Sure, I'm right; they're going to try setting something up: "A little information, Mr. Dolgun, that's all, nothing harmful about it, and we'll be very glad to see you're well compensated for it."

We turned down a narrow side corridor. It was lined with doors strangely close together. Still walking swiftly and scarcely breaking the rhythm of his stride, Kharitonov opened one door and motioned me forward courteously. "This way, please," he said pleasantly. I walked in, still moving as quickly as we had been all along the corridors, and then suddenly came to a halt. I was in a box about four by nine feet. An empty box with a bench. I spun around. "What the hell!" I said, really angry. But I said it to a door that was already shutting hard behind me. A door lined with iron, with a peephole in it. It shut with a clank. I thought, I don't like that sound!

The peephole opened immediately. I went right up to it. I said, "This isn't funny, Major. Open up." The peephole closed again, but not before I saw behind it a dark eye with dark eyebrows. Definitely not the light-skinned major. I waited to hear the bolt pulled back again. I guess I assumed the man was looking for the key or something. I waited as long as my patience could stand it, not very long. But longer than might seem reasonable.

I was very excited. Whatever mixed and unlikely thoughts were racing through my head, all of them meant adventure and great stories to tell. Here I was actually *inside* the infamous Lubyanka. Lots of people told stories about Lubyanka, and lots more speculated about it. I was actually seeing it from the inside, the stronghold of the secret police of Soviet Russia, and no one else I had ever met could say the same. In fact I was giddy with excitement. I was flash-fantasizing all the things I would say when they put it to me that I should become an agent, flash-fantasizing how I would reveal to the world the sinister plans of the MGB for buying off Americans. Maybe I'd be a hero and go on tour in the States, see New York again, get back home. It literally never occurred to me that I was about to begin a prison term that might end with my death. I had no morbid thoughts at all, although of course my heart was beating fast and I was, in a sense, afraid. But afraid in the way you are before a big game: How will I do?

I actually said to myself, "Well, here we come!"

One thing: I knew it was something big and something important in my life.

I supposed the guard with the dark eyebrows was going for Kharitonov. I turned around to look at the box I was in. The ceiling was high, almost three meters. The walls were brown up to shoulder height, then whitewashed. Set in a recess over the door was a single bright bulb, screened by a heavy wire mesh. I looked back at the door. The peephole opened and closed again. Here they are, I thought, and waited for the door to open. Nothing. Silence. Then from somewhere close by a knocking sound and a muffled voice, pleading. The peephole closed. It was very hot in that box.

Still nothing happened. I was getting furious. I pounded with my fists on the door and shouted, "Let me the hell out of this place! I'm an American citizen. I demand my rights. What the hell is going on here!"

Immediately the bolt shot back. A man I had seen in the corridor just before I was shut in, a blue-chinned man with a bad complexion and heavy black eyebrows and a blue smock like a lab coat over his uniform, stepped quickly into the cell. He whispered, "Now, please! Be very quiet. It is not allowed to shout in here. There are others"—he indicated with his head toward the corridor, but I did not know what that was supposed to mean.

But his manner was so easy and polite that it put me off stride for a moment. He went on in a whisper, almost confidential, as if he were respecting somebody else's need for perfect silence, "Don't worry, please. It will only be a moment."

He was like an attendant in a doctor's office: Doctor will be with you in a moment, was what it was like.

But then the knocking somewhere else in the corridor started up again, and a woman's voice screaming out, "But there's no one with my baby! What's going to happen to my baby! Please! Please!" She was muffled by my door's being shut again. That really slowed me down. Despite the heat I felt cold. I was going to knock and yell some more, but the door opened and the blue-chinned man said politely, "Will you come this way?"

I thought, Okay, I'm sorry for that poor woman, but now whatever is going on with me is going to stop. I mean, they'll see it's a mistake, I'll sweet-talk my way through this recruiting business in a minute, maybe I'll even make it to the Aragvi before North decides he's been stood up.

I remember the face of that guard perfectly well. I saw him again years later when they brought me from camp for another interrogation, but he did not recognize me. Now he led me around a corner and motioned to another door. "Step in here." This room was two meters by four, no window, brown walls with whitewash as before, and quite bare except for a table and a straight-backed chair. Now the guard's manner changed. He was still polite in a noncommittal way, but there was no missing the absolute, quiet authority in his voice. The door behind us was locked. I looked up at him and thought of slugging him, but there was an eye at the peephole, and besides we were locked in.

"What is this all about! Don't you know you are dealing with a citizen of the United States of America! I want to know what's going on."

"Be quiet," he said. "Don't worry, you'll know soon enough. Now take everything out of your pockets and put it on the table."

I was going to protest and refuse, but one look at his face made it clear there was no point. Very quietly, as I took off my watch and put my money and cigarettes and lighter and pen and everything else on the table, I explained to him that what was happening was in violation of international agreements, that it was a very serious diplomatic mistake that would create very serious repercussions with the world's greatest power. And then I stopped because I understood, really, that he was just a functionary and besides he was paying no attention and I could save my breath for someone with responsibility.

He gathered up all my things and then said curtly, "Take off all your clothes and put them on the table."

I was licking my lips I was so mad. I knew I had to do it, but I still protested to his disappearing back. He did not turn; he left the room and the door was locked again.

"Boy!" I said tightly, *"Boy!* Just wait. Just you wait!" All the time taking off my shoes and socks, my shirt, my pants, until I stood in the middle of the hot room in my shorts.

I think I was there an hour before anyone came again. The peephole in the door opened quite regularly, and I decided to pretend I did not even notice. It may not have been that long, but my stomach was beginning to churn and the heat was getting me down and it seemed a long time. Then the door opened again, and the swarthy, blue-chinned guy in the smock and a man in a colonel's uniform, MGB, came into the room. The colonel had a piece of paper.

"This is a list of the property we are keeping for you," he said. "My name is Colonel Mironov. I am the commandant of the inner prison. If you need to go to the toilet or would like a drink of water, just call the guard." And he turned to go. I caught his arm but he pulled away and gave me a very hard look. Before I could ask all the questions that were welling up in me, he said simply, "Don't worry"—their favorite phrase—"you'll be fully informed very soon," and went out.

The swarthy guy pointed to my shorts. "Everything off," he said. It was clear he meant it. I sat down on the chair and began to pull them off. When I looked up he had my jacket spread on the table and was ripping the seams with a knife. I just stared. I knew there was no point in it but I said, "Just a minute, there, fella. That's my good jacket." He went on opening the seams as I knew he would. He felt inside the lining and the lapels. He ripped out the shoulder pads.

Then he picked up my shoes and went at the soles with his knife. He pulled out the steel reinforcing shank and put the shoes back on the floor, the soles flapping. Then he took my tie and shoelaces and belt and knocked for the door to be opened. "Can I get dressed now?" I asked. "Not yet," he said.

I sat on the chair. I said to myself, Boy, this is getting to be the big time. Will they be embarrassed when they find out what a screw-up this is!

Then the door was unlocked again and a good-looking woman came into the room in a doctor's white lab coat over a uniform, while the swarthy guard stood with his back to the open door, looking out into the corridor. The woman had an arrogant expression. I was trying to cover myself with my hands. I was terribly embarrassed. She had a clipboard and a pencil. She asked me if I had had tuberculosis, measles, malaria, scarlet fever, syphilis or gonorrhea (I was still composed enough to be insulted by this), diabetes, mental ailments, and so on. Then she walked up very close to me and told me to open my mouth. She examined behind my teeth and under my tongue. She turned my head and looked in my ears and nostrils. She looked under my eyelids. Then she told me to stretch out my hands with the fingers spread, and turn them over. She looked in my armpits. She made me roll back my foreskin, then lift my penis and my scrotum so she could examine behind them, although she did not touch me there. Then I had to turn around and bend over and spread my buttocks.

She did not do an internal examination. "You can dress now," she said flatly, and left the room.

I was taken to a brightly lit room and photographed from three sides with an old camera with a lens cap the photographer removed instead of a shutter. Then fingerprinted. Then led to another room which to my real astonishment seemed to be, and turned out to be, a dentist's office. Two guards stood by me, making it perfectly clear why they were there, and a man in a white lab coat opened my mouth and without a word drilled out a large filling from a molar.

By now I was victimized within the routine of search and preparation. I was red with fury, but holding it because I knew perfectly well none of these men would respond to anything I could say, and if I tried any physical protest they would stop me physically. I knew that before long I would be brought face to face with The Man. I had no idea who that would be, but I knew that I would recognize his function when I met him. I stored up scorn, arrogance, assurance, fury, a whole catalogue to dump on this poor guy, who would not have his job very long when they discovered how wrong they were.

A shower was next, too hot and no way to cool it down, and only a small bit of soft soap that smelled acrid and unpleasant. Somehow I knew I should take this shower seriously, so I used up most of the rotten-smelling soap and washed my whole body thoroughly, even though the shower was so hot it made me gasp. I was in very good physical shape at this time. My weight was 186, very trim, five feet nine and a half, thirty-two inches around the waist. My stomach muscles were hard from exercise, and my shoulders and biceps even harder. I was an amateur acrobat, very good at walking on my hands, played a lot of sports, boxed a bit, and for a couple of years I had been doing the Charles Atlas Dynamic Tension muscle-building course, although I had never been a ninety-seven-pound weakling, like the guy in the comic book ads.

When I got dressed again after the shower, all I had left was my shoes, with the soles slit open and flapping as I walked, my light-gray navy surplus gabardine pants, good heavy material, my navy surplus shirt with epaulets and a hemmed slot in one of the two pockets, two packs of Chesterfield cigarettes, and fifty-three wooden matches. My comb had been taken, but it wouldn't have been much use anyway, because the shower room had no mirror in it, and neither did the toilet when I asked to be taken there. In all the time I spent in prison in Moscow I never saw a mirror. Once, much later, I was taken into an officers' toilet in Lubyanka and there was a large mirror on the wall, covered with a black cloth.

After my shower I was taken over by another guard. I followed his black boots along the carpeted corridors till we came to an old cage elevator, very whiny and full of clanks and rattles, and went up about three floors. Then I remember a thick metal door with a barred window, and an officer who already had a file on me. This officer assigned a cell number to me and we moved off down the corridors again. During this trip, from the shower to my first cell, I became aware that I was, in fact, in a huge prison. I would catch glimpses of long gloomy corridors, lined with doors, each door with its peephole and food slot with a sliding metal panel. All the corridors were carpeted and almost the only sound as we moved along was the guard's clucking of his tongue—the signal used in Lubyanka to let it be known that a prisoner was under escort. Between clucks I could hear the guard breathing through a stuffy nose. All those metal doors were gray, battleship gray, and the effect of the gloom and the silence and the gray doors repeating themselves down the corridors until they merged with the shadows was oppressive and discouraging.

But I still could not take this thing seriously. I knew it was a mistake, and the question was, How soon would they find out their mistake and let me go? When we came around a corner and I was put into another windowless box I felt a bit nonplussed because I thought I was on my way to see someone in authority and get this thing straightened out.

This box was about four meters long and one-and-a-half wide. The ceiling was high and the air was hot. Along one side there was a narrow wooden bench. Above the door was an intense naked bulb, about 150 watts, I thought, in a heavy link-wire cage. The guard was closing the door when I said, "What happens now?"

"Don't worry," he said, "everything will be fine."

I walked up and down in the stifling cell.

After a while I became completely parched in the heat under that glaring bulb, so I knocked on the door for the guard. The peephole opened immediately. I said, "I'm very thirsty. Please give me some water." I remember that I was already modifying my tone and speaking quietly.

He was back with the water in a moment. A pint-sized metal mug. I drained it and took courage from the speed with which he had brought it, and asked for more. In a minute he was back with a refill.

Ten minutes later my bladder began to feel pretty full. Up till now I had not felt any physical needs, no hunger, no toilet needs, nothing until the thirst hit. In fact I think I had gone a bit numb. I may have been more frightened than I like to think. Anyway, I knocked on the door again, and again the peephole opened immediately. "I need to go to the toilet." The peephole closed and I heard the bolt being drawn back. The toilet was in a room across the hall, a trough urinal on the wall and a couple of holes in the floor with metal footplates for squatting over. The guard was new to me. I knew better, but I thought, what the hell, and on the way back to the cell I said quietly, "Listen, do you know what's going on here? I'm completely mystified. I don't know why I'm here."

He ducked his head and said in a whisper, "Don't worry. It will be all taken care of soon. Don't worry, now."

I said, "Well, I'd like another drink of water please."

He did not answer. He locked me in. In a moment the food slot opened and there was the metal mug again.

Whenever I asked for the toilet I was taken immediately, without question.

It is difficult to say how long this went on. It seemed to be more than a day, but I now know that it was not, that sometime in the evening of the day of my arrest they came to get me and take me for interrogation. No food was offered, but strangely I was not in the least hungry.

The guard opened the door, finally, and told me to step out and to follow him with my hands behind my back. We went through several corridors. I began to feel a huge surge of excitement again. I was certain that this had to be the encounter that would explain everything and bring this fantasy to an end.

We came to a corridor with doors more widely spaced than in the cell corridors. The guard knocked lightly on one and opened it without waiting. Inside I was struck by a huge barred window with dark brown curtains. I could see that it was black night outside, though the curtains were closed. I was very curious about the passage of time and so I was staring at the curtains to get some sense of the outside world, when a voice said, "My name is Colonel Sidorov; I am your interrogator."

He was standing behind a very large desk on the far side of the room. There was a shaded lamp on the desk, and bright overhead lights that gleamed on his face. Sidorov was relatively tall, nearly six feet, with a kind of amused, easygoing, slightly cynical expression on a long face that would have been handsome except that it was covered with pockmarks, and I found it a bit hard to look at at first.

"Sit down," Sidorov said, motioning to my right. Opposite his desk there was a small wooden table with a hard chair behind it. About eight feet separated the table and the desk. I sat down and took stock of this man before I said anything. I had had enough time in the cell to get my anger under control, and I was determined to play this with as much control as possible. If they think they have *me*, I said to myself, they've got some surprises coming. The man I looked at was about thirty-seven or -eight. Trim and erect, with a lieutenant colonel's two stars on his shoulder boards and a large dark-blue diamond-shaped pin on the lapel of his military jacket. He sat down behind the desk and opened a file and read for some time without speaking. I had time to see that there was, in addition to the lamp, a phone on the desk and a couple of signal buttons on a sort of electrical panel behind the desk. There were a couple of outlets in this panel, and one wire led to the desk.

Sidorov read the file folder for a few minutes, looking up at me from time to time with this amused expression which put slight crinkles in his well-fed face. Pretty soon I felt I had the situation cased well enough. The next time he looked up with his cynical half-smile I smiled back and said, "Well, I'm glad to meet someone in authority at last, Colonel Sidorov, because it would be just as well to get this little mistake straightened out before someone gets really embarrassed."

Sidorov's expression only changed a hair. His smile came a millimeter closer to a real smile. He held up a finger at me indicating that I should wait a minute, and went on reading.

I said, "Look, I'm sorry to interrupt your reading, but I think you should hear what I have to say, don't you?"

He put down the files. He said, "Yes, yes! That is what we are here for. At least that is what *I* am here for. Do you know why we have brought *you* here?"

"That's the point," I said calmly, still smiling at him to show how confident I was. "I'm here for no reason at all. There is no reason why I should be here and it will be very embarrassing for your government if I am not released right away. When the United States Embassy finds out . . ."

But Sidorov interrupted this speech with a wave of his hand. "Think!" he said sharply. Not angrily. He still had that amused look. More like an algebra teacher who knows you are just a whisker away from the right answer and wants to encourage you.

"Think about it for a moment. Look, I'm sure if you just think a little bit you'll understand why you are here. Then you can tell me about it and I will be glad to, as you say, hear what you have to say."

I had a sudden idea. My accent in Russian was not too bad, but I let it slip a little below its normal level and said hesitatingly, "Maybe I am not understanding you very well. Could we get an interpreter? My Russian is not too good, I'm afraid."

Sidorov's eyebrows went up for a moment. Then he stepped to the door and spoke to the guard. While we waited he read through the file folder, which was quite thick, nearly three inches, and pulled out a cigarette. I pulled my cigarettes out and said in halting Russian, "Would you like to try an American cigarette?"

Sidorov hesitated a moment. He said, "Of course Russian cigarettes are much better" (which is definitely not true) "but just to be polite, yes, thank you."

I said, "I am sorry, sir, but I did not understand everything you said."

He just smiled and took the Chesterfield I offered him and lit mine and then his own.

Quite soon a young junior lieutenant arrived with a stenographer's notebook. Quickly, and in a more serious style, Sidorov told him to tell me I was charged with espionage against the Soviet Union. My face must have shown shock when I heard the words in Russian. But I waited for the interpreter. Then I said in English, pretty emotionally at first, "There's been a terrible mistake! Tell him I've never engaged in any such activities. I'm a file clerk at the American Embassy, for heaven's sake. He's got the wrong man!"

The interpreter's English was not really up to the task. With a strong Ukrainian accent, he translated this as "There has been a terrible mistake. I always engaged in such activities with a file clerk at the American Embassy. He is the wrong man."

I was furious at this stupidity. I yelled at Sidorov in Russian, "No, no, for Christ's sake. This guy's no good. I said I've *never* engaged in any such activities! I . . ." Then I realized I had trapped myself. I think I even spoke *Russian* better than this Ukrainian kid who was supposed to be an interpreter.

Sidorov smiled quite a broad smile this time, showing a good deal of gold. He nodded a dismissal at the junior lieutenant. *"Vsye,"* he said. "That's all." And the kid left the room.

"Let's not waste any more time, Citizen Doldzhin," he said easily, still smiling. "You say we have made a mistake. I tell you we never make mistakes. You say you have never engaged in any espionage activities. I tell you that we can prove it very easily." He picked up the file. Then I saw it was really two soft-backed file folders, one on top of the other.

He said, "It's in here. Places, dates, names of accomplices. All here. We have quite a file on you. Really! It's quite a file. So don't worry." (Again!) "Don't worry about its being a mistake!"

Then he leaned over the desk and looked at me very sternly and said in a very quiet voice, "The MGB does not make mistakes, my friend. We Never Make Mistakes."

He thrust a piece of paper at me. It had an official stamp on it. It was an order for my arrest. It stated that under Article 58, sections 6, 8, 10, etc. of the Soviet Criminal Code I was charged with espionage, political terrorism, anti-Soviet propaganda, etc., etc. But the most impressive single thing about this document was the signature: Rudenko.

General Roman Rudenko was the chief prosecutor of the Soviet Union. I was shaken, and yet impressed with my importance at being charged by the top brass.

It began to look both preposterous and serious to me. I wondered if the embassy knew what had happened to me. They must have missed me by now.

"I would like to make a telephone call," I said.

Sidorov smiled a tolerant smile, and shook his head.

"Look here," I said loudly. "In my country even a common criminal is allowed to telephone his lawyer. I want to phone the embassy and get a representative over here! I want . . ."

"It really does not matter very much what you want now," Sidorov said paternally. "You should have thought about that before you undertook to be a spy in *my* country. Because that is no common crime, and you do not have the privileges of a common criminal.

"However," he went on, still in an easygoing way, "maybe something can be done about that in the morning. It is too late to call there now, and I am required to get some basic information from you."

I took a big breath. I guessed I might as well resign myself to a night in Lubyanka. Besides it would make a better story: How I Was Interrogated by the MGB. I said, Cheer up, Alex, old buddy. They'll be here to get you in the morning. Might as well enjoy it while you can. I nodded my assent to Sidorov.

"Where were you born?"

"New York City. East 110th Street."

"How did you get to the Soviet Union?"

"My father came here in the thirties on contract as a specialist at the Moscow Automotive Works. Later he brought the family over. He was drafted into your army during the war, and I got a job at the American Embassy. That's all. I'm going to get married soon and go back to the States."

Sidorov wrote all this down. At the last he said, "Yes, we know quite a bit about your relations with women here in Moscow, but I think that your marriage seems pretty unlikely now, wouldn't you agree?"

I found myself wondering again if this was just a setup for an approach about doing some work for them. Get the candidate thoroughly intimidated and then suggest that there is a way out if he will be cooperative. It made me madder still to think this might be in their minds. I began to harden myself to deal as coolly and in as controlled a way as I could with whatever they threw at me, and never to get mad again as I had with the interpreter. Stay on top, I thought. So instead of bridling at his taunt about marriage, I just smiled and waited for the next question.

He kept me at it all night. Everything he asked I answered fully and easily. It was all straightforward biographical stuff about school and friends and family and where we lived and so on. There was nothing to conceal and I thought it would make life easier until the embassy representative arrived if I just went along with this craziness.

I knew a lot of time was going by, but I was surprised all the same when I could hear doors opening up and down the corridor and caught a few muffled remarks from guards moving by to indicate that it was morning. There was still no light through the curtains, but in Moscow, close to the longest night in the year, it is still dark until seven o'clock at least. Sidorov came over to my table with the paper he had been writing on and said, "Please read these protocols, and if they are correct, please sign at the bottom of each sheet."

I said, "What the hell is a protocol?"

"This is what we call the original notes I as an interrogator make on the interrogation. We can then refer to them later, as the weeks go by . . ." He paused to let this take effect. "To see if you are consistent and so on. You sign to show your agreement that the notes reflect our conversation accurately. You see, we intend to be perfectly fair and straightforward in this procedure."

I read the notes. I thought, You bastard, you're trying to scare me. I won't let you. I signed the notes with a signature that bore no relation to my own except that it said Alexander Dolgun, in English script, which is, of course, opaque to a Russian who knows only the Cyrillic alphabet and the Russian script. Sidorov scarcely glanced at the signature. He went back to his desk, pressed the button for the guard, and picked up his tunic from the back of the chair.

The guard opened the door and took me back through the maze of corridors to the cell and locked me in. I suddenly felt exhausted. I had only been in bed about three hours the night before. I wondered what Mary had done when I did not show up for the opera. It was *Prince Igor*. I wondered why the embassy had not got through to me by now. There had been a touch of reassurance in Sidorov's tone when he talked about perhaps making a telephone call in the morning.

I stretched out on my side on the narrow wooden bench and put my head on my arm and closed my eyes, thinking I might as well sleep until something happened. I yawned hugely. My eyes were burning a bit. I managed to get into a comfortable position, at least a position less uncomfortable than sitting on a hard chair. I yawned and yawned. Then I became aware of my heart beating. It seemed to be fast and hard. I felt surges of anger rise up, and then I would get them under control.

"Calm down!" I kept saying. "Relax! We'll get this all cleared up in the morning."

But I believe that even at this early stage there must have been some deep, lurking suspicion in a distant part of my mind that I was kidding myself, that things were worse than I would allow myself to be conscious of. In any case, that blessed mechanism that finally releases you from the day and lets you sleep just did not work, that first morning in the Lubyanka. And in the end I gave it up and spent the next few hours striding up and down in my cell, going all over it again in my mind.

CHAPTER

3

THE SECOND DAY IN THE LUBYANKA BEGAN WITH A SORT OF QUIET COMMO-tion in the corridor outside my cell. The sounds were muffled because of the carpeting, but I could hear some footsteps and hushed voices and the sounds of the bars of the food slots going back, and soon my own went back and a mug of hot tea and a loaf of bread were placed on the shelf inside.

In Lubyanka they serve a complete loaf. It is small, dense, rectangular, and, by comparison with that served in other prisons, quite tasty. On top of the loaf were two pieces of sugar—one whole lump and a half lump. The tea was not real tea. It was colored water with a very faint smell of some leaf substance to it.

Although I had not eaten since breakfast the previous day my stomach was tight and I was not hungry at all. I put the sugar in the "tea" and drank it slowly and pondered my situation. I looked at the bread and thought it did not look very appetizing and that soon I would be eating bacon and eggs or steak at the embassy and I could do without that crap.

An hour went by and then another. I stretched out on my side on the narrow bench and tried without success to doze off. Then I paced up and down again, beginning to get a bit resentful at the embassy for not having gotten me out of this mess by now. After a while I knocked on the door and asked for the toilet. I squatted over the hole in the floor and was relieved to find I was functioning all right. Then about half an hour after I got back to the cell the door opened again, and a guard I had not seen the day before took me along the corridors, cluck-clucking as we went, and left me again with Colonel Sidorov.

I was astonished at how fresh he looked. I thought he could not have had more than four or five hours sleep, even if he stayed in the Lubyanka. He had shaved and had a clean shirt, whereas I had slept, or tried to, in mine, had not washed, felt the stubble on my face, which I hated because I always shaved very meticulously, smelled my armpits pretty strongly, and had a powerful desire to brush my teeth.

His manner was still quite straightforward and he still had that amused look. He said we would go on with the biographical details. I asked about the phone call, but he put me off. He asked about my sister, Stella, who had left Russia two years before, and about our passports and all kinds of simple stuff that puzzled me because I figured the MGB must know it all.

Now for some reason this second day of interrogation is less clear in my mind than what happened afterward. It is a jumble of questions of the most ordinary kind of family stuff. Where were my parents born? What relatives did I have in the United States? Where did they live? Etc., etc., etc. I answered it all. Sidorov kept on writing everything out in longhand. We worked at it all day. I remember seeing the light fade behind the curtains, along about what must have been four in the afternoon or four thirty. We did not get through very much material. He had to write it out, and then he would bring it over to me to sign from time to time. It was a slow process.

In the middle of the day sometime he just got up abruptly and left the room. I was taken to the toilet and then came back and sat restlessly in the room while the guard leaned on Sidorov's desk and watched me impassively. I know that I was in quite a puzzled state of mind. I was still certain that someone would come for me soon, but I could not understand the delay. I determined to play a waiting game for at least another twenty-four hours, if that proved necessary, before . . . Well, before what? What could I do? Until the embassy came to get me out, I had to play out this dumb game of Sidorov's. Except that, of course, sooner or later he would get to the point in his questioning, and presumably it was then that we'd start destroying this crap about my being a spy. I thought, Well, if he doesn't get to the meat and potatoes by tomorrow morning, I'll press the issue then. No point getting him mad sooner than I have to. And I may not have to.

When I went back to the cell, shortly after it got dark, there was a plate of cold soup on the food slot shelf, and shortly after I was locked in they brought some thin hot porridge and another cup of so-called tea. I drank the tea. That was all. Still no appetite. And still no ability to sleep, although by now I was feeling really ragged. Beat. And then, to my astonishment, around nine thirty or ten—although I was guessing because I never saw a timepiece of any kind—they took me back to Sidorov.

I had gone through the first pack of Chesterfields. Then, although I was nervous and wanted to smoke a lot, I thought I'd better ration them to myself. I smoked during the sessions with Sidorov, but I never offered him any more of my Chesterfields. My mouth felt really foul now, and I was beginning to smell pretty bad, because the temperature in my cell was quite high and I had had no chance to wash myself. Sidorov looked fresh, again, and must have slept between five or six o'clock, when we quit, and whatever time of night it was now.

More biographical research this night, although he seemed a little less interested now, and repeated himself a lot and seemed to be waiting for something. From time to time he left the room. Then finally after one of these exits he came back and said that was all for now, that I was being transferred to the Lefortovo military prison.

Now, all through this period, despite the tiredness and the suppressed anger, I still felt a kind of excitement at being *inside*. I still felt that the climax was coming, and I still guessed it would be an offer to work for them. I maintained a cheerful exterior, and I always smiled at Sidorov when he asked me a question. From time to time, in the middle of asking about life in New York, the name of the ship we came over on, and all kinds of trivia like that, he would smile and say, "Listen. You must have thought it over by now. Don't you want to tell me about your espionage work? Don't you understand why you are here now?"

I would shake my head with a sort of mock-bewildered smile, and he would say, "Oh, all right. We'll get to it. I have to get all this stuff down anyway," and go on with the personal background.

The guard took me back to my cell. I lay down, and I think I dozed off, because there was a sort of shock when the guard unlocked again quite soon and told me to get up and come with him. When I stepped into the corridor, there were two guards waiting. They took me down in the elevator and along some strange corridors. Then we were in a kind of lobby to what must have been the main exit of the prison, and I saw a clock—just after three. I was given a bundle and told that it was the jacket and tie and so on that had been taken from me. Including my fine broad-brimmed fedora, which, I thought glumly, must be crushed out of shape in this parcel! I still was able to care about such things. Then they gave me the light topcoat I had been wearing when I was arrested and opened a side door and we stepped out into the cold night air.

It felt refreshing and cleansing. In the yard there was a van with its back door open and a sort of ladder of steps reaching down to the surface of the yard. There was a light on top of the wall and I could see that there was a colored advertisement on the side of the van that read DRINK SOVIET CHAMPAGNE, with a picture of the bottle and some fancy artwork. I had often seen vans just like it in Moscow. What I had not noticed before was the two rows of little ventilators on the roof, six in all.

These guards were pretty curt. One of them motioned me to go up the steps into the van, and I saw he had a revolver in his hand. The other guard climbed in ahead of me. There were six small doors flanking a very narrow central passageway—no more than a slot, really. The guard who got in ahead of me held one open and motioned me in. It was a solid box the size of a rabbit hutch. You could not sit down or stand up, just sort of hunker, with your knees near your chin. I hardly thought I could get in it at all, but I was shoved in and the door locked and then I heard the first guard get out and the second one get in, and then the back door slammed and the motor started up and the van lurched off.

I could hear those sliding steel doors groan on their rails, then we moved forward again and I knew we were once more out in the streets of Moscow.

It took, I think now, fifteen minutes. It seemed longer then because I was aching from the cramped position. A lot of my native cockiness was knocked out of me by the way I was hustled into this hutch like so much freight. I had to talk to myself again, to keep from losing control. "Easy, Alex, the last thing you need now is to get mad and bust a gut." By the time the van stopped I had stopped steaming, but my back and legs hurt like hell. I heard someone get out of the front of the van, and I heard the cab door slam. Then, after a short wait, I heard the sound of huge iron gates swinging on their hinges, and the van started up again, lurching over a curb or up a sharp ramp.

All this time I was hunched up in absolute darkness, jostled back and forth by the motion of the van. There was one small compensation: after only a day and a half in prison the clean night air that came in through the ventilators smelled wonderful.

The van stopped again. I heard the back door open. Then the guard unlocked my rabbit hutch. The guard who had stayed inside was out of sight when I crawled out. They never let an armed guard very near a prisoner. It was still almost too dark to see, though my eyes were very sensitive after all this time in absolute darkness. The van was backed up against a door and I was led through a dim corridor to a sort of office where there was a man behind a counter.

"Name?"

"My name is Alexander Dolgun. I am an American citi—"

"Prisoner, be quiet!"

Prisoner!

He had a file and I guess my photograph was in it. He looked in the file and scrutinized my face for a moment. Do they ever get a mismatch? I wondered. Do they ever make mistakes? Or is Sidorov right?

I was given a spoon, a plate, a rolled-up mattress (very thin), a sheet, a musty old blanket, and a coarse pillow. Then I was taken around another corner and into another box like the one in Lubyanka, except that the floor was asphalt, the room felt dank, there was a smell I came to know as the prison smell: ammonia, damp, urine, dirty bodies, a touch of the smell of death.

And then, within a very short time, I was taken out of the box and led to the cell that would be my home for the next ten months. As soon as my guard led me into the main body of the Lefortovo prison I stopped for a moment in astonishment, looking up. "Come on," the guard hissed, "keep moving!" He clanked his key on his belt—no tongue-clucking here—and as we walked I gazed upward into an immense space and had the uncanny impression that I had stepped into the bowels of a great steel ship. On both sides the walls rose up past several stories, each lined with a narrow metal catwalk. In the space between the opposing catwalks, at every level, was a coarse wire mesh stretching across the entire space. Each catwalk, which was just over a meter in width, had a metal handrail on the outside, and if anyone jumped or fell over the handrail he would immediately land unharmed on the wire mesh.

We went around a corner and along a wall. It was painted black but when I put my hand out to feel along it I found it was made of solid stone. Looking up I felt that the huge hall went up to a dizzy height, the successive stories fading so that I could never be sure how many there were or whether in fact I could see any roof, but just an indistinct impression of something vast receding upward. We came to a staircase going up into this cavernous space. The stairs themselves gave me a cold feeling in my arms and back, like a chill in the air, because they were worn down in little hollows, as if millions and millions of feet had passed over them, erasing the stone.

Lefortovo is shaped like a capital letter K—one straight long section, and two wings radiating southeast and southwest from its middle point. The guards took me up these worn stone stairs to the third level, and then, from the midpoint, along to the end of one of the diagonals.

Although the building had a morbid mass to it, a kind of weight that was nearly tangible in the air, I was not so much afraid as immensely curious, with a kind of giddy apprehension. My feelings were not altogether unpleasant. I was increasingly aware that this whole business was not going to be over and done with in the wink of an eye, but then I thought in terms of forty-eight hours, or seventy-two hours, or maybe a week at the most. Now that the initial shock and humiliation had worn off, I still looked on it as a bizarre adventure. It was something like going into a horror movie when you were a young kid, and you knew you might just get more scared than you could handle, but you were propelled by bravado and curiosity. So I stumbled along with my bundles, gawking upward at the vault above or down at the hollowed stone steps or out at the network stretching between the catwalks, a bit giddy from the height and the dark pit below me, thinking that this was a terrific movie and I was *in* it, until we came to the end of the wing, the end of the padded catwalk, and two heavy steel bars were pulled back on a cell door and I was motioned in. I noticed the number on the door as I stepped into the dark room. Cell 111. At first I welcomed the darkness. After the harsh light in the Lubyanka cell, this seemed restful. I thought it was nice that they turned the lights down at night here. But then it was a bit mystifying to discover that the walls were painted black, and the floor was black, and the bed was a black iron cot, and the light in the screened recess over the door was a little twenty-five-watt bulb which did not look as if it would ever get much brighter.

Unlike the Lubyanka cell, this one had a sink and faucet, with a drain going into a toilet that was just a cast-iron inverted cone with a lid. When I took the lid off, the stench was pretty bad and I put it back on immediately.

Usually when you are dog-tired, and I was dog-tired, the physical touch of bedding makes you overpoweringly sleepy. But this thin, hard mattress and threadbare sheet and blanket smelled terrible. Tired as I was, I knew I was not going to sleep easily or soon. I recalled prisoner stories from the hundreds of novels I had read and movies I had seen. *Zenda. The Man in the Iron Mask. Les Misérables.* I thought, Well, better start a calendar. Better keep in touch with the passage of time. I took my spoon and made a single scratch on the hard black paint on the wall opposite the bed. First day in Lefortovo. As I stared at it something caught my eye: scratches in the paint that looked like words, heavily painted over. I ducked to the left so that the meager light from over the door would edge these scratches better and make them more readable. I rubbed away some dust. More words emerged. I picked out a somber message from the past: a poem, an ironic welcome. A sign.

> *Who enters here do not lose hope.*
> *Who leaves do not rejoice.*
> *Who has not been will be here yet.*
> *Who has been here will not forget.*

Well, *I* hadn't lost hope yet, I thought. The poor bastard had a sense of humor, anyway. Probably did a long stretch, poor son of a bitch. Thank God I haven't done anything. I'd sure hate to spend a long time in this dump!

I put the bedding on the bed without unwrapping it. I looked carefully around the whole cell. It was about seven feet wide, I guessed, and twelve feet long, maybe not quite. Beside the door was the conical cast-iron toilet with the wooden lid. It could be flushed, more or less, by running water in the little sink which stood beside the toilet and drained into it. At the far end, if you stood on the bed you could reach up to the frame of a small window with heavy, wire-mesh-reinforced opaque glass. A tiny corner of light from outside showed on one side, but there seemed to be a metal hood on the exterior wall. Below the window was a small, fragile table. I was still standing on the bed when the slot clanged open and the guard hissed in a loud whisper, "Prisoner, if you do that just once more you will be taken to the hard punishment cells! Get down on your bed. And if you cover yourself, keep your hands outside the blanket where I can see them. Do not stand on the bed and do not go near the window!"

I was boiling with resentment. I tried to protest that I was only going to be here for a few more hours anyway, and I didn't know what the hard punishment cells were so that didn't mean anything to me, and anything else I could think of, but he just told me to be quiet if I didn't want real trouble and then clanged the slot shut again. I thought he must be a real son of a bitch after all the polite guards I had had in Lubyanka and the polite manners of Sidorov. Sidorov did not seem such a bad guy, I thought, in the wake of this ugly bastard. Maybe in the morning we can have another talk about contacting the embassy. Maybe he'll realize . . .

I had one last cigarette in my pocket. And I had about a dozen useful matches left. Something had made me hold onto the burned stubs of the others.

I took out my cigarette and smelled it for a while and lit up. The peephole opened. I wondered if this petty-minded slob would complain about the smoking. The peephole closed. Then, about a minute later, it opened again. Then closed. I soon realized it was a rhythm, a quick peek once a minute. The smoke was relaxing me. I thought, Let the bastard look. I went to the toilet and took off the lid and had a satisfying leak. I looked forward to the morning, to getting something done. I thought, Someday I'm going to write about that fantastic shiplike structure out there. What a movie it would make, if only I had a story to put in it.

I felt sleep stealing over me and was very grateful for it. The cell was cool compared to Lubyanka. I pulled the blanket up to my neck, and remembered what the guard said about my hands, and then I drifted off.

"*PODYOM!*" There was a terrific bang on the steel door. "*Podyom!*" Get up! It felt as though I had been asleep ten seconds. The first sleep in over forty hours. In reality it had been, I suppose, an hour and a half. They wake you at six in Lefortovo. I could hardly believe it. I pulled the blanket up over my face and mentally said to hell with it. The next thing

I knew the door had burst open with an awful clang and a hard-eyed man had ripped off the blanket.

"The prisoner will rise when he is told to rise. Hard punishment cells if you do not rise immediately. Now, this is your first day here so I will let it go this time, but I will not let it go next time. *Podyom!*"

Curiously, he did not touch me.

I rose.

I was quite vague in the head and blurry-eyed and heavy-chested. I went to the sink and splashed water on my face. Suddenly for the first time since they took me, I felt hungry. I remembered the smell of the small, one-pound loaf in Lubyanka and actually found myself looking forward to its arrival. Up and down the corridor I could hear doors clanging and bars and bolts being slid and shot home again. Soon the door opened and the hard-eyed man handed in a bucket half-full of cold water and a small gray rag.

"Wash the floor," was all he said.

"Jesus," I muttered to myself, "one goddamn humiliation after another. I better get to Sidorov pretty fast." I was beginning to think of Sidorov as a friend. "He'll stop *this* kind of bullshit," I said out loud.

The slot banged open. The hard-eyed man said, "Prisoner, you are not allowed to speak in the cell. Wash the floor and make sure you dry it well!" He gave me a brief stare to see that I had got the message.

I poured a little water on the asphalt and worked away at it and got it pretty well mopped up. Then I stood up in front of the peephole and when it opened I held up the pail and rag so that he could see I was finished. The door opened. He looked at the floor, grunted, took the pail, and closed the door again.

And then, when breakfast came, I stopped being hungry, because the bread was a damp, coarse lump, sour-smelling and dirty brown. The sugar was sprinkled on top of the bread. The bread was not a complete little loaf, as in Lubyanka, but a chunk cut from a larger loaf. The end grain on the cut looked indescribably murky. But, I thought, I may be here for a while and I'll need some strength to last me for a day or two, so I better eat some. I took a bite of the dank stuff, and then tore off another piece and put some of the sugar on before putting it in my mouth. The steaming cup on the shelf at the food slot looked like tea but had no flavor at all. Still, the warmth was welcome, because out from under the blanket the cell now seemed pretty cool.

My head hurt a bit, and the piece of bread I ate made me feel sleepy again. I finished my tea and sat on the bunk and closed my eyes.

The slot banged open.

The guard said, "Prisoner, you are not allowed to sleep in the daytime.

You are not allowed to close your eyes. You may sit on the bed if you want, but you must keep your eyes toward the door and keep them open. Please try to learn these things quickly or you will have a very hard time here in Lefortovo. You may walk in the cell or you may stand facing the door. But you must not lie down or sit anywhere but on the bunk facing the door. You understand?"

I nodded wearily. I was losing enthusiasm for this game. Let's get to Sidorov and get this stuff over with, I thought.

When it was time to move my bowels I realized there was no toilet paper in the cell; so I knocked on the door and when the guard came I asked for some. He just shook his head. I repeated my request, making it clear I needed some *now*, but he just shook his head and closed the slot. So I learned how to wash myself after the toilet, in the Muslim fashion, with the left hand.

In Lefortovo, when a prisoner is taken to interrogation, he is led through a small anteroom to the building where the interrogation rooms line the corridor. Here there is a large book like a ledger. Covering the ledger is a sheet of fairly heavy iron, smoothed with years of wear by hands and sleeves. It has a slit in it that is placed so that only the name of the prisoner signing in or out, and the interrogator's name, can be seen; any other names are masked from view. There were two things I came to look forward to in the room of the iron book. One was to see the clock. I always knew exactly what time I was taken to interrogation and this gave me a sort of time-fix on the day. That little anchor would become more and more important as the days went heavily by and my sanity became more and more tenuous.

The other thing to look forward to was signing my name. When I signed the protocols for Sidorov, using English script, I felt a little mischievous. I knew perfectly well how to sign in the Russian script, I had done it for various official documents often enough. But I conceived the idea, as one way to keep things a bit off balance, of signing my name differently each day, thinking up a new style of handwriting, either in the Roman or the Cyrillic alphabet, and never giving them the same signature twice. Then, I thought, if this ever does get serious and they make me sign some goofy thing that incriminates me, I'll demand that they compare it with my real signature and then I can claim it wasn't me. However juvenile this was as an idea, it was one of the first of many small techniques I devised for keeping a sort of sense of having the upper hand, and each of these things was important as part of my whole posture, even though in itself it might seem insignificant.

I got satisfaction out of anything that did not fit *their* needs and expectations. Smiling at the interrogator all the time, being excessively polite, the changing signatures: these helped me retain a sense of being in charge of myself and human and not just a piece of meat these guys were shoving around.

So, hands behind the back, look straight ahead, parade along the catwalk sneaking glances up and down through the steel mesh. Downstairs to the first level, treading the cupped hollows in the stone. Across the main wing (the straight line of the K) and out through a wooden corridor to another building, which you entered through the room of the iron book. Sign a flamboyant signature, feeling good. There will be news from the embassy this morning, I know it.

Down a hall, into the interrogation room. Sidorov is smiling. Good.

"There is a letter from your embassy," he said.

"I knew it! That's wonderful!" I reached out for it. Sidorov's manner changed sharply, and he withdrew the letter from me. "It's nothing but a formal note of protest," he said. "They know nothing and they are not going to know anything. They wonder if we would be able to inform them. Hah!"

I was thunderstruck. I probably went a bit pale.

Then something happened; a light went on; I said to myself, He's playing with you, Alex. Don't let him get to you. Get him!

I said out loud, "Well, of course you don't dare show it to me"—I smiled broadly—"because they are about to bring about my release through higher circles and you will be embarrassed. Don't worry." (I enjoyed saying that, I savored the words!) "*Don't worry*. It will all be over soon."

Sidorov was a tough guy. He looked at me with that cynical spark of his. I thought there might have been a bit of admiration in his look. Then his face darkened and he snapped, "Fuck your embassy. That's all you are going to hear from them. That's the end of it. That's all they are good for. You are going to be here for the rest of your life, do you understand that? And even if we let you out some day, you will always be in the beam of our searchlight. It's forever, now, prisoner. So don't tease yourself with any dreams about help from your stupid embassy, because they can't do anything!"

He walked around to the back of his desk and turned away from me to let this sink in. It sank in all right. I felt terrible. Cold. Sick. But at the same time I knew he was putting on an act. I knew he was probably lying (though as it turned out he was not lying), and I knew that at all costs I must not let this act work. If he was the magician, I was going to be the kid who had his eyes on the left hand dipping into the pocket when all the other kids were watching the right hand that was supposed to have the watch and the ring in it. When he turned around again, I was smiling.

"Well," I said brightly, "let's get to work then!"

CHAPTER

4

IF I HAD KNOWN HOW HARD THAT WORK WOULD BE I MIGHT NOT HAVE BEEN so bright. I came back to my cell from that first day, almost desperate to pick up my sleep where it had been interrupted. But when I lay down, the slot banged open immediately and the guard said, "Prisoner, you will not lie down until ten o'clock. Sit up and face the door!" By what I guessed was nine o'clock I was yawning uncontrollably. I wondered if I could last the hour. Then the slot banged open. "Prepare for interrogation!"

I could not believe it! I raged at Sidorov when he came in. I yelled that he could not expect me to remember anything if I could not rest my brain. He heard me out with a cynical smile, and then went on with his questions. I realized that those first night-and-day grillings in the Lubyanka had been just an opening blitz. This was going to continue for . . . for how long? I knew, numbly, that I was launched on the most terrific endurance test of my life. And I made a resolution. I stared at Sidorov and said to him, silently, with a deep, deep anger, "I won't break before you do, you bastard!"

The secret police in the Soviet Union are known as *Organi*—"the Organs." There is a faint sexual implication in the word, although they use it themselves. It is part of the national slang. As such, however, it is not a word that carries any laughs with it, except in the occasional black joke. The Organs and all they stand for, whether referred to that way or by their initials as they changed over the decades—OGPU, NKVD, MGB, finally KGB—are a symbol of repression of such magnitude in the Soviet Union that the sight of their uniform with its purple stripes, the mention of a rap on the door in the middle of the night ("It was the *Organs*, you know"), or any actual encounter with the police themselves seems to take the will to resist right out of most Soviet citizens, and I guess to some extent that is what happened to me too, at the moment I was arrested.

Kidnapped is a better word. When regular police arrest you, they don't need to hide what they're doing. They have the law and the general support of the people with them, and they can openly say, "You're under arrest, charged with so and so," and that's it. But these people never did tell me I was arrested. "Come for a five-minute chat," they said.

And yet I knew what was happening; at least I knew part of it. Not all. No idea how much of my life was in jeopardy. Solzhenitsyn writes about the "rabbits" all over Russia. The ones who never protested. "What's the matter with us?" he wonders in his *Gulag Archipelago*—a nation-state I came to know pretty well. "Why didn't we rise up and resist?"

Well, I think I know why not. It is *because* there is no legitimacy to the KGB and all its preceding versions. In our American society, the fact that something is illegitimate makes it automatically less impressive. But an illegitimate body that is really big and powerful is much more effective in its mass and its capacity to frighten millions of people than a legitimate body. Because it is illegitimate, it doesn't answer to anything recognizable, only to the whims and appetites of its masters; and its masters are always shadowy, indistinct people, or myths like Stalin, so huge that they have infinite power and are not answerable to any law or any system or any body.

People adored Stalin. People want to love infinite power so that it will love them back. People knew that under Stalin millions disappeared in the middle of the night, but most of them said, "It must be for the best." My wife's mother was married to a KGB officer. When she first heard my story, she said privately to Irene, even though she hated her husband and had been deserted by him years before, "Well, Alex *must* have done something terrible or they never would have taken him!" It took her a long time to see things differently.

I knew a pilot in the Soviet Air Force. Peter Bekhtemirov. I met him in camp. He adored Stalin. One night he had had a terrible dream: The Leader had died. Bekhtemirov woke up with tears streaming down his face. He awakened his wife and told her that he had just had the most terrible dream, that Iosif Vissarionovich was dead. He shook with sobs. When he went to the base that day, he was still haunted by the grief of that dream. He confided to some of his fellow pilots what he had dreamed and how it had distressed him. One of the pilots gave him away, and the MGB charged him with an attempt to assassinate Stalin (political terrorism); a second charge was "an attempt to see an anti-Soviet dream." He got twenty-five years. His wife got ten for *not* denouncing him. Nobody believes me when I tell them this, but I know it to be true.

Anyway, the fact that the secret police can and do commit such incredible acts against rationality and humanity gives them overwhelming psychological force in Soviet streets and houses. When the hand of a secret police officer closes on your arm, it is like the hand of an evil god who needs no excuse. And you don't resist.

Now, after a few days with Sidorov, during which I spent as much time as I could complaining about the food and the lack of sleep, but always in as cocky a way as I could muster, and he went over and over the basic elements of my biography to see if they were consistent and to see if he could trip me up and discover if I was hiding anything, we began to get down to business. In the last days of the first week, when I thought I would die if I did not get some sleep pretty soon, he would say, "Listen, we *know* what you were up to. For example, you were employed as a clerk, chief clerk in the file room of the consular section, is that what you said?"

I said, "Of course, you know all that."

"Good. That is correct. We know everything about you, as you will see. Now, a clerk is a very junior position. A clerk does not get invited to parties as the private guest of chargés d'affaires, or to dinners at major embassies. But we have dates in here"—he slaps the folders with the back of his hand, always with the back of his hand—"of your dinner at the Australian Legation . . ."

"The assistant military attaché is a good buddy of mine. You see, I stole his girlfriend away from him, and—"

"The assistant military attaché! Indeed. A young clerk is an intimate friend of the assistant military attaché! That is a bit unusual, wouldn't you agree? Now look here. On this date, you had a private dinner with the Syrian chargé d'affaires, Mr. Baba. The *chargé d'affaires*! Would you say that was normal? And here you are at dinner at the Canadian Embassy, and here at the Belgian, and here at the French? A junior clerk? Can I take this seriously? Can you still maintain you were not in fact being prepared for a very special mission? We know that you were. You might as well save a lot of time and start to tell me about it."

I would hold out my hand for the folders. "Show me some of this crap," I'd say. "Let me see all this so-called proof. Let me see what you're basing all this on!"

But he would pull it away and say, "No, of course not! This is all operative material. You certainly can't look at it."

I would just smile a sort of simple smile, and say, "Okay," as if to say, If I can't see it, I can't tell you anything.

He knew the name of every girl I had ever taken out. Most of my girlfriends had been Russian girls, and now I think most of them were in the MGB, or maybe it is more accurate to say they reported to the MGB and were probably pretty much under their thumb.

I had had a very good time in Moscow after the war. The Russian girls were attracted to Americans. To begin with, we were the great allies, and then we had lots of good cigarettes and we could get nylon stockings and we had money to spend and we liked a good time. It was amazing how many of these good times Sidorov knew about, and amazing how many trivial incidents he could convert into some aspect of my alleged anti-Soviet activities.

There was a diamond buyer from New York who took me out to dinner once. I knew fur buyers and diamond buyers, and they knew each other, and they all had money to spend, and I enjoyed being taken to the good restaurants that I knew about and having them pick up the tab. And I enjoyed talk about America because I planned to go home soon and I wanted to hear all those little bits of gossip and street talk and the kind of stuff you don't get in the papers and in *Time* magazine. Anyway, this man from New York, an older man, suggested that we have dinner at the Metropole Hotel, off Red Square, not far from the embassy, and that I should bring a couple of whores. "Nothing serious," he said. "I'd just like some female company."

I checked around, I remember, and found that there was a sort of exchange for prostitutes in Moscow (where prostitution is still an active occupation to this day), and it was easy to make contact and the price would be, for example, fifty rubles at her place, forty at yours. And so on.

So I got hold of a couple of girls, told them it might not amount to much but they'd get a good dinner and I'd see they at least got a tip. And they were good sports and we actually had quite a few laughs and a fair dinner, because the Metropole was classy but the food in the big hotels was never that good.

The girls went to the ladies' room, and Harry the diamond buyer asked me while they were gone if it was safe to take them upstairs, because he wondered if they might be MGB. I said *I* didn't know. Anybody might be reporting to the MGB. But lots of people took whores to their rooms and got away with it, as far as I knew. In any case, I wasn't interested so it was up to him. And that was all.

Except that the conversation was recorded by a hidden microphone. Sidorov had a transcript of it, and finally made direct references to it, accusing me of trying to reveal the identity of MGB operatives!

I am not sure that was the first piece of concrete evidence that he laid before me, but it was one of the most ludicrous, and to give him credit I think he felt a bit sheepish about it, or maybe he was just using it to confuse me. In any case, he changed the subject pretty quickly.

I said to him, "Anyway, your operatives are clumsy and obvious. They were following me and everybody else in the embassy all the time. We always knew it and I always knew how to give them the slip. You think you know everything about me, but there is plenty you don't know. It has nothing to do with espionage, but you really ought to train your operatives a little better!"

"I don't know what you're talking about," Sidorov said, showing a slight flush of irritation.

I said, "Okay, I'll tell you. I leave the embassy for lunch, right? Or to do an errand? Or to go out for the evening? A plainclothesman in the street follows me to the corner and stays with me till I start down whatever street I'm going. Now, he doesn't want me to know I've got a tail, right? So he drops behind, picks up a phone and calls the booth a couple of corners ahead. 'Watch for a blond young man, one meter eighty, eighty-five kilos. U.S. Embassy.' Or something like that, right? So I'm supposed to think I've lost the tail because there's nobody behind me. The tail is in the front now. Am I right?"

Sidorov did not say a word. Just stared at me with those cynical gray eyes.

I said, "Only I caught on and started watching the phone booths ahead, and as soon as I saw a guy in the phone booth a couple of blocks away I'd wait just long enough so that the guy behind had dropped off, and then I'd turn down a side street, or go into a shop and double back. I could always lose them if I wanted to."

I smiled at Sidorov. To my surprise he smiled back. "Please go on," he said a bit tightly. "This is very interesting."

"Sure," I said. "Your people were always annoying me when I took an embassy car out at night. They followed me around and made the lady I was escorting feel very uncomfortable."

Sidorov shook his head.

"You don't believe I knew?" I said. "Okay. M6–3839. M6–5514. M3–7921. Do you know what those are?" (I was making those up; in fact I had memorized license numbers whenever the MGB cars followed me at night, but I only remembered one now, because it had turned up several times.)

"Look," I said, "if you don't believe me, write this down. M7–2895. Check it out. See if it's not one of your cars."

Sidorov looked at me for a long time, quite seriously. He wrote the number down. He got up and walked around for a while and thought about it.

I resisted the impulse to brag in detail about how I lost a car that was following me. I might want to use the same techniques later, I thought. The block between the Bolshoi and a branch of the Moscow Art Theater was honeycombed with intricately connected courtyards, opening onto the street and to each other through narrow archways. I had studied these yards and knew every possibility. I could lead a tail down Petrovka Street, going away from the Bolshoi, and before I got to the corner of Petrovsky Lane, where the theater is, I would suddenly wheel left into an archway. It was dark in there and slow going if you weren't absolutely sure of yourself. I would turn off the lights because I didn't need them. My followers would find themselves in alleys too narrow to go through. I would jerk left or right and end up going back onto Petrovka through another arch, going the opposite way, or right through the block and out onto Pushkin, or zig and zag to make up the turns necessary to put me out on Petrovsky opposite the theater, while my pursuers were probably still backing out of some cul-de-sac. I compressed this into one sentence and just told Sidorov, "While you're checking, ask him if he was ever able to stay on my tail: then you'll know if he's honest or not, because he never could."

Sidorov tried to get the upper hand back. He said loftily, "Of course all of this is known to us. I was just waiting until you would admit it, I knew you would, and you have. But since you have admitted all of these incriminating things, why not admit that you were engaged in espionage?"

"There's nothing incriminating about giving your guys the slip. They were annoying me. I was trying to have a nice time with a girl. You can't feel relaxed with a girl when there is a car full of MGB following you all the time."

"And why not, if you have nothing to hide?"

"Do you like being followed when you're out with a girl?"

Sidorov's smile dropped. He knew I had overheard him talking to his mistress on the phone in the interrogation room. He used to phone her almost every day—sometimes to say he'd be working that night, sometimes to make a rendezvous. I am sure he never thought I'd be audacious enough to make even this kind of oblique reference to it. He sat there staring at me with his hands on his desk. Then he unlocked his drawer and pulled out a Tokarev revolver and placed it on the desk pointing at me. This must have been a night session. He would never have done that in the daytime.

He got up and walked to my left, to the far corner of the room, holding the gun very lightly, but always pointing the barrel at me.

He said, "I don't think you understand your situation, you stupid son of a bitch. If I wanted to take you out right now and put you up against the wall, that would be it. I may do that. Unless you stop being so stupid. You're so stupid you keep giving yourself away and you don't even know it. This business of the cars. Every time you wanted a car you took it. Just *took* it! Do you think I don't know that a junior employee can't do that sort of thing? Do you think I am blind?!!"

There was no point in explaining a thing like this, because a Russian with Sidorov's experience would never be able to understand the attitude of an American kid who just takes the old man's car if the keys are in it and he knows he won't get into trouble because nobody bothers to check on such things. There were always half a dozen cars in the embassy yard. A couple of new Dodges with their fancy postwar crosshatch grilles and a beige Studebaker unlike any car I'd ever seen before, with the cab sitting on top of the body instead of being part of it and windows all around. And if I wanted a car, I just climbed in and gave the guy at the gate a wave as if I had an assignment. A car made even a drab, heavy city like Moscow a lot of fun to be in. To Sidorov, cars went with authority and official business. It was simply not comprehensible that you would use them for playing around. Unless you were somebody very highly placed.

And that is what he thought of me.

At least I think so. There were times in those early days when I suspected that he would take any credible confession, whatever it might be, whatever relation it bore to the truth. At other times, in fact most of the time, I felt he thought he was on to a really tough customer who had some high-priced goods hidden somewhere and wasn't about to give away the combination in a hurry. So my trouble was, however clever I was, or however right in explaining my behavior and my contacts and all the other trivia he pieced together to make a case against me, he simply thought I was employing the most subtle kind of tactics.

My tactic was to try not to go crazy from lack of sleep, and I found the more elaborate the game and the more I could summon the energy to make Sidorov work, to irritate him, provoke him, make him think he was getting somewhere and then let him drop, then the higher my morale and the more nearly tolerable this terrible lack of sleep. In fact, I was beginning to be frightened about what might happen to me. There would be periods when I suddenly knew that I had no recollection of what had happened in the last few minutes. Dropouts in my mind. Total erasures. Sidorov was showing very little strain. He was getting five or six hours sleep a night, I assumed, in two segments of two to three hours apiece between six in the evening and nine thirty or nine forty-five A.M. And, as I learned from overhearing some whispered remarks to his mistress on the phone, he got a substantial pay bonus for doing night interrogation.

Even Sidorov would begin to sag in the small hours. Three o'clock was a particularly low time for both of us, but in a way it was a good time for me, because after a lot of yawning, which he tried to stifle, Sidorov would tilt back his chair and close his eyes and drift off. At first I would wait a minute to see whether he was really sleeping. Then I would put my head on my arms on the table in front of me and be asleep instantly. When Sidorov woke up he would yell at me. "You're not allowed to sleep!"

"*You're* sleeping," I'd retort.

"*Never mind about me!*"

Then of course, later on, I began to experiment with sleeping upright, to see if my body could learn to hold itself erect. I thought if that would work I might escape detection in the cells for a few minutes at a time, because the guard at the peephole would not think I was asleep if I was sitting upright.

And so it would go, snatching ten minutes here, half an hour there, occasionally a little longer if Sidorov called it quits before six in the morning and the guards left me alone till the wake-up call. But it was too little. Too little. I could feel myself slipping, getting looser and less disciplined every day. I dreaded going crazy almost worse—no, really worse—than dying. Since the end of the routine Sunday Mass and catechism of my childhood, I have never been a church-going man, but I believe in God and I think there will be some kind of life after death. I was afraid of the pain of dying and terribly reluctant to leave the world behind because I liked life a lot, even if it had been pretty tough sometimes. And yet dying would be preferable by far to this terrible thing of going nuts, and that was what I fought against as much as simple physical decay.

Try to go without water for a whole day. Then imagine that your thirst is a desire to sleep. Then you will have ten per cent of what I felt. Stop breathing as you read this page. See how long you can keep from taking a breath. See how desperate you begin to feel as your heart begins to pump hard and your forehead begins to feel strange. Now, still not breathing, imagine there is no air left in the room. The muscles around your chin and neck are straining. Your larynx begins to make involuntary sounds and the bottom of your rib cage hurts. If you are really disciplined and carry this quite far, your vision will begin to blur. That is how badly I wanted sleep. I thought of sleep all the time. I fantasized sleep as a lecher fantasizes the flesh of young girls or a shipwrecked sailor dreams about a steak and mashed potatoes. There was an unending band of pressure around my head just above my eyes. My footsteps were uncertain when I walked and my breath was noisy and short. I found I was licking my lips a lot.

Often when they yelled "*Podyom*" at six o'clock and I had been on the cot only five minutes or ten I wanted to give up right then and beat on the door and yell and beg for them to bring Sidorov, that I would tell him anything, sign anything, accept any humiliation if only I could close my eyes and disappear from the world for a few hours of absolute peace.

Saturday afternoon came. Sidorov packed his stuff in his briefcase and phoned his wife before it got dark and told her he was on his way home for the weekend. Can you imagine what hearing that meant for me? I almost wanted to stand up and bow to him in gratitude as he went out the door. When I got back to the cell I ate the cold soup right away, all of it, as a celebration. Then when the porridge and tea came at six thirty or so I ate it all, taking time with each mouthful, talking silently to myself in a measured way to fill the time until ten o'clock, when I would be allowed, I was certain of it, Sidorov was gone for the weekend, to crawl under the blanket (keeping my hands outside, of course) and sleep. And *sleep*.

I began to hear music playing. Pleasant, waltz-time music. It came from the window. I was sufficiently confused in my mind to wonder seriously if I was imagining the music. But I went to the end of the gloomy black cell and stood by the table and listened carefully and was sure the music came from the window. It was quite clear. I could hear voices, indistinctly, calling out and laughing, and then an unmistakable rhythmic, whispering, scraping sound that I knew so well from years of making it happen under my feet: the sound of skate blades on ice! Somewhere close by was a public skating rink, with music. Right outside the prison somewhere. I could see it in my mind. In fact, years later, telling someone about it, the vision was so clear that I told my friend in all sincerity that I *had* seen it, that I had leaped up to grasp the window frame and pulled myself up until I could peek out through a slit miraculously left for me by an incompetent designer of window hoods, and had seen the skaters whirling about.

In reality what happened was that I counted seconds between peephole openings, stood still staring at the peephole until it was opened, began to count silently as soon as it closed (one-a-thousand, two-a-thousand), and still counting under my breath clambered up on the bed, crouched (I was pretty weak from the small rations and no rest), jumped as high as I could, grabbed the window frame, pulled up (twelve-a-thousand, thirteen-a-thousand, fourteen-a-thousand), kicked against the wall to help me, careful not to put any weight on the flimsy table, wriggled, pulled, got what I thought was a vision of some light from outside, ducked my head, sucked in breath for a bigger effort (thirty-one thousand, thirty-two thousand), pulled like hell as high as I could, realized there was no possible angle from which I could see past the baffles and out to the rink, hung listening a moment to the delicious music (I loved music anyway and at that moment I loved it like God, like Mary Catto, like a great dinner of roast chicken and green peas, like sleep), and listened as long as I dared (forty-five thousand, forty-six thousand) and then dropped to the floor and held my breath so the guard wouldn't see my chest heaving as the peephole opened at fifty-one thousand and I was still staring, immobile, at the door, with my heart beating like the big bass drum.

I remember that I waltzed up and down the cell until bedtime. Although I was so tired my breath was short and my eyes were burning, my morale was as high as it had been since I came to Lefortovo, because I knew I would soon get to sleep, provided Sidorov was not playing games and intending to come back for the usual nine-thirty nighttime start, so I danced or skated to the music. My floppy soles slithered up and down the asphalt. I held Mary in my arms and we spun around and around the ballroom at the Metropole Hotel. The peephole opened rhythmically, every minute. I kept on dancing. When I whirled away from the door I closed my eyes to keep them from burning and tried to guess how close we were coming to ten o'clock. There was a time when I guessed it must be close to nine and I had a terrible apprehension that Sidorov was coming back after all, and my sleep would be stolen from me again. I closed my eyes, fiercely, and danced and danced, bumping against walls occasionally, and humming under my breath. I held Mary very close and whispered that I loved her. In a while I knew that nine o'clock had come and gone, and nine thirty. I knew, too, that it was an easygoing guard on duty that night. I sensed a settling down in the prison. I thought I would chance it. I sat on the bunk and leaned against the end wall, which was against the rules. The peephole opened but the slot stayed shut. If he was going to yell and harass me he would bang open the slot. I stretched out on top of the blanket and kept my eyes wide open. The peephole opened but the slot stayed shut. I pulled the blanket over me and kept my hands outside and my eyes wide open. The peephole opened and the slot stayed shut. I closed my eyes and listened for the peephole to come open again, but I never heard it. I never dreamed. I never heard the music. I dropped a thousand, a million miles into the most profound, world-banishing sleep I had ever known. Not gratitude, not relief, not peace. Nothing approaching consciousness. Nothing I could remember. Oblivion.

CHAPTER

5

In the morning I was drugged with sleep. When "podyom" was shouted through the food slot, I knew I had to move, and I moved, but like a man under water, in slow motion. By now I realized the importance of disciplined routine; so I turned on the water and washed my face very carefully. Then I took off my shirt and square inch by square inch washed my upper body, cupping a little water in my hand and spreading it on, letting it dry a little, spreading some more on, and doing my whole trunk until I began to shiver with the cold. Then my lower body, taking off the baggy long prison underpants they had given me, with drawstrings around the ankles, folding them carefully until I had washed, using the little towel only on the hard-to-dry parts. By the time I had finished all that, I felt cheerful and hungry, almost painfully hungry.

The daily ration scarcely varied. Always, at breakfast, it was the 400 grams of sour bread, a piece of which I usually forced myself to save for later in the day, although I was so ravenous I felt I could eat my own flesh. Then the sugar and the tasteless imitation tea. Since my cell was at the end of the wing, near an elevator, I could hear the mechanism working when it started up in the morning with the tubs of tea and the trays of bread, and by now, even though only four days had gone by, I had begun to salivate uncontrollably at the sound of that elevator.

For a very brief time I fell into the trap of imagining marvelous meals. I would spread out a table with nice dishes and fill them with roast beef and baked potatoes and fried fish and bowls of gravy and white bread and green peas and ice cream and mugs of fresh coffee. As I looked over all this stuff in my mind's eye my stomach began to cry out with hunger. It hurt as if I had been hit. I salivated copiously and swallowed my saliva and began to belch deep, sour belches. Then I realized that this was no good. I was afraid it would break down my mind. I made a pact with myself, under my breath. I promised myself that if images of food like that crept into my mind, I would force myself to think of something else, like hikes in the woods with Mary, or poker games at the embassy, or the streets of New York's East Side. At first it did not work very well because as soon as I went hiking in the woods with Mary she would spread out a cloth and arrange cold sausages and a bottle of wine and cheese and butter and my mouth would fill with saliva again. Or if I walked down a street in Manhattan I would pass a bakery. So then I had to try arithmetic or the names of all the ships in the major naval battles of World Wars I and II. It was difficult to do silently. But I was absolutely determined that every task I agreed upon with myself had to be carried through or else. Failure would be giving in to Sidorov, to *them*. And by constantly giving myself little pep talks I was able to do it.

Easy, Alex. Take it easy. You can do it. You went with no sleep for a week and you can do anything you want. You're all right, boy. You've got guts. You're young and you're strong. These Russian bastards are trying to break you but you're on to them, aren't you. So as long as you're on to them they can't get you.

And this is the way I kept myself going.

I would think, Look. You just have to get through this day. Tomorrow there will be more interrogation. Sidorov is getting madder every day. He may get really tough. Maybe the guards will catch you doing something and throw you into the hard punishment cells. Maybe they'll even take you out and shoot you. But just get through *this* day. That's all you have to do.

In the middle of the morning, that first Sunday, the slot opened and a guard I hadn't seen before dumped three books on the shelf.

I said, "What's this?" But he just closed the slot without speaking. They never spoke to you if they could help it.

I rushed to pick up the books. They were tattered and dirty but they were treasures to me. Even though my eyes were sore and my head not very clear, I began to read immediately. I read every word with the greatest interest. I think I read those books four or five times during the next three weeks.

I have no idea whether the books were selected with a purpose in mind. One was called *Political Prisoners in Tsarist Russia*. It was supposed to be an account of the terrible indignities committed against the human person under the inhuman regime of the tsars. The first thing I noticed was that none of the prisoners I read about was ever prevented from sleeping. I thought that was pretty interesting. I was also fascinated to read references to a code used by prisoners for tapping messages to each other through the cell walls. It was called the prison Morse, but that meant nothing to me. Still, I was beginning to feel lonely enough that it would have been comforting to have someone other than Sidorov to communicate with, even by tapping through the walls.

Another book was Dostoevski's *The House of the Dead*. This was fascinating, in a horrible way. Ninety-nine years before me, this poor guy had been carted off to Siberia for discussing the theories of radical economists. He spent four hideous years there, "like a man buried alive, nailed down in his coffin," he wrote. Reading of his long-past but very real troubles made me feel maybe mine were not so bad after all.

On this Sunday morning I read for an hour, then walked up and down in the cell for a while, then read some more, spacing it out so as not to finish the books too fast. Also, I knew I should have some constructive physical activity to do in a regular way so that I would not get too dependent upon fantasy and keep a good grip on reality. There was a tear in my navy surplus shirt, and I decided that I would figure out some way to repair it. Again from reading old adventure books, I knew that if you were a prisoner you made needles out of fish bones. There were usually fish bones in the noon meal and even occasionally a couple of grams of fish. If I could somehow make a slit or a hole in the thick end of the bone and then dry it out, I might be able to unravel some threads from the prison towel and do some mending.

When the thin soup came in the middle of the day I saved three or four long fish bones from it and attempted, with no success, to bore a hole in the flat part of the wide end with my teeth and then with my spoon. The bone, which was soft from being boiled in the soup, would either split or be crushed completely. Then I tried to sharpen my aluminum spoon by scraping it on the floor, thinking that if I could get it to a point, I could punch the needle eye in tomorrow's fish bones. And then, while I was sharpening the spoon, I realized that it could be made into a crude weapon, if the edges were made sharp, and that led to thoughts of escape, killing a guard and taking his clothes and making my way through the prison somehow—all the kinds of things I had seen in so many Hollywood movies and read in novels.

One problem about killing a guard or any other aspect of escape was that I was getting too weak from poor food and lack of rest. The weakness was not serious at this point, but I knew that if I stayed in this situation very long it would become a very severe problem.

Anyway, a guard saw me sharpening the spoon and took it away, threatening hard punishment. I had been careless about the peephole timing. But even if I had not, I suppose they would have looked at it when I was out of the cell for interrogation.

I got the idea, out of nowhere, for making a more elegant calendar than my scratches on the wall. I would keep the scratches going, for a cumulative record, but I thought I could mold some numbers and a base to mount them on out of this soggy bread they brought me every day, which went very hard when it eventually dried out. I began to work on the calendar that first Sunday, starting with the base. I had enough bread saved for supper to steal a bit of my ration, and I kneaded it and rolled it and pressed it against the floor until I had a small, solid rectangle about eight centimeters long and two wide and one thick. Then I took one of my carefully hoarded matches and used the thin end to bore two holes about halfway through the flat side. These would be the receptacles for pegs which I would make out of the matches and fit into the bottom of the numbers that I would also make out of bread.

With the point of a match, I pressed the year, 1948, into the end of this base. Then I set the little bread block on the window ledge to harden, and wondered if the guards would bother with it. I thought that once it was good and dry I could smooth the surface by rubbing it on my shoes or on the floor, and I began to look forward to starting on the numbers as soon as I could stand to set aside some more bread to make them with.

So, with reading and bread molding and the abortive first attempt at needle making, I passed away most of Sunday afternoon. I was hungry but not too uncomfortable. Once the guard caught me humming quietly to myself and shook his head menacingly through the food slot, but I stopped immediately and he did not come in. It was terribly hard to keep awake, but I guessed that I would get a good night's sleep that night and wondered whether I could make it through the following weekend, or whether I would have to. Maybe the whole charade would be over by then.

I missed the sound of human voices, friendly voices, and it was very difficult to keep from talking to myself. Walking up and down the cell, when my head was turned away from the door, I would whisper very softly bits of remembered conversations, little encouraging messages to myself, little commentaries on what I was reading.

Late in the afternoon a strange guard took me to the shower room. He had a blank face. I tried to talk with him but each time he just shook his head wordlessly and put his finger to his lips. I asked about the weather outside. Shook his head. Asked how often I would get to have a shower. Shook his head, more vigorously. Then I got an idea and asked him if he liked his job. He shook his head just as hard as before, and even made a grimace when he put his finger to his lips, and almost managed to look fierce. But I don't think he had really listened to the question. Wordlessly he pulled out an old pair of hand-operated barbers' clippers and ran them through my soft, week-old beard, reducing it to a stiff stubble and tearing out a good many hairs in the process since the clippers were dull. Wordlessly he motioned and shoved me into the shower.

Even though the soap was the same foul-smelling soft stuff I had used a week before in the Lubyanka, the bath was welcome for the heat and because despite my strict regime of morning washes in my cell, the cold water with no soap still left me a bit ripe. When I looked at my naked body under the shower, I thought I looked a bit slimmer. I determined to keep up the dynamic tension exercises so that my upper body would not go to flab, and began under the shower to press my hands against each other.

The soap was about one-third the size of a small wooden matchbox and I used most of it. Then when the guard was not looking I pocketed the rest to take back to my cell. I did not really plan to wash with it in cold water; it hardly dissolved in hot water. But I was developing pack rat instincts, automatically.

Long before the evening porridge came I was belching long, sour belches of hunger. Then, when it came, I ate it slowly. I chewed every mouthful even though it was watery and thin. I mopped up with the last bit of bread I had saved from the morning meal.

While I ate I found myself thinking about the failure of the embassy to come to my rescue. I felt sad and puzzled about it. Then sadness yielded to anger. How could they leave me in here for a whole week almost, without raising holy hell! The more I thought about it, the madder I got.

Then I thought, this isn't doing me any good. I turned my thoughts to Mary Catto, to help me calm down.

I thought about Mary a good deal as the evening came on. I felt buoyed up by her promise to wait for me. In a way I was excited and strengthened by the thought of the strange coincidence of my having exacted that promise from her. I was filled with longing for her. I wondered for a while whether I should suppress those thoughts for the same reason I suppressed the food fantasies, but in the end I decided not to. The memories of Mary and the other girls in my life were a vital part of my connection with the world outside. They made me feel better, not worse, even though there was a strong rush of sadness sometimes. So by the time ten o'clock came and I was once more allowed to put my somewhat less numb brain to sleep, I felt composed but lonely. Much as I detested Sidorov now, I almost looked forward to the morning, just to have someone to talk to.

Looking back, it is strange that I had the instinct and the will to establish for myself so many disciplines and activities so early, since I was still convinced the whole thing was a mistake and that it would soon be rectified. Sidorov knew very well I was thinking this and he lost no opportunity to cast it in my face and to remind me that "we never make mistakes." He told me that everyone always claims it's a mistake, and, of course, he told me not to worry. From time to time his words would get to me and I would begin to think he might be right; perhaps that is one reason I undertook so seriously to develop survival strategies. Perhaps I had some intuitive sense of the real mess I was in. In addition, of course, I was young and I had read a great many novels and seen a great many movies and I had a young man's natural tendency to try to make life imitate fiction.

Furthermore, there was something about the atmosphere I had been living in that nourished a kind of heady, slightly unreal, playful and daring style of life, particularly if you were a relatively well-paid foreigner to whom all kinds of sought-after consumer goods were easily available and who also had the sense of invulnerability that goes with diplomatic status. At least I had *thought* I was invulnerable up to that point. I would try to explain this atmosphere to Sidorov when he endlessly harped on such things as my way of tearing around Moscow in embassy cars whenever I felt like it, and joining in the social life of the big guns from other embassies and so on. I was not the only one. I may have been a little more adventurous than some, but not more so than others. We all sensed this relief at the end of the war. Even ordinary Muscovites breathed a fresher air and looked forward to better days just around the corner, and for me and some other guys my age there was an intoxicating sense of confidence and optimism that certainly supported a romantic outlook. A good deal of this carried forward into prison, and thank God it did, because it was armor against the weapons that were being ranged against me and deployed with more frequency and more ferocity as time went by. Sidorov never admitted my point about the postwar mood in Moscow. I think he simply did not understand it.

Sidorov's language at night was violent and nasty. In the daytime he was easygoing and even chatty. Often he took time to read a novel or to write a report that had nothing to do with my case. He had a habit of twirling his pen nervously between his fingers, and in the afternoons he would lean back in his chair and twirl his pen and talk about the only real enthusiasm I ever detected in him: soccer and the Moscow Dynamos. The Dynamos were a secret-police-sponsored team, and Sidorov never missed their games. He knew their team members' characteristics and specialties the way an American kid knows batting averages, and sometimes he would spend most of an afternoon on that subject.

But at night he was always hostile and aggressive. I was never anything as simple as *"podsledstvenny"* (interrogatee) but at the very least "stupid *podsledstvenny"* and often "prostitute" or "son of a bitch" and all kinds of combinations. He spewed them out in harsh grunts and piercing yells. He sprayed a lot of saliva around the room as well.

The gun would come out a lot at night. He would brandish it in a wild way, and then sit at his desk and sight me calmly, aiming right between my eyes, and cock the hammer and twitch his finger in a way that looked as though he might accidentally fire it at any time. The Tokarev does not have a hair trigger. In fact, it has a pretty heavy trigger, but I knew enough about guns and about accidents with guns for this behavior of Sidorov's to make me pretty nervous. I never let him see that I was nervous. I just kept smiling. Sometimes I would even wink at him over the gun barrel, and this made him furious.

Once, during this second week, I found myself unconscious on the floor being yelled at by Sidorov. I had no memory of going off to sleep. I mean that it was a complete surprise to hear myself being yelled at to wake up when I was not even in bed. One minute I was staring at Sidorov trying to keep my eyes open; the next minute I was on the floor being roused.

In the cell I had to fight with every bit of willpower I had to keep awake. I tried a few times letting myself doze off while sitting upright on the bunk. If there was a decent guard on duty I might be left like that for a few minutes, perhaps even half an hour from time to time. But decent guards were few and far between. There was one young man with a Komsomol button. (Komsomol is a communist party youth organization.) He was the only guard who would ever chat with me, and that was evidence that he was new at the job. Most guards, when I tried to make them talk to me, simply answered, *"Nye polozhna"*—not permitted. In fact, *nye polozhna* was the single most often heard phrase throughout my entire time in prison. Sleep was *nye polozhna*, speech was *nye polozhna*, laughing was *nye polozhna*, anything human and simple you might want was *nye polozhna*. It was a phrase that could be applied to life. It might almost have been the title for this book. It came to the point where

I would ask a guard for something I knew he would not give me, a cigarette or something outrageous like that, so that I could enjoy saying *nye polozhna* before he did. Not to any of the regular bad guys on my wing, though, or I could count on extra buckets of water dumped on my floor next morning.

The young Komsomol was by nature a compassionate and enthusiastic young man. Later, when I developed the technique that saved my life by allowing me to steal a total of up to two or three hours' sleep every day and which involved a process of what I called "conditioning" the guards, this guy was so easily conditioned, because he was temperamentally sympathetic to my intentions, that he never bothered me at all. And when he first appeared in the wing he would sometimes let me sleep sitting up for several minutes at a time.

Of course he had strict orders not to let me lie down except between ten at night and six in the morning, when I was not usually in the cell anyway, but even this rule he enforced in a manner that could be called kindly. He would open the slot quietly, not yelling or hissing in the sharp, harsh whisper many of the guards favored, but speaking in a quiet, gentle voice: "Prisoner, remember, I am not allowed to let you sleep. Sit up now."

Although I instinctively liked this guy, a man about my own age, I still had to kid him. It was part of my program of keeping a sense of being on top. Kid anyone who was susceptible. I said, "How do you like being in the Komsomol?"

"Oh," he said enthusiastically, "I like it a great deal. It's fine."

"Are you an old Komsomol member?"

"Well, as you can see, I am still very young but" (with evident pride) "I have already been in the Komsomol quite a few years!"

"Well," I said knowingly, "you're in for it, then!"

He stared at me, quite puzzled.

"No, I mean it," I said. "You're in trouble."

"What do you mean by that?"

"*Don't worry!*" I said, trying to sound very mysterious. "You'll find out!"

Actually I believed that he would be bitterly disillusioned, through his work as a guard, about the idealistic picture of the Soviet Union and its system that all those Komsomol kids were fed with. He was not around long enough for me to see if this happened to him. Maybe he did not stick out the job, I don't know. He may well have been arrested for some anti-Soviet activity such as allowing a prisoner like me to sleep for a few minutes. It was not purely a joke when I told him he was in trouble. There was no room for compassion in the life of a guard.

I had made it through the second week. I was muddle-headed and anxious by Saturday night, but I also experienced a sense of satisfaction at having resisted every attempt by Sidorov to get me to admit to the fiction that I was a spy, and a lot of satisfaction at keeping up my smile and refusing to let him see any crack in my armor.

I sat on the edge of my bunk and steeled myself to keep awake until bedtime and the weekend respite at last. I read the poem, as I did most nights when I checked the calendar.

Who enters here do not lose hope.

"Don't worry," I whispered at the wall. "I won't."

Then I checked the calendar, and added up the dates. Twelve days since my arrest. It was . . .

It was Christmas Day.

In my confusion and exhaustion I had missed Christmas Eve. It had gone right by me.

And in my anger and my urgent work of keeping sane and surviving, I had scarcely given a thought to my mother, whose worried face now swam into my vision and engulfed me in sadness. She would have been expecting me for dinner. She would be pacing up and down wringing her hands, worried sick. My father would be saying, "It's all right, dear. It's all right. He probably had to go on a trip somewhere. We'll hear from him tomorrow. I'll give him a piece of my mind for not letting us know."

And then what would they do when tomorrow came and the tomorrow after that and still no word. I found the thought maddening. It made me tremble with fury at what seemed just then a worse affront to humanity than what was happening to me. I mean leaving those two innocent people frantic with worry. I had to get hold of myself. I had to tell myself firmly to cut out this fruitless worry. There was nothing I could do about it. Anyway, I still told myself, though by now I believed it a lot less, I'll see them soon and tell them all about it.

But I think when I finally settled into sleep my eyes were pretty damp.

For the rest of the week I worked at shutting out the images of Christmas and New Year celebrations when they crept up on me. It was too painfully lonely. I found that I could manage pretty well, and the following week I sailed through New Year's Eve and New Year's Day as if they did not exist as anything but marks on the wall.

In the daytime periods in the cell I continued with my bread calendar, which went very well, and the attempt to make a needle, which eluded me for some time. When the calendar base-block I had made got good and hard, it was a bit gray and rough on the surface. So I took off my shoe and rubbed it with the sole until it began to look fairly smooth, and then polished it on my blanket. I polished it every day. After a while it took on a gloss like polished wood. In the meantime I began to form the numbers. I fixed a short piece of match in the bottom of each one for a peg. I made two 1's, two 2's, and one of everything else, so there were twelve of these little figures to mold. I took my time and made a very careful and elegant job of each one. Any that did not turn out just right I ate.

This simple structure gave me enormous pleasure. I never stopped working at it. Often, after several days, I would decide that the 6 or the 8 —that was the hardest one to make—had a certain imperfection, so I would eat it and start on a replacement.

All this time the need for sleep was becoming more and more intense and the fear that I might crack for want of it was a threat in itself. The busywork with the calendar and my still fumbling and unsuccessful attempts at a needle became desperate attempts to stay awake and to stay sane. Sidorov, at my request, had explained that the hard punishment cells were below ground, unheated even in the depths of winter, had no windows and no bed, and that the whole day's food ration was what I was now getting for breakfast and nothing more. So I was determined not to do anything that would land me in conditions that I certainly could not stand up under. That is why I fought sleep so determinedly, and largely successfully, through a second week: fear of that remote, hideous, destroying box in the cellars of this monstrous K-shaped prison for political prisoners—a dungeon worse than anything out of my novels and movies.

Not that my own cell was in any way comfortable. In recounting what happened to me in Lefortovo, because I had a certain measure of success in outwitting Sidorov and outwitting the guards and even outwitting insanity and death, I am often afraid that people will forget what a hell I was living. I see them smiling and nodding cheerfully when I tell about making the calendar, for instance. That was, I guess, a reasonably ingenious thing to do and it gave me pleasure. So I recall it readily enough and tell about it with relish. But this was something that was done in a cell purposely designed to create a waking nightmare for its occupant. It was even called a "psychic cell" and Sidorov made no bones about the fact that it was intended to wear down my morale, because that was his purpose. "You won't last six months at the outside," he often said. "Nobody does, so you might as well start confessing now."

"I have nothing to confess." Etc.

Cell 111. The psychic cell. The black paint was neither flat, which might have had a velvety warmth to it, nor glossy, which might have had a few highlights in it, but just a hard black. The bed was black. The floor was black. The bulb over the door, which when I was allowed to sleep I had to face, was not bright enough to illuminate this black space but bright enough to be an annoyance when I faced it. I considered it one of the components of hell—never off to give you a rest, never bright enough to cheer you.

The cell was cold. There was no source of heat in it. When the outside temperature dropped below zero, frost would form on the floor of the cell. I was warm only when they took me to Sidorov. The cell was airless. It stank of all those prison smells. But most of all it was an environment of almost unrelieved gloom and there is no question that I found it terribly oppressive—so oppressive that for the first couple of weeks it was a relief to leave it, even for interrogation. And then—part of the hell—I would look forward to getting away from Sidorov's taunting and badgering and lies and anger and saliva and into a quiet place, my cell, which almost as soon as I was back in it began to intimidate me all over again with its blackness and its chill.

The peephole was a rhythmic torture at first; later I think I came to terms with it, like breathing. If they had learned to be irregular about it, spring it on me at odd times, let a whole day go by without it, then slam it open, go for an hour without it, then open it every thirty seconds, and so on, it might have driven me quite mad in a short time. But it was very reliable. It could be counted on, even if I did not like it much.

Memory keeps you alive. I firmly believe this. It's obvious you need food and water and air and shelter, of course. But lonely men have gone mad or killed themselves even when they were warm enough and had enough to eat. A man in my position—left in a dark room, not really enough food to keep his furnace going, cold, insulted and abused by the few people he does encounter, so that he doesn't see them as people anymore—needs a good memory to keep in touch with human beings who are somewhere else.

If I had not been able to remember faces, names, the plots of movies, words people had spoken to me, books I had read, restaurants I had eaten in, maps, the face of Europe, rooftops in Manhattan, I could never have survived the Moscow prisons. Labor camps, maybe. There you are with people. In Lefortovo prison, even though I spent nearly eighteen hours a day, six days a week, in interrogation with Colonel Sidorov, I was alone and, next to the desperate need for sleep, aloneness was the strongest sensation and the most feared enemy.

The words of songs were important, all the familiar, romantic, goofy hit songs that we played on the phonograph at the embassy and sang at parties were a lifeline for me.

Sometime in the third week at Lefortovo a new torture was added to the cold and the black and the loneliness of cell 111. Early one morning a strange low rumble started somewhere outside my window and soon grew in pitch and volume until it was a gigantic roar. When I looked at my plate and spoon on the shaky little table they were visibly trembling. Their edges were blurred! I was enraged. I thought that the sound had been designed by a specialist in tortures, a fiendish man who wanted to destroy human will. I admired the genius of whoever invented the torture. Even when I covered my ears the sound drilled through my skull. There was no escaping it. I was relieved when they took me to Sidorov. I wryly complimented him on the inhuman ingenuity of the terrible noise. Irony was never Sidorov's strong point, and he didn't understand me. He said, "I know. It is terrible. They have an aeronautical research institute next door. That's their wind tunnel. Good thing my office is not on that side, I'd never be able to get my reports written."

Poor Sidorov.

So it was a wind tunnel and not a torture device. And yet it was going to get me down. I knew it. I decided I would have to fight that sound the way I fought everything else they tried to break me with. I decided I would learn how to go deaf.

I read once that some people go deaf psychologically after a strong emotional shock. I thought I could train myself to be temporarily deaf, the same way I had trained myself to smile at Sidorov every night instead of showing him how frightened and angry I was. However, I never carried this out, because almost as soon as I thought of it I also realized that this wind tunnel noise was something I could use to help me survive. Instead of fighting it, I would make it an ally.

The guard brought me back to the cell at a quarter past five the next morning. I knew it was earlier than usual because for the last couple of hours Sidorov had been yawning all the time and then when he finally said that was enough for tonight and pressed the button for the guard, the doors in the other interrogation rooms were still closed and the corridors were quiet. Usually there would be some doors open, and since prisoners were being escorted you could hear the keys clanking on the guards' belts along the corridors—the familiar signal to other guards, so that two prisoners would never see each other. The guard would usually hold me back in the room and look up and down the corridor first. But this morning he just motioned me straight out. When I got to the cell I was sure it was still well before six, and I lay down on the cot and nobody bothered me and I think I had at least half an hour's sleep. Maybe three-quarters.

I always used to think there was nothing worse than waking up after a sleep that was too short. But by now I was keeping score because I knew that every minute of real sleep was going to help me from going crazy and keep my memory from blanking out and so keep me alive. My eyes were burning, and I felt real hate for the guy who banged on the door, "*Podyom!*" at six o'clock, not just irritation but real hate, and yet all the same I knew I had gotten a little sleep, and I scored it off mentally as an edge, a bit of an advantage over Sidorov. Sidorov counted on wearing me down, and at this stage I still thought I could wear him down.

A person is made up of his memories, and if you lose that you stop being a person. So even if the body keeps on living, the person is gone. But that is not what I mean; I'm really talking about how memory is necessary for sheer physical survival.

I got up when they banged on the door and shouted *"Podyom!"* There was still no sign of light through the little hooded window. It was January outside in Moscow. I washed my face carefully in the cold water and then I sat for a few minutes on the toilet and closed my eyes in the fifty seconds of safety I could count on between visits at the peephole. This way I actually caught another minute or two of sleep perched on the hard edge of that iron cone.

Then I got up and started to walk back and forth in the cell because as long as you were in motion they left you alone unless you did something strange. And then I began to count the minutes until the wind tunnel would start up because I had decided how I would use it.

It was against the rules to talk in the cell, or make any sound. If you talked to yourself the guard would throw open the food slot and hiss at you. "Shut up, you! No talking! Hard punishment cell for you if I catch you doing that again!" Just for talking! Or if it was a good guard and he caught you whispering or muttering absent-mindedly because you were half asleep all the time, he might just tap at the peephole and wave his finger or shake his head when you looked up. But most of the guards took the opportunity to break their own boring routine, I guess, and throw open the slot and threaten me with the hard punishment cells.

Anyway, they really believed I was an enemy of the people. I found that out later.

Breakfast would come about six thirty. I had figured this out by counting the number of times the peephole opened between *"Podyom"* and breakfast. Once every minute, nearly. I don't claim I was precise about it.

Four hundred grams of hard, damp, sour black bread, with one and a half lumps of sugar and a mug of "tea." Then around seven sometime the door opens again and a guard hands in an old greatcoat from the days of the Revolution, must be thirty years old at least, quite threadbare, and motions you into the corridor and clicks the key on his belt and takes you down some steps and out into the yard for the exercise period.

The yard is divided up by wooden walls. The spaces aren't that much bigger than my cell. I can't see anyone, except a guard looking down from the tower above the exercise slots. I have fifteen minutes for fresh air. If I look straight up I can see the sky and this morning, I remember, it was still dark and clear and I could see a star. I guess lonely people all over the world have looked at stars like that. Is Mary looking at that star? I thought.

There would be indistinct shuffling sounds from behind the boards somewhere across the egg-crate yard. Somebody else having his morning walk. I guessed there were other men looking up at the star and asking themselves if their wives or children or girlfriends could see that same star.

Then the guard came to take me back to the cell, but that was all right because I was waiting for the wind tunnel to start up so I could try my experiment in making it work for me. I counted the times the peephole opened. When I guessed it was getting close to eight o'clock, I thought, All right, now. Maybe after this peephole but before the next one. Then, you know, you don't want to disappoint yourself. So I would say, No, I've probably counted wrong and it's really a few minutes too early. I'll give it three more peepholes.

So finally it started up. Some blurred low noises at first, then a sort of winding noise, and then it would build up to a full roar. The building did not really shake but I could feel it reverberate in my chest. I turned away from the peephole in the cell door and the moment I strode away toward the window I opened my mouth as wide as I could and I filled my lungs and I sang out loud.

I sang

> *Mairzy doats and dozy doats*
> *And liddle lamzy divey*

Loud. I mean really full blast, everything I had. *Fortissimo*. Boy, it felt great!

At the end of the cell I turned and looked back at the peephole. I thought, On the way back where he can see my face, I won't move my lips so much and I won't sing so loud, so even if he looks carefully he won't know what's going on. So now, a little more carefully, Alex, *sotto voce*, is that the word? or *piano*?

> *A kiddley divey too, wouldn't you?*

The effect was fantastic! I mean the effect on me. I was grinning to myself. I had discovered another instrument for my survival. It sounds crazy talking about this childish song as an instrument of survival. But this was a song from America. It was a song they were singing in New York somewhere. Back at the American Embassy on Mokhovaya Street, there was a phonograph with that record on it. Maybe not right now, at eight o'clock in the morning, but the record was there all right and sometime today probably, maybe tonight after work, someone would play it.

> *If the words sound queer*
> *And funny to your ear*
> *A little bit jumbled and jivey*
> *Sing mares eat oats*
> *And does eat oats*
> *And little lambs eat ivy*

I immediately felt less tired. In about an hour I knew I had to go back to the interrogation room. Sidorov would have slept three, three and a half, maybe this morning almost four hours because he had quit early. Slept in a real bed with a pillow and sheets. He would have shaved in hot water. Probably he'd have had an egg or something good to eat and real tea with milk in it. He would know I hadn't slept. He would count on me to be a little crazy, a little lightheaded so he could confuse me. My arms and legs and back would be sore from the hard bed. I wouldn't have much endurance when he began to get at me.

He's had me three weeks now and pretty soon I'll break down and tell him whatever he wants, he's sure of that, I can tell from his face. Although when I just keep smiling politely at him I sense a kind of violence building up.

But this morning I've got the bastard because I can sing and that means I'm still in touch with the outside and I've had half an hour's sleep, maybe forty minutes, and when he sees me he just won't understand why I'm so goddamn cocky and I'm going to be goddamn cocky this morning because I know that bastard is just not going to get what he wants from me and one of these days he's going to have to let me go!

I remember that I walked faster and faster up and down the cell that morning, pivoting on the ball of my foot at the end of the cell, filling my lungs up and singing nonstop. I'm the Lefortovo jukebox, I said to myself.

> *Pardon me boy*
> *Is this the Chattanooga Choo-Choo*
> *On track twenty-nine*
> *Why don't you give me a shine?*

It would be very easy to give in, which is the purpose of everything they are trying to do to me in cell 111 and in the endless interrogation room. I am accused of terrorism, of anti-Soviet propaganda, of espionage. If I confess to these charges, presumably they will stop keeping me awake at night, give me something decent to eat and a bed to sleep in. Well, even if I had something to confess I would never do it. But I have nothing and I'm still completely mystified every time Sidorov says, so confidently, "Look, we know it all, why don't you admit it!" He picks up the thick folders and slaps them with one hand.

"It's all in here. The *sledstvie* (investigative bodies) have made a full report. We know that at a certain period in 1946 you were planning terrorist activities and we know you were recruiting others to work with you. Now tell me about it."

After a while that morning my legs got too tired to walk up and down anymore so I sat on the bunk. This was allowed as long as you kept your hands on your knees and faced the peephole. But I felt good. My optimism was back up again, after slipping pretty low the last few days. I thought I should run a little check list on myself and see how it was going.

> Name: Alexander M. Dolgun
> Age: Twenty-two
> Date of birth: September 29, 1926
> Address: American House, American Embassy, Moscow

All of this out loud in a firm voice, but when the peephole opens I stop moving my lips, just stare straight ahead.

Hands steady? I hold them in front of me. They tremble a little but that's normal enough because I haven't been allowed to sleep all night since . . . I had trouble recalling since when, so I thought I had better work on that. I looked at my wall calendar, a series of scratches in the black paint on the wall of my cell. I was arrested on December 13, 1948. Monday. Moved here, to Lefortovo from Lubyanka, on the fifteenth, and put straight into this all-black cell with one twenty-five-watt bulb in a steel-meshed recess over the door, so it was hard to see my scratches. But they showed the first week truncated, only five days, and then another full week, and another, and then three scratches so it was Wednesday January 5 and that meant I had been two days and two nights without a full sleep. Saturday and Sunday nights they let me sleep while Sidorov went home or wherever he went.

The door of my cell opened and the guard handed in my bucket of icy water and a rag and went out again without speaking. That meant about half an hour left before I would be taken upstairs. I poured some water on the black asphalt floor and got down on my knees and started to scrub. If you did it badly, whatever that meant, they might make you start all over again. There was a woman guard, a truly cruel person, who liked to find fault with the way I scrubbed the floor. Once she came back with a second bucket and spilled the whole thing out on the floor and then yelled at me to hurry and get it mopped up with the rag because it was time to go to interrogation.

She was the one who used to open the door when I was sitting on the iron cone, not grabbing sleep but really using it, with my pants down, completely vulnerable, and yell, "Hurry up, you *sterva!* Why does it take you so long!" *Sterva* is a very unpleasant Russian word meaning "carrion." This squatty, mean woman was the only guard who used filthy language. Others would shout at you but she really was vile, almost as bad as Sidorov, and a lot meaner. Every time I used the toilet she would open the slot and yell at me.

But this morning the guard was a quiet one, and when I finished the floor and stood in front of the peephole with my rag and bucket he opened the door without a word and took it away and locked me in again.

Now it would be five or ten minutes before they would take me upstairs. I was on to Sidorov's daytime/nighttime pattern now. It had become perfectly regular. I decided it was a deliberate trick, to curse and abuse me at night and play a waiting game in the daytime, giving me a chance to let my guard down. The day before he had been carrying on about the Moscow Dynamos again.

Did I ever go to soccer games? Wouldn't I admit that it was a better game than baseball? And so on.

And then that same night he had been at times morose and silent, staring at me angrily to try to unnerve me, and then at other times he'd paced up and down slapping his dossiers and shouting abuse at me. He would say things like, "You are an illegitimate son of a bitch and I fuck your mother. If you don't cooperate with me I will have your balls and then I'll take you out and shoot you personally."

Later on he would build it up to real crescendos, but even at this stage, when he would shout, "The state fucks you, you stupid son of a bitch!" I could sense that his fists were clenching and that worse was to come than just hard language.

At night he would finger his gun a lot, the Tokarev seven-shot revolver. He would take it out and lay it on the table with the barrel pointing at me. That's when he'd talk about taking me out to shoot me.

But in the daytime he was never like this. He'd begin with, "Well, haven't you decided to tell me everything and save yourself a lot of trouble?" Then I would say, "Well, I have told you everything I know, I have nothing more to add. What else do you want?"

Then he would say, "I've got time. We know everything anyway." And he'd hum a bit, and go through his files and read the newspaper, and ask me what I knew about Marxism and Leninism, all in an easygoing, almost amiable way. In detective stories there is a well-known police technique of interrogation, in which a bad guy and a good guy team up. The bad guy terrorizes the prisoner while the "good guy" pretends to look pained and embarrassed at the threats of violence. Then the bad guy leaves the room for a drink of water or something and the good guy puts on a confidential tone and says, "Listen, don't worry, I think I can keep him from losing his temper, just watch out, trust me, he really is a tough customer," and so on, to confuse the prisoner and either weaken his resistance to the tough technique or win him over to the apparent "friend." I suppose the MGB technique was to combine bad guy and good guy in one interrogator. That's what it seemed like.

Well, today I was going to confuse Sidorov some more. I felt up to it. I was a bit lightheaded. I would have to go three more nights with no sleep before it was Saturday. But somehow I knew I would get through it, and somehow I was sure I was going to find a way to sleep during the week.

I stood up again and began to walk. The wind tunnel was still roaring. I grinned at it through the stone walls. "Thank you, friend," I said. And then shouted out loud, "Thank you, friend!" And then I put my head back and filled the time I had left with one more song I could really put my heart into.

> *Oh, give me land lots of land under starry skies above,*
> *Don't fence me in!*
> *Let me ride through the wide open country that I love,*
> *Don't fence me in!*
> *I want to ride to the ridge where the West commences,*
> *Gaze at the moon till I lose my senses,*
> *Can't look at hobbles and I can't stand fences,*
> *Don't fence me in!*

The door rattled and swung open. "Prepare for interrogation," the guard said. He looked up and down the corridor and then motioned me out. He was a relatively easygoing guy, I remember. When he looked at me to motion me out of the cell his eyebrows went up quite a lot because I was grinning quite happily. But he didn't say a word.

CHAPTER

6

SIDOROV WAS NOT IN THE INTERROGATION ROOM WHEN I GOT THERE. I sat on the chair and immediately went to sleep. It probably lasted two minutes, but this time I did not fall off the chair. I was beginning to learn how to sleep in a hard wooden chair without falling off, and to be ready to wake up again at the smallest sound. I had tried it two or three times on Sidorov already but I think he was getting wise to me. He would ask a question and I would say, "Listen, I have to think about that for a minute." Then I would put my hand to my head and close my eyes and doze off, just go to sleep. The first time I came to with a lurch and he knew I had been sleeping. I said, "I can't help it. I'm trying to remember but I'm too sleepy." Sidorov said brusquely, "Keep your eyes open, then." I said, "It helps me to remember. Don't worry, I'll try to stay awake."

I tried it again a day later, in the daytime, and this time I was able to signal myself to wake up in a minute, smoothly, and say quietly, "No, I can't remember," in answer to his question.

This time, as soon as I heard the door opening, I woke up and found

I was sitting up straight, and when Sidorov looked at me my eyes were wide open. Sidorov went directly to his big desk opposite my little table and thumped his file folders down on it. He spread out the newspaper and stood over the desk peering at it and wiping something invisible from his trouser leg with the back of his hand. Then he sat down behind the desk and read for a while without looking at me, and pulled a pack of cigarettes out of his pockets and lit one. I recognized the routine. He smoked for a while and then looked at me for quite a long while without speaking. I have talked to hundreds of prisoners who have undergone interrogation, so I know that this is part of an interrogator's method. Keep you waiting and wondering. Sidorov carried it too far with me because he was not a very sensitive man and had no idea what kind of game I was playing. I have *him* wondering, I told myself.

After a while he said, "Prisoner, come over here."

I went and stood in front of his big desk. He had very gray eyes. I noticed that he had missed shaving just under his nose. After a while he offered me a cigarette. "Here."

I took it and he lit it for me with a kind of courtesy.

"Your own are all gone, aren't they?"

"I told you that. Two weeks ago. More. They only lasted two or three days."

"You like to smoke, don't you?"

"Sure I do, you know that."

"I know a lot about you, my friend."

I waited.

"In the labor camp where I will send you when I'm through with you, there is always tobacco, you can have your own and you can smoke whenever you like. Wouldn't that be better than what you're getting here?"

I just smiled my simple smile at him and shrugged.

"Look, prisoner, I'm going to give you some advice. It won't get any better here. You think you're having a hard time, but it can only get harder if you don't cooperate. Now listen, it's all in here anyway"—he slapped the files—"and I'm going to get it out of you because that's my job and I'm good at it and I've never failed yet. So instead of waiting for a month or two or however long you intend to be stubborn, why not get it over with now? Today. Tell me everything because we know it all anyway, all we need is a few details and a signed statement, and then you'll be able to sleep at night and smoke cigarettes and get decent food and be with other people all day long, and you'll probably get a very light sentence for cooperating."

I heard snatches of music running through my head. I laughed out loud and said in English, "Is this the Chattanooga Choo-Choo?"

"What's that?" Sidorov said sharply.

I said, "Why don't you give me a shine?"

"Prisoner, you are forbidden to speak English!"

I said in Russian, "I'm sorry. I'm really sorry. But this is really marvelous! I don't think you realize how marvelous it is."

He said, "What are you getting at?"

I said, "Listen. You're getting extra pay for night interrogations. If I tell you everything right now, you'll lose all those bonuses. Why should I do that to you after all you've done for me? Besides, if you know everything already, what do you need me for anyway? Why not just send me quietly off to camp? You could spend the next six months writing up your reports at home. Then you could report you've got the confession you needed. You don't need me if you know everything."

Being pretty lightheaded, that all sounded better to me than it really was. But it did succeed in confusing Sidorov for a moment. His face was very blank, and then a trace of anger came into it. But he simply turned away without answering and picked up the paper. "You won't feel so witty later tonight," he said tightly.

I drew on the smoke. It went down deliciously and took the top of my windpipe with a satisfying catch. It was the first cigarette since the weekend and it went to my head which was already floating, and made me very relaxed and dying for sleep. I had to fight off an impulse to say to Sidorov, "Please let me go to sleep! If you let me go to sleep, I'll do anything you want."

But there was no point in even trying that because he wanted details of my spying activities and there simply were no spying activities to give him details on. I couldn't win and yet I felt I couldn't lose either, as long as I refused to give in and show any weakness.

All day I sat in the chair, shifting my shrinking buttocks from side to side, trying to blink away the burning in my eyes. Sidorov scarcely spoke. Once or twice he picked up the phone and called his wife. Sometime in the middle of the day he got up and left to get something to eat. He told the guard to make sure I did not go to sleep. I tried sleeping in my chair without showing it, but as soon as the guard saw my eyes closed he came and shook me. The high morale I had built up for myself with songs in the morning was beginning to wear off. I wanted to get back in the cell and sing some more songs, but I knew they shut the wind tunnel down before six o'clock, and I would have to wait until morning. There was a kind of pressure building up inside my skull. Not a headache, just a strong, incessant pressure connected with my eyes. I knew it could only be cured by sleep. Before Sidorov came back I tottered again and fell off the chair with my eyes closed. Somebody picked me up and shook me vigorously.

"Sleep," I said.

"Talk, and you'll get to sleep," Sidorov's voice said. I opened my burning eyes and smiled at him.

Back to the cell at 6 P.M. Sometime in the middle of the day they have brought the midday bowl of thin cabbage soup with a bit of fish in it. When they open the door of cell 111 and shove me in, the soup is sitting there on my plate, cold, and if I want the bit of protein and phosphorous and other essentials it contains, I will have to eat it right away, cold and insipid as it is, or else do without my hot porridge, which will come almost immediately, since I have only one plate.

That night, or one night soon after, two things happened almost simultaneously. I noticed that my hair was falling out, and I found some information on the bottom of my plate.

In fact, my hair had started coming out at the end of the second week. Years later I was told this could be a result of extreme nervous stress, along with everything else that was happening to me. I was losing a lot of weight, but I could afford a bit of that. But there was no fresh food of any kind. I was sure I would start to get scurvy if I stayed in prison very long. My gums were beginning to get sore. When I washed my face and ran some cold water through my hair with my fingers, a few hairs came away and I saw them in the sink. The next time I was taken out for a shower, when I was drying myself, I saw some more hair lying on my arm. This time there was a whole tuft of it. I had brushed my hand across my head to try to ease the pressure in my skull, and I could literally feel a mass of hair come loose as my fingers rubbed my scalp. I brought down a bunch of blond hair and stared at it. The sight of it made me feel quite uneasy. It was a sign of physical decay. I had been expecting something, but not this.

I felt a surge of panic coming on. I said, "Easy, Alex, that's what they want. To make you lose control." I was enormously tempted to feel my head and see if any more hair would come away but I was terrified that it would, so I didn't.

I thought, I've got to get busy at something new, anything to keep my mind active. I tried drawing in deep breaths to see if that would relax me. My chest felt weighted down with hard straps running around my ribs. I got up and ran some more water in the sink and splashed my face with it, and then decided to wash my plate very meticulously and dry it with my little towel. And this is where the information came from.

I remember a story one of the guys at the embassy used to tell, about some guy who went to jail and was criticized by the warden for keeping a pack of cards instead of a Bible in his cell. Then the guy explained to the warden how the cards had a symbolism that reminded him of all the biblical characters and could also function as a calendar and so on. Well, that's what it's like in prison. You make use of the smallest scraps of information and get a lot of mileage from them. When I was drying this enameled metal plate, I noticed on the bottom the name of the Moscow factory where it was made, and the figures 10–22.

I've always enjoyed number games, and I thought, Here's one ready made. Figure out what this means, 10–22.

Probably when I first saw those numbers I assumed they were the date of manufacture, October 1922. But the plate was pretty new, not worn enough to be a quarter of a century old. I wondered for a while if it referred to the prison in some kind of code. Then, just while I sat and looked at it in my hand, I found myself saying silently that the plate was about twenty-two centimeters across and the inner section about ten centimeters. If that was true, I could prove it by making some sort of tape measure and checking the two dimensions against each other.

Of course, my belt and tie were gone.

I started looking around the cell for something I could use. The towel caught my eye. It was woven pretty loosely of a fairly coarse cotton. It took just two seconds to unravel a thread from across the end, and I got a piece about forty centimeters long. I broke off a piece a little longer than the width of the plate. I laid it across the diameter of the plate and creased it at what I hoped would be the twenty-two-centimeter mark. Then I measured and knotted lengths equal to six centimeters, from the edge to the inner rim; ten centimeters across the inner section; sixteen centimeters from the outer edge right across the inner section; and another of twenty, twice the diameter of the inner section.

I became totally absorbed in this cumbersome arithmetic. From time to time I looked up at the peephole, but what I was doing apparently seemed innocent enough because there was no interruption. Now I measured a thread equal to the difference between the six and the ten, and then folded it in half and found to my delight it was exactly equal to the difference between the twenty and the twenty-two. A small matter, but I almost laughed out loud at my success. All the other comparisons worked. I painstakingly pulled out threads until I had a piece that looked like about a meter, and then divided it up by sharp creases with my teeth into ten ten-centimeter lengths and then divided up the last of these into ten one-centimeter divisions. I now had a ruler.

I at first decided to measure my cell. I said to myself, "I wonder how far I actually walk every day, up and down between these walls?" It was 227 centimeters wide and 351 long. I wondered how many kilometers a day I might make, up and down, up and down, my hands behind my back. I walked from the door to the opposite wall and back. Ten steps, five each way, which meant about seventy centimeters each step. I thought working on a base of seventy might be too much for my mental arithmetic, but if I could shorten the step to 66⅔, so that every three steps meant two meters, then a kilometer would take fifteen hundred steps.

I thought, I'll walk to the embassy.

I did not know then precisely where the American Embassy was in relation to Lefortovo Prison, but I remembered that the drive across town in the middle of the night took about fifteen minutes at a pretty modest pace; so I guessed about eight kilometers. Southwest, I guessed. Let's see how long it takes me to get there.

The idea excited me strangely. In my dead black cell, isolated from everyone but the anonymous eye at the peephole every minute or so, the fantasy of a walk across Moscow to join friends was totally seductive. I had not seen the outside of the prison, but I had heard the gates swing open and could imagine their size. I made the gates my first target and got up and started to walk as fast as I could, estimating a slightly shortened pace, and just feeling my way downstairs to the gates. Up and down the cell. Now I am at the corridor of boxes, another thirty steps, lucky the door is open; and no one is looking and I'm out into the courtyard. It's dark enough. There is a van coming in with a prisoner, I'll just slip behind it, and the gates are still open, and out into the snowy streets and freedom!

A nourishing fantasy. An energizing fantasy. I breathed in the clear, cold imaginary air and hugged my coat around me. (What coat? Oh, I had somehow kept the exercise coat; that would do.) I turned southwest and began to count my steps, up and down the cell. I walked past the skating rink, with the lights and music and the boys and girls whirling around, but I didn't look right or left. I just walked and counted, up and down the cell. Now six hundred paces—it will take twelve thousand tonight, Alex old buddy, and you'd better make it by dawn or they'll pick you up. Keep at it.

Now a funny thing happened. I began to recognize the streets of Moscow—streets I'd driven through with the boys from the embassy, out on the town with a borrowed embassy car. I thought, Easy, I can't have come this far. What's the count? Streets I'd driven along with Mary, with her head on my lap, talking about the future, about America, so far to the west.

Now I'm going southwest, in Moscow.

Then I thought, Jesus! Why not go west, not southwest! Why not walk right out of this God-forsaken country? Let's say it's only six kilometers from here to the outskirts of the city proper, then I can pick up a road west and hide in some farm building in the morning and just head right across Russia until I'm free! Only nine thousand paces to the edge of Moscow, kid. Pick it up now, pick it up!

I turned right at the next street in my mind. I did not recognize the street. But the moon hung low in the west and I headed straight for that. No one in the nearly empty streets paid any attention to me. Why should they? I just tucked my head down against the wind and walked and walked.

The door of the cell opened. "Prepare for interrogation." I thought, Hell! I'm only at 4,150 paces. I'd been walking for an hour. Then I thought, Why stop? I nodded at the guard, still counting, and determined that I wouldn't lose the count because every step would matter just as every minute of stolen sleep would matter. I fell into step behind him with my hands behind my back, my eyes straight ahead, and walked and counted, down the corridor, up the steps to the room of the iron book, signed my name with my feet still moving up and down, and counting, counting, might as well add in every step we can, kiddo, because we're walking home, and on to the interrogation room and into it and down in the chair at last, my legs really tired and glad of the rest now, and I've got 4,450 paces and Sidorov isn't here yet. Now if I can snatch another fifty paces before he gets here, I'm halfway to the edge of the city and then I can finish the trip in the morning before it gets light and I'll have wiped my feet on Moscow!

I got up and started to walk. Sidorov came in on the second trip across the room. "Sit down, prisoner!" he barked. Forty-four-seventy-two and three steps across the room to my chair, 4,475, so I have an extra twenty-five to make up in the morning, now let me see exactly where I am and how many kilometers does 4,475 paces make? Could I do that in my head, I wondered? It's twenty-five paces short of halfway, and I said halfway was, what, three kilometers? Or could I cheat?—because I really started counting after I left the street the prison is on and couldn't hear the music from the skating rink anymore. Or did I? Twenty-five paces is about sixteen meters. Sixteen meters short of three kilometers. Work that out in decimal places and see if we can get some kind of efficiency norm worked out for this on an hourly basis, Alex old buddy, good old American efficiency. And so on. And after a while Sidorov started shouting at me that he had put the same question to me three times without an answer, what was wrong with me anyway.

"I don't get much sleep, you know," I remember saying to him.

It was not a very pleasant night, and it lasted the full time. I fell off the chair at least twice, and the second time they woke me with cold water. I was shivering when they led me back to cell 111 at 6 A.M. and my legs were aching from the evening's crazy enthusiasm, and yet the minute the door opened and the guard beckoned me out of the interrogation room I began to count for sanity, and by the time my breakfast came, although my legs were screaming for mercy, the buildings of Moscow had begun to thin out for me and I was within one kilometer of the edge of the city.

Although it is formally true to say that I was in interrogation sixteen to eighteen hours a day, of course one man could not really interrogate for such extended periods and neither could the prisoner react in any sustained way. In the daytime Sidorov would begin with a pro forma suggestion that it was time to confess, which he would repeat several times during the day without putting much steam behind it. The rest of the time he talked about all those other things. Even at night, when he was earning his extra pay, he did not usually keep at me nonstop. Some nights he went through without a break. Maybe he thought he was getting somewhere and maybe it was part of the pattern of wearing me down, wearing me down. Other nights, most nights, he would go out for a good supper around midnight or one o'clock (I guessed; the only clock I ever saw was in the room of the iron book) and come back wiping his chin and read awhile or work on his files. One night I enraged him by making fun of his needle-and-thread work with the files. They were laced into a soft-backed cover with holes down the side, and when he wanted to enter a sheaf of finished protocols he had to get out a sort of long needle and some coarse yarn and, after unlacing the existing binding, sew it up again. When I suggested that in a well-run military organization an important man like a lieutenant colonel would never be required to do such menial work he flew at me so hard I thought he was going to slug me. He yelled at me nonstop for half an hour. He called me the vilest things he could think of. He said that such a statement proved what an anti-Soviet prostitute I really was, threatened to jam the needle into me in a lot of original ways, and sprayed a lot of saliva around the room. He hated the job of lacing those files and I guess it was unbearably humiliating to be teased about it by his prisoner.

One day during the second week he turned up with the checkbook from my New York bank. It had been in my jacket pocket. He asked me how much was in my account and before I thought better of it I told him it was all my savings, but I did not tell him how much. In fact it was, as far as I can recall, well over a thousand dollars. He pointed out, in an imitation affability that was almost slimy, that the food was so bad in Lefortovo that I would be much better off if I could buy special food. He said he could arrange it if I would sign all the checks. I asked why I should sign *all* the checks and he said that was so he could withdraw small amounts on my behalf from time to time and not risk keeping a large amount of money around. I did not believe him at all, and perhaps he did not expect me to. Anyway, I think before he brought out the checkbook I had been getting a bit tired of the different-signature-every-time game, but now I resolved never to sign anything with a legitimate signature, and of course I refused to sign the checks.

Again, characteristic of the day and night swing, he took that easily enough in the daytime and abused me about it at night.

The serious part of the interrogations began to focus on my acquaintance with military personnel. He kept stressing my friendship with Captain North and my acquaintance with other embassy military people, as if
that proved something. And after a while he began to suggest that I
was well acquainted with a good many Soviet officers too, wasn't I? I said
that the only other contact of any significance had been when everyone
was getting drunker than hell on the night Victory in Europe was
declared and some Soviet Navy officers invited us to drink with them in
the bar of the Metropole. Which of course we did. Sidorov seemed interested in that, and went on to suggest that I had made some very interesting military contacts, knew at least one man very well indeed, and had
tried to do some recruiting.

"We know it all, you know," he would say, always slapping the hand-
sewn files with the back of his hand. "If you do not admit it, you will be
in very serious trouble. Now think about it."

I would, of course, deny it.

He would then go into some other area for a while, but after a pause
or a meal break for him, while I was kept awake by an officious guard,
he often reopened with, "Now, I'm going to give you one more chance to
tell me about your attempt to recruit a certain Soviet officer into your
espionage network," or something like that, always working toward the
idea of an individual. I was puzzled by this because from the way he put
the questions I knew he was doing something more than just fishing. He
had something on his mind. There must have been some event that he
had in mind and was distorting, either purposefully or because he believed
that it would lead somewhere. And for a long time I was at a complete
loss. I just could not think what he was getting at. Then I had a sudden
memory of an event that would be very hard to explain, was in fact partly
illegal, had brought me what seemed at the time precariously close to the
MGB, and for reasons I still can't understand had dropped completely
out of my mind. I had to do some fast thinking. Up to now I had told
Sidorov the truth about everything. If he knew the details of this event
and I lied about it or denied it, then it would seem worse than it really
was. If I told him all about it and he *didn't* already know, then I'd be
giving something away unnecessarily. I decided to play for time. I had to
think it over very carefully. What had suddenly surfaced in my memory
was a trip I had made in the summer of 1946. In the course of it I was
caught trespassing, with a pistol in my possession, on the grounds of the
dacha of the party secretary of the Ukraine. The man I had gone to visit
in the Ukraine was a former friend of my father's, named Michael Kovko.
The name of the party boss of the Ukraine, in those days, was Nikita S.
Khrushchev.

7

MICHAEL KOVKO WAS A UKRAINIAN WHO HAD WORKED WITH MY FATHER IN New York in the twenties and gone back to the Soviet Union in 1929. During the Second World War he was badly wounded and was sent back to Moscow as chief of trophy arms, or something like that. He stayed in the army and because he was an expert on cars and trucks, he was sent to Kiev, the capital of the Ukraine, to run various peacetime transport pools and look after the maintenance.

Somehow, in 1945, Michael Kovko found out my father was in Moscow and came to see him. He was a captain by then. We all met at my father's apartment and had dinner and talked about New York. After that he visited my father fairly often, and I saw him several more times. He was very strongly impressed with my working for the American Embassy. I'm not sure exactly why, but he looked on me with some exaggerated respect. We took a liking to each other. He was only visiting in Moscow for a few weeks. He said several times, "Why don't you come and visit sometime? Meet my wife and my children, see the Ukraine," etc., etc. Very sincere, I thought at the time, and I resolved to do it if the chance ever came.

When Michael Kovko left Moscow to go home to Kiev, I forgot all about him for the time being. But in 1946, with this crazy optimism beginning to blow up all over the city, I thought of Michael Kovko one day and decided, just like that, very impulsively, that I would go and see him when I got some time off from the embassy.

My current girlfriend thought it was a great idea for an adventure. Her name was Dina; she was a graduate of the Moscow Foreign Languages Institute, and very bright and ready for anything. Dina was my first lover and while I was not in love with her the way I later came to feel about Mary, I had a terrific time while we were together and I will always remember her—with certain mixed feelings, as will become clear later.

To travel in the Soviet Union at that time you had to have an official permit for each particular trip, and even Soviet nationals had a hard time getting them, to say nothing of foreigners who had no pressing reason to travel. I thought, what the hell, I've never seen any other part of Russia, I want to go, and I'll do it without a permit, somehow. Dina was all for this. She backed me up. So I started going to the railway stations to look at timetables and watch and listen and see what I could pick up. The stations were packed with people and bundles. Soldiers, mostly, but all kinds of other people, most of them poorly dressed with their belongings wrapped up in rags. You seldom saw a trunk or suitcase. A lot of people were sleeping on benches or even on the floor. Whole families would be huddled together. I saw mothers passing out some pretty meager rations of black bread and cabbage and stuff to their kids. I saw people dressed in clothes from all over the Soviet Union—not fancy national costumes, of course, but you could tell that you were in the center of a huge cultural way-station, from the mixture of clothes and faces and from the dialects and languages you heard spoken.

I started talking with people casually, letting on I was about to go on a trip. I even tried to brazen my way through the ticket office to see if I could lie about a permit and pick up a ticket, because Russians are very sloppy about their bureaucracy, and there are lots of mistakes and slip-ups. But I never got anywhere that way. However, I did learn that a good many people were traveling without permits, and that the way to make arrangements was to find a sympathetic-looking trainman or conductor and offer him a few rubles to fix you up. I was brash enough to just go around the station accosting conductors, until I found a guy who was very easygoing about it and said sure, he could get me on a train, it would cost me a few rubles, etc., etc., and he'd look after me very well.

But he warned me I'd better bring my own food because food was scarce and rationed. I would not be able to get food on the train.

Dina and I were immediately excited. It had taken me more than a month to work it all out, find the right trains and the right station and all the other details, and now we had it, and I claimed my leave, and we got set to go. I packed a big suitcase with clothes and food—canned bacon and fruit and other heavy things, and a bottle of whiskey. I decided to take my two pistols with me in case we got to go into the countryside where I could do some shooting. Dina lived in a small room of her own, and early in the day on the tenth of July, I took a car from the embassy and brought all this stuff to Dina's place. Then I returned the car and went back to Dina's on the bus. I was careful to give the MGB the slip when I was out with the car. They were pretty close behind me going down Petrovka Street, and then I whipped into one of my courtyards, faked a turn back onto Petrovsky Lane through another archway, and when they started out through an earlier archway, as I was sure they would, I whipped right around and backed out into Pushkin Street on the other side of the block. I took a good look to see there was no MGB in sight and headed off for Dina's, in the clear as far as I could see. I knew those blocks perfectly because I had lived near there for a while during the war and I had been all over them on foot.

The conductor had told us how to get into the rail yards by a back way, and had set a time to meet him on the loading platform, a long way from the station proper. There were always cars going around Moscow with government drivers in them, alone, between errands or chauffeuring officials somewhere, and you stood a good chance of being able to bribe one of these poorly paid drivers to take you almost anywhere in the city, so that's what we did. I was naïve enough not even to worry, at this point, about the MGB, although the driver I flagged could just as well have been an MGB as a civil-service driver, for all I knew.

The agreement with the conductor was 200 rubles when we shook hands on the deal, and another 300 when he got us on the train. I was sure he would keep his end of the bargain, because 500 rubles was a very good tip to a Russian workingman in those days, but it was not too hard at all for me to put that much by because I had no expenses and a very good salary. I overestimated his honesty and his good will, though. He promised me a good coach and ended up shoving us on a cattle car. I yelled "What about your promise!" and so on, but he just kept shoving us on and shouting that the train was about to pull out (it was after dark, about ten or ten thirty at night), and sure enough the whole long train shuddered with a long, reverberating rattle the way they do and we could hear the engine huffing and puffing and the cattle car was already pretty heavily populated. "Take it or leave it!" the conductor shouted. We went ahead and climbed on. It was all part of the adventure.

This car had obviously been modified for human transport, and I don't remember whether there were other clandestine travelers like ourselves aboard or not, but evidently the Soviet Union was putting every bit of rolling stock it could find into getting displaced persons back to their homes without disrupting the good coach service for government officials and army officers. There were lots of ordinary soldiers on the car; many of them still had their rifles with them, which proved to be a blessing later on.

It was a nightmare scene in that cattle car. It seemed as though hundreds of ragged bodies had been packed into it. People lay around the car on two layers of wooden shelves. The shelves were crawling with bedbugs and lice, but I had a can of DDT powder and Dina and I made a sort of island of DDT for ourselves. Everyone else had sacks and paper parcels. I think ours was the only suitcase. I wondered if we would be robbed. We agreed that one of us would always stay awake. That was not so hard. The rocking car, the crying women, the stench of bodies that had not been washed for a long time, the bugs, the coal smoke, the wind rushing through the slots, all helped us both keep awake almost all the time.

To try to get through the first night in a reasonably good mood, we drank the whole bottle of whiskey. Next day we were hung over and dying of thirst. The train seldom stopped. When it did I was able to go and fill the empty whiskey bottle and an army canteen with hot water, and we made instant coffee and ate our canned meat and other things, while the others on the train ate dry black bread and looked at us with hostile eyes. We were three nights on that train. The last night, going through the Ukraine, the train was attacked by bandits trying to get stuff from the passengers on the train. We could hear shots several times in the night as the soldiers used their rifles to keep those bandits off.

It was five o'clock in the morning when the train pulled into the Kiev station, or what was left of it after the bombardment it had suffered during the war. There was almost no roof, no storage space, no waiting room— just a platform and rubble and some temporary shacks for ticket offices. But Dina and I were still full of adventure, even though we were pretty tired, and she agreed to wait in the station with the suitcase while I went off to find Michael Kovko. This was the kind of guy I was: I had not written to Kovko to tell him we were coming. After all, he had said come any time. And so at daybreak I set out through the rubbled streets of Kiev with my address book. I had to walk because there was no public trans- portation running, and I think it was about 6 A.M. before I found my way to his building on Levanovsky Street and climbed several flights of stairs to his apartment and knocked on the door, feeling a little rude about it, but kind of high from the successful trip and the strange brush with the bandits in the night and the sensation of being in a totally new place with an extremely good-looking girl as my traveling companion.

I knocked on the door and rang the bell several times, and then I heard his voice. "Who is it?"

"It's Alex!"

"Alex? Alex?" The door opened against the chain. "Alex! Alex Dolgun! Come in! Come in!"

Michael Kovko was in his underwear. He smiled amiably at me and wiped sleep from his eyes.

"Listen, my wife's at the dacha with the kids. The place is a mess. I'll make some coffee. Come into the bedroom and tell me what you're doing here while I get dressed."

I started to follow him, saying, "Well, I've got a girl with me and . . ."

And then I stopped because I was so shocked by what I saw in the bedroom. I immediately felt for the little Japanese pistol in my pocket, thinking, *If I have to* . . . Kovko spoke as if he thought I was embarrassed about announcing my girlfriend. "That's wonderful, don't be shy, tell me about her," and so on. But what had shut my mouth for the moment was the sight of the uniform he was pulling on. It was the uniform of the MGB.

He looked up and saw me staring at the purple stripes. "Yeah," he said, "disgusting, isn't it? Well, they needed a good car-pool man, and they offered to make me a major, and it's not so bad. Same job as the army. Better rank, better pay."

I thought, Boy! The sight of that uniform is pretty potent stuff.

Even though he was an old family friend, the presence of the symbols of that huge illegitimate and unanswerable force had made me want to reach for my gun. I watched while Kovko belted on his own gun and straightened up his room, and he listened to the story of our trip and chuckled at the audacity of it. Then he said he would go and get a car, and we would pick up Dina right away and drive out to his country place where the family was and spend a few days in the woods.

Despite Kovko's affability and frankness of manner, I could not lose a feeling of caution. The MGB uniform nearly overcame human trust. I found myself thinking, If he's trying to trick me I'll shoot him, what the hell.

"Come on," he said, "let's get your girl."

We went out and walked a few blocks until we came to a large building. "MGB headquarters," he said casually. "Don't worry about a thing. I'll tell them you're my brother-in-law. Don't show any papers or anything."

I kept my hand on the gun in my pocket. We walked right up to the checkpoint. Surrounded by MGB! I thought heroically, Well, I'll take at least three of them before they get me. It was a giddy feeling. Kovko told them I was his wife's brother and they issued a pass, just like that. We whisked right through the garage and I never had time for even a little gunfight.

"That's our prison," Michael Kovko said casually, waving up at a stone wall beside the car pool. The garage crew treated him very respectfully.

"I'm taking a car for the weekend," he told them, "and I want you two to bring a truck to get some furniture to go to my dacha."

No questions asked. He sent the two young MGB off to the apartment in a Studebaker truck to pick up some chairs and things, and he and I took a green BMW and went to the station to get Dina.

Like many Russians with means, which includes middle and senior bureaucrats and army officers above the rank of captain, Kovko spent part of the summer in a couple of rented rooms in a small village near enough to rivers and woods to go hiking and picnicking. They called it a dacha but it was closer to a roominghouse. I began to relax once we got into the country, and Dina seemed completely at ease and surprisingly unaffected by the appearance of my friend in his uniform of the dreaded secret police. So that was fine.

We spent long evenings talking and drinking wine, and Dina and I would slip away to bed before Michael and his wife, and then in the morning I would leave her sleeping and Michael and I would take his shotgun and his Tokarev pistol and go off to the banks of the Dnieper River for some shooting. I retained enough caution and good sense not to show him my own pistols, but I always had one with me, the little Japanese .22 in my pocket. Kovko was impressed when I shot a couple of birds with his Tokarev. I was impressed with the Tokarev. I had seen lots of them on officers' belts, but I had no idea what solid, accurate weapons they were.

Sometimes we would take a rowboat across the Dnieper and climb the high bank and roam around the woods on the other side. What we did not know at the time was that these woods were on the outskirts of the dacha being used at the time by Secretary Khrushchev.

At noon or early in the afternoon, we would go back to the village and Valentina, Michael's handsome young wife, would be in the kitchen with Dina, and we would have cold soup and radishes and cakes and tea, and sleep part of the afternoon and maybe go on a picnic for the evening meal, and day by day things became more relaxed and I stopped being nervous about Michael's affiliation with the MGB.

One morning Michael shot two birds with the shotgun. We rowed across the Dnieper River and climbed the far bank and threw the birds into the stream and took turns trying to hit them with the pistol. I could manage it, but Kovko couldn't. He was envious of my skill, but not in a heavy way. He was always joking and always very easygoing. Suddenly, as we were popping away at those poor birds, I heard a noise in the woods behind us. I turned around and got a shock. There were four plainclothes cops with pistols pointing at us, more or less surrounding us. The one who approached us talked in a low, intense voice with a tone of authority.

"Why are you shooting here? Don't you know this is a forbidden zone? Who are you, anyway?" Then he noticed Michael's breeches and the insignia on his shirt. "Excuse me, Comrade Major, would you be good enough to explain? You see, you are on the property of Secretary Khrushchev's dacha, and no one is allowed here."

Michael produced his documents, always jovial, always easygoing. "Sure, sure, boys. Sorry. Didn't realize where we were. Just having a little fun with my friend Alexander here, my wife's brother. You boys are doing a good job, I'm sure," and so on. Very impressive the way he handled them. They became quite friendly and put away their guns and we got out of there in a hurry, but not an undignified hurry. Kovko thought it was funny, but it took me a day or so to see the humor. After all, I had no authorization to be in the Ukraine and if they had ever asked for my papers it would have been pretty dramatic for a while.

I had written myself some letters on embassy stationery introducing myself as a member of the embassy staff traveling on official matters, and would the Kiev stationmaster be good enough to issue Mr. Dolgun a ticket, etc., etc. I had no idea whether they would work. They would certainly not have worked in Moscow, but the farther you got from Moscow, I assumed, the sloppier and more lax things got. I explained my intentions to Michael when it came time to head back. He said I was not to worry at all, that he would fix everything up when we got to the station, and by that time I had relaxed enough to be sure that he would be as good as his word. In fact, he got us on a first-class coach reserved for officials only, with tablecloths and flowers on the table in the diner, excellent meals, and comfortable beds, so the trip back was a lot easier than the trip down, though not as exciting or dramatic. We had left Moscow on the tenth of July and on the sixteenth the travel restrictions were lifted, so we had nothing to worry about on the way back.

We had had a marvelous time. The walks in the woods, the exciting brush with the guards at Khrushchev's dacha, exploring love with Dina, lots of laughter and relaxed talk with Michael and Valentina. I remember that Michael admired my heavy silver I.D. bracelet with its thick chain and the engraving, Alexander M. Dolgun, American Embassy, Moscow. He had never seen an ornament like that anywhere and for some reason thought it was very special. I decided to have one made up for him and send it to him in Kiev. Sometimes he would get a bit drunk and tell me gloomy stories about transporting prisoners, which was, after all, a principal part of his responsibility. One time he had had to take charge of a line of barges moving prisoners down that same Dnieper River where we had been shooting birds and rowing boats. Eight or ten prisoners decided to escape and jumped into the river. The guards made no attempt to recapture the escapees, Michael said. They just machine-gunned them in the river and let the bodies float away. Two got to shore and were recaptured and shot.

Sometimes Dina had gotten up early to go shooting with us, and she got to like the pistol. So when we got back to Moscow I borrowed a .38 with a long barrel and filed down the trigger so it was not too hard for her, and we went into the woods on weekends and did some more shooting, trying to shoot the bottom out of a wine bottle, for example, by firing through the mouth of it without touching the sides. Not that we ever achieved that kind of accuracy, even though I was a very good shot. Some nights I would go back and stay with Dina, and we continued to have a lot of fun together and it might have gone on for quite a long time, even though it was not deeply serious, at least for me.

But one day I was walking in her street, Bolshaya Polyanka. I don't remember why I was there. Anyway, I saw Dina ahead of me and decided for fun not to call out but just to walk up quietly behind her and take her arm and say "Be Quiet! MGB!" in a stern voice, to tease her. I figured I would do that just as she was entering her building, and I paced myself not to get too close until she had her head down fooling with the key. But she suddenly turned in the yard before her house and went into a school building. I followed her up the steps of the school building, and as I went in I saw Dina ahead of me, going into a room down the hall.

There was an attendant by the door of the building and he asked me what I wanted. I said I was waiting for a friend, and I asked him what that office was down the hall. Oh, he said, that's an MGB *spetsotdel*, one of the special briefing rooms where they hold informal meetings with their agents.

I was furious. My first instinct was to wait outside and confront her when she came out. But I realized that I was mad enough to smash her and that would be no good. So I just turned on my heel and walked out of that yard and never went to see her again. She called the embassy quite often for a few days, but I never called her back.

So of course I was pretty sure that this was the episode that Sidorov had in mind when he tried to link me with a particular military man. There were some inconsistencies though. He had never mentioned MGB, and he had never given the slightest indication that whatever he was after had taken place in the Ukraine. On the other hand, while he had mentioned several of my girls by name, he had never mentioned Dina.

I sat in my cell and puzzled it over and it made me feel pretty uneasy because I felt I was going to lose, either way. That trip would be very hard to explain. The coincidence of turning up inside the boundaries of Secretary Khrushchev's preserve just would not be believed. Michael Kovko would be in terrific trouble, if he was not already; unless, of course, he and Dina were in cahoots and they had both given me away. I decided that if I had to tell the story I would leave out the encounter with Khrushchev's bodyguards, hoping that Sidorov did not know that part. Then I decided I would not tell the story at all unless I became convinced that he already knew it. I would have to undertake some fishing myself.

I said, "Look, you know, I am really trying to remember. You think I'm trying to put you off, but I'm trying to remember if there was anything that happened with military officers that could give you this idea I was trying to recruit." I said it in a way that left the question a bit open. Sidorov looked very interested. I felt he was taking the bait and that he sensed I might be about to give something away. I said, feeling pretty risky about it, "Can you tell me where it is these meetings are supposed to have taken place?"

No bite. He said, "I think you'd better tell me that. *I* know, of course, but if you want to save yourself trouble you will tell me everything very freely."

I tried to wait that out and see if he would tell me anything—anything at all—anything that would let me know if he had words like *Kiev* or *Kovko* running around in his mind. No luck.

So then I thought I would try another gambit and try to fix the time. If there was any way of identifying the year and the month, I might be further ahead. I took a deep breath and said, "Now, I think you said we were talking about the summer of 1945," just to throw him off the Kiev trail, if there was any such trail. He was completely casual about it, although he had not in fact mentioned any dates at all. But he must have thought he had, for he simply nodded agreement and waited. I waited. After a while Sidorov repeated, "Nineteen forty-five. That's right."

We both waited.

"Well?" Sidorov said.

"Well," I said, slowly, teasing him, because now I was perfectly relaxed: I would not have to tell him about going to Kiev in 1946. Maybe I had been unfair to Dina after all. Maybe she just went in to use the toilet, maybe the attendant who told me it was a *spetsotdel* was kidding, maybe . . .

"Well! Well????" Sidorov was getting impatient.

Fine. I just shook my head slowly and said, in complete truth, "No. I am sorry. I am trying but I cannot recall anything from 1945. You know, I think you really have made a mistake this time."

It was midafternoon. Sidorov just slumped in his chair and looked disgusted. Then he got up and pressed a button on the panel behind him. When the door opened Sidorov said to the guard, "Watch this scummy prisoner closely. Don't let him get up and don't let him go to sleep. I am going out to have some tea."

Later that night he took it out on me, with rages and gun-waving and a renewed attack on my alleged relations with high-ranking military people. Clearly he was not going to give it up. I might be off the hook in connection with Michael Kovko, but there was something definite that he was aiming for. The more emphatically I denied his accusations and told him, honestly, that I was completely mystified by his line of questioning, the madder he got. I could feel the tension rising and rising. I figured it would be only a matter of days before it spilled over somehow, and I was not looking forward to that.

CHAPTER

8

TOWARD THE END OF THE FIRST MONTH IN LEFORTOVO THINGS BEGAN TO get very bad. Except on the weekends, I was never able to steal more than at the most an hour of sleep every day, and looking back it seems that an hour is too much, it may have been no more than a few minutes some nights. Effectively it was the same as no sleep at all, and my mind began to go blank fairly frequently. The effort to keep counting my steps and converting them to kilometers and remember where I had stopped walking the day before was almost more than I could summon up. My eyes pained constantly, both burning and aching. Sudden bright light was an agony. In the singing periods, I would find myself drifting off into incoherent mutterings and then I would have to lecture myself very sharply to get back on the road. One day I became acutely terrified sitting on my bunk staring at the wall. The wall had been painted and repainted to try to obliterate the scratches of earlier residents of the psychic cell. The traces of half-obscured scratchings combined with cracks running through the masonry made patterns that my mind naturally reshaped into concrete images, the way the interlaced lines in the patterned wallpaper used to turn into ships and animals and cars when I lay in bed as a child. One pattern had begun to fascinate me. If I stared long enough at a certain section of the wall I would begin to see the face of an old man emerge from the random scars and etchings. At first it was agreeable to look for this pattern and relax and wait for the old face to take shape in the half light. Later it began to look like an evil face, but I still looked for it sometimes out of a vague curiosity. What frightened me that day suddenly was that the face, as I stared at it, narrowed its eyes and curled back its lips in a fierce and menacing silent snarl. The hallucination was quite real. The intentions of this evil old creature were clear. He intended to hurt me somehow. But the fear that started my heart beating fast and sent me walking up and down the cell and counting like mad was not the same fear as in a nightmare, when you believe in the terrible things you dream and are in a real way pursued by them. My fear was that I was going out of my mind. I was enormously, morbidly afraid of going crazy.

Sidorov had increased the intensity of his questioning at night. He had begun to suggest that I was particularly interested in certain Soviet naval officers. He told me that my association with a navy lieutenant at our own embassy, Bob Dreyer, a guy I often went out with, drinking and dancing and so on, was suspect because they had long had him marked as an intelligence agent. Not long before I was kidnapped, Dreyer had gotten into trouble over our stores warehouse. The MGB accused him, falsely, of peddling embassy stores on the black market. He was declared *persona non grata* and the embassy had been forced to ship him back to the United States.

Sidorov would say, "We have indisputable evidence that you were engaged in espionage activities with Bob Dreyer. Why do you deny it?"

My answer: "I deny it, that's all."

All this futile dialogue was dutifully recorded on protocols, day after day, and brought across the room for me to read and sign. Sidorov was angry all the time at night. He was angry at each denial, angry at the changing signature, angry at my silences while I tried desperately to shut out my hunger and my confusion and my searing need for sleep by concentration on my arithmetic and my line across the map of western Russia.

One morning when I stumbled into the cell, it was so cold I could see my breath. Now I had to increase the pace of my walking to keep warm, and since I was losing weight on the miserable rations, I had little fuel in my body to burn for warmth.

But even with all these growing threats to my stamina and my mind, I still believed I would find some way to get some sleep and that, once found, it would keep me going in spite of everything they could hit me with.

Sidorov had produced a collection of photographs, mostly of army and navy officers, Soviets, in uniform, and began to show them to me one after another during interrogation, demanding that I identify these unknown men and cursing me when I said I did not recognize any of them.

Over and over again, the same photographs, street photographs taken surreptitiously, formal photographs in a studio, face after face of strangers. Over and over again, with the sense of violence coming nearer and nearer to the surface. "I'm giving you another chance. We know you know some of these men. Point out the ones you know! Those were taken in 1945. Why do you deny that you know some of these men!"

My answer: "I deny it."

Sign the protocol.

Sidorov would tell me, correctly, that I was very knowledgeable about Soviet ships and planes. He would quiz me about this: tonnages, armaments, and so on. I don't know now whether it was foolish to answer him accurately, but I did. If agents in the embassy, and it became clear that in one case a charwoman, as well as many others, had reported on my reading and my conversations, then there was no point claiming I was ignorant in military and especially naval matters. They were a hobby with me and anyone who had been around the embassy would know about it. Sidorov claimed that the books I had taken from the embassy library—like *Jane's*

Fighting Ships and *Jane's All the World's Aircraft* and so on—marked me as a spy for sure and he would not believe me when I told him that in a free country you could buy such books in any bookstore. I told him that thousands of young kids in the States memorized the details of planes and ships just as others memorized batting averages and other baseball details, but he just accused me of lying to cover up my "demonstrated anti-Soviet activities."

And then, around three in the morning, he put photographs on my little table and yelled at me from across the room to keep turning them over until I was prepared to admit that there was someone in the collection I recognized. I sighed and put my head down and began to turn them over. I said, "It's no use; we've done this over and over. I don't recognize anyone. Not one!" I kept turning the photographs over dumbly, placing them face down after I had scanned them. I did not see him come at me until it was too late to throw up my hands or duck. His fist came in hard and caught me on the side of the face with enough force to spin me right out of my chair and onto the floor. I was dizzy with the shock of the blow. I lay as still as I could on the floor with my hands over my eyes and my head pounding. The blow was still reverberating inside my skull. Sidorov barked, "Liar! Liar! Liar!" He came and stood over me where I huddled in the corner. "Get up!" he screamed. "Get up and go through them again and again until you come to your senses and confess you know him!"

"Who? Who?" I yelled back at him, still on the floor. "I never saw any of these men! None of them!"

Suddenly I felt as if my right shin had been cracked open. I sat up and grabbed for it, almost screaming myself, when the toe of his hard high boot landed on the other shin. I felt sick and my stomach began to heave but there was nothing in it to bring up. I got to my hands and knees somehow. My eyes were blurred and red and I could vaguely see his feet scuffing the floor beside me. I was afraid he was going to kick again. I knew I could never stand another blow on top of the first. I pushed myself up as hard as I could, breathing hard and fast to keep the tears back and to keep from yelling.

"The photographs!" he screamed. And hardly able to see them at all, I bent over them again. I had begun to *believe* that there was someone here I should recognize. I knew, too, that his continual insistence that I knew someone in these pictures could lead me to believe it even if it was not so. I was determined not be trapped like that. My hands were shaking with anger and pain, but I started going through the photographs as quickly as I could, identifying the few streets or buildings I recognized, and muttering, "I'll try, I'll try as hard as I can." Sidorov paced the room. I bent my head hard over the pictures so he could not see my face. I worked at composing myself. Gradually I got my heartbeat slowed down and my breathing a good deal easier. I really peered closely at those pictures. I waited until Sidorov got tired of walking and sat down, and then I looked right in his eyes and smiled a big smile. I said, "Maybe you've got some better pictures?" His eyes went very narrow. I was taking the risk of another fist or a boot, but I knew that this was the precise moment when I had to show him he was not winning. He did not get up out of his chair. He did not yell. He just stared. I think there might have been a faint hint of admiration in that stare.

Back in the frigid cell I rolled up my pants and looked at my shins. The left was angry-red and bruised. The right was cut open, and when I pulled up the long prison underwear, a bit of clotted blood was pulled off and a thin trickle of blood began to ooze. I washed it in cold water. It seemed a little before six. My head was pounding terribly. I was shivering and nauseated. I climbed under the blanket and *willed* that there should be time for sleep. For a while my pounding head kept me awake with a sensation of lights pulsing. Then I dropped off and slept for perhaps ten or twenty minutes before the slot opened and that squat, ugly hag yelled at me.

The moment I opened my eyes the pain began again. The hag brought my coat for exercise time, and I said I wanted to stay in the cell, that I felt sick.

"*Nye polozhna!*"

I went out and shut my eyes against the hard light in the corridors to cut down the pain. Somehow I remembered to count. I was in the countryside, dodging towns big enough to have a police station, and beginning to wonder what it would be like when I had to negotiate the border. But that was a long way off. I had only made about forty or fifty kilometers, but it was a relief to have Moscow far behind me.

Breakfast made me more nauseated, but I worked at keeping it down. I feverishly worked a few minutes on my calendar. I prayed for the wind tunnel to start up so I could shout out some curses, tell some jokes, sing a rousing song. At the same time I was afraid the noise might split my head. The wind tunnel did not start. No wing-stress research today, I told myself.

I drank the hot colored water with the sugar in it and I drank a lot of cold water and urinated a lot. I felt my shins. They were exquisitely tender. When I washed and ran my fingers through my hair some more hair came out, a little tuft. Now, running my fingers over my scalp, I thought I could feel three tiny bald spots. That seemed a sign of serious physical deterioration and made my heart beat pretty fast, so I forced myself to sit on the bunk and stare at the peephole and lecture myself silently on calming down. I took long, measured breaths. Somehow, by a quarter to ten, when I signed in at the iron book, the pain in my head had gone down a good deal but when I closed my eyes I could still see lights pulsing.

Sidorov came in late. He said "Good morning," as if nothing had happened. "Are you ready to confess everything now?"

"I have nothing to confess." I forced a smile at that hated face. "You may as well realize that I have nothing to confess and I never will. Then we could talk about something else or you could let me get some sleep!"

"We'll see."

A totally inconsequential day. Sidorov yawned a lot. That was hard on me. I yawned all the time and rubbed my eyes over and over. Almost routinely I fell on the floor, in a dead sleep. Sometimes I think Sidorov left me there long enough to get deep into my sleep before he called a guard to pour cold water on my neck. The shock of the water made my heart beat so hard I thought that I could hear it.

We got through the day. I was helped back to the cell because I stumbled so much. My vision was quite blurred. Strangely, I wanted to read. Words, for human contact. I looked for my books. They were gone. I knocked on the cell door. The woman had gone off duty and a reasonably decent guy opened the slot. "My books!" I mumbled in a piteous kind of voice. He must have thought I was crazy. He just shook his head and closed the slot. The books were never returned, and I never got another issue.

When I ate the cold soup, I immediately vomited. I drank some water and then carefully tried a few mouthfuls of bread saved from the morning. They stayed down. When porridge came I ate it with the greatest care, slowly. It stayed down.

I wanted to continue walking to America but I was too weak. I washed my face several times. I willed myself to sleep sitting up straight and probably caught a few minutes, but then I heard the slot open and the guard said firmly, "*Nye polozhna.*" Somehow I thought that was funny so I laughed a weak laugh at him and said, "I know, I know," and waved him away. I fumbled with my calendar and tried to remember whether I had changed the date that morning. I remembered that I had not made the scratch for the day on the cumulative record, so I did that. Then I tried to add the days up and determine what day this was, to make sure the numbers were right on the bread calendar. But I kept forgetting the totals and gave it up.

Rubbing my head, I got another idea. It came out of nowhere. I felt the bare patches and looked at the hairs on my fingers and suddenly got some energy from a discovery that might save my mind. I knocked on the door again, and the moderately easygoing guard came back and looked in. I steadied my voice as well as I could and told him that I had a serious scalp condition and that if I did not see a doctor soon it could become really bad. I bent over and let him look at my patchwork scalp. He did not answer, but he went away and came back with the block supervisor, who also looked at my scalp. I could hear them confer outside. I remember being cheered, as I always was by the arrival of a new idea for surviving, all the way back to the interrogation room at ten o'clock that night. But the cheer did not last ten seconds inside the room.

Sidorov did not even wait for a denial. He waded into me with both fists, yelling at me that if I did not tell him everything he would kill me with his bare hands.

He sent me flailing across the room trying to hold my balance, which was not very good to begin with. I hit the wall hard and went down on my knees. I thought, I must protect my shins! I must protect my shins! Sidorov picked me up by the shoulders and dragged me to my chair, screaming obscenities. He dumped me in the chair and slapped my cheeks hard, yelling at me to sit up straight. I held my eyes closed against the shattering pain of the lights in the room. He slapped me again and yelled at me to open my eyes. I tried to force a smile but my lips felt numb where his fist had caught me. I wiped my mouth and there was a trail of blood on the back of my hand. Sidorov stood over me with his face close to mine.

"Are you going to identify the man?" he said, with a sudden quiet in his voice.

I did not trust my voice. I just shook my head and mouthed the words, "I can't."

The shock when his boot hit my shin on top of the first bruise made me gasp. The next kick made me yell out loud. "Please! Please! How can I tell you names I don't know! Please! I'll tell you any name! Boris, Andrei, I don't know. Anything, only please don't kick again!"

The fist lashed out again and my consciousness just swam away. I have a vague memory of someone fumbling with a stethoscope at my chest, and fingers peeling back my burning eyelids. Then I know I was dragged down the hall and across to the cell block by two guards holding me under the arms. I would come to and pass out as they dragged me up the stairs. They dumped me on the floor of my cell. I smelled vomit and then realized it was on the front of my shirt. I felt parched and nauseated at the same time. I managed to get to my knees, although the blinding blows inside my skull had sent my balance all off and the movement made me dizzy. I turned on the tap and let some water run down my cheeks and swallowed a little of it. My stomach heaved and it came back up.

My soaked shirt chilled my upper body. I began to shiver terribly. The asphalt floor was terribly cold, but every time I tried to crawl to the bed I felt dizzy and sick.

For a long time I lay shivering on that floor. Then a strange thing happened. The pain receded. I was perfectly conscious. I was standing in the corner of the cell looking down at a shivering, vomit-covered wreck in the corner by the reeking toilet. There was blood on his face and his lip was swollen. There were bare pink patches on his scalp. He moaned with every breath, and from time to time his body arched and his stomach heaved a dry heave. And I thought, That poor son of a bitch! Look how he suffers! But he doesn't cry. He won't give them *that* satisfaction.

I quite clearly stood outside myself and my suffering. It is my clearest recollection of that pulsing and blinding and confused and agony-filled night. For a while I had clarity and peace. I watched my own body suffer. And when the suffering subsided a little and the moans stopped and the eyes opened and seemed to focus, I got back in the body and dragged myself to the bed and climbed in and blessed the warmth of the blanket, and left my hands outside, and slept without moving.

When "*Podyom*" was shouted, I went to sit up, but my head was pounding again and I had to go very slowly. When they saw that I could scarcely walk, they let the exercise period go by. I found I could eat my bread, through a mixture of burning hunger and twinges of nausea. The hot tea seemed to help my head. I wanted to look at my shins. One had red and purple bruises. The other was cemented to my underpants with blood and I left it alone.

When the wind tunnel began to wind up, it startled me and I was afraid that the noise would hurt my head. When it hit full volume, I felt a sudden sense of release and I had a terrible urge to cry, but I was damned if they would see me cry. I thought, Quick! What's the most rousing song I know? And then I limped up and down the cell, feeling stronger as I worked some of the stiffness out of my lower legs, and I sang

> *Roll! Out! The barr-elll!*
> *We'll have a barrel of fun!*

I roared

> *Roll out the barrel!*
> *We've got the blues on the run.*

A great song! A song I came to trust. I could feel the need for tears pushing hard from somewhere inside, but I pushed back with the song.

> *Zing! Boom! Tararrel!*
> *We'll have a barrel of cheer!*

Stomping up the cell like a drum major, I brought my hand up and down with an invisible baton. To hell with them if they were watching. Let them watch. I stared hard at the peephole until it opened and forced a huge smile on my face as the astonished eyes peered.

> *Now's the time to roll the barrel*
> *Because the gang's! All! He-e-e-ere!*

I fully expected the guard to come in. He didn't. That was the first time I realized that the chief reason for the prohibition against talking and singing must be to keep other prisoners from hearing me. From then on I sang openly toward the peephole as long as the wind tunnel was roaring.

Suddenly the door opened and a doctor came in. "What's all this about your hair?" he shouted over the wind tunnel. I shouted back. He motioned a guard and they took me out on the catwalk where the light was better and shut the door against the noise.

I explained as convincingly as I could that this was an old ailment that ran in my family and was brought on by cold. I made up a story. I said that I did not know if it was true, but that two of my cousins were said to have died of brain inflammations after all their hair had fallen out and that was why the whole family always wore hats all the time in cold weather. I said I had been wearing a hat when I was arrested but that it had been taken away. I must have been very convincing. Perhaps my shattered-looking state helped. In any case, the miracle took place. When I came back to the cell in the late afternoon (after a completely routine day with Sidorov, in which he announced that for the time being he would change the line of interrogation and that for the next several sessions we would discuss my work as a file clerk and the nature of the information I had access to), my hat was on my bunk! My beautiful, wide-brimmed, American-made fedora! I savored the word. *Fedora*! The hat was a bit crushed from being bundled up, but the brim snapped out and I soon had it worked into something like its original shape. I parked it jauntily on my aching head and sat on the bunk facing the door. The brim eclipsed the little bulb over the door, and I knew that my eyes were in shadow. The light was so weak I was sure that my eyes would be invisible to the guard at the peephole. When the peephole opened, I sat absolutely immobile. The guard seemed to wait a bit longer than usual, but then closed it and moved off. I thought, he's waiting to see if I've moved when he comes back. I did not move. He was back in a minute. I concentrated hard and sat motionless, trying to guess how long he would watch before he assumed I was trying to sleep. Just before I thought he was going to open the slot and yell, after he watched me for twice as long as usual, I raised my hand and wiped the back of it across my nose. The peephole closed. I spent the rest of the evening before going to Sidorov conditioning the guard that way. Every time he looked in he watched a little longer than usual, and every time I gave a sign of movement at the last moment. I was terribly tempted just to go off to sleep, now that I was confident I could do it without falling over, but I talked myself out of it. *Easy, kid. You had several hours under the blanket last night, even if you were beaten up. Don't rush it. One false move and they'll take that hat. This is going to save your life if it works.*

So you can go a little longer, just a little longer, keep it up, a few more days, that's all.

I began to feel a hard knot in my stomach as the time came closer to go back to interrogation. I gingerly felt my shins and I knew I would scream if Sidorov kicked me again, as I fully expected he would. I did not know how I could possibly stand more of that, but maybe I would pass out again. Or maybe with a new topic I would be able to tell him things he wanted to know without compromising myself, and put off the beatings for a while. As it turned out, the next two nights were not so bad. He tried to get me to admit that as chief file clerk of the consular section I had access to coded information, and I kept insisting that the code room was separate, which he no doubt knew, and that I never saw anything classified, which was not true.

First thing in the morning I put on the hat and went on with the process of conditioning the guards. The nice young Komsomol was on, and he just left me alone. He probably knew what I was up to, I don't know. But he never even lingered at the peephole and I took the chance and got an hour's sleep sitting up. My back ached when I forced myself awake, but my head felt a little clearer. Then came a hell of a day with the woman, who, I understood, would never be conditioned, and then it was Saturday night again.

Sidorov, as he often did, stopped the interrogation early on Saturday, and when I got back to the cell, even though the ugly squat one harassed me for the rest of her duty period, I had the consolation of the wind tunnel, which ran full blast that day until after six in the afternoon. I had another inspiration. I imagined Sidorov striding off down the street outside Lefortovo to his wife or his mistress, and I saluted his retreating back in my mind and shouted out loud, "Sidorov, you bastard, this song is dedicated to you!"

Then I sang all I could remember of

> *Saturday night is the loneliest night of the week,*
> *'Cause that's the night that my baby and I*
> *Used to dance cheek to cheek.*

I sang it ironically, not in the spirit of the original. It was my celebration of Sidorov's departure for the weekend, and for the rest of my time under his care I sang it every Saturday night and looked forward to singing it. It was another one of the little things that seem almost infantile by themselves but provided a growing mass of tiny, essential props for my morale.

My Saturday night sleep was long, dreamless, and a total escape. Stiff muscles on Sunday, but a vigorous walk in the yard and through my mental landscape and road map, and lots more accumulated kilometers. And then came another immense lift to my morale.

I had become aware that I had a neighbor in the next cell. I could hear whispered remarks from the guard at mealtime and the sound of a slot moved back and forth. That was the first indication of anyone in the adjacent cell, and I believe he must have just been moved in there. Then, on Sunday afternoon, while I sat on the toilet and worked away at another fishbone, I heard a sound that gave my spirit a huge jolt of excitement. The simplest of sounds. A series of taps on the wall, clearly coming from the· next cell.

I tapped back with my knuckles. *Tap tap tap.*

He tapped back. Three taps. There was a pause. I heard the peephole open and managed to get up in one motion and walk about concentrating on my fishbone.

Then there was a pause for his peephole. Then another series of taps, quite rapid, but distinctly spaced in double groups: 2,4. Then 1,5. Then 4,3. Then 1,1. And so on. At least, that's what I thought I heard at first. I knew Morse code well enough to recognize that this was not it. But it was a code, no mistaking. Then I remembered my book, *Political Prisoners in Tsarist Russia*. This must be the prison Morse! Damn! Why hadn't that rotten author explained the code! I began to answer in the same patterns, except that some of his groups were pretty long and I could not remember the entire sequence so I would just break down and send a whole series of staccato taps, or two taps and then two more. I was laughing out loud for joy. I had a companion! A fellow human being was next door, a fellow sufferer, someone to make common cause with, someone who would care and understand. I had no idea what his code was or whether it was even in Russian. But it was communication. I became totally absorbed in tapping, listening, tapping, laughing. I paid no attention to the peephole, forgot all about it. The slot burst open with an awful clang. The guard on duty was not friendly but not an extremely bad guy either. He just said in a no-nonsense way, "*Nye polozhna!* And if you do it again, it will be hard punishment cells. Tapping is a very serious offense!" He glared at me to make sure I understood. I said, "I understand," and went over to my bunk and sat down. My heart was beating with excitement. I heard the slot in the cell next to me bang open and knew from the rumble of his voice that the guard was giving the same warning to my new friend. But I knew we could work it out, and I was ecstatic.

I spent some time training the guard with my hat. Then I went to work on the fishbone again and, being so full of high spirits, got an idea that seemed as though it might work. I split the end of the soft bone and twisted the two split ends around the point of a match. I thought that when it dried and hardened I could remove the match and I would then have a workable needle with an eye cemented together by natural bone glue. It took a day for the bone to dry, and when I looped a thread through the eye and started to work on a rip in my shirt, the needle held together. A small success that seemed a triumph. I had lost several buttons from my shirt. Seeing how hard and smooth the bread in my calendar had become, I pressed and molded some bread buttons and pierced holes in them. When they dried in a day or two, I polished them on the blanket until they were smooth as bone and sewed them on my shirt. The needle wore out after a while but it was a welcome task to make another.

My neighbor and I continued our blind correspondence. The next time the wind tunnel started up I tapped as hard as I could on the wall, between peepholes. I knew it could never be heard outside the cell. Back came the answer. Always in the groupings of two numbers. Now I realized that the same figure occurred over and over again like a musical theme. It went: 2,4; 3,6; 3,2 (pause). Then 1,3; 5,2.

I tried returning the same pattern, as soon as I had it memorized. This set off a terrific rattle of taps. I realized that my neighbor thought I suddenly understood the code. I felt impotent and frustrated. I answered with a simple pair of taps. He must have understood. A simple double tap came back.

We found we could get away with tapping while the food was being distributed; that was the only time when the peephole was not opened every minute. In the evenings I began to realize that a new pattern was emerging. My neighbor would start with the familiar 2,4; 3,6; 3,2 ... 1,3; 5,2.

I would answer with a single tap. He must have taken that to mean I don't understand. Then he would begin the following pattern: 1,1; 1,2; 1,3; 1,4; 1,5; 1,6. Then a pause. Then 2,1; 2,2; 2,3; 2,4; 2,5; 2,6. Then a pause. Then 3,1; 3,2 and so on to 3,6. Then it would be 4,1 to 4,6. Then 5,1 to 5,6. I knew there was some kind of key in this. I got out my remaining match stubs. I set them out on the blanket in the number groupings I had heard. My brain was slow and numb from sleeplessness. Something obvious as hell was there. I knew it. But I could not get it. I would answer back a single tap. *I do not understand.* And patiently he began again, 1,1; 1,2; right through the whole sequence.

We had to be very careful not to get caught.

Sitting on the toilet I found I could tap very quietly on the drainpipe, which branched through the wall into the next cell, and get a response. The toilet was to the right of the door, looking in from outside. The guard could not see my right hand down beside the iron cone, tapping ever so lightly.

My friend kept up his attempts at instruction during every meal, but in the morning he would just tap simple taps that corresponded to the rhythms and routine of the day. No code; just an acknowledgment that we were sharing the same experience. Two taps: *good morning*, as I came back from interrogation. (He was always there when I came back; he was not in interrogation then?) Two taps: *going for my walk now*, when they came to take him to exercise. Two taps: *I'm back*. Two little human bits of caring.

I continued to train the guards to believe I was awake under the shadow of the hat. I had to reach the point where they would not wait to see if I moved, where they would simply make a routine stop at the peephole and go on. Once that was established I could dare to try an extended sleep every day. By extended, I mean an hour or so.

Sidorov was trying to work up a satisfactory set of protocols on the information system within the United States Embassy. Sometimes he cuffed me pretty hard on the ears and made my head ring. But for a couple of weeks there was no more serious beating. I still often went out cold in the interrogation room, and then he would slap me awake and curse and yell. But for the time being he did not kick my slowly healing shins.

Almost every day now, I told myself the plot of a movie. A favorite was *13 Rue Madeleine*, a story of commandos and the Gestapo and parachuting into occupied France.

I held my own private screening several times. I found that each time I "saw" this movie I remembered more detail, and after a while I could almost have written out the screenplay.

I started lectures in world geography, calling up everything I could remember about rainfall, population, industry, vegetation, rivers, towns, political structure, and all the rest.

And I trained and trained the guards to think I was wide awake under the hat. Before long I began to give them their mid-term tests and then their final exams. They all passed except that squat old bag and I just gave up on her, but soon, with the rest, I could always get sleep in half-hour chunks, and with the young Komsomol I could sleep for two hours, which was as long as my back held out.

At this point I can predict, I think, what a reader of this page will feel. Relief. "He's got it made. It's all right now."

Part of this is what I felt. Relief, certainly, and a certainty that I was now going to survive. But there was a grimmer side to it. As soon as Sidorov started to beat me, I realized clearly that I was going to be in prison for a long time. I did not think in terms of specific periods and I certainly did not think it would be for the rest of my life. But I knew it was not going to be over soon. I knew there would be more beatings and that I would suffer a lot. I knew I would have to train myself to meet that menace, and the knowledge made me feel numb in the heart. The two or three hours of light sleep I was able to steal each day barely kept me from caving in. I was constantly hungry. My weight dropped steadily. When they gave me back my hat, the hell I was living in became a hell I could survive, but it was still hell. I believe it was at that time that my eyes and my mouth began to settle into a grim cast which is still my normal expression when I am not excited or laughing, and even then I am told it lingers around my eyes. My iron mask never came off, and I can see that it never will.

CHAPTER

9

I HAD TO HAVE A STRATEGY FOR PROTESTING AGAINST THE BEATINGS, AND I decided to go on a hunger strike. I had no intention of starving to death. I just wanted to make the strongest gesture I could, and I guess I hoped that they, whoever they were, would do something about it and make Sidorov stop beating me. I had told Sidorov that I would tell him anything I knew, and apart from classified information at the embassy, I was perfectly prepared to do that. If he indicated any knowledge of the Kiev trip, I would even tell him about that. Nothing I had done, in my own view, had any harm in it. I did not know at that time that there were millions in prison camps all over the Soviet Union who had done nothing harmful. I still assumed that, however long it took, I would some day be vindicated and that they would admit they were wrong about me. But I was wrong about them.

Although I was suffering continual discomfort from the emptiness in my belly and getting weaker and weaker, I remembered how Mahatma Gandhi's prolonged public fast had created a sensation around the world, and he had started as an incredibly skinny little man, so I just started leaving the bread in the food slot when it came in the morning and refusing to offer my plate for the soup or the porridge. I drank the tea for its warmth because the cell was so terribly cold and the hot drink would help me stop shivering for a while and help me sleep. But I ate nothing for three days.

It did no good at all. Sidorov still slapped me around and told me I was a damn fool to try such a useless trick, and at the end of the three days I was dragged, because I could not walk very well, into a clinical-looking room and strapped into a chair and my mouth was forced open first with a knife between my clenched teeth and then held open by a sort of oral speculum while they put a gastric tube down my throat and poured sweet tea and egg yolk and cod-liver oil into me. I realized that there was no point going on with the hunger strike then, and gave it up. The beatings came and went in waves, and I often had that experience of looking at myself shivering on the floor, doubled up with pain, bruised and nauseated, while I watched from outside.

But my mind stayed reasonably clear and my morale was, now that I look back on it, incredibly good. I came to love the invisible nameless being next door who greeted me and said farewells. He tried every evening to teach me the key: 1,1; 1,2; 1,3, and so on. I still could not get it. He persevered. I felt his teaching to be a form of deliberate moral support. Even in his simple double taps in the morning, I heard him telling me to keep my courage up, that I was doing fine, that I would get through, and that he cared for me. That did as much to keep me alive and sane as the sleep I had won myself under the hat. Either one without the other would have left me seriously deprived.

In the periods between beatings, when I was not too much in pain to do anything but escape from myself and watch from outside, I kept my clothes in repair by pulling threads from my towel and mending with my fishbone needles. From time to time the needles would disappear from my cell, but it took only three days for a new one to dry, and I still had my supply of dead matches to use as counters and needle-eye punchers and reminders of days when I could light up a cigarette for Mary and casually flip the match away.

I sang "Don't Sit under the Apple Tree with Anyone Else but Me," and "I've Got Spurs That Jingle Jangle Jingle," and "Anchors Aweigh," and "The Caissons Go Rolling Along." "Roll Out the Barrel" I saved for particularly tough times, and it always made me feel a lot better.

I often wanted to cry for relief but I knew that if they saw me crying through the peephole then they would know I was beginning to crack.

Sometimes I thought, I'm only twenty-two years old, and all this is happening to me! And I often thought, and got a kick out of thinking it, What a story I'll have to tell when I get out! Over and over, when something new and bizarre turned up, even when it was disgusting or painful, I would find some small satisfaction in the anticipation of telling the boys about it.

There came a time when I was afraid for a while that Sidorov knew about my Kiev trip to visit Michael Kovko after all. He said one day, "We have definite proof that in 1946 you were being trained in terrorist activities."

I said, "That's interesting. Why do you suppose I never knew about that?"

That kind of answer always threw Sidorov because he had no detectable trace of a sense of humor and sarcasm was pretty well lost on him.

So he would shake his head as if I had not understood and say, "No, no! I am telling you that *we* knew about it. Now I want you to admit that you were given terrorist training. Otherwise you will be in a lot of trouble."

I said, "What kind of training?"

He said, almost triumphantly, "In 1946 you were unmistakably observed practicing sharpshooting with a high-powered pistol."

If he had sprung that on me a few weeks earlier, before my face hardened, my expression would have given something away, because I could feel my heart begin to beat again and wondered just how much of the Kovko/Kiev story he was on to. Then he said a strange thing which made me feel a little easier again, but more perplexed. He said, "You see, our operatives have been watching you very carefully. Even when you might think you were perfectly safe to carry out your anti-Soviet activities, wherever you went in Moscow we knew what you were doing and had you under observation."

In Moscow! Then it was *not* about Kiev. So what was it?

Again, as in the case of the photographs of military men, I sensed he had some kind of actual event in mind, but I could not imagine what it was. Whenever we had gone to the countryside to shoot, I had made sure to give any tails the slip—unless Dina was an agent after all. And if it was Dina, why would she have given me away about shooting bottles in the woods when she had a much better story in the Khrushchev dacha?

Again, Sidorov became violent. I would reel out of a night's session with half a dozen cuts on my face and both shins screaming with pain. I was not always as sick and confused after the beatings now, because I was less debilitated by sleeplessness than I had been in the first few days of beatings. But I would start to shake with fear if I felt another bout of kicking coming on when my shins had not healed from the last one.

If I could have confessed to something at this point, I think I might have. I had no idea what he was talking about with his sharpshooter training. I finally admitted that I used to take a handgun into the woods and shoot bottles, but he was not the least bit interested in that. It was maddening how evasive he was when I asked him to supply the details I was sure he had, or thought he had. He wanted it all to come from me. I could tell that even if I said to him, "All right, I admit I was training to be an anti-Soviet sharpshooter," he would not be satisfied until I told him where I was trained and who my instructor was, and there was no such detail to be supplied.

Once when I was dizzy with pain from the blows on the head and the kicks in the shins, I shouted at him that I would confess whatever he wanted. I felt kind of crazy. "Put down I'm a Japanese spy!" I said. "I'll sign that! Put down I was born to be a spy. Put down I'm a Roman Catholic pope or a Chinese emperor, I'll sign that! Anything you want!"

He was furious, striding up and down and spraying. "Prostitute! Prostitute! Prostitute! Stupid son of a bitch! I want the details of your training in terrorism and sharpshooting, and I want them now!"

"I don't know what you are talking about!" I shouted back.

Crack! I could hear the boot hit my shin and I thought it must have broken the bone. I doubled up with the pain and hit my head on the table. I lay on the floor roaring in pain and rage, and he came and smacked me on the back of the head with his fist.

And the next day he's all hockey news and soccer and the novel he's reading and maybe another attempt to get me to sign those checks.

To my grief I could not resist any opportunity to tease him or humiliate him. Once, when the interrogation rooms were all in use, I was led downstairs to the courtyard instead of the interrogation wing. A van was waiting with the DRINK SOVIET CHAMPAGNE sign on the side and the six small vents in the roof. I was driven back to Lubyanka and taken to an office that Sidorov shared with three or four other officers. I had been there several times before, usually in the DRINK SOVIET CHAMPAGNE van, and once or twice in a bread van equipped with the same kind of crouching cells. But this time I was feeling cocky because it was an anniversary. Sidorov had told me, right at the beginning probably, saying "Don't worry" when he said it, that no one ever lasted six months under this kind of treatment. By "this kind of treatment" he meant only the solitary cell and the black walls and the sleeplessness, because the beatings had not yet started. Now the reason I felt cocky this particular day was that it was June 15. The weather was warm and I no longer shivered on the floor of my cell when they threw me in it after a hard night with Sidorov. We had passed a few days of relatively easygoing interrogation because Sidorov was preoccupied with something else, and besides I think this bussing back and forth from Lefortovo to Lubyanka put him in a better mood, or distracted him or something. He was always less intense when we were moving around like that. But the biggest reason of all for feeling cocky on June 15 was that I had passed the six months and I was still holding out. Thin and weak and a bit crazy sometimes, but still absolutely determined they would not get me and still able to smile at the bastard who was trying to beat me into the ground.

When I arrived in the Lubyanka office this June 15, two of Sidorov's colleagues were doing paperwork at their desks. As Sidorov was opening his files, another lieutenant colonel walked in and gave some papers to one of the colleagues. He said good morning to Sidorov.

Sidorov said, "Say, by the way, has she confessed yet?"

The other lieutenant colonel said dryly, "You know these old revolutionaries, how stubborn they are. Nothing yet."

"Well," Sidorov said. Then he said, "Did you tell her her husband was shot?"

"Of course not!" the man said. "I have to use the threat of shooting him to try to get her broken down."

They talked as if I wasn't even there.

The man went on, "I showed her some of his protocols, you know. She admitted it was his signature. She said he would never have signed such preposterous stuff so it must be a forgery, and all that same old stuff. I'll get her soon enough. Don't worry." He pulled out a bunch of keys and dangled them in front of Sidorov. "The chief gave me possession of their dacha, you know. You should see the furniture. And a great library. Come and see me when you finish your case." He gave a wave and walked out.

I could see we were not in for a very hard day and I started thinking about some way to make Sidorov look a fool in front of his colleagues.

"Going to talk today?" he asked.

I shook my head.

"All right, all right," he said easily. "We'll see if you change your mind later."

Then he got out his long needle and his twine and his scratchy fountain pen and began to work on his files. He cursed the pen a lot. "This goddamn lousy thing. It puts ink on me, it scratches like a cat, and it won't write, goddamn it!"

One of the interrogators started to laugh at him. "Well, you're a *durak*, Sidorov, a fool. You can get a decent pen if you try. Look here. I got this American Parker pen three years ago. It writes like a charm. Here, try it."

Sidorov took the pen and tried it and admired its smoothness.

I said out loud, "Fifty-eight point ten!"

Sidorov looked up. He had a little wrinkle of bewilderment on his forehead. I had come to relish being able to produce that wrinkle.

"What's that?"

"Fifty-eight point ten," I repeated. "Fifty-eight point ten!"

The Soviet criminal code was famous for its section fifty-eight, the section under which political prisoners were charged with everything from having an anti-Soviet dream to trying to overthrow the government by force of arms. The subsection 58.10, anti-Soviet propaganda, includes a charge based upon bad-mouthing Soviet-manufactured goods, even by implication through praising goods of foreign manufacture.

"Arrest him!" I said, nodding from Sidorov to the other interrogator. "He's committed anti-Soviet propaganda. Praising foreign goods. That's one of my charges. Ten years if you can prove it, and I'll be your witness. Arrest him!"

I underestimated Sidorov. Or overestimated his reticence in front of his fellow practitioners. He just walked quickly across the office, knocked me off the chair with a hard swing of his open palm, and left me on the floor.

After a while he said in a tired voice, "Get up, you son of a bitch." I got up on the chair. I stared at him and he stared back. I wondered what he was thinking. Once again I thought there might have been a hint of admiration for the way I was holding out. But he was angry, too, and tired. Six months, I thought, and this guy is working me over sixteen, eighteen hours a day, and I'm tiring *him* out! My ear was ringing from the smack, but I still felt cocky, though not cocky enough to risk another smack with some smart remark. I became aware, studying him that day, that he had lost a lot of weight too. Not, of course, anything like me. I must have gone from 186 down to 130. But Sidorov's jacket, which he had filled out very well when I first saw him, was hanging loose, and his face, which had had roles of fat under the chin, was drawn. He was doing everything he could in this battle of wits, or battle of tactics, and while he was not exactly losing, he was not winning either. Even though I was weak and hungry and exhausted, I could feel good about the stalemate. I had no idea where this was going to end, but I still felt I could make him stop before he made me stop.

His beatings were not getting what he wanted. His attempts to twist my statements in the protocols (to make me admit things I had not really said by changing a comma or deleting a *not* that I might not notice when I signed) had not worked: I always read carefully, and if my eyes would not focus because he had hit me too hard or because I had not managed to get some sleep because the mean woman was on duty, I refused to sign until I could read clearly. I suppose he may have caught me in minor things but never in anything significant.

So there he was looking tired, and I thought, You bastard, I'm going to win this.

I enjoyed the drive in the Champagne van to Lubyanka and back, despite the pain in my knees from crouching, because in the daytime I could hear the hubbub of traffic and could imagine joining it again one day. I knew that people were watching me spin along Kuznetsky Most, and they thought I was a crate of champagne. And some day I would get out and tell them what I really was.

When I got back in my cell I tapped two taps: *I'm back.*

Two taps from him: *Me too.*

The satisfaction of passing the impossible six months and getting under Sidorov's skin all in one day had given such an impetus to my spirits that I was even thinking more clearly than usual. I had done a lot of work on the tapping code, especially the familiar, daily pattern of 2,4;

3,6; 3,2 . . . 1,3; 5,2. (I knew it so well by memory it sounded like a complete rhythm, a recognizable form, the way Morse code letters come to sound to you when you become adept.) I spread it out on my blanket in match stubs and studied it every way I could. Today I had a feeling that I was bright enough to make some kind of breakthrough. I had tried and discarded a number of approaches. I had tried to pick something out of a remembered story by Poe, "The Gold Bug," I think, in which the frequency of occurrence of certain letters had been the key. That had led me nowhere. There was not enough material to work with. But it had started me thinking about the whole science of ciphers. Could the numbers be subtracted one from another to give a straight 1, 2, 3—right through to 31, for the thirty-one letters of the Russian alphabet? That did not work. I had tried various methods of adding and multiplying, but they led nowhere.

I kept puzzling away at the code. I took the familiar 2,4; 3,6; 3,2; . . . 1,3; 5,2, and used thirty-one pieces of matchstick to arrange these numbers in a sort of checkerboard pattern on my bed, thus:

$$
\begin{array}{ccc}
|| & ||| & ||| \\
|||| & ||||| & || \\
| \quad ||||| & & \\
||| \quad || & &
\end{array}
$$

No luck with that.

Something was nagging at my mind. Why did he persist every night with the arithmetic lesson? 1,1; 1,2; 1,3 and so on to 1,6 until the pattern was completed with 5,6.

I was puzzling away at it when I noticed my mouth filling with saliva and realized that the sound of the elevator had started the conditioned response without my even being aware I had heard it. Now the guards would be busy distributing food. I knew he would start the lesson soon. Patient friend! Keep patience, I thought. I think I'm getting close. I gave him a greeting, a signal to start.

Tap tap.

Back it came: 1,1; 1,2. All the way through.

I thanked him: *Tap tap.*

I sat on my bunk and chewed my watery porridge and forced my brain. The peephole started again. I stared at the wall.

What the hell is it with 1,1; 1,2; 1,3?

Then I thought: Should I read it as 11, 12, 13, 14, 15, 16? And if so, why does he skip from 16 to 21, from 26 to 31, from 46 to 51? Was there something in the interval of five? In groupings of five? But there was also a grouping of six: 11 to 16, 21 to 26.

I wanted to lay out matches for the whole pattern but I did not have nearly enough of them. I set a few matches down on the blanket and tried to imagine how the rest would look. Groupings of five and six. Five plus six is the first number he always sends. Eleven. So what?

Five times six is thirty. So what? There is no 30 in the code.

Wait a minute.

Wait a minute!

If you leave out the "hard" sign, you could say that the Russian alphabet has thirty letters.

Five rows of six letters. Of course! That's what he sends me every night! The whole goddamn alphabet! How could I have missed it for so long? The numbers *have* to be coordinates on a simple grid. A checkerboard! My hands were shaking with excitement. I tried to mark numbers on the blanket with a match. Even though the impression faded almost immediately, I could see it in my mind as if it were still there:

1, 1	1, 2	1, 3	1, 4	1, 5	1, 6
2, 1	2, 2	2, 3	2, 4	2, 5	2, 6
3, 1	3, 2	3, 3	3, 4	3, 5	3, 6
4, 1	4, 2	4, 3	4, 4	4, 5	4, 6
5, 1	5, 2	5, 3	5, 4	5, 5	5, 6

Now! Just substitute the alphabet in the same grid:

А	Б	В	Г	Д	Е
Ж	З	И	К	Л	М
Н	О	П	Р	С	Т
У	Ф	Х	Ц	Ч	Ш
Щ	Ы	Ь	Э	Ю	Я

Oh God! I was so sure I had it! I almost didn't have to fake sitting on the toilet, my stomach was churning so much. How much time before they took me back to Sidorov? I had been so absorbed I had no idea, but I had to tell my friend I could understand him!!

But as soon as I calmed down, I realized I couldn't do it yet because I had not memorized the grid and I hadn't even checked out the familiar morning pattern. I pulled up my pants and went back to the bed and tried to see a mental pattern of letters on the blanket. To help myself I just put thirty pieces of matches on the blanket and then I could mentally place a letter on each match. I checked out the well-remembered message:

2, 4;	3, 6;	3, 2	1, 3;	5, 2
К	Т	О	В	Ы

"*Kto vy?*" Who are you?

Oh, God! A pure rush of love in my chest for a man who has been asking me for three months now who I am, and I can't even tell him. Quick. Piece out the numbers for Aleksandr Dolgun. Look at the thirty matches on the bed. It will be 1,1; 2,5; 1,6; 2,4; 3,5; . . . (Close my eyes and try to memorize it.) Then, dizzy with excitement, I can hardly stand, start for the toilet, forget the numbers, look back on the blanket. Think, No, that's not what to send. Send him . . . send him a question, send him . . .

Oh, no! The door is being unlocked. Not yet! Please!

"Prepare for interrogation."

But it was all right! It was all right! I grinned at the impassive guard. I followed him with real spring in my step for the first time in months. I was exalted. I told myself that I would have a good night in the interrogation room. A *good* night. I would spend it mentally working through the code. By the morning I would have it memorized. Then I could really talk to my friend. Ask him for news. Tell him my hopes and fears. I chuckled to myself as we walked. The guard looked around and frowned. I smiled back at him, a broad, cheery smile.

When I arrived in the interrogation room, Sidorov was staring glumly at the pages of a novel and did not even look up. I sat down in my chair and went over the *kto vy* again to make sure it fit the numbers. It fit perfectly. I began to giggle. It was like giggling in church. The fact you know you shouldn't makes it worse. I giggled and giggled. Sidorov looked up sourly. I was afraid he might want to take it out on me for my afternoon joke about 58.10 but he seemed more interested in his book. He went back to reading. I thought 58.10 doesn't work in the code, but 51.11 would mean, let me see, oh yes, *shcha*. I said out loud, "*Shcha!*" and giggled uncontrollably.

Sidorov slammed his book down. "What the hell's wrong with you!"

"I'm going crazy!" I said merrily.

"What's so funny about that?"

"You wouldn't understand," I giggled.

"Well, try to go crazy quietly. I'm reading."

He went back to his book.

All night long he read. Played right into my hands. All night long I worked on the code. I decided on the question I would surprise my friend with in the morning. I would send, "What is your name?" *Kak vas zvat?* I would open the conversation with two taps as usual. He would reply with two taps as usual. Then I would ask him his name, and the dear, patient invisible man would fall right off the toilet with surprise and delight.

Toward morning Sidorov put his book down and stared listlessly at me. "You thought you were pretty smart today, did you?"

I giggled sleepily.

"Stop that!"

"I'm sorry."

Six o'clock.

Back in the cell, trembling with anticipation. The peephole was very regular and the guard on duty was a very tough customer. I decided against risking the toilet until the meal came. Just two taps, *Hello,* and he sent back the same. Very hard waiting until seven. I laid out thirty matches on the bed as a checkerboard matrix into which I could fit the letters and keep them straight. An age until I finally heard the clanking old elevator and the juice began to flow inside my mouth. I was ravenous as usual. I tore off a hunk of bread, swallowed a mouthful of the hot colored water, stepped close to the wall, held my breath, mentally reviewed the numbers I had memorized for *Kak vas zvat,* and was just poised to tap two taps, *I'm ready,* when he tapped.

Tap tap.

Watch this! I thought.

I began to tap.

Tap tap, Tap tap tap tap

Tap tap

Tap tap, tap tap tap tap.

"What is your name?"

There was a silence from the other side of the wall.

Then I heard a sound like a table falling over, and some sort of faint scrambling sound.

Then, like a waterfall or a typewriter, a regular fusillade of taps from across the barrier of stone.

I looked at my checkerboard of matches. *Medlenno,* I thought— *slowly.*

I tapped it out.

Tap tap, tap tap tap tap tap tap.

And when I had it all out, back came, in agonizingly slow taps, so careful not to run away from me:

D M I T R I

R A G O Z I N

I sent him my name.

Back came

S T A T Y A

"Article." I understood—under what article was I charged? I sent the numbers.

He sent his.

It would have been so easy to become absorbed in this conversation, but I knew it was the most precious possession I had now, and I was determined to risk nothing through lack of vigilance. I sent the word *toilet*, thinking it would be best to be there when the peephole came back into full-time action once the meal was all served, which would be soon. We had ten minutes of it. Pretty laborious stuff, at first. I often had to ask him, *Snova?* Again? And watching my matrix carefully, I was able to pick up his story.

Ragozin was an engineer ten years older than I. He had spent some time abroad in the thirties and, like so many Soviets who did so, got into trouble for it later. Among his articles were 58.4, which I found out much later meant conspiracy with the international bourgeoisie, and 58.1, high treason. He also had 58.10. Everyone had 58.10, it seemed.

Although I was eating up this human contact as if it were food, I knew that I had to conserve myself and take every precaution not to be caught. I sent him, slowly, painstakingly, "Sleep now." And then our own private, comfortable, all-purpose *tap tap*.

I composed myself on the edge of the bunk facing the door.

I set my hat at the correct angle to conceal my eyes in shadow. I waited through two peeps at the peephole just to be extra safe. This guard was a tough guy, but I had trained him well. Not even a pause, just a routine glance. I let my burning eyes close gratefully. It was like going off to sleep with the image of your lover in your mind. I'm sure that for the next hour or so, while I slept bolt upright, the broad smile of achievement and contact, of satisfaction and joy, never completely left my mouth.

For the next several nights Sidorov looked exhausted, and from time to time he dozed off and so did I. Even though I was getting better than two hours of sleep every weekday, unless the woman guard was on duty, I was still close to mental exhaustion most of the time and would nod off instantly whenever there was the slightest opportunity. We did little "work."

One night, when Sidorov caught me a couple of times, he just came over and slapped my cheeks very casually and said in a low, bitter voice, "Wake up, wake up," and went back to his desk and tried to concentrate on his novel.

It was a warm night. When he came back from tea he left the door of the interrogation room ajar to get a little circulation. From a closed room down the hall I could hear the low murmur of a man's voice, and then suddenly a loud scream of a woman, subsiding to a sort of moan, and then a yell that made my scalp lift. I imagined the terrible tortures that must have been applied to her. The voice would subside to silence. Then the quiet man's voice and almost immediately this poor woman yelling and screaming. It was the strangest yell, it had a bizarre tone. I was shaking, listening to it. After a while Sidorov pressed the button and a guard looked in and Sidorov signaled him wearily to close the door and shut out the sound. I was haunted the rest of that night by those screams. At five or five thirty Sidorov pressed the button and when the guard came told him to leave the door ajar for fresh air.

"I'll keep him a while longer," he said, without even looking at me.

I heard the guard go next door and heard the door there open and some quiet words from the guard. To my surprise he was answered by a woman. Then there was a pause. Then the same screaming voice I had heard before began again. But this time I could hear the words and the woman was the interrogator! She was screaming filthy accusations at someone, language as bad as Sidorov's and sounding much more terrible from a woman, all the hideous things she was going to do to this poor man's lower body and so on, and then just a soft, beaten murmur of a man's voice as he answered.

When the guard took me out I saw her standing in the corridor. A middle-aged woman, fifty perhaps, not bad-looking, very composed. She was wearing major's insignia on her shoulder boards.

I asked Sidorov about her the next day. He just shook his head and would not answer. I often asked him personal things in those daytime sessions. He never answered. I never gave up. It was one more way to keep him off balance. What was his wife's name? I would ask, after he had been phoning his mistress. Or how many children did he have? Or did he ever suffer from piles? He just refused to answer. The only thing he ever told me was that he was a law graduate and that the diamond-shaped button on his lapel was a sign of that degree.

As the time went by I tried to think of more and more sarcastic things to put to him. My hatred was growing and growing with every blow and every kick. I used to find myself watching the gun when he played with it to frighten me, and wish for the strength to leap across the room and take it and shoot him or knock him out with it and dress in his uniform and walk out of Lefortovo. I was too weak even to begin such an escapade, but the fantasy was sweet and I replayed it and replayed it and savored my hate. The need to kill Sidorov became a hunger.

I would make an effort to suppress that need and concentrate on my fantasies. Walking home, I had negotiated the Prohibited Zone at the border, dodged dogs and patrols of soldiers, and had made it through the woods into Poland. The sense of freedom and of covering ground helped a lot. Now I had no more Russians to watch out for, even though Poland was an iron curtain country. I concentrated on the map and tried to remember the names of towns and the approximate distances between them. I had to guess a lot, but the heavy black line I was drawing across my mental map of Europe stretched longer and longer.

After several days Sidorov returned to the photographs and the Soviet officers. Realizing, with repeated help from me, that broad general questions propelled by beatings did not seem to be producing what he wanted, Sidorov tried being more specific. He reminded me that I had admitted meeting some Soviet officers and drinking with them on V-E Day at the Metropole. I said, "That's right, but I don't recognize any of them in these pictures."

Sidorov finally showed me one man. "His name is Commander George Tenno," Sidorov said. "You know him. He tried to establish contact with you to give you information, don't you remember?"

I stared at the face. I was so tired and so confused. The face looked familiar. Sidorov's voice was soothing and relaxing. It would be so easy just to say, "All right, George Tenno, that's right, I tried to recruit him and he tried to sell me information," or anything like that. It would have been so comfortable to give Sidorov something he wanted and get off early and go and sleep. Maybe he would reward me with a cigarette or some food. Maybe all this could stop. As I stared at the face of this George Tenno, I decided that, yes, I did recognize him, and yes, maybe I could say something. . . . And then I caught myself. Alex, for God's sake, don't give in. You've gone this far. Keep going, kid. I silently did a couple of lines of "Roll Out the Barrel." I said, I'm getting near the border of East Germany, just east of Dresden. I've heard the East German police are rough and smart so I'll have to be careful. I could smell Sidorov leaning over me, which brought me back to Lefortovo.

"George Tenno," he said. "What was your relationship with George Tenno?"

I took a breath. I looked up at Sidorov. I said truthfully, "I don't know that name. If this is the man you're talking about, I might have had a drink with him or I might not. I don't remember. We all got pretty drunk that day. Didn't you?"

I knew it was coming. He loosened a tooth and I went backwards off the chair. He kicked me and he cursed me. I pleaded for him to stop, but I never admitted anything because now my defenses, which had been lulled nearly asleep, were aroused again to fighting form.

The blows and the kicks that Sidorov hammered on me that night would become part of the cement, years and years later, of one of the finest friendships in my life. But this night they kept raining down as I rolled and ducked and yelled for him to stop until my head began to break into torn, terrible pieces just before I lost consciousness. The next thing I knew I was on the floor of my cell, shivering and wet. The summer was gone. The crisp air of September was outside Lefortovo now, and they were letting it have its way with my shrinking terrible cell. I had been in Lefortovo prison more than nine months.

CHAPTER

10

I WAS NOT ABLE TO SPEAK COHERENTLY FOR SOME TIME AFTER THAT TRE-mendous beating. I remember that at some time Sidorov showed me a protocol, signed by an unidentified operative, indicating that I had been seen drinking with Commander Tenno on May 8, 1945, and that the operative suspected the intentions of this conversation, as Tenno was an intelligence officer of doubtful loyalty and I was under suspicion as a for-eigner. Sidorov asked me if I would like to spend another night like the last one in which we discussed Tenno. I just stared at him with the hard, grim, resigned look that I have come to know now in my own mirror. I do not think I even shook my head. I know I did not answer. He persisted quietly with a few questions about Tenno, and waited a long time for answers. Finally I said, "I have told you all I know about George Tenno." He seemed to know I meant that, which I did.

He wrote a protocol. I read it through severely swollen eyelids. I reread it several times because I found concentration so difficult. My shrunken buttocks pained me on the hard seat and my breath was shallow and noisy. I hated Sidorov so much that I wanted somehow to violate this bland piece of paper on which he depended for his living. But I could find nothing inaccurate in it and I could think of nothing to say and I was too hurt and frightened to tempt another beating so I signed with a shaking and entirely illegible hand and he took it back silently.

By now I was so weak I fell off the chair in the interrogation room or fell over on the bunk in the psychic cell almost immediately after I went to sleep. And so I would be awakened. Days went by when I got no sleep at all, days that I was simply not aware of; certainly I have no memory of them, except a blurred sense of time passing, and a lot of pain, and the cell getting colder and colder as it wore on into autumn.

When I could read again Sidorov showed me another protocol. He had opened the question of the sharpshooting once more and indulged in a few desultory beatings that hardly penetrated the numbness of my body, though they made me terribly dizzy and sick to my stomach. The protocol he finally brought out made me laugh in a way that might have sounded hysterical to Sidorov but was just a relief for me.

I had made friends soon after the war with the Syrian chargé d'affaires. He was actually called Ali Baba. He was an amiable guy and quite a drinker. He was fascinated with America, and I loved to talk about America and boast about its accomplishments. We had spent the Fourth of July together in 1946. I don't remember quite why that was. I know we began drinking at his place, and that his secretary came in while I was telling him about a book I had just read, all about the FBI. I think it was called *Inside the FBI*. I remember showing him how the FBI agents were taught to shoot from the hip, and he thought that was great stuff and I loved having an appreciative audience.

To keep up the dramatics around shooting and cops and that sort of thing, I invited him over to my room at American House, where the second part of Sidorov's story came from. The first part came from Ali Baba's secretary, who, it turned out, was MGB. The protocol Sidorov showed me was signed by her. It had evidently been taken in prison. Apparently she had been arrested for not reporting this incident with Ali Baba, which she, for the benefit of her interrogator, had interpreted as showing that *I* was an intelligence agent of the United States, trained to shoot from the hip. (Her English was not good. I remember that.) They asked her: "Why did you not report this earlier? You might have saved yourself being imprisoned." She answered: "I thought Mr. Baba was drunk and that it was not a serious conversation."

I described the whole day to Sidorov, giggling with relief, although I felt pretty angry at Ali Baba's secretary. She always seemed such a nice girl. Baba and I had left her and gone to my room, where I kept my air pistol that shot tiny darts into a target and looked just like a Luger. We had stood in my room for some time while I showed Ali Baba what a great shot I thought I was. I remembered it very clearly. So did Sidorov. He had a whole protocol on it. Not from Ali Baba, but from an operative with binoculars, stationed on a rooftop half a mile away by the Moscow River, who had observed me through the window all afternoon on the Fourth of July, 1946, "training with a high-powered, high-accuracy hand weapon, possibly of German manufacture."

I told the story to Sidorov. He said, "How can you remember it so clearly, when you can't remember anything else I ask you about?"

I said, "Because it was the Fourth of July, I guess."

He said, "What's distinctive about the fourth of July?"

I said a bit snappishly, "How can you expect to interrogate an American citizen intelligently if you don't even know about our Independence Day?"

I don't remember the beating that followed. I remember him sweeping across the room at me. After that I only remember how I was later.

Perhaps the next day. I stood in front of Sidorov's desk, thick-lipped and aching in every emaciated muscle. I don't recall what it was I had to sign. I just remember that, as I turned away from his desk to stumble back to my chair, I saw from the corner of my eye that he had picked up his rubber overshoe, and I thought, with a dim hope, Maybe he's going home early and I can get some sleep. Then, with my back turned, he brought the overshoe up between my legs with a terrific swing and caught my testicles in a really terrible blow. I had thought nothing could be much worse than those repeated blows on the shins, but this traveled through my entire abdomen as if it were ripping open. I fell to the floor and vomited whatever was in my stomach. It was porridge, I think, so that must have been a night-time session. Sidorov just called in a guard. "Clean that up and get him out of here," he said sourly. I was groaning on the floor but I managed to shriek at him—I did not recognize my own voice—"I will never sign another protocol for you! Never!" It seemed, somehow, the nastiest thing I could think of at the moment.

I don't know what the time sequence was next. It is terribly blurred. I know that I was standing in front of Sidorov's desk once again, some hours or days later, I don't remember. I was trembling with weakness, but I remember the scene with complete clarity, so perhaps I had had some sleep.

He had seven or eight sheets, protocols, that had not been signed yet. I said, "I told you, I'm not signing any more protocols!"

I picked the sheets up and tore them in half and strode back to my chair. Sidorov grabbed the overshoe and let me have it between the legs again. This time he was less accurate and I was not paralyzed by the blow. I was stung into an anger so total that it took account of nothing. I leaned against my chair. I looked around. Sidorov was standing with his back to me at the desk, picking up the torn protocols. I called on every remnant of strength I had, for just this one moment, and swung the chair at Sidorov's head to kill him at last. But I was too weak; it was a poor blow, slow and badly aimed. He heard it coming and ducked and turned, and I just grazed his forehead. I saw that I had drawn blood, but I was dismayed that I had not crushed that hateful, pock-marked skull. Sidorov just knocked me down. He looked a bit frightened. He signaled for the guard. I said, "I'm going to kill you, you know."

Sidorov said, "No, you're not. You're going to the hard punishment cells for the maximum. That's twenty-one days and you'll never come out alive. I'm through with you!"

They dragged me out. I yelled going through the door, "I'll get out of here someday and I'll kill you!"

They dragged me across to the prison and down steep stone stairs. I remember being thrown in an absolutely bare cell. It was terribly cold. There was no bed, no sink, just a bucket with a lid. No window. Gray stone and black asphalt. I lay on the floor and shivered and called out with the loudest voice I could make, shaking and quivering though it was, *"I'll kill you!!!"*

I knew I could not survive that cell. I had only a shirt and trousers. The temperature was below freezing. Outside it was late October and Moscow dips way below zero Fahrenheit in November. When they brought me water my hands shook so hard that some of the water spilled on the filthy floor. The next time I looked it was frozen.

At night they brought in a wooden pallet for me to sleep on. I was dying for sleep but shivering too hard to do more than doze off, wake up, doze off.

I knew with complete certainty that I could not last five days in that cell, let alone twenty-one, and I thought confusedly that I had better keep a calendar to see how long I did last. It never occurred to me that I would not know the outcome. I was too confused.

The morning came and I did not even have a running nose. They brought me bread and water. I deliberately spilled a little more water in the corner. Later, when it froze, I skated on it, sliding around on my shoes for exercise and warmth. I sang all my songs at the top of my voice and nobody bothered me. I fainted often, and came to shivering on the ice. My only clothes during this period were my prison underwear of light cotton, and the shirt and pants I was arrested in. There was no blanket at night.

I believe I never stopped shivering, if that is humanly possible.

After a few days they brought hot soup made with salt herring. I drank it all down before I realized it was saturated with salt. I tried to ration myself on water, but I was too weak to be disciplined and I drank the whole cup right down. By nightfall I was screaming for more water. Before morning I began to have hallucinations of swimming. Was it in the sea or in a lake? Did I drink the water I was swimming in? Was it salt or fresh? I just remember the shock of coming to my senses and realizing that I was stroking feebly on the bottom of my cell, weak but frantic swimming strokes. Sometimes the cell would fill with water. Every third day they brought the salt-herring soup and I was so starved I ate it even though I knew I would go mad for water.

The days passed in almost total confusion, except that I forced myself to mark the wall every morning when they brought the bread. That was the one clear moment in the day. Incredibly the strokes passed five, and then ten. I shivered, slept a bit, skated on my rink, what else I don't know. Once I wanly tapped out a message in code on the wall. There was no response. I was so lonely I would have been glad if a guard had come in to tell me to quit tapping.

I think they took my bucket out once a day. I know they never spoke.

The strokes on the wall passed twenty-one. They passed thirty. I had been in the cell a month. I think some days I was delirious all day, but I am not sure of much except that I often said, *Hold on, Alex, hold on till the end!* I expected The End.

Forty-one days. A mouse has come into the cell. I will catch it and eat it. It comes in through tiny holes in the bottom of the cell. If there is one mouse there must be more. I salivate at the thought of chewing on the live mouse. I wait for him on the floor. He comes out of his hole and sniffs at me. I try to catch him but he slips through my hands. I wait with infinite patience, day after day, for my mouse.

Then I watch myself lying, shivering on the floor, covered in filth, a skeleton waiting for a mouse. I watch for hours, but the mouse never comes to the man on the floor.

I lie on the floor and stare at the mouse. He runs in the hole. I cannot find the hole.

Forty-nine days on the wall.

I am trying to catch the mouse and they are watching me through the slot in the door, but they won't come in and help me get the mouse.

By now I know there is no mouse, no hole, but for a while I keep on trying to catch him. Then I give up trying to catch him. He still comes in through the hole in the wall that does not exist.

They are watching me through the slot in the door.

Fifty-two days on the wall, and I will die soon, and that's all right, but I still do not have a cold or a runny nose.

The door of the cell opens.

"Prisoner, get up!"

I can make it to my hands and knees. They help me. Not kindly, not roughly, just get the prisoner moving. I think there is a doctor with them. Was that later? I stand in the door of my own cell, 111, the psychic cell. At least there is a blanket and pillow here.

I did not understand their words. Wrap up the blanket and pillow? Will they take them away from me? I thought. Then I realized I was leaving cell 111. Something still alive inside me said, Alex, you made it.

They're moving you.

You got through it.

You're going to be all right! You have survived and the bad part is finished now. I was lightheaded, still shivering uncontrollably, but something akin to happy, floating.

I think they took me upstairs on an elevator. That is the impression I have, though the memory is not clear. I know that it was the sixth floor. I was surprised at that. I thought I had worked out the layout of Lefortovo from my frequent trips to interrogation by different routes to avoid meeting other prisoners, and I had somehow figured that there were only five floors. This sixth floor had a small corridor with a wooden floor and looked centuries newer than the other parts of the building. When we reached the cell (it was 216, and I still see the number) the guard did a strange thing. He stopped and opened the peephole and peered in. My chest caught in the way people describe as your heart skipping a beat. There could be only one reason for looking in the cell. There had to be another person inside. I was not going to be alone. After two months shivering on the floor in the hard punishment cell with never the sound of a human voice, I was going to have company!

The cell door was pushed open. It had a polished wooden floor and was bright and airy with a big window. My eyes were unfocused from the sudden transition to light after fifty-two days of near darkness. I saw the shape of a man on one of the two beds. As the door was locked behind me he got up and came toward me. He looked ferocious, and for a minute I had a terrible misgiving. Quarter-inch stubble of black hair, black stubble of beard, intense eyes, very old, faded army breeches. I thought they had put me in a cell with a murderer. The apparition put out a strong hand. I took it in a bewildered way. He shook my hand firmly and gently, and said in a soft voice and clear, musical Russian, "Let me please introduce myself. My name is Orlov. Captain Grigori Orlov."

CHAPTER

11

SEVERAL TIMES DURING MY INTERROGATION SIDOROV HAD TRIED TO INFLUENCE me with the promise of better meals, a full night's sleep, and company in the cell if only I would confess. I was certain, whenever he mentioned putting me in a cell with someone else, that the person would be a stool pigeon and I would have to be extremely careful of what I said because all of it would be reported. They knew that a prisoner kept alone for a prolonged period and then suddenly given company could not refrain from talking. I could not stop talking to Orlov. I told myself the man was a stool pigeon, but I thought, I don't care: it is such a joy to talk. And Orlov seemed so genuine and so sympathetic and so interested that I just let it pour out and out.

He had been saving some extra bread and sugar for himself. He immediately offered them to me. "I ask you not to hesitate," he said. "Just eat it all up. There will be more." He was gravely courteous. I got over the shock of his strange appearance quickly. I realized I must look monstrous myself. I took a deep and heartfelt liking to Orlov, and although I have never seen him since he left me in that cell a month later, I still have warm feelings for him.

For the first few days in cell 216 it was all sleep and talk, with me doing most of both. The expression "verbal diarrhea" is the same in Russian: I had it. I told Orlov my whole life story. I grew sentimental and expansive over my wonderful Mary, who would be my wife as soon as I got out. I boasted about the way I handled Sidorov. I remember that some feeling of caution made me withhold the story of Dina and the trip to Kiev, but I think that was the only thing I censored.

Orlov chuckled over the story of my Valentine's Day visit to Zagorsk. Zagorsk is a beautiful old city forty miles or so from central Moscow. It has a collection of medieval monasteries and churches and so of course it is a strong tourist attraction. Mary and I and a man my age from the Canadian Embassy and his girl, who worked at the British Embassy with Mary, went there for the Valentine's Day weekend in 1948. The Canadian boy and I shared a bedroom and the two girls shared another. After we went to bed the girls took advantage of Valentine's Day custom and slipped notes under our door proposing marriage. Mary's letter promised that she would make a fine man out of me, help me cut down my drinking, make a very happy life for me and so on, and if I refused her I would have to pay a forfeit of a dozen pairs of nylons or something like that. The trouble was we boys were so absorbed in our own conversation that we did not see or hear the notes come under the door. The girls went back to their room and lay there breathless and giggling for some time. Then they began to get madder and madder when we never replied. We saw the letters for the first time when we woke up next morning and the girls were so furious they would not speak to us.

My outpourings to Orlov were a mixture of precious, treasured trivialities like the Zagorsk trip, and bitter, angry accounts of the terrible year that had just passed. As I talked he listened gravely and attentively. He was on extra rations because, as it turned out, he had come to Lefortovo from a prison camp to give some desired information. He always shared his extra ration with me. He had a few cigarettes and offered one from time to time. Tobacco was a luxury I had not had for months and it was ecstasy to light the first one up, although it made me cough and go dizzy.

"Well," Orlov said, when I had pretty well exhausted my story some days later, and was rested and quite happy and relaxed in this bright warm cell, and had stopped shivering at last, "I think you had better prepare yourself for camp, and I can be helpful."

I did not like the sound of that. I said, "But they are through with me now. They have nothing on me. Surely they'll have to let me out soon?"

Orlov looked a little embarrassed and avoided my eyes. Then he said, "I really am afraid you will have to face the strange reality you find yourself in. Yes, I am afraid you will have to do that. If they truly found nothing against you, your sentence will not be a very long one, that is exactly true. But you will truly and unavoidably be given a sentence. It is not possible for the Organs to arrest a man and then free him. They never make mistakes, you know; I believe your diligent interrogator informed you of that fact?"

I just stared at him blankly.

He said, "Look. Cheer up. Camp is not fun, but after what you have come through with such shining courage, if I may say such words, you will do very well there. There are two kinds of prisoners in camp: the kind who die quickly and the kind who make life quite acceptable for themselves and survive very well. You are truly and definitely not the kind who dies quickly, and I will give you some hints about how to manage."

I pulled myself together. I thought, Well, at least the interrogation is over and if I survived a year of that hell, another year in a prison camp can't be so bad. I was interested to hear Orlov speak, now that I had stopped my outpourings, and he began to make himself known a bit through his fairly elaborate way of talking. I asked him about his own background.

"You see, I am an economist, and a good one. I helped organize the agricultural economy around Saratov. We were truly very successful. We had such a truly splendid harvest of wheat in 1938 that I was given the Second Order of Honor by the state. I was truly a very loyal and patriotic man. I volunteered for the army on the second day of the war. I was made a senior lieutenant and sent to the front very quickly. I was captured late in 1941. The Germans treated me very badly in camp. I know something of the kind of life you have had, truly I do."

We sat and smoked in silence for a while and I watched the memory of that bad experience darken his face. Then he went on.

"A strange thing happened. Some Soviet officers came to see me in camp. They were dressed in German uniforms and they looked well fed and happy. They told me confidentially that I would be starved to death unless I agreed to work for the Germans. I said I could never do that. They said there was nothing to it, that they were sure there would come a way to escape someday and rejoin their units. They did not consider themselves traitors. Clearly they could not serve the Soviet Union again if they died in prison, and they were just going to be careful not to do anything for the Germans that would compromise their loyalty.

"It was truly a seductive argument. It seduced me. I agreed. I was taken to an intelligence-training camp and fed well and taught the German language, which is truly a difficult language to learn. I got a uniform and eventually a sidearm and joined an intelligence unit called NORD."

I said, "How could you work for German intelligence without compromising your loyalty?"

Orlov scratched his head and looked miserable, and I felt sorry for having asked. After a while he said, "I always counted on getting back to my own troops somehow, my own people, and turning over German intelligence to them. We were assigned to a Colonel Krause. His unit was stationed at Mogilev. He was a specialist in recruiting Soviet POW's and deserters into the German Army. I am truly sad to have to tell you there were many deserters. Conditions in our army were very bad in many cases. A lot of those boys came from the country. They were not educated. They wanted full bellies and girls and vodka to drink, and they hated their officers and they knew nothing of the Soviet and they had no politics, and all they truly wanted after a while was to survive. So they deserted."

He looked dejected, talking about this period of his life. I was going to suggest changing the subject, but I guess he wanted to get it off his chest. He said, "Truly, I would have to use these words, I would have to say that what I did was not different in fundamentals from what those illiterate boys did. I did what I did to survive."

I felt sorry for his guilt, and I told him so. I also felt a bit contemptuous of his treason, but I did not say that.

He said, "I was in touch with all kinds of classified German material, in Krause's unit. And now I am beginning to justify myself a little, because they kidnapped Krause in the U.S. Zone in Berlin last month, and I am here in Moscow to meet him and confront him. They will take me to Lubyanka for the confrontation. To some extent I can truly redeem myself in the eyes of the state now, I think. But I felt so guilty at the end of the war that I went west instead of east, through the British Zone, and then ended up in Liège. I had been there before, on furlough. I got married to a lady who ran an inn. It was a nice life, a comfortable life, and I thoroughly and confidently expected to end my days quietly as an innkeeper.

"One day a man came in who spoke Russian. He said he was an old émigré. I was just like you when you first came to this cell a few days ago. I was entirely and totally needful of human communication in my native language, and I truly told him my whole story and asked him to come often to talk. He came again the very next day, very punctually. We began to drink together. The next thing I knew I was waking up out of a drugged sleep on a Soviet plane. He was an agent, don't you see. I even paid for the drink that knocked me out," he finished ruefully.

For his collaboration, Orlov had been given ten years in labor camps, and life had been pretty hard in Dubravlag, one of the Potma group of camps where he had been since late in 1945. But his interrogation had been easy. He had held nothing back since he felt himself a loyal Soviet and needed to pay for his sense of guilt. So no beatings, no sleepless nights, and reasonable rations. Now, because he was freely giving the interrogators information about the German colonel and had agreed to be taken for a confrontation with Krause, he was given extra rations and quite easy treatment. Because he shared those rations with me I began to regain my strength quite quickly. My buttocks began to develop a little cushioning again and my thighs to fill out.

It was like a holiday in cell 216. Sunlight flooded the cell every afternoon through the frosted window. The cell was small, less than three meters square, but the light and the pale beige walls gave it a larger feeling. I wallowed in sleep every night, and the feast of talking went on and on.

Occasionally a guard would come in the morning and take Orlov away for the day, but I never left the cell. I started doing push-ups and dynamic tension exercises again, and although I trembled with the exertion of two or three push-ups at first, I made very rapid progress. My muscles began to tone up, and I steadily gained weight, though of course not very much weight. Orlov, on his days away, was put in a Champagne van, and once in a Meat van—we both laughed about that—and was driven to Lubyanka for his meetings with Krause and his interrogation. He was always cheerful when he came back, and would talk about the joy of hearing the noises of the city around him as the van pushed its way through daytime Moscow traffic.

He began to tell me about the life in camp, and gave me some rules for survival that I never forgot. Some of them were inverted parodies of the kind of puritan schoolbook sayings we used to get when we were kids. "Never do today what you can put off till tomorrow," for example, was one of a series of little sermons about conserving energy. "Never tell the truth if a lie will do," as part of dealing with, and confusing, your captors. He told me that it was important to find an income-producing occupation, that there was always some need to be met in every camp and if you could find a way to construct or steal some needed objects (loaves of bread if they put you to work in the kitchen, for example), you did not hesitate to do so and to sell what you could to your fellow prisoners in exchange for other survival items.

He warned me to watch out for common criminals and laughed when I told him that had been my first assumption about him.

"They are truly very tough boys, Alex. They are organized all over the Soviet Union. They have their own code of rules, which is very strict, and if you find yourself in a camp where political prisoners and common criminals are mixed, be careful, because the 'coloreds'—that's the name they are known by—live by stealing from the politicals. The coloreds call the political prisoners 'fascists,' you know, and they call themselves *urki*."

"*Urki?*"

"That's their name. Now listen to me, Alexander Mikhailovich. These *urki* have one large advantage over the political prisoners. You'd better know about this. The *urki* come to prison ready-equipped, if I can use those words, for survival. They have a code of laws that binds them together. They understand each other's way of thinking. They have lived underground outside in a way that teaches them how to cooperate against a hostile world, and when they come inside it's not that much different for them."

He wagged a finger at me for emphasis. "They consider themselves loyal Soviet citizens who happen to live by a different code, by the way. They think all the politicals are enemies of the people."

"That's why they call them 'fascists'?"

"I guess so. The *urki*'s only sin is getting caught. Some of them have patriotic slogans tattooed on their arms. They are a crude, hateful, antisocial gang, Alexander Mikhailovich, but they hang together and that makes them strong."

"And the politicals?"

"Entirely different! Entirely different! Every political is convinced of his own innocence and convinced of every other political's guilt. They have no street experience in cooperating for survival. They are thrown into confusion by their imprisonment. They distrust each other. They are completely incapable of organizing, you see. So they are the perfect victims for the *urki*. When they were outside, the *urki* practiced their trade on a suspicious, distrustful, disorganized society of 'civilians.' Inside they do the same thing. So watch out!"

Orlov asked me if I had ever been tormented with salty food, and I told him about the herring soup in the hard punishment cell. "Watch out for that," he said. "Sometimes when you are in transportation they will use it to drive you truly crazy. They are obliged by the regulations to give a certain number of grams of meat or fish, you see. So they give salt herring. Then people go crazy for water. Sometimes they will give the water and refuse to take you to the toilet, so you either develop terrible pain in your bladder, and maybe get kidney problems from holding in your water, or you relieve yourself on the floor. They will punish you for that, of course."

I missed Orlov a great deal when he went to Lubyanka for the day, and we fell to talking together when he got back at night like old companions who had not seen each other for years. I was becoming deeply fond of him for his old-fashioned manner and his courtesy and his careful, understanding way of listening to me and his unselfish sharing of his food. While he was away, I busied myself with exercise. I picked up my walking where I had left off, in Germany, west of Stuttgart, heading for the Rhine valley and the border with France. I made some more needles and carefully repaired my clothes with towel threads.

It was about a month after my stumbling arrival in cell 216. I was much stronger now. My mind was alert and ready for anything. Orlov went out early one morning for another session at Lubyanka and I was doing arm and chest dynamic exercises when the door opened suddenly and a voice came from outside, "D. With all your belongings. Outside!"

I wondered for a moment whether it had anything to do with Orlov, whether he had been talking about me and had procured some kind of change for me. I could not imagine what. I was sure, incidentally, that Orlov was asked to report on me, but I doubted that he would ever report anything harmful, not that there was much to report, except my hatred for Sidorov and my attempt to outwit him and eventually to kill him. And I had already been punished for that.

They took me out to the courtyard. I was pleased in a childlike way to see a butcher's van standing there, with colored pictures of pieces of meat on it and six little ventilators on the roof. Nothing was said. I was word-lessly motioned inside and I could hear that a guard had climbed in after me, just as in the first ride to Lefortovo. It seemed like another turning point. The fact that I had been made to bring all my belongings made me certain that I would never see Lefortovo again, and my heart was singing. I began to hum quietly as we rolled through the streets of Moscow:

> *Over hill, over dale,*
> *We will hit the dusty trail*
> *As those caissons go rolling along!*

Outside I could hear traffic sounds, the bell of a trolley, a bus's exhaust, and best of all the voices of free people talking as they jostled by the van at a stopping point. Once someone even bumped the side of it going by and slapped a hand on it, quite oblivious of the kind of meat it was carrying, I thought to myself.

I was held in a box downstairs in Lubyanka. I was feeling quite sad about not saying good-by to Orlov. I assumed that I would be put into a solitary cell again, now that I had spilled my guts to Orlov for their benefit, and while that thought was a bit discouraging, I felt strong enough for solitude again. It was like a sort of accounting system. Just as I had considered any five-minute block of sleep I could steal in Lefortovo to be money in the bank against my need to keep alert and ahead of Sidorov, I considered my holiday month with Orlov to have built the account up to the point where I could stand several months on my own again, if it came to that.

After a short while the door of my box opened and I was told to bring my bundle and follow a guard. I was amused to hear the tongue-clucking again. I followed him to a cell on the third floor, cell 33. To my pleasure, the guard stopped outside the cell and opened the peephole and looked inside. I was to have company after all. I had a sudden moment of guess-

ing it was Orlov. But I was wrong, because I was never to see Orlov
again. Instead, there were *two* strangers inside, a tall, rather courtly-
looking man in his fifties with gray hair and bushy eyebrows, and a
short, dark man in his thirties. I felt very excited. The cell was quite
large. It had been a hotel room in the old days when this building had
been the Insurance Hotel. I walked forward briskly with my hand out,
imitating Orlov, and said, "Allow me to introduce myself. My name is
Dolgun. I am an American citizen." I addressed the older man first. He
gave a little bow, very courteously, and said simply, "Igor Krivoshein."
That was a familiar name from Russian history: a Krivoshein had been a
minister under Tsar Nicholas II. Krivoshein stepped back and waved the
other man ahead very politely. The dark-haired guy grinned a big, toothy
grin and shook hands very warmly. He was much less reserved than
Krivoshein. He said, "My name is Feldman, and I bet I know all about
you!"

I raised my eyebrows. Feldman said, "Sure. I read about it in London.
You were picked up outside the American Embassy, right? Sure, sure. I
read the story in some paper, I don't remember.

"I was a correspondent for *Red Star*," he added. "I used to get a bit
loaded with my English friends and tell anti-Soviet jokes. I thought they
were pretty funny jokes. One of my English friends turned out to be not
so English and not so friendly, and here I am. Fifty-eight point ten."

Krivoshein had fought in the White Army in the Civil War, and when
they were defeated in the Crimea he had found his way to Paris and
settled down to work as a taxi driver. Quite a comedown, he said, for a
man descended from a famous Russian statesman. During World War II
he served in the French underground and began to dream of going home
again, because he was terribly homesick for Russia and was sure that
things would change after the war. Sure enough, Stalin, in 1946, announced that Russian émigrés were forgiven and invited home. Krivoshein
was immensely happy. He set out with his French-born wife and child,
got to Moscow, and was given a place to live and a job in Sverdlovsk,
in the Urals, about fifteen hundred kilometers east of Moscow. He
worked in a garage. One day his boss told him that he wanted Krivoshein
to make trips to Moscow for him to get parts and so on, and that he
would go with him on the first trip to help him along. Of course, when
they got to Moscow the boss turned Krivoshein right over to the MGB,
and the only puzzle is why they bothered with the Sverdlovsk honeymoon.*

I stayed with these two only for three or four days. The cell was

* Just as this book was going to the typesetter, I received news that Igor
Krivoshein has been able to leave the Soviet Union, and is living in France again.

bright and smelled of fresh floor wax because every morning we were
given a brush and a bit of wax and told to polish the parquet floor with
it. In the afternoons we were taken up on the roof for exercise. There was
a high parapet around the roof, and guards in boxes, so you could not
see the streets of Moscow below, but you could hear the traffic and the
voices of people and once I even heard children laughing. I continued
my exercises every day and discussed the possibilities of the future with
Feldman and Krivoshein. Feldman believed they would get one-to-three-
year sentences and found that tolerable. I was appalled at the cool way
they looked at the prospect of years of confinement, but to them it
seemed to be natural and acceptable. Although Krivoshein used to sigh
gloomily and say, "Never expect anything good from the MGB!"

Both had signed Article 206, termination of interrogation, and neither
had had a rough time in interrogation.

Feldman said, "Dolgun, I don't know how you did it. I admire you
very much. Very much. I really do. I thank God they did not take you to
Sukhanovka."

I had never heard of it.

"To tell you the truth," Feldman said, "I'm not even sure it exists. But
the rumor is that there is a prison called Sukhanovka where they take
only big cases. Big guys they caught in some treason or other, or guys
the Leader wants to put away or get a confession out of that he can use
against one of his enemies. It's the kind of place people talk about with
hushed voices. But you see, I've never heard of anyone coming *out* of
Sukhanovka. I've heard of them going in there, but never coming out."

I said, "It could not really be any worse than what I got."

"Perhaps not," Feldman said. "But you came out."

I tried to get them to guess what was going to happen to me next.
They would not. They said I should wait till I heard whether or not I was
to get a trial, what the verdict was, what I was convicted of. "But I
haven't done one thing!" I protested.

"Is telling jokes about the Soviet Union doing anything?" Feldman
shot back bitterly.

I did not have long to wait. I think it was the fourth day. The door
opened. "D. Come out." I was taken to an interrogation room where an
air force major was standing by the curtained window. For a second I
thought it might be a confrontation with one of the military officers that
Sidorov was always referring to. But it turned out that Kozhukhov, this
"air force" major, was really MGB and, like many of their officers, wore a
uniform of the regular forces as a sort of disguise, and to reduce the number of purple-striped pants that would otherwise be swarming the streets
of Moscow and every other city in the Soviet Union.

I was sure I had seen this man before. He had distinctive Eastern features, and something about the eyes gave me either a strong *déjà vu* or an authentic memory that made me uneasy but which I could not place.

After the formalities of identification and so on, Kozhukhov showed me Sidorov's collection of protocols on my interrogation. They came in four volumes. I skimmed them. I had read that stuff before. Then he gave me a form to sign, Article 206, termination of interrogation. That was a heart-warming phrase; I think I even signed with my real signature.

But I remember distinctly that I transferred none of that warm feeling to Kozhukhov. There was something wrong about him. Yet his next words were, on the face of it, very reassuring.

He said, "All the charges under Article 58 have been withdrawn as unfounded or unproven. You are now charged under Article 7.35 as a socially dangerous element."

That did not sound like much to me. Maybe it would mean that the embassy would have to send me back to the States, which would be fine. I asked Kozhukhov what happened next, and he said, very formally, he could not possibly know that, he was only an interrogator, and they had simply asked him to see me and show me this article for my signature. I signed and went back to cell 33 in high spirits.

Feldman and Krivoshein burst into smiles when I told them it was 7.35. They pumped both my hands at once and laughed, and Feldman almost jumped up and down with excitement.

"This is wonderful news! Wonderful news," Feldman said. His eyes were shining. He said, "The very worst they can do, the *very* worst, is five years' prison camp. Why, lots of guys only get five years of exile. This is great!"

My face must have fallen because here in the cell among friends I was totally off guard. I could not believe my ears. "Five years!" I said incredulously. "Five years in prison camp for being a socially dangerous element?"

"What's the matter?" said Krivoshein. "It couldn't be better, you know."

I thought of what Orlov had said, how the MGB never made mistakes. I had been so sure they would let me go now. Five years out of my life. For nothing. Five years without Mary. Five years seemed like eternity. The bottom had just dropped out. It was to get worse. I spent a gloomy weekend trying to get my spirits up and trying to get Feldman and Krivoshein to speculate about better possibilities, but they were genuinely irritated to find that I was not rejoicing at the lightness of my likely sentence.

On Monday I was taken to the interrogation room again, and again it was Major Kozhukhov. He said very offhandedly, as if he were telling me it was raining out, that fresh evidence against me had turned up, and that charges 58.6, espionage, and 58.10, anti-Soviet activities, were being reinstated.

At first I did not understand this at all. I said, "Will that affect my sentence?"

Kozhukhov said, "Oh, there is no sentence yet. We are going to resume interrogation."

He let that sink in. I felt very cold and a bit sick. I said in a very low voice, "I'm not going back to Colonel Sidorov in Lefortovo, am I?"

"No," he said. "I will be your interrogator this time."

"Here in Lubyanka, then," I said.

"No," he said, looking at me with a very unpleasant smile. "No, I am transferring you immediately to Sukhanovka."

I felt dizzy and terrified. I tried not to show it. I do not know if I succeeded. I do not remember saying good-by to Feldman and Krivoshein, although I must have been taken to cell 33 to get my things. I do remember that it was a DRINK SOVIET CHAMPAGNE van again.

Anger helped clear my head on that cramped ride, which was a long one. I could tell from sounds outside that we were leaving the city, and by the way the speed picked up after a while that we were on the open road. The ride took about an hour and a half, as far as I could tell. When the van finally stopped, I heard a squealing iron gate, then a moment later my cubicle was unlocked and I stepped out into very bright sunlight. It was January, cold and clear and fine. I caught glimpses of a high yellow wall with barbed wire around what seemed a good-sized compound, and a building that looked very much like a monastery, which is what it had been for a long time. I was hustled inside. Someone, a guard, shoved me into a small closet so narrow that standing straight up I almost touched the door and the back of the closet at the same time. There was no room to crouch or sit. There was a weak bulb in a caged recess high in the gloomy little vertical coffin, and through the food slot there was a hairline of brighter light from the corridor. I wondered why they even bothered with a food slot in a ridiculous little holding cell like that. I waited an hour for them to come and get me for the usual arrival procedures of bath and searching and the rest. When they did not come and I was becoming extremely uncomfortable, I knocked on the door and called the guard. The peephole slid open. "I want to go to the toilet," I said. The door was unlocked and I stepped into the corridor, blinking at the light. The guard motioned for me to follow him along the corridor to the toilet a few steps away. I tried to get him to talk to me, but he just put his fingers to his lips and said "*Nye polozhna*" in a low voice. I asked if he would at least tell me when I would be taken to my cell, but he just shook his head, no.

Back in the closet my feet began to hurt and I tried resting my knees against the door and my back against the wall behind me. That relieved my feet for a while but hurt my knees; so I stood up again and moved from foot to foot. Soon the food slot opened—toward the outside: it had no shelf—and a small plate of soup was passed in. It was not much but it was delicious. I knocked in a moment and the empty soup plate disappeared and was replaced by a small plate with a tiny sliver of delicious veal cutlet and a spoonful of delicately fried potatoes, steaming hot and nicely seasoned. I could hardly believe it. I ate them in two mouthfuls and knocked, and when the guard took the empty plate I said "Thank you!" and I meant it. I had not tasted food like that for over a year. I wondered what would come next. What came next was one cup of water. Then I realized soon that there would be no more food. My appetite had been so aroused by those excellent teasers that I had given in to the kind of food fantasies that I used to suppress all the time in Lefortovo. Now I had to try to suppress them again, but those delicious salty tastes lingered insistently in my mouth and forced me to think of food. I asked for more water, and when he brought it I carefully rinsed out my mouth before swallowing, and washed away the maddening taste.

By the time evening came, I was acutely uncomfortable. A new guard brought me a bowl of excellent hot porridge, extremely tasty, about a tablespoonful. I ate it carefully and then knocked and asked for the toilet. This guard spoke when he took me out. "This way," he said. I thought that was a good sign, so coming back from the toilet I said in a conversational way, "Listen. When am I going to be transferred?"

He said casually, "You're transferred."

That's all. Just, "You're transferred."

Of course I did not believe it, and kept waiting to be taken to a cell. But nobody came. I became very sleepy but there was no way to get any kind of comfort. I would lean my head against the door and angle my hip to one side. Then I would sleep for a few minutes and wake up with a terrible pain in my back. I tried with my knees against the door but that was acutely painful. By morning I could not stop my knees buckling. I asked for the toilet as often as they would take me—three or four times a day—just to get a chance to sit down, although it was only a hole in the floor with footplates to squat over, and I would just let myself go down onto the cold floor until the guard, who watched the whole performance, ordered me to get up again. Walking was difficult and painful, and yet a relief.

It never occurred to me that I should keep a calendar, so I made no scratches. I remember examining mosquitoes clustered, immobile, in the dust around the corners at the top of that box, and wondering if they were dead or hibernating. I remember that the third morning I began to force myself to keep count of the days, but there was nothing to scratch with anyway, although I might have made lines in the dust around the mosquitoes with my finger, but I did not bother. I could not believe it when the morning of the fifth day arrived. I would lose consciousness and wake up to the intense pain in my kneecaps, extending through all the muscles of my legs. I realized of course what they were doing to me with those tantalizing tiny bits of food, and went back to earlier Lefortovo disciplines of taking tiny bites and chewing them a long time to make them last. They had no impact on my yawning stomach. The saliva flowed at a terrible rate whenever the food came, and I developed a kind of compulsive swallowing reflex. Five days I was kept in that box. On the fifth evening I was taken to a cell, shaking, my legs terribly swollen, my knees a total agony. A folding bed was pulled down from the wall and I was given a clean blanket and pillow. But the pain was too great to sleep for more than a few minutes, until it was nearly morning. My feet and lower legs had gone numb, and as sensation returned to them they at first prickled lightly and then began to be very hot and to ache all over with a deep, dull ache.

I was overwhelmed. I could believe that nobody ever came out of this hellish place. I could not collect myself and recover my one-day-at-a-time attitude which had gotten me through before. I came near to panic. I forgot all my survival devices. I just could not believe this was happening to me and yet I saw that it was. The element of fear was profound and very debilitating.

It was a Friday night when I arrived in the cell. I think some time toward morning I must have regained some of my composure and control over myself. I realized that it was a weekend and that I would probably be left on my own. I still had my measuring string, which I had kept rolled in my pocket. It was too light and flimsy ever to be discovered in a search. Even if I turned my pockets out, I could tuck it up in an upper corner of the pocket in the same motion as turning the linings out, and it was never discovered and never taken from me. I began to tell myself to get organized as soon as the bread and hot water came in the morning. The bread was good but small, perhaps 400 grams. I forced starvation out of my mind and began to measure the little cell. It was exactly 1.56 meters by 2.09, just long enough for the two narrow beds that were made of heavy wood reinforced with iron and hinged to the wall like horizontal doors. The cell was designed to contain two people, then. Between the beds, and under them if they were ever both down (mine never were), was a narrow table one meter long, an inch thick, and only six inches wide, somewhat the shape of an ironing board, mounted on one-inch pipe sunk in the concrete floor. At opposite corners of this little table and bed support were round stools on pipes, a handspan below table height, less than eight inches across. That was what I had to sit on during the day. Try it. If your buttocks are not well-cushioned it is painful. I was not allowed to sit on the table.

The bed, when it folded up into the wall in the morning, had a spring lock, which was opened again with a key at ten thirty at night. The cell was cozy, not cold. The window was large, frosted, and locked with heavy bars and mesh. It was closed. The guard opened a small panel above it for a few minutes each morning, and later in the year as the weather warmed up a bit, I could smell the pines outside. Most of the day the cell was stuffy and by morning, especially if I had been allowed to sleep, the air was so heavy it made my head ache.

There was an iron pail with a fitted iron cover. No sink or toilet.

At ten thirty the block commander came with a key and opened the bed and silently indicated that I should help lower it. It was very heavy. If I had left my hand accidentally on the stool or table as it came down it would have crushed the fingers. The straw tick was clean enough. You had to sleep facing the door, of course, with your hands outside the blanket, a standard prison regulation. In the morning the guard ordered me to push the bed up into the wall, and watched until it was up and the lock clicked shut.

These were monks' cells. Somehow I later found out there were sixty-eight of them in this old stone building, still providing mortification of the flesh, as they had for centuries, though with a different purpose in mind.

In the morning, after breakfast, the door was opened and the guard said one word: "*Opravka.*" Toilet. I had to take the bucket to the toilet and dump it there and rinse it out. The toilet was one of eight doors in the short corridor, four on each side. The others were cells. In the toilet, to rinse out your bucket, was a barrel of chlorinated water and a mop.

When I was taken back to the cell I began walking and counting again —I was almost across the border of France by now—but walking was slow and difficult because, with the stools and the table and the cramped size of the cell to begin with, I could make only two steps to the end, a half-step sideways around the end of the table, two steps, a half, and so on. I still have a habit of walking two steps, a half step. In Sukhanovka I had to face the door while walking; so I walked into France, at least part of the way, looking over my shoulder.

When Monday morning came I was taken out at nine thirty, through a frigid wooden corridor with frost on the walls, into another building where the interrogation rooms were. I thought as I walked and counted, If everything else about this place is horrible, what in the world will the interrogation be like? Kozhukhov gave me no time to speculate. As I came into the room he tripped me with his foot and sent me tumbling to the floor. He laughed a kind of coarse, coughing laugh. As I tried to get up on my hands and knees, he put his big, jackbooted foot between my shoulder blades and roughly shoved me down again. I turned and stared at him. Wide Mongol cheeks and a constant cruel leer. He said harshly, "You will find that Sukhanovka is nothing like the Sunday picnic you had in that kindergarten called Lefortovo! Now, get to the table and start answering questions fast because I have no intention of fooling around like some of my colleagues."

I said to myself again, Well, here we come.

CHAPTER

12

THE HUMAN MIND HAS A NUMBER OF SAFETY VALVES, AND MOST OF MINE have worked well and often. I am not even sure *safety valve* is the right expression, because while there is the release of pressure that comes with jokes and memory devices and fantasy, there is also the suppression of things that you cannot tolerate very well when you are weak or needful. I suppressed for a long time, working on this book, my suicide plans in Lefortovo, under Sidorov. I suppose, in the sense that such suppression relieves pressure, there is a kind of safety valve function. In any case, it is certainly the most difficult kind of labor for me now to dig down into my memory for the terrible experiences, and when people ask me about prison and especially about camp, and I have to tell stories of some kind, the ones that surface quickly are usually funny—funny characters or narrow escapes, and so on. But the perception of myself as someone who twice coolly and deliberately planned the destruction of his own life is something that I "forgot" until I had to deal with it. I was able to keep it "forgotten" in reviewing the Lefortovo experience; I cannot do so in the case of Sukhanovka. Even though the actual planning and preparations were to come a long time after these first few days in the most feared, legendary horror prison of Russia, the memory of what I planned there surfaces the moment I see the geography of the cell, and with it the memory of my earlier plan in Lefortovo, which was less elaborate.

It was a contingency plan, and it was not accompanied by much emotion when I worked it out. In fact, the words *plan* and *worked it out* are too sophisticated. What I decided, very simply and straightforwardly, was that if Sidorov got to be too much for me and I became convinced that I was going to break down and become a tool for him to use as he pleased, to fabricate whatever humiliating lies he wanted, or if I became convinced that one day I would lose the strength and the will to keep up the disciplines and strategies of survival that I had developed and that therefore I was going to die anyway, I would simply step up on the iron cot during the break between peephole visits and throw myself headlong off the bunk in a dive of the kind we used to call "the dead soldier" when I was a kid, with my arms firmly at my sides, in a way that would bring me down head first onto the cast-iron toilet. The lid of the toilet would be off. The edges of that cast iron were rough and sharp enough so that sitting on it with my almost-disappeared buttocks had become a pain made bearable only by the joy of tapping messages next door, and I was sure that my skull would be caved in by the impact and that I would die quickly, unconscious at the very end.

It was not a good concept after all, because by the time I began to feel seriously that I might have to use it I was far too weak to have any assurance of launching myself sufficiently accurately at that ring of rough iron with enough force to do the job completely, supposing I did manage to hit the rim at all.

Here in Sukhanovka the prospect was much more serious and the plan much more elaborate. The bed that was let down every night with the block commander's key was terribly heavy. In the first few days, before I was dehydrated with fever and stunned with sleeplessness and exhausted by starvation, I was actually able to lift it back in position when the guard ordered me to do so in the morning. It was a hard, grunting job to lift it the first few inches, but then when it passed the forty-five-degree mark it was not too bad, and I could bang it into its spring latch without much difficulty. Later, and not much later either, I could not help the block commander lower it at night and I could not budge it off the stools it rested on in the morning. At some point I realized that if I could find a way of unlocking the bed myself, I could use it as a weapon for my self-destruction.

Each day I was taken once to the toilet and ordered to carry my bucket, which contained a twenty-four-hour collection of urine. In the toilet I was given a tiny scrap of coarse paper to use as toilet paper. Instead of using it, I washed myself and palmed the paper. Then, back in the cell, I hid the paper and slowly began to accumulate quite a few of these little scraps. I had decided that I could make a chewed papier-mâché out of them and use it to block the hole the latch sprang into, so that when the bed was put up, the latch would *appear* to spring, but the bed would be actually staying in position only because it was vertical. I had noticed that it stayed balanced in the vertical position before it was latched. Having prepared it before the guard put it up in the morning, I would then wait until he was safely out of sight, pull the heavy iron and wood frame toward me until it was just barely balanced on its hinges and tending to continue outward in its arc to fall down on the small round stool, then, before it could get moving, quickly kneel and place my temple on the stool so that the hundred pounds of wood and iron following down would instantly crush my skull. It was not pleasant, of course, to make such a plan and to begin to hoard paper in aid of it, and yet it gave me a small but psychologically necessary handhold on some element of control over my future. And it gave me access to an escape route if what was happening got beyond the point where I could bear it.

I have mentioned fever. It was something like malaria, and I don't remember now where it came from, but I think it had been a recurring problem when I was a child. Very soon after the brutal Kozhukhov once again began the long review of my personal history, I woke up after a short half-hour's sleep one morning and realized that my cheeks were hot and my lips dry. I asked for the doctor. She came—middle-aged, tired, long face, sympathetic eyes—and shoved a thermometer under my arm. It read over 40°C—nearly 105°F—and I was very frightened. The doctor told me sadly there was nothing she could do for me but give me aspirin. I was stunned when I realized that meant no relief from interrogation.

In fact, Kozhukhov treated the fever like a joke. I pleaded with him. I told him I was sweating and that the fever was dangerously high. I told him my head and joints were aching, and he could see the parched lips and the high color. He just laughed. He said, "I'll help you to cool down, then!" He stepped to the window and threw it open. Outside the late February air must have been below zero. Kozhukhov put on his woolen scarf and his army greatcoat and his fur hat and heavy gloves. Then he just laughed hugely at me. I think the laugh was spontaneous. I think he found the situation quite funny and enjoyable in a crazy way. He tried to continue the interrogation but most of the time I was shivering too much to answer him. He finally closed the window, not out of any humanitarian intention but because the shivering and the chattering teeth slowed down his work and made progress impossible. But the next day he would say with a hateful grin, rubbing his hands together in anticipation, "Got a high fever again today, have you, prisoner? Well, we can bring that fever down very easily. You'll see. We are much better than those doctors. You'll see." And again he would put on his coat and open the window and laugh to see me tremble out of control.

So I am not surprised that sequential, chronological recollections of Sukhanovka scarcely exist. I went downhill quickly, losing weight and losing clarity. I remember the kinds of things Kozhukhov concentrated on, but I recall few of the actual conversations. He had a dirty mind. He would question me in detail about the sexual part of my relations with the girls I had known. I recall that I told him about Steve Sage and me going to Gorky Park and picking up a couple of girls in the rowboat we rented; we offered to take them home, very gentlemanly, but of course expecting that there might be some drinks and some fun when we got there. My girl lived miles from the center of Moscow, and by the time we got there it was almost time for the last tram back. Furthermore, she showed me the house where she lived with her parents and sisters but did not invite me in, so that was a terrible waste. I got on the tram, but it stopped somewhere in the outskirts and the conductor cleared the car: it was the last stop. I asked her how to get to central Moscow and she just waved—"That way." And I started walking. After midnight.

Some time later I was passing through a very dim street, and I saw three young men waiting at the corner. I thought they were probably looking for trouble. They followed me for a while and finally a couple pulled ahead and cut me off and asked for cigarettes.

"I don't smoke," I said politely. "Sorry."

I was looking frantically for a sign of a cop or a house I could dash into or any source of help or safety. No luck. One of the guys asked the time. I said I had no watch. He said he could hear it ticking. I backed up against a wall with a big drainpipe so that I had my back and one side protected, and I said toughly, "All right, you guys, what do you really want?"

"Your coat," one said. He pulled a knife and came toward me. I kicked out, not at him but at the guy beside him. I got him in the crotch and he went down, but the knife got me over the eye at the same time. I felt blood come out, and I let go with a hard right to somebody's jaw and then ducked and ran. They did not come after me. For a while I thought I had been blinded in my left eye. I wiped it with a handkerchief and saw a lot of blood and found it was coming from my forehead, just over the eye, and I could still see all right. A cop at a subway station took me to their feldsher —a medical assistant—and the feldsher clamped the cut. I told Kozhu-khov about the girls but not about the fight. He thought the story was a waste of time.

I told him another one about a beautiful half-Chinese girl Steve Sage and I picked up at the bar of the Moskva Hotel. She worked as a bartender and knew only three words of English: I love you! We got friendly and proposed having a party, and she agreed to bring a girlfriend —in fact, we ended up at the friend's apartment. It turned out pretty well, with lots of caviar and cold meat and wine and records on the phonograph, and plenty of giggling and stories and all the rest, until the friend's es-tranged husband came to the door and threatened to break in and kill us all, and Steve Sage and I went out the second-floor window. Steve and I had both grabbed champagne bottles as weapons in case the jealous husband got in, and we found we still had them when we jumped out. There we were running like hell through Moscow, clutching champagne bottles in our hands. Kozhukhov thought this was a great story, although he was disappointed that it did not have any real sex in it. The one thing I did not tell him about the adventure with the champagne bottle was that the jealous husband was an MGB colonel. I *wanted* to throw that at Kozhukhov, to humiliate him. If I had thought of it with Sidorov, I would have thrown it at him. I might even have added something provocative like, "It wasn't you, by any chance, was it?" and taken my kicks and blows just for the satisfaction of getting at him. With Kozhukhov it was different. I was desperately sick most of the time, and I never had the feeling that Kozhukhov cared whether I lived or died. Sidorov had been determined to get information from me. Kozhukhov, I felt, was determined to be cruel to me, and if information came along as well, then that was gravy for him. The end product did not matter; it was the experience of the day he lived for. So I thought if I pushed him too far, he would beat me hard enough to kill me and never think twice about it. In fact, he did not beat me as badly as Sidorov. I was too much of a whimpering mess of fever and emaciation most of the time. I got very little sleep. I was unconscious a great deal of the time and many days went by with almost no conscious activity on my part, although I think I almost always managed to put a scratch on the cumulative calendar.

At some point Kozhukhov began asking me about another girl, an artist named Ella I met at a party with Joe O'Brian from the embassy. She said she wanted to paint my portrait, and we had some pretty friendly times in her studio apartment until I realized that she was bleeding a lot of money from me. We'd be lying there in bed on a sunny afternoon, and she would say things like, "Listen, I need twenty rubles—I'll give it back tomorrow."

I always gave. Then after a while I realized she never gave it back. I was embarrassed to ask her about it, but after a while I got the message pretty clearly: she was never going to give it back. She was an old-fashioned gold digger. So I stopped seeing her.

This had never been an important relationship to me, although Ella was beautiful and very active and had a great sense of humor. But we were not together long at all. I was surprised that Kozhukhov was zeroing in on her. He kept describing her, her features and her figure, the location of her studio, and finally the location of our first meeting after the initial cocktail party, where we had made a rendezvous in a subway station. He knew where I had stood, where she had stood, what we had each been wearing. I began to re-create the scene in my mind as he talked about it. Finally in my memory came the clear view of the MGB tail who had been on me that night, and I finally knew where I had seen Kozhukhov before. He had been the tail.

He said, "By the way, did she ever borrow any money from you?"

I was embarrassed still about the way she had taken me, so I said no.

He said, "Come on, tell me, didn't she get some money out of you?"

I thought, Boy, he knows a lot! Then I guessed why he knew, and I said, "Are we by any chance milk brothers?" That is a Russian expression for two men who have shared the same woman. He just laughed and went on asking me if Ella had gotten any of my money, and when I kept protesting crossly, "No, for Christ's sake. Why do you keep on about that!" he finally said, "Well, I'll bet she did, because she borrowed a whole lot from me and I never got it back!"

That was before life with Kozhukhov became nearly impossible and the thoughts of suicide began to form in my mind again.

Kozhukhov was very abusive. His language was worse than Sidorov's— not in quality, which would not have been possible, but in quantity: the nonstop spewing of dirty, ugly words.

He tried to get me to say that I had attempted to persuade a Soviet employee of the U.S. Embassy, Morris Seltser, to defect to the United States and had helped him with his plans to escape the Soviet Union.

As we moved off the casual areas of girls and other acquaintances, Kozhukhov's manner became more deliberate. When he asked me about Seltser, he moved around the interrogation room with deliberate, measured steps. He held himself in a military posture. His army breeches were tucked precisely into his high boots and he would place each foot before the other in a hard, emphatic way, as if to say, "I'll show you, prisoner. I'll get it out of you." His square chin he held forward with a kind of grimace drawing down the corners of his mouth. He worked at looking cruel.

Unlike Sidorov with his vague suggestions, Kozhukhov came right out with it, naming Seltser and specifying the charge. I denied it. Kozhukhov said he had been a boxer and would demonstrate a few of his punches to help me remember. His favorite was a hard jab on the biceps, repeated to the point where my arm would be swollen and completely useless. I said I remembered Seltser all right. He was a deferential man; during the one and only conversation we had, he called me Mr. Dolgun and I called him Morris. He was a messenger and handyman who made a good living selling secondhand goods around Moscow, some of which he got out of embassy employees who liked his pleasant ways. A carton of cigarettes would bring 200 rubles in those days; Morris would get some cigarettes at the embassy —as well as clothes—and pay the embassy employees prices they thought were pretty good.

I had never played this black-market game. I thought it was bad stuff. Except for my little pistol collection, which I got from trading cigarettes with diplomatic couriers and other embassy people and never with Soviets, I never sold any of these things for money, although I gave a lot of presents to my Russian girlfriends. But I talked with Morris that day about his success in the trade, and he boasted that if he had been living in America he would have been a millionaire because he was so good at buying low and selling high. He liked to boast about it. And it turned out that this was the only source of the accusation that I was helping Morris Seltser escape to America, this remark of his about being a millionaire if he lived in my country.

Every day Kozhukhov would hit me. The beatings did not go on and on. I was too weak. One or two blows would keep me in agony for hours, and the sleeplessness was, of course, the principal weapon. Sometimes Kozhukhov would smash me with the edge of his open hand right under my nose. I would go temporarily blind from this blow, and my eyes would run and sometimes my lip would bleed. And all the time I denied and denied trying to persuade Morris Seltser to defect, until one day Kozhukhov brought me a protocol that showed my room had been bugged the day Morris and I had that conversation. The protocol said that he tried to buy flour from me. Most of the flour I was able to get I gave to my mother, but I was always a soft touch and I gave a bag to Morris, even though I knew he would sell it for a lot of rubles, and that was when he said, "If I lived in the United States," etc., etc.

I was furious with Kozhukhov through my fear and weakness and fever and pain. I yelled, "Is *this* what's supposed to prove I was trying to make Seltser defect? Are you serious!"

I even laughed at him. Faced with this outright crap, I found the daring to laugh at him and taunt him. My self-respect would not let the opportunity go by, even though I would suffer for it. Kozhukhov did not hit me for laughing. I supposed he had been told to see if there was anything behind that innocent conversation, and had done as much fishing as he thought was worthwhile and finally completed what he had to do by showing me the protocol. In the end he probably felt not sheepish, but a kind of what-the-hell feeling. He could not possibly have believed in what he was doing. It was orders.

By the end of February 1950, my buttocks had shrunk to wrinkled skin and sitting anywhere was painful. I probably weighed less than Charles Atlas' famous ninety-seven-pound weakling by this time, but I was much too feeble for any dynamic tension exercises. I walked a little in the cell and continued to move across France toward the border of Spain. I was never taken outside. For that whole period in Sukhanovka, I never saw the sky, although by the end of March the smell of pines coming in through the window when it was open for those few precious minutes each morning gave me visions of an outside world and gave me a little hope, somehow— just knowing that such things as pine trees still existed. The prison was deadly quiet. It was carpeted throughout. At first, being left alone in that cell with the terrible heavy beds and the round stools was oppressive not just because of the stuffy air and the harsh light but also because of the absolute silence.

Later I began to hear a buzz of voices, and slowly, over a period of time, I discovered that the cell opposite had two prisoners in it, and that they must have had a very special status because they were allowed to talk, and also, as I soon discovered by listening at the door, they were taken out for exercise periods every day. I envied them both privileges and came to feel hatred for them because they had and I had not. One day I nearly screamed in rage because I heard a soft voice at their food slot opposite asking them to choose books from a library list. "Here's the catalogue, what books do you want to order this week?" the voice said. I would have given one of my tiny loaves of bread away for a book, even though my eyes were almost too sore to read and my body was shrinking into invisibility. (They had a phrase for this. I was taunted with it on several occasions. The phrase is *tonki, zvonki i prozrachny*. Literally, it means "thin, ringing, and transparent," like a crystal goblet—so thin you are invisible.)

I was told later that some very senior officials serve their sentences of ten or fifteen or twenty years in a closed prison like Sukhanovka, never going to a slave labor camp where they might form a faction and find themselves allies they could use during their captivity or later in freedom. I never found out who these two were. I hated them worse than ever the day I realized that the noise I could hear was beds going down and I knew that they could raise and lower their beds when they wanted to.

Toward the end of the week I would pass out with increasing frequency, sometimes coming to on the floor of the interrogation room with a doctor peering at me, sometimes on the floor of my cell with a guard's key tapping at the food slot to wake me up. On Saturday Kozhukhov would usually let me go early and go off to Moscow where his friends were. I often heard him making dates to meet in bars, on the telephone in the interrogation room. It was hard to believe that such a man had friends. I am not sure I ever met anyone else I felt that way about.

When Kozhukhov went to sleep in his chair at night, as he often did, he would wake up in a fright that lasted long enough for me to perceive it. Then he would rage at me and the flow of filth would run for several minutes without interruption, except maybe for a punch on the biceps or a hand edge blow on the upper lip. I believe he was frightened because he thought I would sneak up on him and kill him while he slept. In fact I went to sleep the moment he did, sometimes succeeding in staying on my chair and sometimes waking up on the floor at the end of Kozhukhov's hard boot.

As time went on I became more and more useless to him either as a victim of his sadism or as a source of information. Because I was losing consciousness so frequently, he would terminate interrogation at one or two in the morning and I would be allowed to sleep until six. Then, just before six, I would hear others being led back from interrogation, some screaming for pity and help, some moaning, some silent, some—from the faint sounds of dragging—unable to walk. I knew what that was like. It was like me.

One man who moaned and cried a great deal was in the cell diagonally opposite mine. On a Saturday evening when I was beginning to compose myself for the relief of a long sleep and a day ahead without Kozhukhov I suddenly heard the dull thud of boot heels on the carpeting and then the whispering of many voices. Then there was the sound of a cell door opening violently and a pause and a loud call, "Bring a stretcher! Hurry!"

Finally more boots and scuffling, and after a while urgent angry whispers: "*No!* You fool! It won't fit the door that way. Twist it around. Turn it that way! God, what a mess. No! No! Lift him sideways. What a mess! What a mess!" And so on. I was listening intently at the door, moving away only when I heard the soft footfall of the guard approaching for his peep, and then back again to hear all I could. There were quiet, indistinct sounds of the cell door opening and closing a few times, and a sound of water being poured, and after a while silence.

I stayed by the door listening for explanations. It may have been some hours later, I cannot be sure, when the guard on my block took a few minutes off from his boring routine to open the door between our block and the next and gossip with his colleague through the half-open door. I could catch a few whispered words. "Seemed all right . . . stood facing the door . . . quiet . . . what happened? . . . blood all over . . ." I assumed a suicide.

I began now to go deeply into the thought of my own suicide. Although with the frequent total collapses I was possibly getting more sleep than I had had in Lefortovo, the fever and the microscopic meals were slowly draining all my physical strength and with it my will to resist. That was the standard I had set myself: when that will was gone, then it would be time to die. The guards' whispers about my unknown neighbor unnerved me a little. Somehow they made me lose confidence in my ability to kill myself—not my courage to undertake the act, but my physical ability in strength and coordination to bring it off and not bungle, like the prisoner I once read of or heard of somewhere who had thrown himself from an inadequate height and succeeded only in popping out his eyes and breaking his neck, so that he lived on for years a blind and paralyzed derelict. I would rather rot away or yield or anything but that.

And yet I could not imagine going on. Although I was not cold anymore because spring was coming, still I shivered much of the time anyway. My stomach hurt all the time, as did my head and my knees and elbows and back. Mental clarity was rare. I have no picture of whole days during that period, unlike my recall of the Lefortovo experience. And there came a point where it suddenly and dramatically seemed infinitely worse than even the freezing hard punishment cell in the basement of the K-shaped dungeon. I do not even remember where I was when it happened. Did they take me for baths at Sukhanovka? I think they did, though I do not remember a bathroom as such. What I do remember—and I still feel the shock that came with seeing the sight that will still form itself horrifyingly in front of me if I let it—is that somehow I was naked. It must have been at the bath. I looked at my shrunken body and I saw a devastating thing: my knees were thicker than any other part of my legs! I nearly fainted to see this. The terrible thing that swam into my mind was a photograph in *Life* magazine of some survivors of Belsen or Auschwitz—some one of the Nazi extermination camps. The staring creatures were not really people. They stood or lay or clung to fences, surrounded by the bodies of those who had died the morning of liberation or perhaps the day before, and some of those bodies had been torn open for their livers and other soft parts. These were not human beings in the photographs, though they had been human once. They stared out of deep, dark eye sockets, but I believed they could not see or comprehend anything, and I thought at the time that such a life was worse than death and was more obscene than anything that could be imagined. That photograph had made me shudder, and now I was in the photograph. I could not see my face, but I imagined it to be a staring, vacant face in that photograph. I shook with my fever, and I thought, Is this a life that is any better than death? And then I thought, If I am able to ask that question, does that mean I am pretty close to the end? Had I better try to remember where I have hidden my scraps of paper, and chew them up, and plug that lock on the bed frame? Oh God, I think I said—where have you gone to, Alex Dolgun? You could take anything once. If you've gone away somewhere, why keep the body living?

I know that I came very close to plugging the spring lock. I do not know how close. I know only that, sometime in late April or early May, I knew that The End had about arrived. I was able to be almost dispassionate about it. I could say to myself, "Alex, you did everything you could. Now it is time to rest, forever."

Hazy and delirious much of the time now, and in the midst of the red mist around my eyes, one morning the door to the cell is open and I am aware that a woman in a physician's smock is there and that I have never seen her before but feel a strange, dreamy affection toward her. Someone has told me to get up and get my things together. I think I try to do this, but it must be clear that I cannot raise myself. My lips are too dry to speak, when I try to speak, and my head is throbbing with the fever so much that I can scarcely make out any words.

I am in a van, on a bench. There is a bundle beside me that I vaguely recognize. The van lurches and I look up and I can see outside it, and it is moving, and trees in early leaf are going by. The lurch almost knocks me off the bench, and a uniformed guard beside me holds me up. Not kindly, not roughly, just an object: Keep the prisoner off the floor.

But the prisoner slides gratefully onto the floor and loses his senses. Then the sound of car horns and tram bells, and I force myself awake and pull up and catch a brief glimpse of the streets of Moscow, and of people. I recognize Kalyaevskaya Street. It seems very strange to recognize a street.

Someone tells me where we are. Butyrka prison. It is an old and notorious prison. Orlov had spoken of Butyrka. "A slack place," he said. I have a sense of pressures easing. I remember nothing of arriving there, only that after some days I became aware of waking up from endless sleep in a firm comfortable bed with many other beds around, of people speaking in soft voices, white-smocked medical people moving about, tubes taped to my arm, and of the marvelous and unfamiliar sense that I was not hungry and that my mind was emerging from fog into clear light again.

CHAPTER

13

THE HOSPITAL WARD IN BUTYRKA WAS, AFTER ALL, A CELL. I WAS STILL A prisoner and, although slack, Butyrka was still a prison. The doctors and feldshers moved quietly and professionally around the ward and dealt with the patients in a straightforward and businesslike way, so that while they were not harsh you certainly could not say that they were sympathetic either.

Once I was conscious again and the fever subsiding, they began feeding me sweet tea and soft-boiled eggs and cod-liver oil, and every day I felt tiny new increments of strength come to me. I determined to try to stay there as long as I could. I had the strongest sense of having come very close to the Absolute. An astonishing wave of confidence and optimism returned. I began to believe again that I had a future, not an easy or miraculous one, but a future I could handle. I *knew* that I would survive because I had survived.

Slowly the blur of people around me in the ward sorted itself out into individuals, and I remember the two nearest me, although the names have vanished. One was a professor of Russian history who had been arrested for anti-Soviet propaganda and drug addiction and was suffering strong withdrawal symptoms. He had been taking veronal. On the other side was an Austrian who spoke English with a heavy accent. I pleaded with him to speak to me in English, even though we would have made out better in Russian. He said he had been in charge of agriculture in the Ukraine, for the Germans, during the war. Then he had gone back to Vienna, and one day when he was transferring a large amount of money, perhaps $25,000, from his residence to a bank in the American Zone of Vienna, a car full of MGB swept him off the streets; he was knocked out, and came to on the way to Moscow. He was tried as a military criminal, but it seems all they really wanted was the dollars. He had met Orlov in camp.

Every day I got shots of calcium chloride, which made me feel deeply and comfortably warm, and glucose and vitamins. When the fever started slipping back satisfactorily, I began to worry that I would be shipped out, so I learned how to keep my fingers in my teacup when they brought the thermometer in the morning, and to hand the feldsher the thermometer with my hot fingers on the bulb. That usually maintained my apparent temperature at around 39°C (102°F) or 39½°, and so kept me in the hospital bed quite satisfactorily. I sent it up higher in the evening than in the morning because I remembered my mother telling me that sick people run a higher temperature at the end of the day and that sleep cools you off.

I kept no track of the days. I was too grateful for rest to worry about the passage of time. No scratches on the wall, no mental attempt to re-member. I think I was in that hospital three weeks, but it might have been two weeks and it might have been a month. I knew I would be discharged soon, even though I was still emaciated and weak.

They took me one day to a sort of interrogation room. I was pleased in a vague way to see a civilian at the desk, since for a year and a half now I had seen only uniforms and medical smocks. Somewhere along the line they had given me an additional name, Dovgun, which they hyphenated to their version of Dolgun, so that I became for their obscure purposes Dovgun-Doldzhin. No one ever explained this appendage: it was a given. The civilian behind the desk, a very self-important-looking man, asked my name, and corrected it to Dovgun-Doldzhin when I gave him only Alexan-der Dole-gin. He then went on to read away the next quarter century of my life as if he were prescribing cough medicine:

"Alexander M. Dovgun-Doldzhin, by decision of the Special Commit-tee of the Ministry of State Security [the MGB], on the basis of your espionage activities and other anti-Soviet activities, you are deprived of freedom for twenty-five years in IRT." ("Corrective labor camps," he explained. Later I would hear, over and over again, "Through hard labor you become free!")

Strangely, I was neither stunned nor even surprised. A mild anger was the strongest thing I felt. He presented the order to me and told me to sign. I refused: signing that thing would mean agreeing with it, so to hell with them.

"Sign!" he said. "Otherwise it's the hard punishment cell!"

I shook my head.

He brandished the pen at me.

I shook my head again and said, "*Nye polozhna!*"

He looked completely baffled, and I felt I was getting back together again.

I never did get the hard punishment cell and I guess, having gone to the trouble of putting me back together again with drugs and vitamins, they probably thought it would be illogical to turn around and murder me right away. But it is hard to say, because everything in this crazy system seems illogical at heart. Maybe my avoiding hard punishment that time in Butyrka was no more than sloppiness and bad management, or absent-mindedness, or maybe the threat had never been meant in the first place. There is no way to tell.

I had not seen my face for a long time. Occasionally back in Lefortovo the sun used to drive some light through the heavy window in a way that would allow me to catch a bright streak on the side of my face so that I could take the lid off the cast-iron toilet and see an indistinct glimpse of my drawn cheeks and sunken eyes reflected in the water. Now I did not want to see what I looked like. I just wanted thighs thicker than my knees. I had become compulsive about feeling those great knobbled joints with my fingertips, and stroking the wilted flesh above and below them and the sharp shin bone with its rough scars from Sidorov's boots. I wanted to feel flesh growing back on my thighs and calves, to get me out of that nightmare photograph.

I often thought, as I lay in that hospital, and in the crowded cell afterwards, of those strange experiences in prison where the cell walls seemed to disappear and I would be outside looking in at my own body. I knew that whatever source had provided me that gift, it had been a gift of life, but now I wanted to get back into life with all of myself. No more removals, but just let's get going and see where it takes us. If I had known where that would be, perhaps I would not have been so eager, but life was beginning to move in my veins again.

The crowded cell, after the hospital, had twenty-five beds, and more than twenty-five people, so there was sleeping in shifts and much lying on the floor. I remember no individuals from this cell because I was there only a day or two at the most. I remember only two things: I saw people playing chess, and the sight was very cheering; and now, beginning to be a little less indifferent about my sentence, I went around the cell and asked every single man what his sentence was. One man had ten years. Every other person had twenty-five years' "corrective labor," five years' exile, and five years' deprivation of civil rights, which meant that you could not vote in a Soviet election for the one candidate you can choose among, and you risked instant imprisonment for the slightest misdemeanor during that period.

Everyone I spoke to, all around the packed cell: "Twenty-five, five, and five. Twenty-five, five, and five." I was the only one with twenty-five years who had not been given the extra five-and-five.

The men in the cell talked about *etap*. It meant a shipment of prisoners to labor camps anywhere across the huge eastern expanses of the Soviet Union. I said I hoped they would not send me north to Siberia. I still shivered when I remembered the hard punishment cell in Lefortovo. Other prisoners spoke about the equal terrors of the desert south. I was told that from now on, as we moved through transfer prisons and on and off trains, we must learn to recite the prisoner's prayer. When a guard wanted to call you out he would call your initial: "D!" In fact, they said, "On D!" Then all the initial D's must come to the door of the cell and recite their prayer, consisting of full name, date of birth, length of sentence, and section of the criminal code under which they have been convicted. Hence, "Dovgun-Doldzhin, Alexander M. 1926. Twenty-five years. Fifty-eight point six. Fifty-eight point ten." That was my prayer, and I would recite it hundreds and hundreds of times in the next years. Thousands of times, perhaps.

I believe that on the second day in this crowded cell where I was trying to convalesce, the guard came to the door and called for the D's, and two or three of us recited our prayers, and the others were told to go back, while I had to bring my bundle and follow him for the *etap*. But when we got out onto the train platform, I collapsed unconscious and the officer in charge of the convoy refused to accept me. He said I was too weak to stand transportation, and that he would not accept the responsibility for having a corpse in his care when they got to Kuibyshev, which was evidently to be the first stop. So back in a van to Butyrka, still pretty confused in the head with all this sudden action after a period of rest, and glad to have another few days to try to get my strength back before going on a train trip.

But finally I had to face it. It was decided (by whom? Who was so wise as to predict my survival, so medically sophisticated? Nobody ever examined me, as far as I recall) that I was fit to travel. I was shoved into a Black Maria and taken to the station with a dozen other men—in age from seventeen to fifty, in physical condition from wrecks like me to guys who looked strong and healthy and good candidates for survival, even if I was not. I learned that looks are deceptive.

A Stolypin railway car is another masterpiece of the deception of the security system of the Soviet Union. It is painted to look like a mail car.

Since sometimes there are four or five or more such prison cars on a train, nobody is fooled into thinking that Soviet citizens have suddenly been infected by a prodigious fit of letter-writing, but nobody will officially admit that there is such a thing as a Stolypin car.

They were designed to the orders of a tsarist minister, and they carry his name. They are converted from old coaches, and in place of four-bunk compartments giving onto the corridor, there are four-plank cells, ostensibly meant for a maximum of sixteen prisoners but seldom carrying fewer than twenty, in my experience. At each end of the corridor there is a toilet. Guards patrol the corridor. You are not allowed to talk to prisoners in the next cell, but you can talk all you want to your own, and I enjoyed that. I was lucky to be one of the first to board the train and to occupy the plank across the top bunks before the cell was filled. Filled is the right word. The guards responsible for operating the train used boots and rifle butts to shove the incredible number of twenty-nine people into our four-person compartment. Men lay in the tiny space beneath the lower bunks. Men lay on other men in the middle and upper bunks. Some stood packed together in the space between, with their heads uncomfortably bowed under the planks I lay on. Arms and legs and bodies were mixed together.

The stink and confusion were terrible. I think we were two or three days on the first leg. The dominant smell was urine, and the floor was always wet. I had been dehydrated by a violent three-day attack of diarrhea in Butyrka and, while my bowels were beginning to come under my voluntary control now, I was feverish again almost as soon as we were put aboard the train, and the dehydration persisted all the way to Kuibyshev. Sleep was a haphazard affair, but at least, if you could find any way to compose yourself and drop off for a while, the guards did not bother you. The weather was warm and got warmer as we traveled east and then south. The frosted glass window in the cell was fastened shut, but the cell door was just open bars, and once out in the open country where curious civilians could no longer see what kind of mail was being carried in such mass loads to eastern Russia, the guards for their own sakes threw open the windows in their corridor and we could see the countryside sliding by.

After we had been compressed into the cell, a guard came around to the cell door and called out our names; when we answered with our prayers, the guard checked against the file, which contained a photograph of the prisoner and his transportation details, including the destination. I was lying on the top bunk against the bars so I was able to peer down at these files. I saw my own when it came. The destination was marked as a *steplag* (steppe camp) in the Kazakh Republic, at Dzhezkazgan, but that meant nothing to me at the time. I also noticed in red pencil on the corner of my file, in huge letters printed by hand, SKLONNY K POBEGU—likely to attempt escape. I thought that was pretty funny, given my physical condition, but I was glad to have the reputation all the same.

The Stolypin cars in our convoy were pulled to another location after we boarded, and there we waited while a passenger train was connected on behind. Then, after a long delay, we began to move. And at the end of the day we were taken to the toilet one by one and yelled at and abused by the guards until we did what we had to do. The door of the toilet was open all the time. In the evening the people in our cell tried to work out a rotation system, so that everybody could get a little sleep. I found myself watching an old priest down below me, who occupied himself with prayers and with concern for a pair of very fine-quality heavy felt boots he was carrying, one stuffed into the other. The boots were awkward for him to handle. Other prisoners cursed if he let them bump against them or fall on them, and yet he could not manage comfortably to hold them on his own person.

Finally someone said, "Look, Father, put the boots on the floor. Nobody can get away with them here!" There was some laughter at this and finally the bearded old fellow accepted the idea and the boots were shoved under a bunk. Sometime that night or the second night some prisoner managed to use the boots for a toilet and left a big pile in one of them. This would violently come to light at Kuibyshev on the third day.

Before boarding the train we had been given rations for the trip: two days' supply of bread, sugar, and, as Orlov had predicted, several pieces of salt herring. I warned everyone close to me against eating the herring. Some understood. Others thought I was lying in order to get their herring. Others knew I was right but were too hungry to do without it and went right ahead, even eating the pieces rejected by those like me who knew what it would lead to.

Within two hours there were cries throughout the car, begging for water. The guards strolled up and down and laughed at the poor pinched faces pressed against the bars, pleading for a drink. All the guards on the trains were overtly cruel and abusive. In prison, both in Lefortovo and Sukhanovka, and of course in Lubyanka and Butyrka, all the guards except that terrible woman had been more or less correct. They did their job in a straightforward way and left the abuse to the interrogators. But there was a change when we boarded the train. These men were coarse in their appearance and brutal by temperament. Perhaps it was a requirement for the position. Usually the brutality was expressed in the crudest, most direct form, with kicks, rifle butts, and curses. Sometimes it had a kind of low-grade ingenuity. This group on our car withheld water until the screams became a constant wail and then brought all the water anyone wanted, and sat back to watch the fun that began in half an hour or so when bladders began to cry out for relief and people went into silent agonies or else humiliated themselves by wetting their clothes at last, or urinating on the floor. One poor fellow let go through the bars into the corridor. In seconds the guards had pulled him out while he was still doing it, one beat him about the head and shoulders, screaming curses at him; when they shoved him back in the cell, he was still feebly dribbling through the rough slit in the front of his trousers. He had been a captain in the army.

In the night I got into conversation with another man on the top layer, incapacitated like myself, but not from exhaustion and illness. He was a cripple and his crutches were kept just outside the cell, where he could get at them to go to the toilet. This old man was going to prison for whatever time he had left in life. The sentence was ten years and he was already seventy-three and feeble. His name was Nikiforov, and his crime was writing letters to Stalin, reporting on conditions in his community as they actually were. He always read the papers, he said, and he could tell from the glowing speeches the Leader always made about the marvelous state of things in the Soviet Union that someone was keeping the truth from the great Father and Teacher, and that he, this old fellow, would set that right by writing to the Leader directly and telling him how things really were.

Nikiforov was not totally naïve. He knew that his letters might be intercepted and that officials afraid for their jobs might seek him out and punish him. So he never signed the letters and he mailed each one at a different mailbox. Since he was a cripple, his range of operations was not very big, and the MGB tracked him down by the following technique: they knew from the postmarks the district in Moscow from which the letters all came. They made a search from apartment house to apartment house. It would have been impossible to enter every apartment, so they went to the building management offices and asked for the files of complaints. In Moscow you can complain about the water service, or lack of heat, or electrical problems only in writing, and the building management committee must keep all the letters. The secret police sent out agents with samples of the old man's handwriting, and simply kept looking through tenants' complaints until they found that handwriting.

His interrogator boasted to him about this masterpiece of detective work, Nikiforov said. The old man did not seem to think it strange that such a massive manhunt had been deployed simply to entrap the man who wrote the truth to Stalin.

Kuibyshev is about six hundred miles east of Moscow, almost in the foothills of the Ural Mountains. It is built along the middle reaches of the Volga, where it drains Lake Kama and begins its thousand-kilometer run southward to Astrakhan and a shallow, many-mouthed delta spreading nearly fifty miles out into the Caspian Sea. The Soviet government fled to

Kuibyshev during the war, when the Germans were at the gates of Moscow. Stalin had gone there secretly, though the propaganda had him bravely holding on in the capital. The U.S. Embassy was there for a while as well. I have been told it is a fine city, but all I saw of it that morning was cobblestoned streets and poor, shabby houses with peeling stucco and loose boards and no paint. In the distance we could see some taller buildings and we sensed it was a good-sized town. The guards made no attempt to conceal us from the population here. We were simply dragged out between lines of armed soldiers with huge German shepherd dogs snarling and pulling on their chains, and marched through the town while people stared or more often went indifferently about their business. I had to be helped by other prisoners and when I fell down, which was pretty often, the guards would scream at me and at the poor guys who were helping me, to get me up and get going. The march was perhaps two kilometers and by the end I was being dragged because I could not walk.

When we came to the yellow stone wall of the prison, with barbed wire along the top and watchtowers with machine guns, and they opened the huge gates and marched us in, I was able to look around and became aware that there was an immense group in this convoy. There were women as well as men. Some of the women were carrying babies that were a few days to a few months old. It was a bizarre scene—several hundred men and women, some in their teens, a few gray and bearded and near death. Some were vigorous and sleek, though most were pale and thin and weak like me. Some were clearly new, "from freedom," and were dressed in good clothes, with all their buttons intact, clean and free of tears and patches. Others wore the worst shredded rags. The smell of dirty bodies was heavy even in the open air. We all sat on the ground, or lay down, waiting for the next order. Some of the prisoners, particularly women, went around seeking news—"Where did you come from, brother? Potma? Have you seen my husband? Vasili Grigoryevich Kravchuk? No? And you, brother, where have you come from? Moscow? The Lubyanka? Did you hear any news of my husband? Vasili Kravchuk? No? And you, brother?"—piteously going from person to person. Occasionally there was a buzz, and heads came together, and faces shone faintly through their own filth and despair, and you could tell that contact had been made.

I watched all this from the ground.

After an hour or more had passed, a major of the MVD came out. It was the MVD, the ministry of the interior, that was responsible for the security of the prison camps. Its army was a branch of the Soviet armed forces. It was separate from the MGB, the ministry of state security. The major told everyone to stand up and form lines. People helped me up. He then called for silence. When he got it, he called out in a loud voice, "All *chestnyagi* step forward!" From the two or three hundred people gathered in that dirty yard, perhaps thirty or forty men stepped forward. I do not think there were any women, but I am not sure. I tried to figure out what the word *chestnyagi* meant. All I could tell was that one of them had been in my cell, and that I had surmised from his manner and the tattoos on the backs of his arms that he might be a professional criminal and not a "fascist," or political prisoner. Most of the men in the group who had identified themselves as *chestnyagi* looked relatively healthy and their clothes were in good shape. The major nodded to a group of guards and the *chestnyagi* were led away separately. All right, I assumed, professional criminals.

Then the major called out again, "All *suki*. Step forward." Again I did not recognize the word. Again the twelve or fifteen men who responded were marginally better dressed than the average. There was certainly no one in totally derelict rags. The average age in the two groups was younger than the total average. I asked the old cripple if he knew what the words meant, but he did not, and no one else near me knew.

Once the *suki* and the *chestnyagi* were out of the way we were taken inside. I think the women with babies were separated from the main group, but more than two hundred men and women were lined up in the large barrackslike building with showers rigged along one wall, and told to undress and put their clothes on the floor in front of them. The women screamed and protested but the guards just came up and smashed them in the face if they hesitated about undressing. Soon we were all naked, two hundred sweating, dirty, scabbed, pale, skeletal, vulnerable human bodies. A file of fifteen or twenty unarmed guards had marched into the room and stood in a line facing the several lines of naked prisoners. The guards were laughing and joking about the physical characteristics of the naked bodies in front of them. "Hey, look at the boobies on that one, she must be new." "Not much here for you, Boris." "That one's so long you could tie a knot in it. Reminds me of you, Sasha," and a lot of just coarse, insulting stuff, mostly aimed at the women. The women whimpered and tried to cover themselves. When the guards were lined up and all our stuff was in poor little piles in front of us, we were told to take a step backward and the line of guards moved forward to search the bundles. The old priest stood next to me, his felt boots on the floor in front of him. They did not give away what they contained because the stink in the room was already too strong. When the guard plunged his hand into one of the boots to search it for contraband, he pulled it out again with a yell. It was smeared with brown halfway to the elbow. "You bastard!" he yelled at the old priest, who was just as amazed and even stopped praying. The guard just stepped up to him, wiped the filth all over the old man's face and beard, and then knocked him down and kicked him hard in the ribs. The poor old priest lay doubled up with pain, moaning and clutching his pale, wrinkled belly.

Soon we were led, men and women in separate lines, to a long, low table where two trusties with hair clippers came along and made us raise our arms. They clipped our armpits, our heads, our beards. Then we had to step up on the table while they went to work on our pubic areas. The women were almost all crying and pleading for mercy, while the guards and trusties with the clippers made lewd remarks like, "Move your lip to the left a bit there, sister. Smile, now." Another one said, "This one has more hair on her tits than she has between her legs. Do I get to do her tits too, Sergei?" There was terror and humiliation in the big room. After the shaving we were herded to the showers, men and women together. There were screams and yells of rage as we were scalded with terribly hot water for several minutes. Our clothes were hung on hooks on wheeled carts like those in the garment district in New York, our other belongings put on shelves at the bottom of the carts, and these carts were wheeled into a huge oven where they were disinfected with heat. Afterward we had to scramble through totally unsorted jumbles of trousers and skirts and stockings and boots to try to find our own. Then the men and women were finally segregated into groups and taken outside again and lined up facing several long stone barracks buildings.

The cell that I and about fifteen others were taken to opened directly on the yard. It was cell number 12. At the door we formed a line and one by one repeated our prayers and then were roughly pushed inside. I stumbled going across the threshold and fell against a jumble of people just inside the door. I rolled on the floor and ended up against a wooden pole. I pulled myself up by grabbing this pole, found it was a support for some sort of long bunk, or shelf, and grabbed a space to sit down.

My first impression was of bedlam. The cell reverberated with chatter. Later I counted and found that we were 129 people in a cell sixteen feet wide and about forty feet long. Two layers of bunks, which were nothing more than hard plank platforms, ran down each of the long sides and across the end. At the far end was a large window, open in the warm air, with bars on the outside. In the glare from the window it was hard to see the far end of the cell clearly, but I know that it was already packed with people standing on the floor and sitting or lying on or under the sleeping platforms. By the door, at the opposite end from the window, was a large wooden barrel that served as a urinal. The floor around it was damp, as the barrel was too high to use without difficulty unless you were very tall. The smell of urine would have been suffocating if the window had not been open at the other end of the room.

I remember that several people came up to me almost immediately to hear news from outside. The first question was always, "Are you from freedom?" And then, even when I explained that I had been in prison for a year and a half, many still wanted to know what it was like outside; they had been in prison for five years, ten years, some for twenty years.

For some reason I was standing up. Perhaps I had been squeezed off the crowded bunk. I was weak, but sitting on hard wood with my buttocks gone was not comfortable and I know that I often stood up to relieve the pain on my hip bones. The talk around me went silent suddenly and the heads of the people who had gathered to hear my meager news swung around toward the central part of the room. Then they moved away from me anxiously. I saw three dirty, ragged young men advancing toward me, grinning wickedly. They stepped up to within a couple of feet of where I stood, hanging on to a bunk support, and looked me over with insolent eyes. I still had my navy surplus gray gabardine trousers, and even after a year and a half of prison they were in much better shape than most prisoners' clothes. These toughs were *shobla yobla*, the lowest of the *urki*, or criminal class. They were very nasty-looking guys. They looked at my pants with obvious interest. The one in the middle said to the others, "Look, brothers, he has my trousers on!" He started to feel the cloth.

I said, "What the hell are you talking about? These are mine. Hands off!"

The leader kept pushing at me roughly. "Now, look at this, brothers! A common thief wearing my pants! And claims they are his own! Well, well!"

Then he grabbed a bundle from one of the other young jackals and held it out to me, a bundle of rags. "*These* are your trousers," he said between his teeth, holding them under my nose and pushing his face very close. "Now give me mine and give them to me quick," and thrust out two fingers as if to jab them in my eyes.

I had been up against tougher guys than he for a year and a half, and I was certainly not going to take this lying down. I was too weak for a good swing, but I held tight to the post with my left hand and brought my right up from below in the hardest and fastest uppercut I could manage. It hurt my hand like hell because it connected beautifully, right on the button, and the kid went down on his back. He looked astonished and he looked ready to kill. The other two began to close in and they were still grinning, but the grin had hardened a lot and their hands were held out like wrestlers'.

The room had gone absolutely silent. All the friendly people who had been so eager to hear my news had melted away. I felt totally alone in this weird crowd. The guy on the floor got up, rubbing his chin. There was blood on his lip. He spread his hands and held the other two back. His eyes looked murder. "I'll take him," he said curtly. He took a step toward me. I tightened my grip on the post. I was trembling but I figured I could at least duck and butt him in the stomach with my head, and then go for the crotch of one of the others before he got me. I was pretty scared, but I was pretty mad, too, and quite ready to throw myself at them, as feeble as I was.

But it never happened. A loud call from the back of the room, where the glare from the window hid the speaker from me, stopped the *shobla yobla* cold.

"*Off!*" this voice said, very clear, with great authority. "Lay off, now. That man is a *dukharik!*" *Dukh* is the word for "soul," but it means pretty much the same, in this context, as the English word "guts."

"Bring him to me," the voice said, more quietly. I was squinting into the shadow under the glaring window to try to see who this was. All heads in the room were looking either at me or toward the invisible speaker at the end of the room.

The *shobla yobla* were cowed. One of them said, almost deferentially, "The *pakhan* calls you. You better go see him," and then he led me to the other end of the room.

Pakhan is underworld slang for "the chief." In rank and authority, this guy has the status of a robber king. In the Mafia he would be like the godfather, but I do not want to use that word, because there is a godfather in the labor camps and that is an entirely different thing. Besides, a *pakhan* can arise anywhere and does not have to be linked to a particular family. He is a man widely recognized in the underworld for his skill and experience and authority. To meet such a distinguished, high-class *urka* is a very rare event.

The man I saw on the lower shelf at the end of the cell when I got close enough not to be dazzled by the light from the window was impressive in every way. He was well over six feet tall. He had wide shoulders and strong brown hands. He sat cross-legged on the bunk in boots of fine black soft leather, very high boots, with blue trousers tucked into the tops. His whole suit was a rich blue and made of good cloth. He had a pink shirt and a flashy striped tie and a handkerchief in his jacket pocket. Perhaps the most astonishing thing of all, since I had just come through the most rigorous search and knew that anything as innocent as a teaspoon would be confiscated in case you had an idea of making a weapon from it, was that this man had in his hand a large polished hunting knife with a handle made of laminated discs of different-colored plastic. With the absolutely classical manner of a movie tough guy, he sat there on the bunk slicing pieces of smoked meat from a big chunk and popping them in his mouth. Not only that, but he had *white* bread, which I had not seen since December 13, 1948, almost eighteen months earlier. He looked me over with an amused smile, but a very friendly kind of amusement.

The *pakhan* said, "Here, sit." Immediately people made room beside him. I took my jacket out of my bundle and made a cushion out of it and sat. The *pakhan* looked me over and I looked over all the people around him. There was a short, fair-haired guy sitting at his right hand, and from time to time someone would come up and whisper to this short guy and the short guy would whisper back, or just nod or shake his head, and the supplicant would go away. He looked like the *pakhan*'s grand vizier, and that is almost exactly what he turned out to be.

The *pakhan* cut off a slice of smoked sausage and put it on a slice of white bread and handed it to me. I gobbled it down. I had not eaten such good food since my last breakfast at the American Embassy.

My benefactor opened his eyes at the speed with which his gift disappeared. He cut off another slice of meat and made a sandwich and offered it, and while I gobbled it down he waved his hand and a mug of water appeared, which he passed to me as soon as I had licked the last grease and crumbs from my fingers. He waited until I had drunk, then he said simply, "Well?"

I said, "I'm an American citizen. I was kidnapped by the Organs. I've just come from Sukhanovka. I've got twenty-five years and I think I'm going to Dzhezkazgan. My name is Alexander Dolgun."

"Then I call you Sasha the American, okay? This"—indicating the grand vizier—"is Sashka Kozyr." *Kozyr* is Russian for "trump." "He is my deputy. My name is Valentin Intellighent. You can call me Valka."

I said, "Thanks for the food. I really don't understand how you get all this stuff . . . and the knife? What's going on here?" I was totally mystified. Valentine the Intelligent just laughed.

"I will explain it to you sometime," he said in a very good-natured way, but also in a way that made clear that *he* was the chief and *he* would decide the order in which things were supposed to be done.

"Listen," he said, "if you're an American, you must have seen lots of movies, yes?"

I nodded.

"And you talk like an educated man, like myself, yes? Read a lot of books? Read novels a lot?"

I nodded again.

"Good. I think we may be able to have a good business relationship."

The *pakhan* grinned widely at my bewilderment. Then his mood shifted and he became very serious and intense, peering at me directly with only a hint of a mocking smile around his dark eyes. He was very handsome, his black hair was neatly combed, and he was clean shaven. With that knife, I thought. It looked sharp enough.

"Now listen," he said seriously. "Can you squeeze a novel?"

I said, "What do you mean, 'squeeze'?"

He said, "You know, 'squeeze' is our slang for 'tell.' Can you tell us novels, narrate the stories, same with movies? We have no storyteller here, and we need stories. Life is empty without a good story to keep you going every day. Can you do that?"

I said eagerly, "Sure I can. I've spent the last year and a half telling myself all the movies and novels I could remember. I'm getting very good at it."

"That's excellent!" Valentin said. "I'll call the brothers around and we can get started."

I said, "Valka, wait one minute. I've just come in on *etap*. I'm exhausted. I've been starved for a long time, and the food you gave me makes me very sleepy. My brain is pretty foggy. I hardly had any sleep for two nights on the train. I could do a much better job of squeezing movies if I could get a good long sleep first."

He looked disappointed for a moment. Then he nodded decisively and said, "Of course. I want the best. You sleep, and when you are ready I will feed you some more and then we can get started."

He made them clear some space on the top shelf at the side of the cell near the window so I would have air, but not right in front of it where I might be uncomfortable because of the breeze or the bright light. Some of the *urki* looked pretty ugly about giving up their space to me, but they would not dare let the *pakhan* see their anger. They were surly, treacherous thugs; and Valentin Intellighent stood out among them like a diamond. He was a civilized and intelligent criminal. They were illiterate and subhuman. But they had absolute respect for the authority of their extraordinary *pakhan*. He got some coats and things and helped me make a sort of pad to stretch out on, and a good soft pillow of crumpled cloth in a small sack. He climbed on the lower bunk and stood with his head close to mine. He said, "Sasha, you look terrible. I should never have thought of making you work right away. Sleep as long as you want. Nobody can hurt you because I am looking after you."

I was just quietly amazed. I could not speak because I felt grateful and embarrassed and there was a lump in my throat at so much kindness in such a cruel place. Valentin Intellighent turned around and held up his hand and said quietly to Sashka the Trump, "I want silence."

Sashka the Trump jumped up on the top bunk and whistled sharply through two fingers. The chatter in the cell died down quickly. The deputy called out, "The *pakhan* is speaking."

Valentin Intellighent looked around the cell to make sure everyone was attentive. There was not a sound. "Good," he said after a moment. "That is the way it is to be until I say so." He pointed at me. "I want silence in this cell because a Man is sleeping!"

He had used the word *chelovek*, which is like *mensch* in German. The way he stressed the word it meant a Man with a capital M, a Person. "*Chelovek spit!*" A Man is sleeping! I felt elated by the compliment. I looked around the cell with my eyes half closed. Prisoners were collected in little knots, conversing in low whispers. Just before I drifted off to sleep I got some insight into the prosperity and style of my newfound protector. Over in the corner two of his *urki* serfs had engaged three new Estonian arrivals in earnest whispered conversation. It must have been very fascinating. The new arrivals were obviously politicals, obviously fresh "from freedom." Their characteristic Baltic sacks were quite full, beside them on the floor. They were totally unaware of what then happened. A third hoodlum sat on the bunk behind the Estonians. He took off his shoe. He pulled from some mysterious hiding place a tiny strip of broken razor blade. Later I learned this was called a *moika*, that it was a standard weapon among the pros and they could almost always conceal one well enough to get through any search. This was what Valentin Intellighent shaved with, as it turned out. The third *shobla yobla*, as I watched, deftly gripped the *moika* between two filthy toes, extended his foot, and silently slit the Estonian's sack from top to bottom. Then with a continuing deftness that I found a delight to watch, like watching any good acrobat, or magician, or juggler, he retrieved with his agile foot several sausages, a loaf of bread, some handkerchiefs, several paper packets that probably held tea—in fact, he got everything that the sack contained.

Other politicals looked on meekly and made no attempt to intervene. They would have been beaten up if they had. I had an inward chuckle and said to myself, "Business as usual." Then I closed my eyes and went off into a very relaxed and definitely happy sleep.

CHAPTER

14

VALENTIN INTELLIGHENT WAS AS GOOD AS HIS WORD. THROUGHOUT MY STAY in the cell where he ruled like a feudal duke no one tried to do me harm, no one stole from me, and I found that Valentin was not only a benefactor and protector but a subtle and fascinating talker, an exact and relevant adviser, and a loyal friend.

During that first afternoon, I woke from my deep sleep foggy in my head and weak in my limbs but desperate to urinate. I climbed down stiffly from the upper bunk, and a young man immediately leapt up to my place with a silent sign indicating that he would guard it for me. I limped down the cell toward the barrel. Before I was halfway there, three politicals had accosted me. "Listen," one man said very severely—he was a naval officer and still in the uniform from which his shoulder boards had been ripped—"what the hell do you think you're doing with those thugs? We know you're a political, like us. Those rascals will rob you tonight when you're sleeping and dump you on the floor by the urine barrel. You're crazy to trust them!"

Another one said, "You should be with us. Those colored bastards will slit your throat for a kopek."

I said, "Well, all right, suppose I join you. Will you guarantee to protect my life?"

"God, no! What do you think you're saying? We can't protect you. We have no power!"

I said, "You can't protect anyone else either. I saw a couple of poor suckers get robbed of everything they had a while ago, and none of you lifted a finger. There's over a hundred of you and only twenty pros, and you just sit on your hands while they rob you blind."

No answer. I pushed them aside and went to relieve myself. To hell with them. There was a strange sight at the barrel. Two *urki* were holding a forty-year-old man by the arms, with his mouth smothered by a strong forearm so he could not cry out. A third was punching him with rhythmic silent punches in the stomach. The poor man's eyes were bugged out and his face was purple. As I came up to them the punching stopped and one whispered in the political's ear, "If you make a sound when we let you go it starts again!" The political shook his head vigorously. They let him go. He clutched his stomach and bent over and scuttled away. The thugs moved sullenly aside as I was undoing my fly. "What was that for?" I asked.

"The bastard shit in the barrel. Can't you smell it?"

I could not, because the urine was so acrid and powerful I think it masked anything else, but I could see a contribution floating on the half-full contents.

Back at my corner the *pakhan* was waiting to give me a hand up. "How's it going?" he asked me. I just grunted and nodded and went right back to sleep.

The next time I woke up I smelled porridge. The evening meal was coming in, served from big barrels and passed in through the slot. The pros got theirs first, of course, and the political rabbits hung back meekly and waited until Valentin's minion gave them permission.

"Hungry, Sasha?"

It was Valentin. I said, "Very."

"Want some extra porridge?"

I was surprised, although by now I should not have been. The thought of filling up on the warm stuff made my mouth fill up with saliva. I said, "Sure I do. Wonderful."

He sent word to the door. The trusty on the barrel passed in twelve extra portions of the watery gruel, and they were brought over in relays by the criminals. For the first time since I was kidnapped, I ate until I was full.

When I finished I was terribly sleepy again.

Valentin came up and looked at me expectantly. Then he said, "Not really ready yet eh, brother?"

I shook my head.

"Sleep," he said.

When I woke up again it was dark in the cell and still quiet, with occasional whispers from different corners and levels. I felt hungry again, but in an easy, agreeable way. And I felt bright and optimistic and interested in company.

I sat up and looked for the *pakhan*. Sashka the Trump caught my eye and signaled that he would fetch the chief. Valentin came over, smiled warmly to see me looking rested and alert, and cut me off some bread and smoked meat. He said, "Do you feel like a cup of real tea?"

Tea was forbidden in prison, but by now I expected anything from this man. I nodded eagerly with my mouth full of white bread and greasy meat.

"I mean *real* tea," Valentin said with a mischievous look. I just shrugged and nodded. I had no idea what he meant.

He signaled to one of his *shestyorki*, a deputy of rank just below that of Sashka the Trump, and the *shestyorka* began to build a curious bonfire on the concrete floor near the window. The principal fuel was plastic toothbrush handles, stolen from the poor politicals. Certainly it was clear that none of the *shobla yobla* ever used a toothbrush. The plastic smoked and stank, but most of that went out the window. The deputy held a tin cup full of water over the fire until the water boiled. Then he put in a chunk of pressed tea, like a plug of tobacco almost. He let this steep for several minutes. Then while some of the low-class *shobla yobla* and others watched hostilely from a distance, a select group composed of the *pakhan*, Sashka, the deputy who had made the tea, and I took sips in turn from the steaming cup. "It's called *chifir*," Valentin said. "It'll wake you up."

Wake me up! It nearly blew my head off! I began to understand how these guys could survive in prison without their drugs. Soon my heart was beating very fast. I was really wound up. Valentin grinned at me. "Ready?" I nodded back. The deputies and a few of the more nearly civilized *urki* gathered around. A few politicals came nervously to the edge of the little group but kept a respectful distance. I looked over the group. I felt center stage. I'm sure my eyes were shining. My heart was going like a long-distance runner's, from the effects of a few sips of the *chifir*. I started: "During the war there was a house in occupied France that contained one of the deadliest Gestapo units the Nazis ever put together. The address of this house was thirteen rue Madeleine."

They were spellbound. I had told myself the plot of *13 Rue Madeleine* so many times that I could see individual shots in the movie as I told it. I remembered the expressions on the actors' faces and the tones of voice they used. I could describe at length the cruel face of the Gestapo villain and the clothes the heroine wore and the plane used in the bombing raid. At the end, when the hero was about to be tortured by the Gestapo at 13 rue Madeleine, and his best friend, the second hero, had to go in on a night raid and drop the bomb that would save him from the agonies of torture and also keep his secrets safe, I thought Sashka the Trump's eyes were shining a bit more than was natural.

It was light outside. With all the extended descriptions and the talk about the inner feelings of the participants, and the extra stuff I put in so that non-Americans could understand every shade and nuance of the story, I had talked all night. The *chifir* had really kept me going. Some of the men were yawning but nobody went to sleep. I was elated at their reaction. I thought, Alex, kiddo, if you don't go back to embassy work you can always go into the storytelling business.

The *pakhan* stood up and shook me warmly by the hand. He said, "The guards have just changed their shift, and we have a shipment of something I think you will enjoy very much." One of the others handed him a package. He undid the wrappings and produced several packs of fresh, strong Russian cigarettes. He opened a pack and offered me the first smoke. Then the rest were handed around and we all smoked and exhaled and grinned at each other with great satisfaction. My head spun a bit from the impact of the tobacco. It was already spinning with the feeling of security and success that I was catching from Valentin Intelligent.

When breakfast was brought to the cell, Valentin turned my portion of black bread over to his *shobla yobla* and gave me some more white bread and greasy smoked bacon. He put some stolen tea into the colored hot water we were served, and we made a pretty good breakfast. After breakfast, the whole cell was taken out to the yard for exercise and to go to the toilet. Four prisoners—politicals, of course—shoved long poles into brackets on the side of the urinal and carried it outside and up a slope to the latrine building. The latrine was a six-holer, and everything went into a kind of trough that drained into a hole in the ground at the end of the building. It looked as though a larger latrine building was in the works, because there were boards and long lengths of pipe stacked against this low wooden structure, which stood not far from the outer wall of the prison. Next to the wall was a fire zone filled with rolls of barbed wire, and Valentin Intelligent explained to me that if a prisoner stepped inside the fire zone the guards on the watchtowers would shoot without warning and shoot to kill.

Before and after our turn in the latrine shed, the two of us walked together, my arm about his shoulder for support, around and around the big yard, sharing our life stories. He was a "bear-killer," he told me, a *medvezhatnik*, which is underworld slang for a safe-cracker. That put him in the top professional class. To rob an individual of even a large sum of money would be beneath him, he said, unless it was a very special caper, like getting a hundred-thousand-ruble payroll away from an armed escort. Occasionally he had tried, with good success, hijacking whole carloads of goods and reselling them on the black market, but his real love and the great challenge and great opportunity for an elegant job was an "unbreakable" safe, and he claimed he had broken many of them. I believed him. He was one of the most alert and quickest men I had ever met. He had that faculty of knowing what you were about to say before you finished a sentence, and of answering a question before you had completely asked it because he intuited its direction. He had immensely keen hearing and sharp eyes. He had been orphaned as a boy of eight or ten and been on his own since then, but he had never lost the manner of speaking he had learned in his home, since his father and mother were both professors, and that is why his professional name was Valentine the Intelligent.

I asked him about *suki* and *chestnyagi* and he laughed. "*Suki* are a creation of the MVD," he said. "Those bastards can't stand the way the *lyudi* have organized themselves, and they've been trying for years to break us up."

I was struck by his emphatic use of the word *lyudi*, which is the plural of *chelovek*, and can mean The People. As he continued to talk, I gathered that this was the way the *urki* described themselves and that when he had called me a *chelovek*, telling the rest of the cell that a Man is sleeping, he had in effect made me an honorary member. Later I realized that all the *urki*, the criminals, normally reserved the words *chelovek* and *lyudi* for dramatic occasions when a little self-glorification was in order. Valentin usually used the word *urki*, which is pure underworld slang and has no English equivalent. "You see," he said, "somehow the MVD consider us enemies of the people, like the fascists. We're loyal Soviets. We don't want to overthrow the system, for God's sake. We just happen to be in a different field of endeavor; we get a very good living from the system. We don't stir up trouble like these other worthless scum" (waving an arm at the groups of politicals who watched us curiously as we went by). "We just do what we can and stick together and if there is another war we'll help out the best way we can and so on and so on. But the *urki* are organized and the fascists are not. You can see that. We get the guards to sell the stuff we liberate from new arrivals, and we split with them, and they buy us good food and tobacco in town and make sure that we have what we need. Their commanders tried to wipe that out by punishing the guards they caught, but it never worked and they know it won't. So they tried another plan.

"They went into the camps and began to terrorize some of the less staunch *urki* by violence and threats, you know, until they had some of the poor guys so cowed they'd do anything. Then they were very cunning, those bastards. They forced some of these *urki* to do jobs that were absolutely against the code of the underworld."

"What jobs?"

"Anything that helped the prison. You must never help build a prison wall or put up barbed wire. No self-respecting *urka* will ever do that; the rest would rub him out. So they forced them to break their own unwritten laws, do you see? Forced them to be a foreman in a work project. Absolutely taboo. Every *chelovek* knows that. Accept a job like that and you've practically committed suicide. These were the *suki*, then. They had to be separated from the rest of the criminals or they'd have been rubbed out fast. The *suki* are the MVD's converts. The *chestnyagi*, the unconverted, hate their guts.

"So the MVD always separates the two groups when there's an *etap*. They don't want their precious converts wiped out. All the same the war goes on in camp. Any time a *suka* is discovered, he usually loses his head."

"Literally? Somebody cuts his head off?"

"That's right. Or strangles him. It's the code.

"By the way, that's a very fine hat you're wearing," he said parenthetically. "Is it American?"

I told him the story of the hat and how it had saved my life.

"It's very fine," he said warmly. "Here, let me see how it feels on me."

He tried it on. It fit pretty well and looked superb with his flashy suit.

"I certainly like that hat," he repeated.

I was not feeling bright and I failed to get the message, but for the moment he let the matter drop, though he wore the hat through the rest of that first morning's exercise.

From time to time other *lyudi* would come up to Sashka the Trump, who walked around the yard in front of us, never very far from his chief. They would speak to him in a low voice and sometimes he would shake his head and then the fellow would go away, and sometimes he would nod and come and tug Valentin's elbow and speak to him quietly in his ear, and Valentin would listen and either nod thoughtfully or give Sashka the Trump a firm double pat just above the elbow, or else say a few words back to him in an equally confidential tone. I never heard any of these exchanges, but Valentin explained to me that they were sometimes information about movements of people or goods, sometimes intelligence about developments in the camp, sometimes disputes about the division of spoils that he was called upon, as *pakhan*, to render judgment on. He said they tried to keep all these things quiet unless something came up that needed larger discussion, and there was a tradition of respecting the *pakhan*'s confidentiality that simply was not broken.

I felt badly tired out by the exercise period and took a nap when we got back in. When I woke up, I saw a lot of expectant faces looking in my direction. I was enjoying the prominence. I asked for a drink and a deputy brewed some more explosive *chifir*. Then I indicated to Valentin that I was ready. He gathered my audience, passed me a lighted cigarette, and nodded to me to go ahead. I thought I would try something a little shorter, so I told them a short story I was sure they would love. I cannot now remember whether it is fiction or whether I read it in a newspaper or a magazine, but I have a feeling that it really happened. It is about a movie company coming to New York to make a film about a bank robbery. They negotiate at length with a major bank to get permission to film the bank. They arrange with the NYPD to provide lots of cops to keep traffic from bothering them and keep passers-by from interfering when they see the guns and the masked bandits and all the rest. They set up cameras and lights on the appointed day and then calmly go ahead and rob the bank under the unconcerned eyes of New York's finest, who think all along that they are protecting a bunch of actors and technicians from public harassment, and that all the screams and yells from inside the bank after the getaway cars drive off are part of the act.

My story was a sensation! Every time my cigarette went out I was handed a fresh one. Sometime in the afternoon, hot water appeared from somewhere, and we had fresh tea. When the midday soup came Valentin shredded some excellent Baltic cheese into it with his famous hunting knife, and I found it a delicious dish. Hardly anyone in my audience moved as I spun out the story and dropped a little hint here and a little hint there so that they could think they were guessing at the ending without being steered there by me. When I came to the punch line, the getaway, and the picture of the cops standing around with their faces getting redder and redder when they finally found out what had happened, there were deep chuckles of satisfaction. One of the *shestyorki*, the deputies, kindling a toothbrush-handle fire for more tea, slapped me on the back and said they certainly hoped I had more where that came from. I was a hit and I loved it. But my throat was sore from talking so long and smoking so much, and I explained that I would have to let it rest until the evening. They were disappointed as hell and started a clamor for another story right away—it was too long until the evening, what the hell did I think they were feeding me so well for? It was all said in a good-natured way, but they meant it all the same, and I was relieved when Valentin intervened and decreed that I should indeed rest my voice and build up my strength for a good all-night session. So I declined the *chifir*, which would have kept me awake. I climbed up onto my reserved spot again and caught a little sleep, and then just sat quietly with Valentin for the rest of the afternoon and nibbled white bread and bacon and listened to his advice on prison life and his bits of lore and his secrets for getting on.

He said, for example, that if I ever heard guards in a transfer prison talking about India, to avoid going there because that was the cell where the *urki* were who collaborated with the guards, and it meant that politicals would be put in it for a few minutes "by mistake" (because in most cases politicals and professionals were segregated). By the time the "mistake" was discovered and rectified the poor political would be very much poorer.

I said, "Valka, you go where they send you. How could I get out of it?"

"Oh, faint, fall down, something like that, get sick, just don't go."

"And if I can't stop them putting me in such a cell?"

"Oh, that's easy."

All the other *urki* listening to this chuckled and exchanged knowing looks. "Go ahead, *pakhan*, tell him," one said.

"Of course! He is my brother, after all," Valentin said expansively.

"Now, Sasha," he said to me, "if you saw a clean white handkerchief lying in the mess by the piss barrel over there, would you wipe your dirty feet on it?"

"Of course not," I said. I wondered what he was driving at. Everyone else laughed when I said it.

Valentin said emphatically, "Of *course* you would!" and laughed very gaily, and all the rest laughed again at my bewilderment.

"Listen, Valka, is this some kind of riddle or something? I don't get it," I said. I was embarrassed about it.

"Just remember what I said," Valentin answered. He was still chuckling. His eyes were very merry and he was clearly teasing me. He would not say any more about the riddle.

When supper came, I was again asked if I wanted extra helpings, and again I ate them greedily. Then I was almost overcome with sleep. I told Valentin and the others I would sleep for an hour or two, until dark perhaps, and that suited them. I think they liked stories in the dark best of all, even though there was a bright light over the far end of the cell. I started out with what seemed like a comfortable and refreshing sleep. But after about an hour I was awakened with terrible cramps in my belly. I knew exactly what was happening, and it alarmed me a good deal because of a scene I remembered vividly from the day before. All that greasy bacon and the pressure of those many dishes of watery porridge had begun to exact a price. There would be no trip to the toilet for at least another eight or ten hours, and I had seen what happened if you tried to use the barrel.

I decided to confide in Valentin. I beckoned to his deputy and asked if I could speak to the *pakhan*. Sashka the Trump went prowling off in the chaotic cell and came back with Valentin. I whispered in his ear the way I had seen Sashka do it. "Valka, I've got a terrible attack of diarrhea. What'll I do!"

He was silent a moment. He looked very grave. Then he said quickly, "Anything happen yet?"

"Not yet, but I can't hold out long."

Valentin turned and beckoned to his deputy and they put their heads together for a moment, then looked at me, then called over the two other deputies. They conferred not more than half a minute, and I could see that my friend was giving orders. The others nodded. Valentin came back to me. He said, "Can you sing?" I was getting used to puzzles from him. I said, "Yes, so what?"

"Good," he said with a mischievous smile. "Go with them."

Sashka and the two deputies helped me across toward the barrel. When we got there, they hoisted me up to the edge of it and made a sort of human screen in front of me, so that my head appeared above their shoulders but the lower part of my body was concealed. They began to sing a ribald song about drinking and women. "Sing!" one of them told me.

"I don't know the words!"

"Just open your mouth and pretend you do," he shouted.

I was struggling to lower my pants. I certainly did not want to fall backward. I got my pants down. Things started to work. Suddenly they all lit up cigarettes at once and puffed away furiously as they sang. After a while I said, "Thanks. We can go back now."

I was out of breath with suppressed laughter. I had a good smoke and a cup of cold tea, and then Valentin's inner circle gathered around, and for a teaser I told them a short story called "The One Million Pound Note." They loved anything about money. Then I started an Ellery Queen mystery that I remembered fairly well, and it lasted through the night. Every hour and a half or so the deputies and I would repair to the urine barrel for a smoke and a round of loud and vulgar singing. And that's how we got through the night.

The next day in the yard Valentin made a further gesture of his confidence in me. He told me about his escape plan and invited me to join it. I was thrilled. My heart began to beat wildly. Halfway through his explanation of the plan I had another attack and had to dash to the latrine shed and beg to break into the line-up. When I came back he went on and explained how the latrine was to be our take-off point. He had already managed to stack in a pile some of the long iron pipes that were lying beside it. The plan was to hide in the latrine building and at night use the pipes to pole-vault over the wall. I said I would have to build up some strength first, and he agreed that we should wait for that to happen because he really wanted my company.

"I'll tell you honestly why I admired your hat so much, Sasha," he said with a very frank look, but an amused look as well. "I wanted it for my escape. I figured with a hat like that I would look like some big party official and nobody would ever accost me. But if you come along it will work for all of us. And that is not why I invited you. I just thought about it while you were telling us that mystery story overnight. I like you a lot and I think you should join us."

I thought about that for a while. I said, "What kind of a life could I have outside, though? I'd be a fugitive all my days."

"I've been a fugitive a lot of my days, you know," Valentin said. "It's not so bad. I escaped from the orphanage after my parents . . ."

He stopped and walked in silence for a while. Then he said, "The truth is my parents were party members. They got caught up in some plot or other. I never knew what it was all about. As far as I know, they behaved like perfectly normal people. But they were arrested for treason and then they were shot, so they must have done something terrible."

I could not believe that naïveté. I said, "Lots of perfectly innocent people were shot during the purges, surely you know that!"

He looked quite offended. "Stalin would never permit that!" he said emphatically. I realized that he was completely serious so I let it drop. It was then that I knew he must believe that I was a spy and therefore used to all kinds of fugitive and clandestine ways. My knowledgeable tales of criminal life in America must have reinforced his impression. I decided to let it ride for the moment.

"Valka," I said, "how much time have you done in prison all together?"

"If you count the orphanage, which I certainly do, almost twenty years."

"And you're not forty yet."

"Thirty-eight, that's right. I made my first escape when I was eleven."

"But isn't that a terrible life?"

"I miss my women. And wine. I miss wine a great deal. But you can see that I live very well in prison. It never lasts very long. And when I get out there is no way that I can have the women and the wine and the good suits unless I live my life with the *urki*." He gave a short, ironic laugh. "Can you imagine me working in an office? I'd be crazy! That's the real slave labor.

We've got a very good *malina*, a hide-out, right here in Kuibyshev. There's a girl waiting there for me. I'll take my chance, and I hope you'll cast in with me. It can be very good, our life."

I said I would and we shook hands on it. We walked the yard hand in hand. There is nothing homosexual about this in the Soviet Union. Men who are good friends do it openly, and it is perfectly natural. The same with women.

When we came back to the cell a bizarre game was in progress. Two of the *shobla yobla* had their pants off and were lying with their buttocks in the air on an upper bunk. Another stood by with a pack of matches. Every so often one of the guys on the bunk would say, "Now," and the third guy lit a match and held it over his pal's behind while he passed gas and a blue methane flame shot up in the air. The politicals looked disgusted, while some of the younger *shobla yobla* laughed and applauded. My own digestion seemed to have settled down. Through that day, rather than telling stories as such, I answered questions about crime in America, the electric chair, the FBI, weapons, the careers of outstanding criminals, the techniques of safebreaking (I was hardly an expert, but Valentin expressed polite interest so I kept on with it).

Then Valentin would tell one of his exploits, how he had stolen a whole carload of sugar—I think it was sixty tons—and sold it at a very good price. Others would, in effect, ask permission and then recount some of their exploits. One told some grisly stories of how prisoners mutilated themselves if they heard they were to be transported to a particularly notorious camp such as Kolyma in Siberia. One, he said, shaved dust from an indelible pencil with his *moika*, put the dust in his eye, and deliberately blinded himself. The eye ulcerated and had to be removed. And still they sent him to Kolyma. Another nailed his scrotum to the bunk and yelled, "Kill me, you bastards! Take me away, kill me!" They simply pulled out the nail with a claw hammer, poured iodine on it, and put him on the train.

Several of the younger guys talked sadly and sentimentally about their mothers. Most of these men were tattooed, some quite extensively, and many of them had MOTHER on the back of a hand or a forearm. Valentin asked me about my mother. I said, "I don't know. She's in Moscow, I suppose. She hasn't been very well. I have no way of communicating with her, and I don't know whether she even knows what's happened to me."

"Write her a letter."

I laughed bitterly at the cruel joke.

"I'm serious," Valentin said. "Listen, don't you think I can get it out? Write her a triangle. Now! Come on." And he told Sashka to get a piece of paper and a pencil.

A triangle is just that: if you are too poor for envelopes and stamps, you fold your letter into a triangle and the Soviet post will carry it anyway. This started during the war, as a way for soldiers to send mail when they had no envelopes or money, and it was still accepted in the fifties. I wrote, not really believing it would go through despite Valentin's assurances. I told my mother that I was fine, that I was going to be in Central Asia, at Dzhezkazgan 292 (I had seen that number, too, on my transport file and thought correctly that it was a postal address, but incorrectly, as it turned out, that it was complete). I asked her whether the embassy had given her my personal belongings, because I thought she could sell them to help eke out some kind of meager subsistence. And I asked her to get in touch with Mary and say that I was fine and that she should not feel compelled by her promise to wait for me. That made me very sad, but even with thoughts of escape in my head, I knew it would be many years before I would see her again, and I did not want her to be imprisoned by a promise I had extracted as a joke. It seemed a poor joke now.

Valentin took the letter and gave it to Saska, who went immediately to the cell door, where I saw him slip it through the slot to a guard. I said, "In truth, Valka, all I want to do is get out of the Soviet Union as fast as I can, and if that means coming with you for a while, as a first step, then I'm for it."

"But why would you want to leave the Soviet Union?" he said. He was really surprised.

That night I began my longest tale. It was serialized over many nights. In the daytime, between lots of sleep and lots of food, I would talk crime in the U.S.A., but at night it was time for real craft, and I embarked on Victor Hugo's gigantic *Les Misérables*. I do not recall now how long it took to tell. Several nights. I know that I often lost my way in it and had to go back and pick up threads here and there. It did not matter. The younger ones particularly, but I think all these men, who had lived outside the law all their lives, were caught up in and moved at the story of Jean Valjean and his relentless pursuer. It was no difficulty for them to see themselves rowing in the galleys. The story was utterly real to them. I think each could see himself as the beleaguered central figure, battered by the injustice of a society that would not let him live his life the way he wanted to live it.

My diarrhea never completely disappeared, and after a while I began to worry about getting up enough strength to go with Valentin and Sashka. From time to time I was slightly feverish. My appetite stayed good. I ate well and put on quite a lot of weight. I was strong enough to do some exercises and to walk easily. My muscles were growing again and taking on some tone. But I could not imagine pole vaulting from that latrine-shed roof, and the prospect of a long run at top speed afterward, assuming I did not break a leg or get shot, was quite impossible. I confided this to Valentin one day. He looked terribly disappointed, and I believe he really was. I said, "If I can't go, and you're ready to go, I want you to have my hat and my tie." I had shown him the tie I was arrested in. It had been crushed in my bundle but we "ironed" it under my "mattress" and Valentin wore it alternately with his own much flashier one. He was pleased. He knew that hat would help him, and he thought the tie would look more respectable than his own if he wanted to pass as an official. But he insisted on holding out a little longer.

It was no use. My fever began to rise daily. I had recurring bouts of diarrhea and began to be a bit dehydrated. Then news came in the morning that put an end to speculation. There was to be a continuation of the *etap* to Dzhezkazgan. I was to be on it, of course, and so was one of the *urki*, a young man named Vasya.

"I'm not going *there!*" he said. He then began a very strange procedure. He got a needle from someone, and a piece of fine thread. He ran the thread between his filthy teeth several times until it was well coated with plaque. Then he rolled up his trousers and ran the thread under the skin on the top of his thigh, just into the fatty tissue, not deep enough to draw more than a tiny drop of blood, and drew it out again. I asked Valentin about it. He said, "By tonight you'll see. He'll be really sick. And you'd better be, too, because you're in no shape for *etap*."

I said, "I don't have to fake it. I'm sure my fever is pretty high. In fact, I haven't been letting on, because I didn't want you to worry, and besides I wanted to go with you, you know."

He looked me hard in the eye. He said, "It's too bad, my brother. We could have had a good life."

There was a pause. Then Valentin said, "You'd better start putting on a show. The *etap* goes tomorrow." We talked a bit longer. He helped me with the scenario. I gave him my beloved hat and my tie. We shook hands. Then I wrapped up my bundle and went over and lay in the wet around the barrel and began to moan and clutch my stomach. Every once in a while a guard looked in. We waited until this performance had been seen several times. Then Valentin pounded on the door and told a guard to get a doctor, there was a sick man in here. He was right. I really felt terrible by now. Valentin had warned me that it would be an all-day matter. By late afternoon I did not have to pretend at all. My stomach was cramping heavily, and I was covered with cold sweat and shivering. By early evening the doctor still had not come, and I was good and sick. From time to time Valentin would come and stand where I could see him and give me an encouraging wave. Around suppertime he brought Vasya with him and indicated that Vasya should come over to me. He came and squatted down uncomfortably beside me. His face was flushed and his eyes were very bright. He peeled back his trousers, "Look," was all he said. I looked and almost vomited. His thigh had swollen till the skin was tight. It was terribly discolored. The infection was raging but there was absolutely no sign of the wound that induced it. He took my hand and put it to the skin of his thigh. I was burning with fever and he was much hotter. "Did you ever see such a *mastyrka?*" he asked me proudly. I had never seen a *mastyrka* of any kind, but I had heard those terrible tales about what prisoners did to themselves to avoid transportation, so I guessed at the meaning of the word. "Congratulations," I said feebly.

The doctor came. Vasya had a fever of 41° by then and was incoherent. I was at 39° and had vomited twice. They brought stretchers. They took us to another building, where there was a small hospital. Just after dark the second night in the hospital I heard a terrific fusillade of shots echo among the buildings. Later that night I was shaken gently awake by one of the prisoner orderlies. "Wake up and hear what I have to say, *chelovek*," he whispered. I forced myself awake.

"The *pakhan* and Sashka and a guy called the Tiger made their try tonight. You probably heard something?"

I nodded weakly, fearfully.

"The Tiger is dead. Sashka got it in the leg, but he made it over the wall. The *pakhan* made it, too. Good night, *chelovek*."

I slept.

CHAPTER

15

THE MAN IN THE NEXT BED WAS "SEMICOLORED." THAT MEANS THAT HE WAS a political prisoner who had picked up some of the ways of the *urki*. He introduced himself to me in a flowery way as Baron Laszlo something (I don't recall his last name), and for all I know he may have been a baron. By instinct he was an operator who bought low and sold high to whoever was paying. Because of his behavior in prison, although he was really a political, the authorities treated him like one of the *urki*. He had a kind of slippery, oily quality and an elaborate courtesy that I found a bit suspect.

The Baron had been in prison since the end of the war, he told me. He had peddled information during the war to whoever would pay for it. He worked for the British, the Swiss, the Germans, double-crossing all of them all the way whenever he could make more money. Toward the end of the war, armed with secrets from all the others, he began to sell information to the Soviets.

When the Red Army was marching into Budapest, the Baron's friends urged him to flee westward. "Why should I?" he had replied. "After all, my employers will soon be here!"

Sure enough, the Russians came and he identified himself to the Soviet commandant of Budapest. The commandant told him that the Soviet Army highly appreciated his intelligence reports and that he was to be rewarded in Moscow for his cooperation. He was flown to Moscow, given a tour of the city, and then taken to MGB headquarters. There a general said to him, "My dear Baron, that you worked for the British, German, and our intelligence we know. For whom else did you work?"

They gave him ten years. He was astonished. He had thought he was among friends. But he was smart enough to accept a situation when he saw it. He confessed everything without reserve and had an easy time over a year and a half of interrogation—largely bragging about his exploits, I imagined. He confided in me. He said he had heard he was about to be sent in an *etap* to the dreaded Kolyma camps. He had asked one of his *urki* friends what to do about this. On the advice he received, he had peeled a clove of garlic, bribed from a guard, and inserted it in his anus. "A sure way to send up your fever, my friend! I commend it to you. It never fails. They brought me in here with thirty-nine degrees this afternoon!"

The doctor who came to examine us was also a prisoner, and an old hand. He finished with me, prescribed drugs for the diarrhea and the fever, and a heart stimulant, and turned to the Baron. He examined him very thoroughly. Then he waved away the feldsher who was accompanying him, and spoke very quietly to the Baron. I was just able to catch what he said, but I pretended to have drifted back to sleep.

The doctor said, "Baron, I respect you very much. I am going to keep you here until the *etap* is over, but remember, there is always another *etap*, and you can't get out of all of them. By the way, you could have confided in me and saved me a lot of trouble; you could have told me you had a piece of garlic up your ass. I would have kept you here anyway." Then he chuckled and patted the Baron on the arm and went on his way. I gathered from this experience that a prison doctor would collaborate with some kinds of prisoners as long as he had some medical evidence he could show the authorities that would justify hospitalization. I filed that away as information that might become useful later on.

Parasha, the prison telegraph, confirmed the escape of the *pakhan* and Saska, and the death of the Tiger. There was also a report that there had been a mistake somewhere along the line and that three *chestnyagi* had gotten into a cell full of *suki*, who had promptly hanged the three unconverted. *Parasha* is also the name for the urine barrel—a gossip exchange center.

The Hungarian Baron left the hospital, presumably with a garlic-free rectum, as soon as the transport he wanted to avoid had gone off, and I never saw him again.

The doctor kept me on, sympathetically, for three or four days after my fever had subsided, and did his best to feed me up and restore my strength, but when the next transport was formed, the next *etap* for Dzhezkazgan, there was no avoiding it. We were lined up in the yard. It took some time to assemble the forty or fifty prisoners, and while we stood there I saw a man going up and down the lines with a letter, asking people their names. Someone pointed to me. The man came over. He said, "You Doldzhin?" I nodded, amazed. He handed me the letter. "It's been here a couple of days," he said. "I guess you almost missed it."

I could not believe it. It was from Moscow, from my mother. I was so excited I tore the letter getting the envelope open. There was not much news. She was very noncommittal, said that she'd got my triangle and was glad to know I was all right, and that she would try to get a food parcel sent to me. The weather is fine, she wrote, and that was about all.

And yet it was like nourishment, like a warm bath, like a drink of wine. I felt immensely stronger. A new wave of hope swept over me. All the way to the train I grinned as we marched through the streets of Kuibyshev. I think I was still grinning when they jammed me like a piece of meat into the Stolypin car. There was now a chance that someone could start working on my behalf; they now knew where I was.

What a vain hope that was! And yet it kept me buoyant as the train worked its way still east and further east into the Urals and then across them.

There was a handsome military man in our group, a former Hero of the Soviet Union, with his shoulder boards ripped off now and his spirit destroyed. And there was a former minister of state from Armenia who had been incredibly fat and had lost it all during his interrogation. Now he was flowing with rolls of loose skin. He could have walked naked through the streets with modesty because his belly folds hung down halfway to his knees. This man confided to me that he had hidden a roll of money in his crotch, and that it had never been found because the folds were so deep that by just squeezing the muscles a little he could conceal it perfectly. His name was Khachaturian; I remember it because I was interested in the work of the composer with the same name.

Going through the Urals, whenever the guards opened the windows, we had been able to see the hillsides covered with spring green. It took slightly more than a day to reach the next transfer prison, in a small city called Chelyabinsk, and the memory of my first hour inside that prison will never leave my mind.

There were eight political prisoners in my group, including, of course, the Hero of the Soviet Union and the Armenian minister of state with his scrotal money pouch. We were lined up, as usual, and segregated from the professional criminals, who had been the largest group on the train.

A couple of guards came out of the building and said to the men who had searched us, "Where to for these?" Someone said, "India."

I fell down on the ground clutching my stomach. I rolled around and moaned and said, "I've get a terrible fever; I think I'm dying."

Suddenly there was a terrific blow from a boot in my wizened buttocks. I leapt up yelling. The guard who had kicked me laughed coarsely and said I would have a long wait for a hospital bed when I could dance like that. I yelled that I had a terrible fever. I had, too. I had felt it coming back during the train ride; my lips were dry and my head and joints ached. I yelled at them to feel my head, get a doctor, take my temperature, they'd see! They just cuffed me into line and herded us along a corridor and down some stairs until we stood outside a cell marked 49.

There was a terrific noise from inside, a constant chatter almost like a collection of animals. At the door they heard our prayers one by one and then shoved us inside. I was number five in the line. When the first man walked in there was a pause and then a cheer went up. Then the second. A pause. A cheer. As the third man went through, I was able to peek inside the cell. It gave an impression of enormous confusion, of bodies milling about, and strangely I thought at first they must all be naked. But what struck me was that on the floor by the barrel, just at the edge of the spatterings of urine, there was a gleaming white handkerchief spread out, exactly in the path of anyone walking into the cell. The number three political walked in, daintily sidestepped the handkerchief, and then a cheer went up. The man in front of me gave his prayer. I was beginning to feel nauseated and unsteady, but I was fascinated with the handkerchief. I remembered Valentin's riddle. I remembered him telling me that *of course* I would wipe my feet on it. Now I guessed why. I still wanted to get away from that cell, but if I was stuck with it I had at least one piece of information no one else seemed to know. Provided it was valid. Well, my *pakhan* had never let me down before. I stepped up and gave my prayer. I said, "Look, I'm burning up with fever, I—" but the guard just sent me flying with a hard shove. I thought, Well, okay, here goes.

I carefully wiped my feet on the handkerchief.

No cheer. Then I looked up.

I can still see it, although at the time I could hardly believe it; it seemed as though the fever was distorting my vision.

What I saw was exactly like an overcrowded monkey cage in a big zoo. What seemed like hundreds of bodies were hanging by an arm or upside down by two legs from the bunks or the bunk supports, scrambling up and down like young apes, lying in grotesque postures, eating with their fingers, chattering and gesticulating, and all of them naked except for underpants, and sweating in the hot cell, and all of those naked, sweating bodies tattooed, it seemed at first, from head to foot.

Except for my consignment of politicals, there was not a fully dressed human being in the cell.

Three or four dirty, ugly men immediately ran to me as I stepped away from the hanky. One took my bundle, very clearly not to steal it but to help: "Here, let me take this off your shoulders, brother, you look like a wreck." They led me to a bunk. "Welcome, brother, sit down, we'll get some tea and then you can tell us your story."

I just wondered how long I could keep up the deception. I certainly was in no way a brother to these disgusting hoodlums. There was not a tattoo anywhere on my body. Maybe I could plead fever and stay dressed. God knew I was beginning to shiver quite a lot.

Tattoos are a cultural mark of those members of Soviet society who pursue, as Valentine the Intelligent had said, "a different line of endeavor." I had seen elaborate tattoos on hands and forearms in Kuibyshev. Here I saw a complete gallery of designs on exposed flesh. One guy had a cat on one buttock and a mouse on the other; when he walked the cat chased the mouse. Many were erotic. There was, of course, the common wreath or ribbon with a girl's name and flowers and hearts. One man had his whole back covered with an elaborate floral design supporting the proud motto: I WOULD DIE FOR MY MOTHER. One had a different girl's name on each of his ten fingers and on each of his ten toes. Several had tattoos on their penises that said SHALUN, which means "little rascal," or "imp." One had SLAVE OF THE COMMUNIST PARTY on his forehead. I wondered how loyal a Soviet citizen he was. Another had a completely black chest, peppered with irregular tattoo marks that seemed to obscure some vague shape. I could not resist asking him about it as I sat on the bunk collecting myself and getting my wind back and sipping the bitter *chifir* one of them brought. He said it had been his life's pride, a full-sized portrait of the Leader, Stalin, which the bastards had filled in after he was arrested, saying it was disrespectful. "Disrespectful, my arse! I *love* the Leader! These bastards don't know what respect means!" he told me.

I told them about Kuibyshev. I won some time, before they started asking me about my own career in crime, by telling them how the *pakhan* had escaped. Many of them knew Valentin well, and all of them without exception knew his reputation. They looked at me with great respect when I told them that I had been invited to join the escape, and clucked in sympathy when I said I had been hospitalized and had to miss out on it. By now I thought I had gone about as far as I could with my masquerade. I let my shivers become a little more pronounced than they needed to be, and I said, "Brothers, I'm afraid I'm desperately sick; the fever is coming back; I hope I don't infect anyone!"

They fell away from me. But one bold fellow with stars on his nipples and a snake coiled around his belly came up close, and although he looked very fierce he had a soft voice and the manner of a nurse or a doctor. He felt my head with the back of his hand. He said, "Brother, you are really in bad shape." Then he turned around and called for silence. He called out, when everyone was listening: "One of The People is close to death, brothers. He must have a doctor, quick!"

Without a pause some of these monkeys ran to the open windows and began to yell. Others pounded on the cell door, yelling. "Urgent cry for help!" They yelled, "A *chelovek* is dying! It's terrible! Help! Help! These tormentors won't let us have a doctor! Help! A doctor! Help!"

Pandemonium.

Amid all the other yells, I could hear screams. Now that they had satisfied their curiosity about me, they were turning their attention to my fellow politicals. Here it was no discreet bag-slitting with a *moika*. They simply knocked the poor fellows down, and while one or two held the victim, others stripped off his clothes and searched his person.

The once-fat Armenian minister was on his back with his struggling legs held apart, squeaking like a puppy. They found his money roll and there was much laughing and rejoicing. Within minutes the poor fascists were struggling to cover themselves in the filthy and ill-fitting rags that the *urki* had given them in exchange for their clothes. The former Hero must have tried to fight because he was sitting on the floor looking stunned, trying to stanch the flow of blood from his nose and shaking his head in a pitiful way.

Shortly the cell door was unlocked, and a senior officer came in with two or three guards. He shouted, "This is terrible! There has been a terrible mistake!" Then, as if he were furious with the guards, "Get these political prisoners out of here, you fools! Don't you know this cell is only for coloreds?" As the bewildered fascists were led from the cell with what was left of their rifled bundles, the major apologized to each one: "A terrible mistake. It has never happened before. These blundering fools will be punished, you can be sure." The guards smirked at this. One political, bolder than the others, said, "What about getting our stuff back, then?" But the officer just kept on clucking about the terrible mistake as if he had not heard, and the guards shoved and prodded the seven men out into the corridor. As the door was closing on them, the officer stuck his head back in the cell and winked at the *urki*.

As soon as this performance was over, the *urki* set up their cry for a doctor again. "One of us is dying!" Some of them took the heavy wooden cover off the urine barrel and banged the door with it until I was nearly deafened. There was at least another ten minutes of this noise, and then the door opened again and the prison doctor (a prisoner) and the block commander came in. The doctor took my temperature and felt my pulse. I was dragged off to the hospital. There he did a more thorough examination, gave me some quinine and aspirin, and discharged me, and I was taken to a cell for politicals, with twenty or thirty men in it. I felt sick, but I was relieved to be out of India with my bundle intact.

I was in that cell less than a day before the next leg of the *etap* began. It was long enough to get a sinister foretaste of the next period of my life. There was a tall, emaciated man in the cell who paced up and down incessantly and coughed as he walked. His face and body looked wasted, and his clothing was striking and unpleasant. It consisted of a black cotton jacket and trousers and a black cotton cap. A rectangle was cut out of the left breast of the jacket and a strip of white cloth sewed in. There were letters and numbers on the white patch, something like CB 551. The same cutout patch and numbers were sewn on both arms, on the front of his cap, on the left leg of his trousers, on the back of his jacket.

He was old and weak, and yet he kept pacing, coughing, pacing. I asked him his story. He stared at me out of cavernous, miserable eyes for a long time before he answered. I had to keep walking with him because he could not stop.

They were sending him to Spassk, he said finally, a camp for the dying. He had silicosis from the copper mines and certainly could not last long, he knew that. The only consolation was that you did no work in Spassk, or so he had been told, but perhaps that was a lie like everything else. The numbers were worn by prisoners in all the camps where he had been for seven years, in Dzhezkazgan. Yes, he was terrified of death, but it could not be worse to die than to live in the living hell of Dzhezkazgan. I was horrified and told him in a kind of gasp that I was going to Dzhezkazgan. He just shook his head and coughed heavily but said nothing more, and when I tried to get him to talk again later, he refused.

This walking Death made me deeply afraid. I had stopped shivering from the fever after the drugs I had been given. Now I quite literally started to shake from fright. Somehow I got hold of myself, and began the old pep talks. "Remember what Orlov said," I reminded myself. "Some die quickly and some survive very well, and I am not the kind to die quickly. Remember the dungeon in Lefortovo. If you can survive that, you can survive anything. Remember to find an enterprise to earn your bread. Watch out for a friend. Remember the maxims for conserving energy."

I was able to rediscover some shreds of the old optimist and start cheering up. Gossip arrived that helped the process, just because it was fascinating and distracting. This was in the spring of 1950, and there had been another major purge. A group of party bosses in Leningrad had been arrested. Many had been shot, along with their families, and many others sent to camps. Here in Petropavlovsk there was a whole wing, it was said, reserved for the wives and children of these men who were purged.

By the time we were loaded back on the train I had pulled myself together. I was still physically weak, but I felt morally tough and even a bit adventurous once again.

Soon the green-treed hills were left behind and the train labored as we began to climb through grassy steppe land. At first the cities and towns retained their Russian sound: Kokchetav, Akmolinsk, and so on. Then the names began to sound more Asian: Temir Tau was one stop, and then Karaganda, early in the second day. Not long after Karaganda, the grasses began to thin out and there was nothing to see but flat expanses of rock and sand. The guards told us maliciously that it was called Bet Pak Dala, the Dead Steppe, and that we'd all be part of it soon enough. We were very high. This land is all more than two thousand feet above sea level. At night the car was freezing and the guards wore their greatcoats while we all huddled together. In the daytime it was over a hundred degrees.

At three o'clock on the third morning, the train stopped at a station that seemed to be in the middle of empty space. The first sound I heard was a continual barking of dogs, as if the train had run into a huge kennel. When we came out, there was nothing but flat rock reaching off into the darkness, and milling dogs pulling at their leashes, and dozens of guards in tropical uniforms, shivering a lot in the cold because it was not dawn yet, and holding back their German shepherds.

They sat us on the ground and came around to us with file folders and heard our prayers. Several of us were judged too weak to walk the eleven kilometers to camp and were put into a truck with several guards. The sky was brilliant with stars. By the time we got to the camp it was beginning to get light in the east. We were unloaded beside a huge stone wall that seemed to stretch for half a mile in each direction. There were watch-towers and barbed wire on the top, and a great gate a hundred feet or so from where we were told to sit and wait for the rest of the prisoners, who were marching in convoy from the station. The gate was timber, about four meters high. Outside it was a rough wooden barrier, a pole with a counterweight like a railway crossing barrier.

When the sun came up, it was hard and sudden. It was like a stab, only the warmth was welcome. You could feel it immediately.

Almost immediately after the sun appeared, there was some noise from inside the gates, and in a moment they swung open. A thin, tired horse appeared, drawing a flat farm wagon with wooden wheels. Ten or twelve corpses were stretched out on the wagon. Somehow I found this normal. I was watching indifferently until the wagon stopped and two guards appeared with axes. Then I felt quite sick. The guards methodically walked from corpse to corpse and swung the axes up and down. Soon each skull was split wide open. The man leading the horse tugged the reins and led it off. Each corpse had a small metal tag wired to a big toe and the metal tags waved back and forth as the wagon moved away across the steppe.

I began to feel as though I was hallucinating again because I could hear music, a band, playing some kind of bravura march. It sounded weak and the instruments were not well tuned, but the rhythm was fast and I was sure it was coming from inside the gate. I had a sense of deep cosmic horror that made me dizzy. In the distance I could see the silhouette of the corpses on the wagon. The band seemed to be playing some kind of grotesque farewell. Then it got worse. Out of the gate came, in lines of five abreast, a column of *walking* corpses in black cotton jackets with white number patches. They could hardly drag themselves. Their faces were pale and drawn and expressionless and they stared straight ahead. Somehow I learned that they were from a hard punishment barracks called BUR. The band is for them, then, I thought. They marched, or shuffled, away into the distance surrounded by guards and dogs. All directions seemed the same in front of this flat wall on top of this flat rock. All directions led away from the prison except the one in through the gate.

The band kept playing. Now in one of the distances I saw a black line approaching and heard more dogs. It was the rest of our *etap*. When it arrived, we were formed into columns of five and marched through the gate. We passed other columns of prisoners marching out. They looked a little better than the group from BUR, but only a little. Most were tanned. All wore the black jackets with the number patches. Unlike the column of the walking dead men, some of these looked at us—some in curiosity, some indifferently, some cordially, some, I thought, in pity.

I was terribly thirsty. I asked for water repeatedly, but no one paid any attention. Guards were going around with files and papers again, checking on each prisoner.

Inside the walls the camp appeared to be a village of low stone buildings, plastered white, with low-pitched slate roofs and a barren dirt road or plaza running between them. This road or street stretched straight away from the gates, and what gave the appearance of a town was the movement of people back and forth between these buildings. One building was much larger than the others. It turned out to be the mess hall and kitchen. The rest of the buildings were mostly barracks. On the right was a small bathhouse and another small building, the bakery.

The music, when I found it, peering around in the shadows inside the walls because the sun was still very low, came from a pitiful little band of prisoners lined up near the *vakhta*, the guardhouse, sitting on a bench, playing away with desperate eyes—a tuba, a trumpet, a drum, an accordion, and a violin. They were still playing the same march. The eyes of the brass

players looked profoundly hollow over their puffed cheeks. The whole
picture was so bizarre I still felt myself in a kind of dream state. Am I
really seeing this? Human ghosts with numbers on their arms. Faces of
death playing a lively march.

I began to feel more real again with the touch of rough hands searching
us. Our bundles were searched and their contents registered, and they
were taken away to storage. Prisoners going to the toilet or the mess
hall or back to their barracks came and tried to talk to us. The guards were
not too severe about stopping them, so some acquaintances began to be
made.

We were taken by fives to the supply room after a hopeless bath with
half a pail of water, since water was very short in the camp, and given our
black clothes and numbers. My number was Ess Ya 265—in Russian letters:
СЯ265. It would remain the same all the time I was in Dzhezkazgan. The
clothes were badly worn and we were told they were called thirty-third-
term clothes: that they had been worn for thirty-three full terms. They
seemed threadbare enough. The numbers were painted on by prisoners
with brushes and pots of black paint.

The next several days passed uneventfully except for talk. This was the
quarantine. I was glad of the rest. After that we were sent for "medical
examinations" and then assigned to our barracks. I had almost no buttocks.
I discovered that this was desirable. If you had buttocks, you were assigned
to the copper mines, which meant silicosis and early death. If you had no
buttocks, you were too weak for the copper mines, so they would send
you to outdoor construction or the rock quarry. The medical examination
was conducted not by a medical man but by an MVD noncom; it consisted
almost entirely of having your buttocks squeezed.

Then we were assigned our barracks number and turned out into the
road between the barracks and the other buildings. I was to go to barracks
number five. I had to ask the way. When I got there I was supposed to
look for the chief of the work brigade I was assigned to, known simply as
the brigadier. His name was Vtyurin, and he showed me where I was to
sleep, on an upper bunk in section one of the barracks.

The barracks were long, rectangular buildings divided into four normal
sleeping sections for the work brigades, two at each end of the building,
and a central section which was part wash house and part barracks for the
pridurki, the soft-job workers, who were assigned to the hospital or the
various administrative posts that the MVD delegated to prisoners. There
was a corridor on each side of this central section, and an outside entrance
to each of these two corridors. You could walk from, say, the south corridor into work brigade sections one and two, and from the north corridor
into work brigade sections three and four. Only one corridor had a door to
the *pridurki* barracks, and both gave onto the washrooms. The washrooms

had long troughs. You lifted a lever and a trickle of water came down to wash with, when there was water. The barracks had two layers of bunks. If the camp was crowded, as it was when I arrived, the spaces between the sets of bunks would be boarded over to make a continuous sleeping platform. In this way each section held about 120 to 150 people—between 600 and 750 altogether in each barracks, including the *pridurki* administrative workers.

I had been provided with a pillowcase, a blanket, and a mattress case— just a sort of flat bag. It was up to me to find the stuffing, and for the first several days I slept on the wood with nothing but two layers of thin cloth beneath me. I began to think about finding some sawdust or soft earth or something to stuff it with, and speculated that perhaps there was an industry for me in mattress stuffing, if I could find a good supply of something desirable.

The first person I got to know in the barracks was a Moscow biologist serving the second of two ten-year sentences because he had dared to disagree with Lysenko and his famous theory that environment and behavior can change hereditary characteristics. His name was Vladimir Pavlovich Effroimson. We became very friendly in prison, although years later when I tried to look him up in Moscow he refused to see me because I was American and he feared a third term. But here in Dzhezkazgan, on our first meeting, he gave me some extra food he had saved and began to explain the camp routine to me. He seemed a man who knew his way around, and I decided to stick close to him at first, for as long as I needed his help. After we had talked for a while, he asked me about my case. That was always the way. Like Ragozin tapping through the wall in Lefortovo, it was Article? Section? And within minutes of any encounter you were always launched on an elaborate version of your prayer. It was credentials. It placed you, so the other person knew who he was dealing with. It was like, What do you do and where are you from, in a normal world.

As soon as I told him my story, Effroimson said, "Well, you're in luck. There's a man from the U.S. Embassy here in camp."

My jaw must have dropped. I said "Quick! Tell me! What's his name?" I assumed it would be poor Morris Seltser. Effroimson said, "Victor S———."

"Victor! Impossible. He was shot in 1941. I never met him, but I heard his story all the time. His wife was Armenian. She was a kind of a lost soul in Moscow. We gave her a job in the embassy as a clerk. The Organs told her Victor was shot."

"Well," Effroimson said, "then you'll have the pleasure of your first conversation with a dead man, because there he is over there!"

He pointed out the window, and I looked out toward a barracks across the street. A tall, lanky guy was bending over slightly, in conversation with a shorter man. He had a very low number, which meant he was one of the first lucky ones to get to Dzhezkazgan. I was terribly excited. I excused myself to Effroimson and dashed out into the street.

Now this was Sunday. Most Sundays in camps were workdays like any other workday. But from time to time there was a free Sunday. It was usually interrupted by harassment from the MVD administration, with barracks emptied for searching, and line-ups of prisoners in the streets outside for haranguing and intimidation. But I was lucky to hit a free Sunday, and one, as far as I can recall, free not only of work but of interruption from the administration. If it had not been for this Sunday of getting acquainted with people and with routines, it might have taken me a lot longer to get to know my way around, because on normal workdays the prisoners would be exhausted by bedtime and much too cranky at 5 A.M. to explain this strange new world to a new arrival. Only on a free Sunday could I have had time to make an important contact with a man like Victor S.

I came up behind him and said very formally in Russian, "Mr. S———?"

He turned around and looked at me curiously and not discourteously. I immediately said, "You're from Moscow?"

"Yes."

"You worked at the American Embassy?"

"That's right."

"Well, so did I. My name is Alexander Dolgun"—and into the extended prayer, article, section, all the normal elements of first meeting.

After a while I said, "Listen, I heard all the time that this was a death camp, and I thought it was pretty horrifying when I first got here. But you look in good shape. How come?"

He laughed. "For some reason or other, my dossier was marked EXTREMELY DANGEROUS when I first came down to Karaganda. That was in forty-two, you know. There were no camps for politicals then. 'Extremely dangerous'! I don't know why. But they never dared let me out of camp to go to work. *Pridurki* from the first day. Always in camp, always a better chance to steal food. No copper mines. Different now. They know I'm not dangerous. So I get some hard assignments. But I know my *tufta* now. I get along."

"*Tufta?*"

"*Tufta* means filling your work quota without really doing any work. Look, I can give you some hints, but mostly you'll have to figure it out for yourself, depending on the job you're on. If we work together sometime, you'll never have to work at all, believe me. But you have to know how to do it, and if you don't learn you'll be dead before you're out of school!"

Then he said, "Who's your brigadier?"

"Vtyurin."

"Well, I don't know him. But you better make friends with your brigadier. That's the beginning of successful *tufta*."

I said, "I've only just met him, but I'll take your advice." Then I said, "By the way, I saw your wife just about two years ago. She thinks you're shot, you know."

Victor gave me a funny look, then a short bitter laugh. "Good," he said. "Let her think it, if she really does. But the bitch will say anything if it serves her purpose."

I was surprised at the bitterness. "But she's been working as a Soviet clerk in the embassy and she drove us nuts weeping and complaining and asking for help."

"Does she get it?"

"Well, they give her some food, or some money. They feel bad about what happened to you."

"She takes food home from the embassy and the Organs don't pick her up for black marketeering, is that it? And doesn't that make you think?"

I had never thought about it before. "I guess because you were an employee there, the Organs think she has good reason . . . I don't know," I said a bit lamely.

"Of course she has good reason," he said bitterly. "She's on the best of terms with the bloody Organs. It was my wife who put them on to me."

Victor S. had gone to Kuibyshev when the American Embassy moved there early in the war. He worked as a translator in the economic section. He was a Soviet citizen. He and his wife quarreled a good deal, as husbands and wives often do, but she was a vindictive woman and decided to have the ultimate victory. She told the MGB that Victor was a German spy. After all, he had a German name. They picked him up and gave him a rough time. He had nothing to confess to and so he was treated very roughly. But in the end, on no evidence at all, he was given twenty years for espionage.

It seemed strange standing there in the hot sun chatting easily with Victor, who was almost an old friend even though I had never seen him before. We talked in English. His English was perfect, and hearing and speaking my own language for the first time since . . . well, when? I could not remember when, but it gave me an enormous boost. Despite the corpse wagon and the reputation of the camp and the stories of the terrible copper mines, I began to sense again that warm, good conviction that I could handle anything and that I must surely come out on top. After a while, although I hated to leave the sound of the English words, I told Victor that I wanted to get myself organized in the barracks, and get started making friends with Vtyurin, my brigadier. We shook hands warmly. I could see that we would be good friends. We promised to keep an eye out for each other and take every opportunity to get together and talk some more.

It took me some time to find Vtyurin. He was very matter-of-fact. He said that it was very hard work in the quarry and that he was very insistent about the quota's being filled. He did not seem much interested in my being an American, unlike almost everyone else I had met up till now, so I thought I was not going to have much luck there. I fell into conversation with two Muscovites, Boris Gorelov and Vadim Popov, who were in for terrorism and propaganda because in their school days they had formed a group called the Black Guard; they had put out a few juvenile pamphlets proposing a new democratic power and pushed over a few kiosks in parks and knocked out some street lights. They were about sixteen when they did this stuff. Popov, along with Gorelov and some other students, was turned in several years later when he was in the medical institute and confided his childish pranks to a girl he had fallen in love with. She turned him in. Twenty-five, five, and five. The girl got it too. Twenty-five, five and five, for associating with known subversives. Popov thought that was pretty funny.

While Popov and Gorelov and I were talking, there were suddenly loud shouts from outside. The water tank truck was coming to fill the reservoirs. Everyone who had a cup ran out to catch drippings from the hose. I had no cup. I was thirsty all the time, those first weeks. Popov gave me some of his catchings. I think everyone was thirsty in Dzhezkazgan until much later when the water supply was improved.

About nine o'clock there was a loud ringing sound from someone banging a bar of iron on a piece of steel rail that was hung up in the center of camp. This announced the night count. Soon we were ordered out of the section by a bunch of shouting, hostile guards. The only one allowed to stay in was an old cripple, whose job was to stay in the barracks all day and keep it clean and empty the *parasha*, the urine barrel, and keep an eye on things. The rest of us were taken out, counted by fives, marched in, and counted again. The guards made up their count with strokes in pencil on a plywood board, which was then scraped down for further use. I do not know why they never used paper, but throughout the system a piece of board seems to be the preferred object to mark the count on. After we got inside again and the second count was made, there was a flurry of cursing from the guards and we all had to go outside again because the count did not tally. I got the impression that the guards were not too bright and had difficulty counting anyway. It took three counts, that first night in barracks number five. Finally we were locked in. It was ten o'clock. I scrambled up to the top bunk that Vtyurin had assigned me. I was very tired and even the flat boards felt good. I was cheered by the encounter with Victor S. I felt he was an ally. Effroimson, too. It was going to be all right. The four very bright bulbs in the ceiling were a nuisance, but I pulled my meager blanket over my face and stretched and sighed and yawned and felt the grateful approach of sleep.

Then I sat up with a start. I had been bitten on the leg. I threw off the blanket. I could not see anything. Then I felt a bite on the belly. I yanked at my shirt. A bedbug ran out and disappeared. Then I was bitten on the foot, then on the arm, then on the back, several bites. They kept coming. I began to thrash around. Bedbug bites sting me very severely, and the first bites on my arm and stomach were already swelling. My next-bunk neighbor sat up and said crossly, "What the hell are you doing?"

I said, "I'm going to kill these goddamn bugs!"

"Don't be crazy," he said. "Look at the wall."

I stared at the whitewashed wall. It was not white anymore. A mass of black insects was migrating down the wall. I screamed and jumped off the bunk. Angry prisoners snapped at me to for God's sake shut up. The wall seemed to move. It made me feel as though my eyes had gone wrong. I was a bit nauseated. I began to shiver again. The room was cool, but not cold; there were enough bodies to keep the temperature up, even though it was dropping outside with the darkness and the open windows were letting in the cooling air.

I went to the table by the door and the *parasha*. I pulled every bug that I could find off my body. I sat down at the table and stared at the bugs on the wall and crawling up the bunks. Every once in a while a prisoner would stir and try to wipe away a sting. But most of them slept soundly. Once in a while there was a moan or a cry; nightmares were beginning to play around the snoring barracks. I put my head on my arms on the table and tried to sleep. There was a sudden touch on the back of my neck, and I started up, terrified. I looked up. There were bedbugs on the ceiling above me, and some dropped off now and then on me and on the table. From time to time I dozed off, but even if I was not awakened by bites I would start up anticipating them, or imagining that another bug had landed on the back of my neck. It was a bad night. Around one in the morning, there was a huge commotion suddenly in one corner of the cell. Sleeping prisoners woke up angrily and then leapt from their beds. I watched from the table. I was quite puzzled at first. Then I made out from the shouts that there was a lethal spider in somebody's bed, and they were trying to kill it. Shouts of triumph. Success. Then whispers: Get back to bed before the guards look in!

But it was too late. The door was flung open and two MVD stamped into the barracks. "All right! All right! Why is everyone out of bed? What is happening here?"

"A *karakurt!* A *karakurt!* We killed it!"—and one timid-looking man with baggy, too-large underwear flapping around his skinny frame brought the deadly specimen forward on a stick for the guards to see. The spider was put on the table beside me. It was about three centimeters long, long black furry legs, tan on top, black on the bottom with a perfect tan cross. *Karakurt* is Kazakh for "black death." The guard picked up the spider gingerly on the stick, shooed everyone back to bed, and went out again. In ten minutes he was back with two captains and a major wiping the sleep from their eyes. I was shooed from the table. I could scarcely believe my eyes. They held an investigation, on the spot, into the killing of the spider! Someone speculated that they might have been afraid that the prisoners would extract the venom and use it for terroristic purposes. None of it made any sense to me.

The bedbugs seemed to thin out toward morning. I dozed off for a while with my head on my hands, and then the rail clanged with its powerful beats at about four o'clock, or four thirty. Guards opened the doors immediately and began to curse and yell "*Podyom,*" and threaten hard punishment to anyone caught still in bed in two minutes. Clearly they were serious because everyone leapt out of bed, cursing and scrambling into their clothes and rubbing their eyes and yawning. The sleep period was only six hours and these were men who worked hard, breaking rock and carrying timbers twelve hours a day.

The brigadier organized us for breakfast. One man was dispatched to the kitchen to get the bowls for our twenty-five-man group, another to the bakery with a list of live prisoners to collect the day's allotment of 700 grams of bread per person. No one had died overnight, but someone told me to make sure that, if someone near me died, the death was concealed from the guards until the bread ration had been picked up.

Curiously, there was no head count in the morning. We were allowed to go to the toilet building more or less as we wanted to, and the brigadier was responsible for getting us into the mess hall when there was an empty table, getting our soup into us, and getting us out fast to make room for the next brigade. No spoons were issued. I had to borrow one from Gorelov after he finished his cabbage soup. That gave me another idea for an enterprise.

Some brigades were assigned to different projects every day, depending on special needs. Others, like mine, were on permanent assignment. By a quarter to six we were forming columns of five inside the gate, and the sorrowful orchestra was beating out its up-tempo march. The column was marched out of the camp and halted again by the barrier. Here a head count was made and marked on the boards in pencil. Then the MVD in charge of the convoy called out in a loud voice, "Prisoners! On the way to the work site you will keep close column. Hands behind your back. One step to the right or one step to the left will be considered an attempt to escape, and the convoy has orders to shoot without warning. Remember! One step to the right, or one to the left!"

And the prisoners intoned back, "Or one step upward."

No one paid any attention.

Dogs were yelping all around us, and as soon as the order was given to march, there began a torrent of commands and counterremarks from the prisoners: Pick up the pace. Slow down, we can't manage! Get moving or you'll get shot! Hold back and wait for the column to close in. Pick it up at the rear there!

A constant kind of bickering, enriched with the snarls and yaps of the excited dogs.

It was a long, long march. When we started out, the sun cast long shadows behind us. An hour and a half later, arriving at the work site, the shadows had shortened and the heat was beginning to be unpleasant. Five kilometers, perhaps five and a half. The first view of the quarry was a pair of watchtowers silhouetted against the yellow sky. Then the barbed wire, which was invisible from a mile away, began to appear, until I could see a fence that seemed to stretch forever in both directions. As we came closer, a gate of poles and barbed wire appeared between the two watchtowers, and more towers could be seen along the fence, which now seemed to curve away from us. There was still no sign of rock or tools or a pit or anything that resembled a quarry. Before the guards unlocked the gates, the entire column was counted by fives and then ordered to lie down on the ground, while the guards assigned to the watchtowers went off to their posts. This took nearly half an hour. I realized that some of the watchtowers were very far away. The rest was welcome. I was tired out by the walk and could not imagine digging rock. Then the gate was unlocked and we were led inside, counted again, and taken to the lip of the biggest excavation I have ever seen in my life. It must have been nearly two kilometers across, perhaps one and a half, and about one kilometer wide, oval in shape with a spiral truck road winding down to the bottom. The bottom was almost half a kilometer, 1,600 feet, below the surface. I was given a sledge hammer I could hardly lift and a chisel, and led to a rock face deep down in the pit. Here we had to break rock out of the quarry with our chisels and pile it up ready for the dump trucks. The unbelievable daily quota was three cubic meters for each person. My heart sank. I knew it was impossible for me to break up three cubic feet, let alone three cubic meters.

I looked around me. Everywhere men were wearily lifting their picks and sledges and slamming them feebly against huge rocks. It seemed like the labors of Hercules. I could imagine the rocks doubling in size each time I broke one. I tried to lift the huge sledge and it slipped sideways and pulled me over with it. I lay panting on the ground. The brigadier's assistant came over and started to yell at me to get up.

"I don't think I can," I said. I was not *that* weak. I just felt discouraged and wanted some time to think about a way out of this impossible task. The assistant got furious. He was about to haul off and kick me in the ribs when a man came up and took his arm and spoke in his ear. The assistant shrugged and went away without the satisfaction of his kick. Gorelov, my friend from the Black Guard, who had somehow been able to call off the brigadier's goon, helped me to my feet again and took me by the arm.

"You better stick with me for the day," he said. "Anybody in your shape who actually tries to lift a sledge is either crazy or too young to be outdoors by himself."

We both laughed. "Anything you say," I told Gorelov.

CHAPTER

16

THANK GOD FOR GORELOV THAT DAY! HE HAD BEEN LUCKY AND HAD received some food parcels from home, and had strategically given more than half of what he got to the brigadier. This got him both a lower quota, and a blind eye to his *tufta*, his cheating on the quota. Gorelov had devised a way of building a hollow mound of stone that looked like three cubic meters, or six if he was in partnership with someone, but which really contained only about a third of that amount. Working hard, he could do almost two cubic meters by himself, so that first day, taking pity on me, he built the hollow square mound, and when the sun became unbearably hot he put me inside in the shade to rest and went on working on his own. The sun made the rock so hot we had to wear gloves to avoid blisters. Gorelov built the square against the wall of the quarry, so he had to make only three sides and a rough roof. The roof was hardest, but he sloped the structure so that a few big stones across the top would do to close it in.

I had my own shirt under the black jacket, and sometime during the day, when we stripped in the heat, my shirt was stolen. There was a brigade of *urki*, and Gorelov went off to find their leader. This guy at first denied that any of his boys had stolen my shirt, but after we talked awhile he became friendly and promised to get it back for me before the end of the day. "I've got influential friends," he said, and laughed, and went back to his *urki*. At noon we were led up to a higher level where there was a primitive field kitchen: an iron stove on wheels with a simmering kettle of porridge. It smelled delicious as we came up, but when it was ladled out it was so thin you could drink it like water. Gorelov explained that the field cook, a soft-job prisoner, was given an allotment of a third of a bag of crushed grain to make his porridge. Some he kept back for himself as a privilege of the job. Some he gave to his brigadier to keep things sweet in the barracks. The *urki* always managed to steal a little more. By the time he put water in the kettle to make up the noon meal, there was almost nothing left for the prisoners.

Gorelov had secreted a package of his own and shared it with me. White bread and fat, greasy smoked bacon, running with oil in the burning sun. The bacon made me anxious. I thought that it might have been too much of Valentin's greasy meat that triggered my diarrhea the first time. But I had no choice: it was eat meat or starve and I chose to eat.

Back at work, we were joined by a young guy who was half Chinese. His father had been in Shanghai working for the East Chinese railroads. Stalin invited all Russian émigrés in China to come home, and then arrested them. This boy got twenty-five years. No reason. He joined Gorelov and me, and together we began to enlarge our hollow stone structure to look like nine cubic meters. The half-Chinese worked very well, and by mid-afternoon we had an acceptable pile, and a good place to hide and smoke and talk in the shade. And by then my diarrhea had started up again, as I had feared it would.

From time to time, the brigadier's assistant would check up on us. Other brigadiers were sending goon squads around to step up the work pace with threats and curses and occasionally blows from a stick. Gorelov had bought us peace; so we just lay around the rest of the afternoon and got to know each other. After a while I broached the subject of escape. The way my two companions looked at each other suggested to me they had something in mind. I pressed them about it, and after some fencing and testing, they decided to let me in on it and take me along if I wanted to go.

They had made two knives from scrap steel and hidden them in the tool shed at the quarry. They planned to kidnap a civilian truck driver late in the day when the trucks came for the loads of stone. They would bind and gag him, using the knives to intimidate him, and hide him in the tool shed. They were prepared to kill him if they had to, but since the drivers were free men and not part of the MVD, they bore him no ill will. They would then jump in the truck and drive toward the gate. Just before they reached it, they would build up speed and trip the dump so that the road behind would be strewn with rocks and the dump box would tilt up and provide a shield against machine gun bullets from the watchtowers behind them. Then they would crash through the gate, which was only wire and poles, and just keep going out into the desert. I said I thought the radiator of the truck would be punctured going through the gate and they would burn out the engine almost immediately. They disagreed. So we passed the afternoon, between bouts of my running outside to find a rock to squat behind, chatting about this plan in a relaxed way. I thought it was too fantastic to come off, and privately believed they were just talking.

Late in the afternoon the young *urki* leader stuck his head into our hide-out and handed in my shirt. I felt in the pockets. Some sugar and tobacco that Effroimson had given me were gone. "Sorry," said the *urka*, "I guess my guys have liberal tendencies." He winked and went away.

I was beginning to feel terrible. I was sore from so many bowel movements, and terribly thirsty. Gorelov and the half-Chinese took turns getting water for me. At six we made our way with the rail gang up the long spiral road to the gate. The climb was extremely difficult for me and I was apprehensive about the march back. We had a chance to rest on the ground while they rounded up the guards after the head count was made, and I began to feel I could make it after all.

It was a bizarre walk back. We had not gone more than a kilometer before I felt another attack coming. I whispered to my neighbor, "Will they let you stop? My bowels . . ."

He shook his head violently. "Don't try it. They shot the last guy."

In the end I just had to keep on walking and let it happen. I felt humiliated, but no one said anything about it, so I guessed it was not the first time.

Then there was a commotion up ahead in the line. The convoy soldiers began to curse the prisoners and threaten to shoot. There was a kind of wavering in the line ahead that came closer and closer to us. Then I realized the men ahead of me were stepping over something. It was a body. One poor man had collapsed, and the convoy just kept us marching. Finally they halted the march and detailed two prisoners to pull the fallen man out of the line so they could have a look at him. One soldier kept his rifle pointed at the pitiful shrunken figure, while another felt his heart and peeled back the eyelids. "He's dead," the soldier said shortly, as casually as if he had said, "It's hot out." Four prisoners were ordered to pick up the body and carry it back to camp. Everyone was exhausted, and carrying an extra load was a terrible task. The soldiers stopped the column every few minutes and assigned a relief group to take over the body. It was past eight o'clock when we got back to the gates.

As soon as the count was made and we were turned loose in the compound, I went to find Victor and ask him how I could wash out my pants. He found me some water, and while I was cleaning up the mess he told me that I just might be able to talk my way into the hospital on the basis of the diarrhea by claiming it was the fever again. He could see how feeble I felt, and he said, "You won't last in the quarry, even with a clever *tufta* artist like your friend Gorelov. So you better get into that hospital by hook or by crook."

And so, after another night fighting off the bedbugs and catching what sleep I could, I grabbed my bread when it came and went straight to the hospital without the rest of my breakfast.

The man who examined me—a prisoner, of course—was sympathetic. There was a great line-up of would-be malingerers, with differing schemes for appearing to need hospitalization, and some genuinely sick men. When it was my turn, the doctor shoved a thermometer under my arm and asked me my story. "I think it's another malaria attack," I said, trying to sound very sick. I was sorry I had not brought a mug of tea with me to heat my fingers in, or a clove of garlic, although garlic was the rarest of treasures in camp and ought not to be wasted in the wrong orifice.

The doctor looked at me very carefully. He said, "You're not Latvian, by any chance?"

"No. I'm an American."

"An American!" He seemed delighted. He immediately started speaking English, almost without an accent. "I've been dying to find someone to talk English with," he said warmly. "Now, we are not allowed to put you into the hospital for diarrhea and . . ." He looked at the thermometer. "Hmm, no fever. I guess you knew that. Let me see."

Then he said in a loud voice, in Russian, "This looks very serious. Wait in the surgery. I want to do a more thorough examination."

When the rest of the line was processed, a few minutes later, he came into the surgery seeming in a great hurry. "Now, listen," he said in a whisper. "I am allowed only a small quota each day, and I'm over it now. I've got to make you really sick if you're going to stay here. Would you be willing to give yourself an infection if I promise to cure it for you later?"

"Anything!" I said. "I'll do anything to get in here. What's the plan?"

He said, "You've got a boil on the back of your arm, not a bad one. I'm going to lance it for you and give you some of the pus on a matchstick." He moved quickly and deftly; I scarcely felt the probe. Then he handed me the match with a big, unpleasant drop of white matter on it.

"Hold that," he said. "I have to cut you now. Can you stand it? It won't be very nice."

"Go ahead," I said. I was fascinated.

Again, with a speed and deftness that I found amazing, he made an incision on the inside of my arm. It was made in a way that produced little blood.

"I can't do the next part," he said with a half-humorous, half-serious look. "My professional ethics won't let me infect a wound. But you can. I'll look away."

I stuck the match in the incision and wiped the pus off inside. Then Atsinch, which was this doctor's name, sent me to a feldsher to get a bandage on the cut. He explained that he could keep me overnight, but by morning he would have to justify bringing another patient into the ward, and by then I should have a spectacular infection. I remembered Vasya's leg at Kuibyshev and felt faintly sick. But I had formed an immediate trust and liking for this soft-spoken young surgeon with such marvelous hands. I was sure that he could manage anything.

Atsinch sent me to the barracks for my things, and told me he would do a very thorough examination as soon as I got back, to see what else he could find that might let him keep me in the hospital for a good long time.

As I was going out the door, I turned back and said to him, "Dr. Atsinch, why are you doing all this for me?"

"I told you," he said easily, with a big smile, "I've got to practice my English or I'll forget it."

We became very good friends, Arvid Atsinch and I. It began with the unbelievably soothing connection he could make with his patients through his fingertips. He went over my whole body meticulously, and everywhere he touched me I had the feeling that the process of healing began at the point of contact with those fingers.

My legs had been swollen for some days; he pressed the puffiness along my shinbones and a depression remained when he took his finger away. "That's got to be connected with something," he said quietly. Eventually he found it. He did a most meticulous examination of my heart, by percussion and with the stethoscope, over and over again tapping, listening, tapping, listening, pressing, closing his eyes as if his fingers could look inside my body.

Then we sat down and he wrote out a very extensive history, always speaking English, of course, and occasionally asking me for the English word if he had forgotten it.

He liked the colloquial ways of the language, and he announced right at the beginning that he would call me Al, if that was all right with me.

"Al," he said, "this is serious, but it is good news in a way, because I am going to be able to make a good case to the medical administration to keep you here for some time. If we let this infection develop in your arm, along with the edema in your legs and the way your heart sounds, I think I can make you out to be a real mess. But you'll be able to walk around and do light work, and if you like I'll give you some medical training because I need another assistant, and then we can work together and talk English all we want."

"Wait a minute," I said anxiously, "what's all this about my heart? Are you serious?"

"Well . . ." He paused for quite a long time, looking very serious, so that I became a bit alarmed.

"Let me ask you about your treatment before you got here," Atsinch said. "I have the impression that you've got a fundamentally very strong body, a very healthy body. But it seems to me that it has been very badly abused recently; am I right?"

I told him about the beatings and the sleeplessness and the cold and the starvation.

"Perhaps that explains it," he said. "The left ventricle of your heart is quite enlarged. Without an X-ray I can only estimate how much, but it seems to me to be about four and a half centimeters. That's pretty serious. I can't believe that you could survive a lot of hard physical work. I think you have what we call congestive heart disease, and with your dystrophic diarrhea and your general weakness, it means that we will have to start some very extensive therapy."

That suited me. It meant rest and food. Atsinch found me a bed and a hospital gown. He started vitamin injections and intravenous glucose right away. By the time the hospital administrator, an MVD captain, came to check me out, I was plugged up with tubes and had a huge, purple infection in my right arm. The captain was evidently impressed, as Atsinch had planned. I was allowed to stay.

Arvid Atsinch began my medical training later on that very first day. He asked if I felt up to making rounds with him, and gave me a white smock and a stethoscope to wear around my neck. We saw men with tuberculosis and silicosis, men with dysentery and men with bowel blockage. We saw a great variety of wounds from the mines and the quarry and the construction sites. Fractured skulls and limbs, eyes and fingers and toes lost, lacerations and scrapes and burns. Atsinch believed very strongly in vitamin injections; right away he taught me how to sterilize the skin with alcohol and pinch up the muscle or stretch it out, depending on the kind of injection, and how to clear air from the syringe before quickly plunging in the needle. The patients were mystified at the language we spoke, but Arvid Atsinch was always kind and made a real effort to make every man feel better. To the patients, I was clearly another physician: I had the uniform. They would say, "Thank you, doctor," when I made the injection, and look at me with a respect I did not deserve.

I saw that Atsinch watched me very closely too. He said, later in our first day together, "You know, Al, I think you have the makings of a physician. It is really too bad you never studied medicine. But I'm going to teach you as much as I can while you're here with me. It may be the only way you will ever survive camp, with that heart of yours, to have a skill that will keep you out of the mines."

What an irony that was. Arvid Atsinch's own exquisite medical skill would be, not too many years later, the very thing that took him into the mines and to his death. I would see a lot of deaths in my years in camp. One had already taken place almost under my feet. I would get hardened to death as a fact, as a part of the environment. I would feel grief for only a very few, but Atsinch's would be one of them. He was the first man I became strongly attached to in camp. He was a lifeline to my own roots because of his command of English. He was a teacher by instinct, and a good one. He was a passionate democrat. His father had been a minister of state in Latvia, before the Soviet take-over, and Atsinch often talked about the excellence of the democratic system in that small republic. His father had been shot after the take-over.

He was as committed as I to finding ways to survive the rigors of camp. But he said, "Survival is no good without moral integrity. You survive at *almost* any cost. The *almost* means that indecent methods are outside the range of acceptable cost. If you survive by stepping on others and lose your compassion, then you're not worth saving."

Although he was only a few years older than I, I found myself looking on him as a guide and accepting his teaching unreservedly, whether it was medicine or philosophy or politics. When he entered the ward, faces lit up. Most of our patients were in pain most of the time, and Atsinch's presence seemed to relieve that pain. I think much of it had to do with his moral clarity. I had considered myself a kind of natural democrat. Atsinch was the first one to put into my head ideas about the moral basis of democracy. I don't think I had ever done any serious thinking before I met Atsinch, and the person who starts your mind working in a serious way is someone you remain grateful to. He believed strongly that a man deprived of liberty tends to degenerate morally. That was why he kept stressing the point of survival with decency. He tied that theme into the whole of history. He knew more history of the English-speaking world than I did, and virtually gave me a course in the history of England, which he saw as the story of a people gaining moral strength through the development of institutions to protect and enlarge liberty. I had never really understood before what an *idea* was, in this sense, and it was as if I were taking off dark glasses and for the first time finally getting a clear look at the world. This was an invigorating experience: even in the midst of those terrible surroundings, my outlook on life became more optimistic. I was growing as a human being probably faster than I ever had before, and it felt just fine.

It was a curious experience to be learning medicine as part of my own therapy. Atsinch was always teaching, always showing and explaining, sometimes about what was happening to me, sometimes about other patients. He seemed to be fulfilled by having a pupil—maybe even disciple is not too strong a word.

A day or two after my arrival at Atsinch's hospital, he told me that he

wanted to begin a program of colonic irrigation with potassium permanganate to try to make some headway against my stubborn diarrhea. He
assigned a feldsher to perform the operation, which was to be simply a
matter of a huge, ten-liter enema, to be repeated several times over several
days. I was alarmed at the idea of such a volume of liquid being pumped
into me. Atsinch warned me that it would be very uncomfortable for a
short while, but that I was to expel it all immediately and then I would feel
all right again. He gave me a couple of cigarettes to keep me calm and
occupied throughout the procedure, and the feldsher and I went off to the
toilets to get on with it. I lay down on a bench and lit up a cigarette. The
man inserted the tube, held a funnel well above me, and began to pour. I
could feel the warm water slowly beginning to fill me up. The pressure
became strong after a while and breathing was uncomfortable, so I assumed
that the ten liters must be almost in. Then I heard the door of the toilet
open, and a strange and very commanding voice said, "What is going on
here!"

I turned my head and almost swallowed my cigarette, because three
MGB officers in full uniform were standing there staring at this strange
sight of a man on a bench with a pail draining into his backside. Somehow,
with the effort of turning and the difficulty of breathing and the surprise
of our visitors, I was seized with a sudden fit of coughing. Perhaps I had
swallowed some smoke. The coughing sent terrific spasms into my swollen
abdomen. The contents of my lower bowel started to spurt out the funnel
that the pail was pouring into. The startled feldsher did not have the
presence of mind to lower the funnel. Perhaps it was fastened to the
ceiling, too. It began to spray all over the room, the feldsher, and the MGB
colonels. If I had not been coughing, I would have been seized with laughter, and the laughing impulse probably kept the cough going for a while. I
saw the colonels back hastily out of the room, wiping purple liquid and
brown and yellow fragments off their impeccable uniforms. The feldsher
was terrified, and when I thought about what I had just done, I began to
get a bit scared too.

But nothing came of it. The MGB were a commission of inspection,
looking for malingerers. They acknowledged that they had burst in un-
announced during a medical procedure and took no punitive action. There
was something about Atsinch's presence, though he was a prisoner, that
won respect even from the Organs. And I won respect from the whole
camp, and a title: they called me the Man Who Shit on the Organs.

The next morning Atsinch brought me with him to the dispensary
where the outpatients came, and where everyone hopeful of being admitted
lined up. He began to teach me some rudimentary pharmacology, and I
continued giving injections under his supervision. One of the first patients
we saw that morning was Effroimson. He said all he wanted was aspirin,

and Atsinch told me where to get them and how many to give. When I brought them to Effroimson he leaned close to me for a moment and whispered in my ear, "I don't need these at all. I just wanted to tell you that Gorelov and the Chinese boy tried their escape yesterday. They made it out the gate all right. Then they ran out of gas about thirty miles out on the steppe. The Organs have a small search plane. They found them pretty fast. They are very badly beaten, but people think they'll survive. They've been locked in the BUR. That's all."

He nodded politely to Atsinch and hurried out.

Later I told Atsinch the story. He shook his head. "They may be lucky and they may not," he said seriously. "Usually anyone who tries to escape is shot and they throw his body outside the gates for all of us to look at until it rots. Even if they're not shot, those boys won't have any fun from now on, and they might have been better dead. It's hard to say."

Atsinch thought that I was doing very well with the injections. He asked me if I was squeamish at the sight of blood. I said I didn't think I was, and he said good, that he would like me to start in the operating room, and learn to assist him in surgery, which was his real specialty. Our first case was a mine injury. A man was brought in with a messy head wound. Several chunks of loose ore had fallen on him. There was a lot of blood, scraps of loose flesh, and a soft depression in the skull itself. I found that I was not sickened by this grisly stuff, but I was very excited and nervous. I tried not to show this. Atsinch handed me a straight razor and told me to shave around the wound while he got instruments and dressing ready. My hands were a bit shaky. I had never used a straight razor before, and I didn't want to admit this. The man was conscious but a bit dazed and very frightened. That made two of us. He was seated on a chair beside the operating table, facing the back of the chair and leaning on it. When I first applied the razor it cut into a bit of loose flesh. I don't think he could feel it because the blow must have numbed the whole area, but he sensed my uncertainty and said in a very loud voice, "If you don't know how to do it, don't do it!" His manner was very commanding. I looked to Atsinch for help. He quickly took the razor and I watched him shave the man gently and cleanly in about thirty seconds. Then he took forceps and cleaned out the wound and lifted off several bits of flesh, and put on a dressing and sent the man away to a bed. It took only moments. I had begun already to fancy myself a budding physician, but the amazing skill and sureness of my friend's hands took some of the cockiness out of me. I knew I had a long way to go to achieve *that* kind of perfection, and probably I did not have the talent to begin with. But I was experiencing the joy of learning all the same, and just about the best companionship I had ever known.

Many of the people we operated on had committed *mastyrka*. There were frequent amputations of fingers or toes. Several people came with suppurating arms or legs that showed no wound, and I often talked with them when they were recovering and sometimes got them to admit that they had infected themselves with the thread through the teeth, or in other ways, in order to get a week or two of rest and better food. I asked Atsinch how this met with his standards of morality and survival at *almost* any cost. He laughed. He reminded me that he had taught me my own *mastyrka*, and that as long as it did not mean turning away a person who seriously needed help, he could not fault these people and even admired the ingenuity of some of them. "I do think amputation is foolish, though," he said. "That really does dishonor to the human body. I wish they would stick to infections."

There were too many patients in the hospital most of the time, sometimes sleeping three people in two beds, with one poor guy on the ridge between two cots pushed together. The patients kept the place clean, and we had prisoner orderlies assigned to bring meals and clean out the O.R. slop pails and so on, *pridurki* who were probably stool pigeons, so we were very careful what we said when they were around. They were undoubtedly frustrated at our speaking English all the time. There was a morgue attached to the hospital, and on the third or fourth day Atsinch took me there and began to show me how to make superficial incisions, because the incising and draining of abscesses and phlegmons from *mastyrka* wounds was so common he thought I should be able to do it on my own. He gave me a handbook of anatomy and began to guide me through it.

When a patient died, we were able to conceal it through at least two meal periods and collect his ration to be distributed to all the other patients. Atsinch was very scrupulous about this distribution. Then, when the death could no longer be concealed, Atsinch was required to perform an autopsy and write it up. He insisted I attend. I found the first few unzippings of the abdomen pretty hard to take, especially when one of the first we had to do was a man I recognized from my barracks. But even here Atsinch's presence and his manner put me at ease. He quietly and lucidly described the pathological conditions he discovered, and as he showed me a diseased liver, a tubercular lung, arterial failure in the heart muscle, emboli, sclerotic blood vessels, and all the myriad manifestations of the body's disintegration, my distaste and disgust soon gave way to an intense interest. Atsinch quizzed me regularly on everything he showed me. I had a quick memory and I knew that I was a very good pupil.

All this time my infected arm was kept just active enough to show any visiting MGB, and my colonic irrigations were continued because the diarrhea was very stubborn. My edema began to go down and my muscles to build up. I began exercises again, dynamic tension, and plenty of fast walking up and down the corridors of the little hospital. Atsinch continued to give me intravenous glucose and vitamins, so even though the food ration was not generous I was able to build up some flesh again. When the MVD administrator made his regular visit, I was always in bed looking miserable. Atsinch said that if I was seen making rounds and giving injections, there would be trouble and I would be sent back to the quarry.

Because Atsinch lives so warmly in my memory, and because he was such a strong personality in his quiet and unspectacular way, I find I am writing about the hospital as though he were the only physician, but that was not the case. Albert Feldman was an ophthalmologist who had trained with Filatov, the man who pioneered corneal transplants in the Soviet Union. Feldman had fifteen years for publicly praising religion (he was an orthodox Jew) and criticizing the official atheism. Feldman was jealous of the English connection between Atsinch and me, and tried to get me to teach him English. He shared the view of many prisoners that war between the Soviet Union and the United States was coming soon, and that the United States would send planes to drop arms to all us camp prisoners. He wanted to be ready to meet the Americans in their own language, and he was not alone, although it was forbidden to study a foreign language in camp and English was particularly taboo. Poor Feldman was a little bit nuts and almost blind, ironically, and he kept vocabulary notes scrawled in huge letters on all sorts of odd scraps of paper hanging out of his pockets and stuck inside his glasses and everywhere. Everyone knew that Feldman was studying English. If it had not been Feldman, who was clearly harmless, he might have had his sentence extended and been thrown into hard punishment cells, because studying English meant you were expecting the Americans and were prepared to collaborate with them. Evidently it was different if you already knew English, because Atsinch and I were not bothered. But Feldman escaped punishment only because he was old and feeble and nearly sightless. The stool pigeons saw his vocabulary notes, the MVD saw them. He was never touched. Yet every time he asked me some question about the language he would say anxiously, "For God's sake, don't let anyone find out I am studying English!"

Feldman taught me a trachoma procedure and a bit about general eye care, but I never spent very much time with him.

Westerners find it strange that in a prison camp where life was held in such low value, where people were deliberately overworked, shot without warning if they literally stepped out of line, skull-bashed after they were dead, harassed at every turn of their lives and in every way treated with the utmost contempt, there should have been a hospital at all, and one staffed with dedicated and skilled doctors. I have to explain over and over again that the hospital does not represent any concern over the welfare of the prison inmates. It represents only one concern: that regulations be met. It is laid down in Soviet law that within any prison there must be medical facilities of such and such a character for every so many prisoners; that out of so many prisoners you are permitted a quota of so many bed patients; that a person with a fever of more than 38°C is to be hospitalized, and so on. Someday a bureaucrat who wants to find fault with another bureaucrat may investigate to see whether these regulations are being met—so they are maintained purely for bureaucratic reasons.

My only regret about the hospital was that my comfortable and interesting life there had to come to an end. Despite Atsinch's benign neglect, my arm infection healed itself. I was—by camp standards—manifestly healthy to anyone who cared to look. My edema was gone. My dysentery had stopped. Even my heart sounded better, Atsinch told me with some surprise. He could no longer keep me hospitalized, he said, and he had found out that there was no way possible at the moment for him to get me an official job as a feldsher trainee. So rather than create trouble for both of us, he would discharge me. "You're strong enough to handle a great deal, I think," Atsinch said. "We will see each other often. I'll put on your sheet that you are to report for examination every day for the next two weeks, and we can keep some glucose coming. And vitamins. And then we will see what happens after that. Good luck, my friend."

And I regretfully packed my little sack and went to the administration office to pick up my new barracks and job assignments.

CHAPTER

17

BECAUSE OF THE ENLARGEMENT OF MY HEART, ATSINCH HAD BEEN ABLE TO get me listed as Category Two for the work assignment, so that I would not be sent to the mines even though my buttocks were now perceptible after all that glucose and rest. They reassigned me to the same barracks and the same brigadier, Vtyurin. I had passed the whole summer at the hospital, and now the days were getting short and the nights were very cold. Vtyurin's brigade had been assigned to the railroad station unloading bricks and cement and lumber. It was hard work and *tufta* was difficult to invent. I had lost my friend Gorelov and had not found a way to bribe Vtyurin.

It was not long before my confidence began to slip again. The work was much too hard for the amount of food and rest we got. People died every day, especially the older men. As the weather got colder the rate of deaths increased. We were issued gloves and padded jackets and trousers, but they were badly worn and not much protection as the temperature began to drop. My hands were always cold. At those altitudes, with no bodies of water and no vegetation to moderate the temperature, September slips into winter very quickly. Cold, numbed fingers could not hold onto handles and levers and timbers and crates, and there were many accidents, often fatal. One man was crushed when we were rolling logs off a flat car, using two logs as a ramp. He was buried when twenty or more logs let loose at once and he was not fast enough. The guards shoved his body out of the way on the platform and the blood-stiffened mass was waiting for us to carry it home when night came.

My bowel problems came and went. Friends in the barracks tried to persuade me that it was not fats but the lack of fats that triggered the attacks, and I was given fat bacon from food parcels to try to stabilize myself.

Now it was dark when we stumbled out of the gates at six o'clock in the morning. The convoy stood around with machine guns cocked. The dogs steamed and barked continually. You had to take off your mittens and open all your padded clothing for a search, no matter how cold it got. Many men collapsed in uncontrollable trembling during the search and had to be dragged along by their fellow prisoners until they could get the blood moving again.

Another man was pinned under falling logs, and prisoners were forced to carry the screaming, bleeding wreck back to the camp. The camp was referred to as the Zone. Two guards with dogs were sent to escort the makeshift stretcher party to the Zone. The man had a fractured pelvis and multiple internal injuries. Atsinch kept him alive a few weeks and then he died. Many died easily because they had lost the will to live. My will to live was strong but I was afraid I felt the weakness returning, and I saw so much death that it began to seem a real possibility to me.

The soldiers who guarded us had thick felt boots and sheepskin great-coats over their padded jackets and trousers. They had thick fur mittens. They would steal wood from construction projects and make fires to keep themselves warm, and when it got down below zero degrees Fahrenheit they allowed us to make fires too, if we could scrounge some wood. The guards did not care where the wood came from. You could steal anything as long as it was not a weapon. Everyone took wood back to camp to eke out the meager fuel ration we were allowed for the barracks stove, and the guards always demanded that twenty-five per cent of what we brought back be turned over to them for their private use. They just picked every fourth row and said, "Hand it over." We all complied. If we had refused they would have forbidden us to bring any wood for ourselves; they made that perfectly clear.

I remember a very cold day when we were unloading window frames. Some guards made a fire with the frames, and soon prisoners were doing the same. We burned half a carload of window frames to keep warm that day.

The cold made it harder than ever to get up in the morning. It made us more fatigued because we burned more food to keep warm and had less left for energy, and of course it was terribly hard to walk out of a barracks that was at least above freezing—if only barely—from body heat plus the glow from our poor stove, into the bitter, dust-laden wind or blowing snow at five or ten above zero. People who stayed in bed only minutes after *podyom* had their numbers written down and in the evening they would be told to collect their belongings. If they came back from their stint in BUR, the hard punishment barracks where they were taken, they looked terrible and many had bronchial diseases from the prolonged confinement in those unheated cells. Many simply did not come back. New *etaps* arrived regularly and new living bodies replaced the dead.

People were taken away to BUR when contraband was discovered; this usually meant hardware that had been or could be converted into a knife or any sort of weapon. Many prisoners made little knives from odd bits of steel. Many were caught, either given away by stool pigeons or discovered in the regular searches that took place when we were away at work. The knives were always concealed around the beds, and often found, and their owners taken away. But people kept on making knives for everyday use, not for weapons. In our barracks there was a Moscow lawyer; some of the illiterates could not tell the difference between a lawyer and a prosecutor, and so they took him for a bad guy, the kind who puts you in prison, and treated him very badly. A group of Ukrainians who were convinced he had been a prosecutor decided to fix him. They just got the idea lodged in their minds that he was bad, and they found great satisfaction in his persecution. They made a long, sharp knife and concealed it in his bunk, without his knowing about it, but in a way that a search would easily discover. The plot backfired though. The knife looked so vicious that when it was found the lawyer was thrown into a cell full of hardened prisoners who had tried to escape or refused to work or been caught in anti-Soviet talks; they were leading a relatively comfortable life in the BUR, with no hard labor and occasional extra bread smuggled in by friends from camp. They were delighted to have a lawyer in their midst and made friends with him in return for lessons in the law. When he was finally returned to the barracks, he pleaded with prisoners going to construction projects to get him a piece of steel so he could make another knife. The Ukrainians were totally baffled by the whole thing but they left him alone after that.

One night, just at midnight, I was asleep on my top bunk, with a cloth over my eyes. I felt my leg being tugged. It was an MVD. "You Ess Ya 265?"

I said I was.

"Get your stuff and come with me."

I said, "I haven't done anything!"

"Get your stuff!"

He took me across the frozen compound. Snow was beginning to blow a lot now. I was shivering when we got to the dining hall. Several MVD were there, including an officer. They made me strip and they searched all my clothes and then made me dress again. I kept saying, "What is this all about?"

"You'll see, don't worry," was what they said. It was familiar in a distressing way.

The officer opened a file folder and asked me my prayer. I gave it. "Everything's correct," he said. They took me to the bread window. "Seven days' allotment," the captain said. I was given several loaves of bread, ten lumps of sugar in a newspaper twist, and two salted herrings. I realized this meant *etap*, and I asked where?

"None of your business," the captain said.

Eight more prisoners were brought in. Some were given five days' allotment, some three, some four. I was the only one with seven. I put the numbers together in my mind. Some of them were told they were going to another camp. I deduced I was going to Moscow. This made me terribly excited because I thought perhaps I would be released now. Then I got scared because I also thought they might be taking me there to shoot me. I cannot imagine why I thought that, since shooting was not uncommon right here in Dzhezkazgan.

I was dying for confirmation of my guess. I said quietly to the captain when he came near me, "It's the center for me, isn't it?"

He smiled then. "Good guess," he said.

I said, "In that case I should get the rest of my personal belongings. They're in the hospital." That was a lie but I had to say good-by to Arvid Atsinch.

I was taken across to the hospital. The thin snow had thickened a little. I found Arvid and woke him up and told him. His eyes shone. He said, "Dear Al, dear friend, they're going to let you out! I know it!"

He rustled around and found some tobacco and soap and sausage and matches and made up a farewell package. He embraced me warmly. He said, "Whatever you do, write about us. Tell the world about us. People have to know." I promised I would. The guard cursed and called from the doorway, and I saluted Arvid and went back to the dining hall.

The next time they took us outside it was snowing hard. Making our way from the mess hall to the gate was a struggle. There is a corridor right through the wall beside the gate, with a guardroom built into the wall itself. The others were led past the guardroom and outside, and I was kept back and told to sit in the guardroom. That was fine with me because there was an electric coil in there, a homemade affair of just a few feet of wire hung on a frame, and loose ends plugged into the outlet. When I was finally taken outside in the stinging snow, the other seven had been searched again and were loaded into a van. The van drove off. I stood there with several guards and their machine guns and dogs. I felt quite important somehow, but nobody would tell me what it was all about. The snow was so heavy that the lights along the wall disappeared about a hundred feet away. I began to shiver violently. One of the guards began to curse the van for being late. They took me back into the guardroom. We waited half an hour for the van. The van had a large central space and one cell. They put me in the cell and seven soldiers sat in the larger space. At the station I was put on a Stolypin car attached to a waiting train, and into a cell half the size of a normal Stolypin cell. I was alone in that cell. It had an outer door of solid wood and an inner door of steel bars. The wooden door was kept closed while other prisoners were shoved into the coach. Then, when none of the others could see me, the door was opened again after the train began to roll, and two guards stood outside with a master sergeant and a senior lieutenant. The officer said, "Prisoner, you must understand that you have nothing in common with the general convoy on this coach. I am the only one allowed to speak to you. You must speak to nobody else even if you are spoken to. Whatever you want, call me. If soldiers in the general convoy speak to you, ignore them."

So. There was a special convoy, seven of them as it turned out, assigned to look after me!

Somehow this confirmed my fear that I was going to Moscow to be shot, and I began to shiver again, although the cell was very warm. Soon I talked myself back into a tentative optimism and went to sleep. It was pleasant to sleep in a warm place, I told myself; I was much better off than my poor buddies shivering in the barracks. I like the sound of a train at night, and I had lots of room to stretch out. With various reassuring thoughts, some of them illusions, some real enough, I slept pretty well. In the morning I was not rushed to the toilet. Later when I asked for water it was brought immediately, and when I asked for more they brought it whenever I wanted it. There was no harassment throughout the trip.

My cell was beside the toilet, and I could overhear the other prisoners speculating about my closed door when they were taken to the toilet in the morning. There were two popular rumors, said by their supporters to have come on the best authority. One was that I was an American general captured in Korea. The other was that I was a leader of the Georgian government who had tried to flee the country and was being taken to Moscow to be shot.

At Chelyabinsk they took me in another solitary van to an MGB prison, and marched me across the sidewalk between a double line of soldiers. I heard a voice from someone in the street say, "Look! Numbers!"

I thought, *They haven't seen numbers before!* I let on my sack was heavy and that I had to shift it, and swung it so the big patch on my back would show. A woman's voice said, "Look at that! So young! How terrible he looks!!"

They put me in a solitary cell for a couple of days and brought me a daily food ration, so I was able to keep my travel rations aside.

Back on the train, now that I knew I could go to the toilet whenever I wanted, I treated myself to herring, and drank lots of water.

Finally I was taken off the train in Moscow, early in the morning, and put in a plain gray van with the same kind of solitary cell and again an escort of seven soldiers. I thought, Whatever this is going to be, it's important. I was apprehensive, but not really frightened anymore, just terribly curious to get on with it and find out what it was all about. After a few minutes the van stopped and I heard the familiar doors of Lubyanka. The sound gave me pleasure, strangely enough. The man who searched me was the same blue-chinned man who had searched me in that same room almost two years earlier. He did not recognize me, but he looked at me a bit strangely and took out a razor blade and began to cut the numbers out of my padded jacket. I screamed at him, "What are you trying to do! Don't you know they shoot you for that?" My old sense of mischief was getting back in shape. I said, "You can get in deep trouble for that. That's my secret name. They'll never let you get away with cutting that out!"

The blue-chinned man stared at me in real consternation. He did not say a word but he put the jacket down and left the cell. After a while he came back with an officer. The officer said, "Does the prisoner have civilian clothes?"

"Yes."

"Put those in storage and issue his civilian clothes."

So when they took me upstairs I was back in my navy-surplus gabardine pants, and my poor worn shirt with the epaulets and four bread buttons.

The office they took me to was surprisingly rich in its decoration and furnishing. A thick elegant carpet, good hangings on the wall, excellent polished mahogany furniture. We went through it to an inner office that was even more plush. The guard knocked quietly and then pushed the door open and motioned me into a chair. A man of medium height sat writing at the desk and for a long time he wrote and said nothing. I knew the routine so I waited and studied him. I studied him very carefully—I remember doing it; but I cannot remember his face. I have every reason to remember this man. I can remember his words and the sound of his voice and the clothes he wore, but not his face. I don't know why that is. The other men who interrogated me are very clear. I can see Sidorov's pock-marks as if he were here. I would know him anywhere. But this man—General Ryumin, I would find out later—has no face for me, no features at all, as if a nylon stocking were pulled over his head. Even more vague than that—a faceless face. I can't remember him.

I remember his suit. An elegant German suit. There was a good, broad-brimmed hat on the hatrack with a British label in it. I thought, Time for a tease again. Ryumin was still writing and was quite surprised when I broke the rules and said in a strong voice, "Fifty-eight point ten."

"What's that?" he said.

"Fifty-eight point ten. Section one. Praise of foreign, non-Soviet cloth-ing." I nodded at the hat. "And your suit," I said. I was getting pretty fresh again. "And I bet your tie, as well."

Ryumin got up and came around the desk and stood in front of me. He hit me hard with his palm on one cheek and the back of his hand on the other, with a whipping motion. He said, "I have heard accounts of your cockiness. A repetition is not required."

He went back to his desk.

"Why do you suppose we have summoned you?"

I said I had no idea.

"Well, of course, you have your twenty-five-year term, and in a sense we are through with you. But we are very much interested in the opera-tions of American intelligence here in the capital and throughout the Union. We know most of it, you understand, but we believe you can supply some important links. We do not propose to create any unpleasant-nesses for you. Eventually you will go back to camp. We expect you to talk very freely and have no uneasiness about your American friends, because of course two years have gone by and all the personnel have dispersed to their homes or other postings. If you cooperate fully, we will house you comfortably while you are here, in a cell with congenial com-panions. We will give you an allotment of 200 rubles a month so that you can buy extra nourishment and machine-made cigarettes. So tell me, what do you say? Will you make your best contribution to our investigations in this matter?"

I just stared at him silently.

"Ahh," General Ryumin said. There was a long pause.

"I suppose you are able to recall the Sukhanovka prison," he said.

I had trouble getting my voice to work. I tried not to show it. I said, "Very well, of course."

"Of course," Ryumin said levelly. "Of course you do. I have to con-gratulate you on your passing of that test. You came through your sleep-less nights and those innocuous little beatings with flying colors. I am not being sarcastic. I know of nobody who did as well as you. You have my respect. I know your endurance. . . ."

All this in an almost congenial tone. Which then changed to a very quiet and hard and intense voice.

"I know your endurance and I know how to break it down very rapidly. I have the full authority to use every means and method of physical and mental torture to get your confession. I am quite prepared to use them. I will beat you to death if I do not get your confession. . . ."

Then he leaned back on his chair and resumed the easygoing tone again. It is so strange that I can see his gesture and remember his elaborate, wordy way of speaking and everything he said, but I cannot see his face. He repeated his words slowly but with an almost amiable tone. "I will beat you to death if I do not get your confession."

He put his fingertips together and waited. I was unable to talk at all. I just stared at him until my throat came out of spasm. Then I said, "What confession? I thought you just wanted some links in your picture of United States intelligence in this country."

"Ahhh," said Ryumin. His fingers were still together.

"You mean I am supposed to be one of the links?" I asked him, trying for a lofty tone.

"Ahhh," said Ryumin.

I said, "I will tell you what I know. It's not much. I had nothing to do with intelligence operations. I was a clerk in the consular section. You know that. I am willing to talk but I can't say what I don't know." I was trying hard to keep the fear out of my voice. I was not succeeding perfectly.

"It is altogether up to you," Ryumin said after a while. "I will give you a few days to think it over. Then if you have not decided to cooperate, you and I will pay a visit to Sukhanovka together, and then it will not take very long at all."

He pressed a button. A guard came. I went to my cell in a daze. It was strange that only after I got back to the box cell and went over the encounter in my mind did I realize that there had been another man in the room with us, a colonel of the MGB in uniform. He had been invisible to me for some reason until after I left. Perhaps I imagined him there, although I was to meet him soon after.

The next day at noon I was taken to Ryumin again.

"Will you cooperate?"

"I told everything in my last interrogations. There is nothing else."

"It is your life."

Back to the cell.

Next day at noon.

"Have you thought it over?"

"Of course."

"And you will help us?"

"If I had anything more to tell. But even if I had, I've forgotten a lot in two years. I've been beaten and starved. I've been sick. That doesn't help people remember. What is it you want?"

"The full story of your intelligence work and your espionage work in Moscow."

"There is nothing to tell."

"It's your life."

Back to the cell.

Next day at noon.

"Well? What about it? Nice cell here in Lubyanka? Nice food? Nice companions? Or torture and death at Sukhanovka?"

"Let me ask one question," I said.

"Ask it, then."

"Why? Why do you bring me back? Why all this special treatment on the train? What do you hope to gain?"

"The truth, of course."

"You say you know everything. You only want links."

"Ahh." Ryumin got up and walked back and forth for a minute.

"All right, I'll tell you," he said. "I don't know why I should, but perhaps it will help you to understand you *must* cooperate."

He pressed his fingers together and I believe the faceless face stared at me for some time before he told me.

"We are going to have a public trial. We have ample evidence that the U.S. Embassy has been engaged for a number of years in wide-ranging intelligence activities. We know that you participated in them too. In the trial we will expose certain Soviet citizens who have unfortunately collaborated with you and your colleagues. You know who they are. This has been ordered from the highest level. Do you understand?"

"Don't you think that even if I had anything to tell, knowing about that trial would really shut me up?"

"I don't evaluate the situation in that manner, no. I believe that when you appreciate how irrefutable my orders are, you will understand that you have no way to avoid cooperating. Nobody can resist the highest Soviet power."

I said, "Witnesses at public trials usually disappear afterwards. They are shot so they can never recant."

He looked angry for a moment. Then he said, "Not in your case. I will never need you for a witness. I just need you to lead me to those traitorous officers. And to give me material to flesh out the skeleton we already understand very well."

I thought about that for a moment. I began silently to try concoctions that might save my skin but would never be credible outside Ryumin's office, not in the States, anyway. Something so obviously phony that my people would know what was happening. I was not thinking clearly. I said, "I really have told you everything I can think of."

"It is not good enough," Ryumin said flatly.

I tried a last, hopeless gambit.

"If you're worried about my phony signature on all the protocols, I'll sign my right signature. Would that help? Or I'll make something up if you want. But I don't know anything that I haven't told you."

Ryumin flew up out of his chair and yelled at me. "We have no desire to be misled by your phantasmagoric inventions! We want the truth and we will have the truth!" He pressed the button. He jammed it hard with his finger, jammed it repeatedly, so that his finger bent and went white at the knuckle. He said, very hard, "So! I will see you in Sukhanovka! You can blame only yourself for what happens next!"

There was snow at Sukhanovka when I got out of the van. My cell was number 18. I truly believed when I came into it that it would be my last home in the world. I smoked heavily for the first few minutes until I remembered that the window would be open only twenty minutes a day. I thought, I can save my tobacco for the interrogation room. It was some sort of defense against the realities that must be waiting for me in that room. I was deeply, terribly afraid.

It must have been eight thirty or a quarter to nine when the cell was opened. "Prepare for interrogation."

I sensed a deep, deep inner fear. I suddenly found the strength to look at myself and see that I was on the point of giving in. I said, "No, Alex. Never."

The fear persisted.

I said, "Try! You must! You've done it before! It can't be worse! *Try!*"

Somehow I pushed the fear back and brought some determination forward. I walked out of the cell quite steadily. By the time I arrived at the door of the interrogation room I had summoned enough willpower and energy to achieve what I wanted to achieve, and when I walked through that door I had covered my face with a large and radiant smile.

CHAPTER

18

GENERAL RYUMIN WAS NOT IN THE ROOM. THE MAN WAITING FOR ME WAS the same MGB colonel I had failed to see in Ryumin's office four days ago. He had a high balding forehead and a chunky, humane face. He said, "Please sit down. My name is Colonel Chichurin. I will be your interrogator."

I caught myself being astonished. I thought, Watch it, kid. These guys are full of tricks. There's a horseshoe in the glove somewhere.

Chichurin's technique, however, was consistent with his appearance and his manner. He spoke quietly, never got angry, and never hit me. He began with a lot of general questions about life in America and about my political attitudes. He told me several times that I was in for a lot of trouble, but in a kind of gentle, scolding way. We covered a lot of the old ground, and it was clear that he was familiar with the protocols from my time with Sidorov and Kozhukhov. Sometimes, for days and nights and days, we would discuss world history, psychology, medicine, anything but the issue of my espionage and intelligence activities. I could not tell whether he was stalling, waiting for me to take the initiative, or just trying to wear me down. I could not figure it. At the beginning of each session he would say, "Are you going to confess today?"

I would say, "There is nothing to confess." The rest of the session was small talk.

There was no sleep except Saturday and Sunday nights, and I very soon began to go unconscious and fall off the chair again. I had lost the knack of sleeping while sitting up. There was no way to steal sleep in the cell, and Chichurin never knocked off early. He once complained about my keeping him from seeing his family, and about how tiring it was to sleep on the couch in the interrogation room.

So it seems that several weeks went by uneventfully, except that I acquired bruises from falling off the chair, and my mind was pretty confused much of the time. I started counting steps again. I remember crossing Spain. I made a scratch calendar on the wall, but I was often too vague to remember whether I had marked it or not, and so sometimes I am sure it was marked twice or maybe three times in a single day, and sometimes not at all.

I had lost the urgent sense of fear, but I still felt that the sleeplessness and the tiny meals would finish me off. I knew I did not have the resources that had kept me alive though the first session in this hellish place. It was just a matter of time.

One night when I arrived in the room Chichurin brought out a photograph of Michael Kovko. "Do you recognize this man?" I did not bat an eye.

I said, "He looks familiar. I don't know. My memory is poor. I might have met him sometime. I'm very confused."

Chichurin purred at me. "Now I am sure you know him very well, don't you?"

"I can't say. I don't know."

Chichurin took the photograph back. "We know all about your trip to Kiev with Dina, you know. You might as well admit to it."

"Oh, *that!*" I said. "Nothing wrong with that. Just a holiday."

"Please!" Chichurin said, not really loud, but firmly. "Please do not try my patience! I am a very patient man. This was a clandestine trip. We know that, and we know that you bribed a trainman for a place on the train. We know that you spent two weeks in Kiev and in the countryside around it, and we know that your host was Michael Kovko, and that he was a leader in the Ukrainian underground movement. Now. Don't you think you'd better tell us how you went there to organize U.S. support for the movement? We know that was your purpose."

I told him everything about the trip except the shooting incident and Khrushchev's bodyguards. I told him about Michael Kovko's association with my father in the States. He kept insisting that we had gone into the country in order to have privacy for our illegal plotting, and I kept insisting that it was for picnics.

He really got quite irritated as I kept telling him the truth. He *believed* I was on a mission. I could tell from his attitude. He just thought I was a stubborn holdout. He said, "Don't think you're protecting Kovko, you know. We've got him, and he's already sentenced, so don't hold back on his account."

He finally gave it up.

I realized, after many weeks, that Chichurin was a kindly man at heart and had little stomach for his work. Twice when he came back from his midnight dinner break he brought me bread and butter and smoked sausage. I still had tobacco, and when I asked him for a bit of paper to roll a smoke he always got out a pack of Astra cigarettes and gave me one. When he went to dinner he never made any special comments to the guard about watching me, and I often stole a half hour's sleep, which probably saved my life. Later in the interrogation he would doze off at night and so would I, and when he woke he never got angry, he just told me to wake up now, and went on with the questioning. He told me he had been in

SMERSH—counterintelligence—during and since the war, and that he had only recently been seconded to the MGB. I came to believe that he was sincere and loyal to his country, and trying to do his best to get this stubborn spy to spill his story.

Despite Chichurin's easy ways, I had no real store of stamina to resist starvation and sleep deprivation. And so I was in pretty bad shape after a few months. I talked to myself a lot, and hallucinated vague things, and went completely blank for long periods that are of course completely lost to me now.

One day a fly appeared in my cell. It must have been getting on into April, with warmer weather that brought out the flies from crevices in the stone. For hours I watched and waited with a kind of desperate patience. I wanted to capture the fly. For company.

I got her. I ripped a thread out of my towel and somehow, with slow painstaking motions, I tied a loop around one of her wings. I called her *her* because I think she had ovipositors on the end of her abdomen, but she may have been a drone, if flies have such things, or a worker. The important thing for me was to have someone to talk to. I would give her some of my sugar in a drop of water and praise her when she took it. With the thread on her she was unable to fly, and when I was taken to interrogation I tossed her on the window. She was invisible against the pattern of wire mesh in the cloudy glass, and they never found her when they searched the cell. But they could see me talking to her through the cell and occasionally I would hear the door being unlocked and get her hidden in time before they burst in.

"What are you doing?"

"Nothing."

"You're doing something strange, what is it?"

"I don't know. I'm too confused."

But one day when I came back from interrogation the fly was gone, and I was called to the block commander's office and given a long, moralistic lecture about my terrible behavior, a talk in which no mention was made of the fly. When I would say, "What is it you're complaining about?" he simply said, "You know! You know! And you must never do such a terrible thing again!"

Every ten days I was shaved with dull hair clippers, face and head. I collected soap after my baths, and made a large ball of it. Every few weeks the ball would disappear and I would start again. I thought about my suicide plan again, and began to collect toilet paper. I think I was not very serious about the suicide at this point, but I kept it as an option.

I became terribly agitated when Chichurin told me that the Organs were planning to arrest my parents if I did not confess. I learned only long after that he was lying: they were already in prison. But of course I had no way of knowing that. I told him I would confess anything, make up anything to save my parents, but he got really angry for a while and said that it had to be the truth. Fabrication would not do. He was serious. Again I tried to think of fabrications that would stand up to scrutiny.

I was wearing down, and the terrible thing was I didn't care. I had stopped smiling long ago. My sense of humor had vanished. I noticed that it had gone and felt sad.

Chichurin seemed to be more and more agitated. He smoked a great deal, and kept giving me cigarettes and urging me to hurry up and confess.

Then one night he just shook his head and sighed when I came in and finally told me that General Ryumin was coming that night. He smoked nonstop and coughed a great deal. A guard came and said something to him. He sent me away with two guards. By now they had to hold me up anyway; I was not able to walk by myself. We came to a room with the number 13 on it. I was too stupefied even to think at the time how corny that was. Inside there was a thick Persian carpet with a thinner runner lying on it in the middle of the room. There were dark stains on the runner. The window was covered with very heavy draperies. There was a wall of exquisite walnut panels behind the desk, with a thin slit running up it and light coming through. When I sat down and tilted my head sideways I saw that there was another room behind with a sink and a faucet.

Then the wall moved. In fact it was an electric sliding door. Ryumin came out chewing on some snack, and the wall closed up again. He said, "Well, well, so here you are."

Chichurin came in, and Ryumin told him to close the window and pull the drapes all the way across. He said, "Would you like to change your mind and talk?"

I was dull and indifferent. I simply repeated that I had nothing to say. He opened a drawer and took out a rubber club about two feet long and an inch thick, with a leather strap which he turned around his wrist. He said, "I think this will advance the process of changing your mind. Now cries will rise up to heaven. Chichurin, are you sure the window is secure? Prisoner, take off your trousers and lie on the floor."

I felt no fear. I think I believed I would feel nothing. I had felt so little for so long, except dull aching fatigue, that I could not believe it would hurt that much. I did not take my trousers off and Ryumin did not make an issue of it. I did not lie on the floor. I stayed on the chair, dull and inert. "Do you just sit there?" Ryumin yelled. He knocked me off the chair with a blow to the head. It hurt like hell. I roared as I fell on the floor. Ryumin yelled again, "Aha!"

He told Chichurin to sit on my legs. He said, "I have a Cossack method of beating. I draw as I hit. You will never have felt such pain! Ever!"

I vowed to count every blow and exact revenge on this man for each of them. But counting was not possible.

The thing was terrible. I broke my fingernails on the rug. No buttocks, the blows went right on the sciatic nerve, blew up inside my head, all over my body, total explosions of pain. I passed out.

Water splashed on my face. A stethoscope on my chest. "How's his heart?"

"I think you may continue, General."

"Prisoner, will you confess now?"

"To what, for God's sake! Anything, just tell me what! Please tell me. I have nothing to—"

The terrible explosions again. I have no idea how many blows. Only total pain throughout my body, and the broken fingernails. I must have yelled but I have no memory of it. When I came to again they were sitting on chairs. Somehow I knew it was three o'clock in the morning. "Take him away," Ryumin said. As I was dragged out he said, "We will meet again."

I had three hours to sleep but there was no way to escape the pain. They put up the bed at six and I was left all day in the cell.

I made up a song, a kind of persistent doggerel song about all the terrible things that were happening to me. I sang it to myself all day in a low whisper. I walked a great deal because my buttocks were too sore to sit. They burned. When I finally dared to feel them with my fingers they were swollen and ridged with welts. I was shivering from fright at the thought of being called again to Ryumin, but I found that if I sang determinedly, and as loudly as I could without being heard, I could stop the shivering.

For weeks I had been constipated. Suddenly as the evening came on and I knew that nine o'clock was approaching, I felt a sharp pain in my belly. I scarcely made it to the pail. I realized that I was utterly, totally terrified deep within me. I began to laugh uncontrollably. The guard opened the slot peephole and yelled at me to stop. I could not. He ran off and came back with the duty officer. They slapped my face until I shut up.

At nine thirty they came for me again. I could not walk at all. They dragged me to Chichurin's room. He said, "Don't you think you had better confess now? You don't want any more of *that*, do you?"

"Please! Please! Don't let him do that anymore," I pleaded with him. "I have told you everything I know. There is nothing more. Please! *Please!!!*"

Ryumin sent for us at midnight and they began again. I cried and pleaded and lost consciousness several times. A so-called doctor applied a stethoscope and told Ryumin he could go on. Then unconscious again, and somehow back in the cell, lying on my stomach, drifting in and out of oblivion, then fiery pain, then oblivion again. I tried to take my trousers off in the morning, to examine myself. They were glued to my wizened buttocks with blood and the slightest attempt to move them was exquisitely agonizing, so I gave it up.

At some point a woman doctor examined me in a clinic of some kind; I remember that she had a white coat. She must have got my trousers off somehow. She was not the one who came to the sessions with a stethoscope. She said, with some shock, "How did you get all those lacerations on your buttocks?"

I flew into a rage. I said, "I sat on a red hot stove, you ignorant bitch!"

She just pursed her lips and started pouring on iodine, and then taped on dressings.

They left me alone for a while. A few days, or perhaps only one day. I was fuzzy and blanked out most of the time. Chichurin started at me again, and for a month or so I saw him every night and spent all day in the cell. I got a bit of sleep, I think. I must have, or I would have died. But not much. The whole period is blurred. Chichurin pleaded with me to try to remember, to withhold nothing, to do anything to avoid the terrible beatings. I am sure he was sickened by my condition. After some weeks he said one night, "You are a fool. Ryumin is coming back."

I was not surprised. I sat in terrible silence all night while he pleaded and urged me to talk, numb with waiting.

The swellings had almost gone but the skin was still tender when Ryumin began again. After the first blow I knew I was through. I screamed, "All right. I'm ready. I'll confess!"

He kept hitting me.

I screamed, *"I'm ready!!! I'm ready to confess!!!"*

He yelled back, "Start confessing then!" And hit me again.

I said, "Please! I need time to collect my thoughts."

He stopped hitting me. I was dragged to another room. They left me with a guard for about forty minutes. I worked my mind harder than I ever had. It had to be a story about Bob Dreyer and myself and that George Tenno they had been talking to me about before. When they came I told them Dreyer and I had been trained together and Dreyer had tried to recruit Tenno. I made up code names for both of us. Ryumin and Chichurin both took notes like mad. I tried to surround the fantasies with as many facts as possible, to make them sound plausible, but I put in false dates so that if it came to trial everyone would know that it was a lie. I had nothing to go on except the questions they had put about Dreyer and Tenno and a few others, and it was hard work.

They seemed extremely pleased. After an hour or so Ryumin said, "Take a rest. Have a smoke."

He gave me cigarettes, a whole package, and a box of matches. He pressed a button and sent a guard for food. The guard came back surprisingly soon, with a full plate of excellent roast meat and vegetables and a big mug of real tea and some white bread and butter. When I had told everything I could safely fabricate they asked no more questions. They praised me warmly. Chichurin gave me three packs of Astras and told the guards to take me to my cell.

I was allowed to sleep all night. For ten days I had all the sleep I wanted. The food was not increased, but because I could rest I seemed less starved. My welts began to heal. I saw no one but the guard.

Then one night, "Prepare for interrogation."

I felt a twinge of apprehension. Suppose there had been a fault in my fabrications?

At least it was not room 13 I was taken to. But when Chichurin came in, his face looked genuinely anguished.

"You are in worse trouble than ever, now," he said gravely. He said nothing more, and I didn't ask. I was too frightened to speak.

At midnight we went to room 13. Ryumin came in. "You tried to cheat us, did you!" He knocked me flat. He danced around me with the rubber truncheon. "Confess that you lied!" he screamed. After two or three of those explosive blows, I said, "Yes! Yes! I lied. I don't have any truth!"

He kicked me in the jaw. There was a tearing pain right through to the back of my neck. A stream of blood poured out of my mouth onto the carpet. I looked at it in horror. My eyes were blurred with tears, but I could see that there were two teeth on the stained runner.

When I came to I was very fuzzy. I remember that I said, "All right, I will tell the truth. Everything. But I need to get rest first because my mind is blanking out." Ryumin brandished the club. He said, "Now!"

I had spent those days in the cell working up a new story. They did not like the story. They sent me to wait in another room. Then I was dragged back to 13 and the beatings began again. I was sure I would die. I was rolling about so hard to escape the blows that Ryumin hit himself on the leg and swore and hopped up and down and then came at me with new fury. Twice I rolled too far and the truncheon landed on my belly. There was a ripping sensation and a deep pain that would not go away, as though there was a continually crushing force on my testicles.

I screamed out a third version. Out of some desperation I found another way to try to be credible. The blows stopped; I passed out several times. Each time a feldsher listened to my heart. At 3 A.M. he said it was too weak to continue. Water was splashed on my face. I felt a needle in my arm and the pressure of some injected fluid. And then I found myself bleeding on the floor of cell 18. My stomach was hugely swollen. I had a high fever and my pulse rate seemed to be terrifyingly fast, perhaps 200. I looked at my stomach. The tight, distended skin was blotched with blue and purple. I was shivering out of control. I said, "I'm going to die now." But I banged on the door and yelled for a doctor. It was the woman. I remember that her face looked very worried. She went away. I heard the motor of a van. A stretcher came with a lot of men. I screamed when they put me on it buttocks down. They rolled me over.

I woke up in Butyrka. A tube was taped to my arm. I passed out again. I woke up again after several hours. I was stiff in every joint and my skin felt like parchment that would tear if I moved. I saw a face with long whiskers in another bed. Then I went off again.

After a while I came to again. I began to examine my body. I had a terrible shock when I looked between my legs. My scrotum was swollen to the size of a child's football. It was like two fists in a bag. A part of my intestines had descended into it.

The man with the whiskers was an Austrian colonel. He told me that I had been given huge injections and continuous intravenous feeding. He himself had suffered a mild heart attack during interrogation. He had been brought back from camp for questioning on some details about the Austrian military, some things that had been missed years before when he was first kidnapped. The interrogation was easy and friendly, but he had developed high blood pressure and then had the slight attack.

After two weeks, during which I slept almost all the time, I was taken in a wheelchair to an interrogation room. Chichurin was there. He seemed very anxious. His sympathetic manner had gone. He was distracted and very formal. He gave me a fifteen-page protocol to read. Out of all my fabrications he had written up a confession. It was cleverly done and I could see that it would probably withstand scrutiny and satisfy Ryumin.

Chichurin had composed it himself. There was a litany that went: Q. "Is it true that prior to your arrest the American intelligence service was preparing to spring you into action?" A. "Yes." Q. "Were you assigned to strike up acquaintances with military personnel?" A. "Yes." Q. "For what purpose?" A. "For the purpose of persuading them to divulge information." Q. "On what subjects?" A. "On Moscow defense installations."

And so on.

Q. "Is it true that it is only because of the vigilance of Soviet security operatives that you have been prevented from carrying out your assignments?" A. "Yes, that is very true."

Half a page or more in praise of the MGB.

I handed it back. I said, "That's very interesting but I'm not going to sign it."

Chichurin said with a sigh, "Then it will all start again, you know."

I said, "When is the trial?"

He shook his head. "There isn't going to be a trial."

"Why not?"

He just shook his head.

"Why do you need this confession, then?"

For the first time he became really violent in his manner. "Sign it, you stupid son of a bitch! Sign it or Ryumin will be here tonight, hospital or no hospital! Sign it! Sign it! Sign it!"

I thought, *I have twenty-five years anyway.*

I thought, *No one will ever believe it anyway.*

I thought, *I am never going to allow myself to be tortured again.*

I signed. *What the hell. They've got me anyway. Why didn't I do it long ago, and avoid all that pain?*

Then I thought, *No, Alex, you gave them one hell of a run! And all they've got for their trouble is a pack of lies that nobody will ever believe.*

And besides, they've lost interest.

It was true. A month ago they had been slavering over this show trial. Now they had lost interest. I could tell from Chichurin's manner that something had changed, something had happened, perhaps another purge in his own bailiwick, perhaps someone has fallen out of favor, perhaps . . .

Chichurin told me at this point that Ryumin was the immediate number two to Viktor Abakumov, the minister of state security. Abakumov, of course, was Lavrenti Beria's right-hand man. While I was rereading the protocols two more MGB officers came in and whispered to Chichurin. I overheard the name of Ryumin and of Minister Abakumov. There was reference to a telephone call. Chichurin picked up the protocols in an absent-minded way and walked out of the room in a daze. I never saw him again.

It had been a relief to sign. It was over. Maybe I could get back to—I laughed a bitter laugh at the word that had come to mind—my *comfortable* life in camp. I thought of Atsinch, and assumed I would see him again, because it would be a long time before I could be let out of the hospital.

For a while I was in an *etap* cell with about a hundred others awaiting transfer. One tall man in a ragged army uniform could not straighten his knees when he walked. They had hung him over a trapeze device, as a torture. They call it a triangle. It works in some way to dislocate the knee joint. He is the only person I have ever met who survived Sukhanovka.

This time the train went through the Urals by a different route and we stopped at Sverdlovsk. I was put in a cell with twelve or fifteen older *urki*. I was afraid that they would take what little I had left in my sack, including my good trousers, but when they saw the black Dzhezkazgan prison uniform with the numbers they treated me with respect and consideration. They had heard about Dzhezkazgan. They seemed more politically aware in this summer of 1951 than Valentin and his cohort a year ago. We had many thoughtful discussions about the system. They were more cynical. One had SLAVE OF STALIN tattooed on his forehead. STALIN had been partly obliterated but was still legible.

After Sverdlovsk there was a brief stop at Petropavlovsk, and then the train arrived at Dzhezkazgan in the sweltering heat. I was weak and still in pain but my morale was good. I was certain I had seen the last of interrogation rooms and the last of Moscow's prisons. I began to wonder about the many friends I had made in those few short months in camp, Arvid Atsinch especially, of course, but also Effroimson and Feldman and Victor.

The *etap* was a small one. The few dozen others on the train were marched away from the station and a single guard waited with me. Soon the van came along. As I was helped into it, I had the strange awareness that for a moment I had found myself thinking I was back "home."

CHAPTER

19

I WAS DISAPPOINTED TO FIND MYSELF IN A STRANGE CAMP. IT WAS STILL Dzhezkazgan, of course, and I had no good reason to think that of the six compounds in the area I had any proprietary rights over the one I had been in. But I was disappointed anyway. This one was several miles from the first compound, and I had to resign myself to the probability that I would not see any of my old friends again.

In the quarantine barracks I met a young Muscovite with whom I felt comfortable and friendly from the first moment. His name was Edik L. He had been a student at Moscow University. Once in a study hall he overheard a group at a nearby table telling some of the anti-Soviet jokes that have always been around underground among students in Russian society. Example: A rabbit is caught trying to flee across the border. The MGB interrogate the rabbit. "Why did you want to leave the Soviet Union?" his interrogator asks him.

"Because," says the rabbit, "I heard that all camels are going to be castrated."

"But you are a rabbit!" remonstrates the interrogator.

"Sure," says the rabbit, "but just try to prove that after they've castrated you for being a camel!"

This is the kind of thing these students were giggling over at a table near Edik's. Three of that group were arrested soon after because the fourth was an MGB informer. Edik was arrested for *not* having informed.

He was state's witness on the first day of the trial. The next day they tried him. Fifty-eight point twelve. Failure to inform the authorities. Twenty-five years.

They brought a sort of personnel questionnaire around the quarantine barracks one day. I was determined to try for a *pridurki* job if possible, and failing that, a skilled job of any kind that would keep me out of the mines and away from the quarry. Conservation of energy is the first prison law, Orlov had told me.

So on the forms where my profession or trade was to be entered I put down boldly: PHYSICIAN. They had no way to check. Then, since we were offered three options, I put down MECHANIC as number two, and out of some strange whim I can't explain now, except that it sounded like a nice, soft, sit-down job, LOCKSMITH as number three. I did know a bit about cars, which justified the mechanic, but I had never seen the inside of a lock.

Edik put down ELECTRICIAN as his first choice.

Through the grapevine we found out quickly that our camp was near a village called Krestovaya, and that it was one of three under the same box number and administration. Next to our camp was a KTR or *katorzhane* compound, reserved for people sentenced to extreme hard labor, most of them war criminals, which certainly meant they had been captured by the Germans, and probably meant that some of them had collaborated. Their numbers on the white patches were all prefixed with KTR. I still had СЯ265.

On the second Sunday we were released from quarantine. I said so long to Edik and went out in search of the hospital before I was even assigned a barracks number.

Like the first camp compound, my new prison home had stone walls two meters thick and nearly six meters high. About one and a half meters from the wall there was a barbed-wire fence almost as high as the wall. Sloping down from the top of the fence on the inside was a kind of tent of barbed wire, which stretched to the ground at a point about nine or ten meters from the bottom of the fence. Two and a half meters farther in from the barbed-wire tent was a single thick wire on short posts, marking a forbidden area between the compound and the barbed wire. This area was known as the fire zone, and we were repeatedly told that anyone stepping over the wire into the fire zone would be assumed to be attempting escape and would be shot without warning from the watchtowers. In the space between the wall and the barbed-wire fence another thick wire was strung about five feet above the ground from wall to wall around the camp. Every night German shepherds were leashed to the wire as an additional precaution against escape.

Even if you came within a few feet of the fire zone, the guards on the watchtowers might yell at you and point their guns. Occasionally, it was said, a watchtower marksman had been known to relieve the monotony of his job by shooting down a prisoner who had strayed close enough to the wire for the guard to be able to tell his commanding officer that he had warned him to stop running into the fire zone before he shot him.

There was a closed gate in the wall between us and the KTR camp next door, which was really part of the same complex, and although there was no barbed wire along this dividing wall, the fire zone wire was there and the same warning applied.

The hospital was near the main gate, adjacent to the mess building. I made myself known to the physician in charge, a man name Shkarin, and within a few minutes he had brought his two colleagues, Kask and Adarich, to meet me and to examine me. I was still in appalling condition. They needed no excuses or *mastyrka* to hospitalize me. They were interested in my description of the training Atsinch had given me, and discussed among themselves the possibility of adding to that training enough to qualify me as a feldsher because they badly needed additional help.

Kask was an Estonian who was known to everyone in his native country for the daily medical broadcasts he had made on the radio. He was the laboratory man: blood tests, urine tests, pathology, and so on. Kask did many of their autopsies. He spoke good English and on that basis we became friendly right away. The third man, Adarich, was a surgeon from Minsk who had been in camp since 1934. He was impressed by my scrotal hernia, but warned me that surgery might be a mistake until I was a lot stronger, and suggested I try to live with it for the time being. In addition to the hernia and general debility, I had an exudative pleurisy and a fever of nearly 39°, so I qualified for admission.

There was a surgery, a lab, a therapy ward, some offices, and an out-patient clinic and dispensary. And a morgue. The hospital served all three camps in our group—our own, the KTR next door, and a ZUR two kilometers away, which was the Zone for hardened escapists, persistent malingerers, and so on. While I was mending in that hospital, Adarich began where Atsinch had left off, and on days when I was feeling up to it I went to the morgue with him and learned how to make an appendectomy incision and how to suture it up, how to amputate toes and fingers, which was common procedure in the winter because of frostbite, and so on.

I got to know the hospital supply clerk, Kuznetsov. He complained that his greatest fear was that he would be given a sentence for theft on top of his political sentence. His spoon supply always dropped by the exact number of patients discharged on any given day, and he had a hard time replacing the spoons. He would buy them from prisoners for bread and sugar and other supplies, if indeed any prisoners had spoons to sell. Spoons are never issued in camp. You use your fingers or drink from the rim of the plate. Kuznetsov was sure that he would be caught short of spoons one day, or caught buying them with hospital rations, and that would be the end of him.

I resolved to steal a spoon too. I remembered my earlier notion of somehow getting into the spoon business if I could only get a supply. Bribe a guard in standard "colored" fashion? Imitate my friend the *pakhan?* I did not know what it would be, but I had identified one more critical shortage and I was sure I could make something out of it.

I was discharged from the hospital after two weeks. Adarich the surgeon said he was trying to find a way to get me assigned to the hospital, but he warned that it might take some time. In the meantime I was put on a construction brigade, working on buildings in a wired-off open zone not far from Krestovaya village. It was called DOZ, meaning a woodworking plant, although many other components of buildings besides doors and windows and furniture were made there.

At first it was very hard going. The days were characterized by a continuous hot, dry wind that blew dust and sand everywhere. Many of the prisoners were badly choked up by the dust. It settled on buildings and seeped through cracks into the barracks. It turned everyone's short-cropped hair gray whenever their hair was not covered by the regulation cap. It obliterated the numbers within two or three days. At the gates of the camp as you went out each morning there were always two or three men with pots of black paint waiting to touch up your number. If a man was a painter or an artist by profession, he was assigned to paint numbers in the morning and to decorate the officers' quarters with paintings of ruby sunsets or waterfalls or ships at sea by day. I regretted my inability to draw a straight line, let alone a picture.

My brigadier was an easygoing guy and had the *tufta* well organized at the DOZ. When he saw how feeble I was, he helped me to goof off for the first week or so, until I felt better. So I prowled around and acquainted myself with everything that went on in the DOZ. I watched men operating metal lathes and thought that that looked like a soft touch. I watched the arc welders, and it looked as if you could make a few rubles or extra grams of bread if you could think of some things to manufacture. I saw the locksmith's shop, full at the time regrettably, but it looked like a soft touch too.

I saw that there was a very good supply of aluminum in the cables the arc welders used. I thought that if I could learn how to melt it down, I might be able to mold some spoons. I did a little talking around to some prisoners who seemed to know what they were doing with metal, and picked up some ideas without giving my own away. I also found some good hiding places where you could spend part of a day without being rousted out to work, and some other hiding places where you could conceal tools or bits of scrap aluminum wire.

I built two shallow boxes for my foundry, stole myself some scraps of aluminum wire, fashioned a rough crucible from some thin steel from the stove works, scrounged some good charcoal and diesel fuel to fire my forge, and was ready to get into business.

The next day, which would have been two weeks or more after starting work at the DOZ, I brought my spoon with me when we were marched to work, and got some sand and cement and began to experiment with a foundry mold, using the spoon as my pattern. Now, I knew almost nothing about foundry work. It was like starting from scratch. If I had not been so determined to get into business for survival reasons, I would never have stuck with it. The bottom of the mold was all right. I would press the spoon into the moist sand and put the open-ended second box with guiding sticks on the sides on top of the first box, fill it with sand, push a stick through the sand (through which I planned to pour the molten aluminum later), compact the sand so that it would not fall out when I lifted the second box, remove the spoon and put it back in place. Of course the sand did collapse and fall out as well. Finally, whether by trial and error or divine inspiration, I hit upon a mixture of sand, cement, and soot that worked beautifully. The sand stayed in place! I melted a few grams of aluminum in my little crucible and when the first spoon came out of the mold, covered with grains of sand, rough and ugly, like a spoon that had measles, I was as proud as a new father. I found some emery cloth and polished it until it was perfect. The next morning before breakfast I took it to Kuznetsov. He was delighted. It was perfectly obvious that this was not one of his own spoons he was buying back. Two patients had died in the night and he had their bread ration. He gave me a whole ration, 450 grams, and said he could use all the spoons I could bring him. I was in business.

Soon I learned to line the sand mold with a dusting of powdered ash, which prevented the sand from pimpling the spoons, and then I made a two-spoon mold, and was able to turn out two spoons almost every day.

One of the spoons I traded to an ex-German war prisoner for his German water flask. Then I sold spoons to Kuznetsov for cooking oil, which was always easy for him to dispense into my flask. We had such a terrible shortage of oils and fats in camp that people were always very tired from lack of calories. I soaked my bread in cooking oil and found it very tasty then, though it would not have seemed very good two years earlier. The body seems to be able to create a taste for substances that it needs.

One day I got into conversation with one of the painters at the gate who were always there to touch up faded number patches. His name was Pavel Voronkin. He had gone to China as a boy when his father was working on the Russian railroad to China in the early thirties. Like

Gorelov's Chinese friend, Pavel, now a grown man and established artist, was arrested after he came back in response to an official invitation to repatriate. Voronkin had casually told a Russian neighbor once about an American movie he had seen and been impressed by, a war movie, I think it was, starring Robert Taylor. There may have been a misunderstanding, or perhaps there was not, but in any case when he saw the protocol containing his charges and his conviction, it was for associating with a known U.S. agent, one R. Taylor! Later on in my development of the spoon business, after I had made and sold several hundred spoons and the market began to go a bit soft, I got Voronkin to sculpt a nude woman with provocative breasts and buttocks and belly, just the size of a spoon handle. He made it in wood, and I fastened a spoon bowl to it and began to cast erotic spoons, which sold very well.

It was not possible for my soft brigadier to protect me indefinitely. It would not have been fair to the others, he said, because *tufta* could stretch only so far. I would have to do some work. This turned out to be carrying stone for the masons, and it nearly killed me. I had forgotten how weakened I was. I knew I had to find something else as soon as possible. So I approached the brigadier in the machine shop, a man named Zyuzin. He was an accomplished guitarist, whose bunk was close to mine. I visited him in the evening and listened to him play the guitar. I expressed a strong interest in the music. I asked him to teach me to play. He was pleased and flattered. He began to teach me simple chords so that I could play what he called "dog waltzes": rudimentary tunes like "Dark Eyes"—just the chords, of course.

After we had made friends over the guitar, I expressed a sort of offhand interest in joining his brigade. He liked me very much by now, and thought the idea of my moving into his brigade was just fine; we could do music together every night and so on, and so somehow he was able to arrange the transfer. I told him I knew everything about machine shops.

My first job was threading nuts, big ones. This involved turning heavy taps into the rough-cast blank of the hexagonal nut, which was held in a vise. It looked easy and was terribly hard. But even before I had to tackle the hard steel with my weak hands, I ran into trouble when Zyuzin sent me to the supply room to get the taps for the nuts. "Go get the *metchiki i vorot*," he said—"the taps and a tap-handle." I heard *metki u vorot*, which means "the marks at the gates." It made no sense. The supply room was baffled and sent me to the paint shop. They were no help. I tried the blacksmith shop. No help. I finally had to admit to Zyuzin that I couldn't find any marks at the gates. He thought that was pretty funny. "But don't be embarrassed, Alexander Mikhailovich. I knew you were putting on an act with all your fancy words about your machine shop experience. You'll learn enough here. I'll help you, too. Just be honest with me from now on so I can keep you out of trouble."

So that was all right.

But the job itself was a lot less all right than I had hoped. Of course it was much better than lifting heavy blocks of stone. But the norm for a nut tapper is 185 nuts a day. They are big nuts, over an inch thick. You wind the tap into them by hand, cutting through the heavy blank. It takes several cuts, starting with a coarse tap and finishing with a fine one. This means that, working nonstop with about ten or eleven actual working hours at the vise, if you could stand that, which nobody could, you would have to turn out a nut about every three minutes. It takes all the strength a weakened man can muster just to turn the tap. The first day on the job I made thirty-five nuts. The second day fifty nuts. I broke a tap at least twice an hour at first. I got blisters on my hands. My arms and back ached all night. And most seriously I was getting tired out. Although I was still grabbing time in the meal break to turn out a couple of spoons, and still able to buy extra bread and oil with the products of my foundry, I was just not strong enough to begin with. For too long the only exercise my muscles had experienced was flinching against blows. I had no tone in my back and shoulders and arms. I began to worry that this job would defeat me, and although I tried desperately to meet the norm, because Zyuzin had carried me for the first few days well beyond even his considerable capacity for *tufta*, I never made more than 130 nuts, and 120 was more usual. If I could have got it up to 150 there would have been some way to justify keeping me at the job, but I knew I could never make it.

So I stopped spoonmaking for a few days and used my lunch breaks to see what I could find out about softer jobs. Arc welding looked easiest. You just put on the face mask and the gloves and made seams in the metal. Nobody seemed to mind if you picked up their tools and fooled around during lunch, so I gave it a try to see if it was tricky. I made a few seams on scraps of steel, and they looked okay to me. After all, I had no standards to judge the work by. I practiced as much as I could to see if I could consistently keep from either getting the electrode stuck by working too close, or losing the arc by working too loose. It began to come after a while and I let Zyuzin know that arc welding really was one of my skills, no fooling this time. Zyuzin just looked suspicious and said there was a line-up for arc-welding jobs. This confirmed my guess that it was a soft job. I told him to put my name on the list. I said, "By the way, I see you need a drill press operator. That I can certainly do. I had lots of experience in Moscow." I lied.

So I got on the drill press. I connected it up incorrectly the first morning. The electrical cables got tangled in the drill mechanism and I shorted out the whole shop. Zyuzin sent me back to threading nuts, but I kept haunting the arc welders whenever I could, partly to learn more about their craft, and partly to steal bits of their grounding cable, which had excellent aluminum wire in it for my spoons.

If it had not been for Zyuzin's skill in *tufta*, I might have died in the DOZ. That must sound an exaggeration, but this is how it works. If you made your norm you were given a basic ration, known as 100 per cent, and this was sufficient to keep you going. If you dropped below your norm, you got a lower ration. With lower rations you would be too weak to maintain whatever percentage of the norm you had been achieving, and so your ration would be lowered again. Finally it would be reduced to the starvation ration. At that point, without some supplementary food, a prisoner would simply starve to death. I had supplementary food, but I feared that I would get so weak that I would have no energy left for making spoons, and besides the market was uncertain. But somehow Zyuzin managed to walk the tightrope very well. He kept me and all his brigade at least at the base rations by satisfying the MVD that his norms were being met when they were not, juggling books, keeping from being caught, keeping his brigade loyal to him so that no one would be tempted to turn informer. All of us would watch out for informers and see that they were stopped before they had done their work.

Informers were usually killed. There was a prisoners' committee called the People's Council of Justice, a sort of special soviet that undertook on behalf of the camp as a whole to execute these destructive people. The commonplace saying in camp was, "The stool pigeon walks with an ax at his back," and it was not just a figure of speech. The standard practice until mid-1953 was for a nominee of the Council simply to walk up to the condemned man in the yard, say quickly and quietly, "The People's Council has condemned you to death," and stab him before he knew what was happening. Professional criminals preferred beheading to simple stabbing. I met a man who had been serving a short sentence for robbery and had lost a big bet at blackjack. His payoff was that he had to behead the camp commandant. He never hesitated. Found the man in the yard and stepped up behind him with a knife and did the job. Why he was not shot I do not understand. Why he ended up in our camp is clear: killing an MVD is a political offense. When a professional was assigned executioner by the People's Council, consistent with the ethic of audacity among the coloreds, he would sometimes take the severed head immediately to the nearest guard and say, "Here! I got the dirty stool pigeon. He's one of yours!" Then he would hand over the head and stoically take his three months in hard punishment. If it was winter that would likely be the end of him.

In 1953 we were made to sign a document we jokingly called "the peace treaty." This was simply a declaration that any prisoner known to have killed another prisoner would be summarily shot without trial. When that was promulgated, the execution of informers went underground. One technique was to arrange to have the electric wires cut in the barracks. Almost as soon as the lights went out, there would be a scream that died off into a rasping breath and silence, or sometimes the muted sounds of a man struggling whose mouth has been stopped with an arm in a padded jacket and whose limbs are pinioned. Once a hoarse whisper reached my ears from a nearby bunk: "*Ivan Sergeiyevich Rostov, you are condemned to death by order of the People's Council,*" and then some unpleasant gurgling sounds. After that I heard the soft padding of bare feet as the unknown executioner or executioners slipped back to their bunks. This all took seconds from the time the light died. And seconds later cursing guards would be in the place with torches or lanterns, rousing someone to build up the fire while the wires were fixed. They would go around flinging off blankets until they found a blue strangled face or a pool of blood and a gaping throat. One man in my barracks was executed with drills from the quarry.

This sort of thing confirmed what the guards had been taught to believe about us, that we were killers and enemies of the people. In the evening, after the constant desert daytime winds had died down, voices carried with a strange rising and falling strength. And I remember that often, sitting on the toilet in the evening silence, I could hear the guards handing over the watch in the towers around the camp. They had their own prayer: "Sentry number forty-one. Post number three. For the defense of the Soviet Union. Guarding terrorists, spies, murderers, and enemies of the people. Sentry forty-one delivers the post."

Then the reply: "Sentry number nineteen. Post number three. For the defense of the Soviet Union. Guarding terrorists, spies, murderers, and enemies of the people. Sentry nineteen accepts the post."

They called it out in a loud clear voice. The ritual never varied.

At the work site the guards often came in and walked around the shop or the welding yard or wherever we were working. They looked at us as if we were exhibits in a zoo. They were rotated from post to post frequently, and from camp to camp, to ensure that they formed no friendships with the prisoners. It would have been bad for morale if the guards discovered that we were human beings and that most of us were serving our sentences for modest offenses or for no offense at all. Solzhenitsyn, who was in a camp in Ekibastuz, recounts a conversation between a guard and a prisoner.

"What is your sentence?"

"Twenty-five years."

"What did you do?"

"Nothing. I did nothing at all."

"You are lying, prisoner; the sentence for nothing at all is ten years."

To an outsider this seems like a joke; it was not a joke. The guards believed that the correct sentence for people such as us, when we had done nothing at all, was ten years. They were wrong, of course. Twenty-five, five, and five was more common.

After a while I told Zyuzin I simply could not manage the nut threading. It was a matter of physical endurance. If I had started strong I would have been all right. As it was I was falling behind by 70 per cent and I knew that, ingenious as Zyuzin was, I would be giving him trouble if it got much lower than that, and it had to get lower because I was getting weaker.

Zyuzin agreed. He made me a locksmith. The norm was four locks a day, but nobody could ever manage more than two and nobody made trouble about it. There was no problem of physical strength. It was just a time-consuming job, though not very difficult. We had a pattern to follow. We cut out simple keys. We made a simple, flat sheet-metal box, drilled it, and set in springs and other parts we had cut from the patterns. The blacksmith shop made the springs and I think we made everything else. They were crude locks for desk drawers, and one key would open all the locks. I soon got the hang of it and turned out my two locks a day, until the sheet-metal supply dried up. I went to Zyuzin.

"No more sheet metal. What'll I do?"

"Use your ingenuity."

"Can't make locks out of ingenuity."

"Look. There is metal around. If the gauge you need isn't delivered, find out where you can get some and get it. Only don't tell me about it. All I want to know about is finished locks that work."

"You mean steal it?"

"I don't want to know anything about it. Don't steal it. Just get it wherever you can get it and don't get caught."

I stole it from the stove works. They were making wood-burning stoves with a sheet metal that was just about exactly what we needed. Here's a good example of how *tufta* can work beautifully if your nerves are good: Once the stove makers had completed a stove, it was written down in their norm sheets, and they were through with it. Stoves were picked up for delivery by civilian drivers once a week or so. There was no difficulty juggling inventories at this stage because everyone stole stoves, including the MVD. So I just stole a whole stove, knowing that the man who made it would not be penalized, and probably no one else would either. The hardest part of my career as a locksmith was stealing stoves, and the hardest part of that was the physical work of carrying them. I hammered out the rivets, flattened the bent sheets, cut them for the lock box, and kept on making two locks a day. One stove would last me about two weeks.

Then I got a brainstorm. I remembered some of the things my father had told me about techniques of mass production. I went to the brigadier. I said, "Zyuzin, how long could you go? A week? Two weeks? Without having to measure my output?"

He said, "What are you getting at?"

I said, "Suppose I produced you three locks a day, but you wouldn't see any finished locks for three weeks?"

"But nobody's ever made three locks a day. Two and a half is about the best possible."

"I think I can make three. Can you wait three weeks to do your count?"

"Go ahead," he said. "I think I can fix it."

I started a production-line system. First I made a pattern and hammered out boxes, only boxes, until I had sixty of them. That took me a week. Then I started on the inside parts for sixty locks. That took me nearly two weeks. Keys one day. Latches the next. And so on. But then it took only one day to assemble sixty locks from all these parts. I took them to Zyuzin in triumph. His reaction was disappointing. He just took the locks and noted the number. All he said was, "Okay, keep it up." He looked worried about something and distracted.

I said, "What's wrong? What's bothering you?"

"Oh, no problem really. Some son of a bitch is stealing stoves and the supply room is mad as hell. Must be one of those civilian drivers."

Now I had more energy; there was nothing physically demanding about lockmaking except lugging those stoves around. I began to take off at lunch again to make spoons. Zyuzin caught me stealing ground cables for the aluminum, but he was tolerant about it when he found out that it was going into spoons, and I helped him feel better by letting him have part of every liter of cooking oil Kuznetsov passed out to me in the dispensary.

The lock assignment was completed a few weeks later. Zyuzin said he reckoned I'd have to go back to threading nuts; there still was no opening in arc welding. I had seen a lot of the blacksmith shop when I went to pick up my springs, and I thought the smith himself had a pretty good touch. His assistant had to wield a heavy hammer, but he mostly held onto things with a pair of tongs, or did fine work with a small hammer, and I had watched a lot and got the idea I could handle that pretty easily, so I asked Zyuzin, What about the blacksmith shop?

He looked surprised. "Are you sure?" he said.

"Sure; I know all about it."

His face showed what he thought of that statement. He was getting to know me pretty well. But he was still friendly and tolerant and so he sent me to the blacksmith shop. "There's always a demand for apprentices," he said.

It was terrible. I was assigned to an old Estonian blacksmith named Arnold. Arnold was small and wiry and very competent. I was supposed to help him cut metal. I wielded the hammer, of course, and could hardly lift it. He held the chisel. I had a knack of somehow striking the chisel in a way that would cause the handle to break off and the hot blade to fly through the window.

Arnold was shocked. "How the hell did you do that! That never happened before!"

I went to get the chisel. It had smashed through the glass window and disappeared in a snowdrift outside. Then Arnold sent me to the supply room for a new handle. I brought the turned wooden handle back to the forge. The blacksmith heated up the chisel, thrust the handle into the enlarged socket and immediately dunked it in a barrel of water to shrink it onto the handle.

Then he set up for another try. The bar of hot metal was laid on the anvil and the blacksmith seized the chisel and signaled me to strike. I could hardly lift the big hammer, that was the trouble. I just could not hold it straight. It came down at an angle. There was a sound something between a shot and a breaking guitar string, and the chisel disappeared. We both looked around. There were no new panes of glass broken. It was not on the floor anywhere. Finally, knowing it was crazy, I went out and looked in the snowbank. There was the chisel, right where it had been before, and it must have gone through the already broken windowpane.

Arnold said, "How can anyone so sloppy be so accurate?"

We tried again, and for a while I managed to hit straight on. The next day I broke a couple of handles, and the next day a couple more. They quite often went through the same window. The other men in the forge began to call me Dead-eye Dolgun. Arnold the blacksmith was too kindly to complain. He was the kind of man who hated to cause trouble for anyone, but he looked increasingly pained each time I shot a chisel out the window. The one who did complain was the supply-room man. We were exhausting his supply of chisel handles and he was going to face trouble when he asked the administration for new ones. Three years on the job and he had never given out a chisel handle. I broke thirty in two weeks.

One day, coming back from the supply room with a fresh handle, I saw a commotion out in the arc welders' yard. The door opened and they carried in a dead guy with burns up the sleeve of his padded jacket. He had electrocuted himself.

I dropped the handle and ran to Zyuzin. I forgot all about my kindly Estonian boss. I guess he just stood there and wondered what hole his apprentice had fallen into and whether he had fallen in the same hole before several times. I pleaded with Zyuzin to give me the dead arc welder's job. Zyuzin tried to get himself off the hook. He called the chief engineer, a civilian. The man said, "Can you do a figure-eight bead?"

"Sure, easy."

"Can you make a double seam on two pieces of rail?"

"What do you take me for?" I said indignantly. "This is baby stuff!"

"All right, come and show me," the engineer said.

We went outside. I was completely confident. I had been practicing. He gave me a mask and a machine and pointed out the two bits of rail I was to weld. "Call me when it's done and I'll see if you're any good," he said, and went inside.

I thought, *This will be a cinch!*

Then I remembered the poor guy they had just carried out, and told myself to be careful, to take every precaution. I looked at all the eleven other arc welders to see if there was anything I had not noticed before. They were all looking at me. Suddenly I felt very embarrassed, so I pulled on my gloves and shoved the mask down over my face. I couldn't see a thing. I pulled the mask up again and got the rails together and set the electrode as close to them as I dared and then pulled the mask down and moved the electrode in to start the arc. Immediately I got it too close and it stuck. I wrenched it loose. I started again and made the beginnings of a bead, but I was overcautious now and the arc kept going out.

I was sweating inside the mask. I lifted it for a moment and looked around. The other arc welders were still looking at me. I pulled the mask down again. *Steady, Alex. This can be very important.*

Sweat kept getting in my eyes. I would lift the mask to wipe it away, catch the amused looks from the other guys, shrivel up with embarrassment some more, and try again.

It took me nearly an hour to make those two seams.

I called Zyuzin and he called the engineer. It was lunch break now, and the other welders had gone. The engineer picked up a sledge hammer to see if he could break open my weld. Suddenly he put the hammer down again without using it. He bent over and and examined the weld more closely. Then he swung his boot six inches and gave it a light kick. It fell apart.

I was mortified.

The engineer laughed. He said, "I'll show you how to do it right. You've got the basic idea but there's still a lot to learn."

He was a very sympathetic guy. Over the lunch break he showed me how to make a simple seam that would hold, and then he gave me some work to do and left me to it.

Actually I learned welding quickly and moderately well. Moving the sheets and rods and rails of steel was hard work and I was unsteady on my feet, so that I often weaved around like a drunk. But once I settled down in the welder's crouch, I seemed to be all right. I had no overalls for some time; the dead man's were too small for me. One day I failed to notice that sparks from the work had ignited the padding in my winter pants. Soon the whole crotch was smoldering and I still did not notice it because there was always smoke from the work. Suddenly I was jumping up and down and yelling because my crotch seemed to be on fire. I had to leap into a snowbank to put it out.

My job was to make components for a staircase in a basement some-where, cross-gridded steel plates for the steps, and I-beams for the sides, and so on. We had a pattern. We would chalk it out on the material, cut it with the arc welder, and then start assembling. I staggered whenever I had to carry anything, but for some reason I was able to laugh at myself as if I were watching someone else. Although by the end of the day I was ex-hausted, I found the long march back to the Zone a cheerful time because it meant going home, to rest and food and friends. I would carry stolen boards and pieces of joists and studs home for the fire, and when my line was singled out by the guards for confiscation of the wood I was philo-sophical about it. I had begun to understand and accept that there were certain costs you had to pay for survival, and that you had better accept them and not fight them. Many others bitched and got sour stomachs when the guards took their wood. I marked those people down as less skillful survivors. Their bitching just used up energy.

When a guard was unnecessarily cruel and made someone take off his boots and his footcloths in the snow when it was ten below zero during the search, I got mad inside, but I never let it show. What was the use?

One afternoon I heard a few shots ring out. All the welders stopped and looked up and stared solemnly at each other and then went back to work. Later that afternoon I cut my hand on a piece of ragged-edged steel and went to the first aid post to get it bandaged. Inside the post was the young kid they had shot for getting too close to the fire zone. His jacket was on the floor and where the bullet had gone in there was a neat round hole and where it came out there was a sort of explosion of cotton padding and blood and fragments of flesh and bone. The arm was severed above the elbow. Only a tendon held it on. They kept him in the DOZ for several hours with a tourniquet on, and by the time he was taken back to Adarich there was no way to save the already morbid arm. This sort of thing gave me twinges of anger, but even such extremes of violence did not upset me profoundly. I knew that I was living in the midst of a totally inhumane society where survival was the first duty and where too much tender-ness of sentiment or resentment or rage would only sap my strength and perhaps affect my judgment. Eternal vigilance, I told myself. Don't let it get you down to the point where you forget to watch out for any advantage.

One day Arnold the blacksmith came into the yard and stood watching me work for some time. I just dimly saw a pair of legs through the mask and went on with my work. When I looked up, the wiry old man was smiling at me in a very friendly way and I was glad to see him. "Things are not the same in the forge anymore, Alexander my boy," he said. "I have had the same chisel handle for three weeks now, and some of the spice has gone out of our life."

We both laughed over this and I pulled out my tobacco and he got out some scraps of brown paper and we rolled ourselves a smoke and sat on a snowbank for a short break.

"I've been watching you work, Alexander," Arnold said. "I am surprised at how well you are doing. Please don't be offended."

I laughed and said there was no offense.

Arnold said, "I have an idea for making some money to buy extra food. Do you think it would be difficult to set aside a few round bars and some angle irons from time to time?"

I said I thought not.

Arnold explained that he had been talking to some of the civilian drivers and some of the free workers who came into the DOZ. They were very disgruntled because the government had lured them to come and work in Dzhezkazgan by describing Krestovaya as a model town with all the latest in apartments, furnishings, recreational facilities, and so on. When they arrived they found cold, half-finished apartments, badly made (by slave labor of course), and no furniture and no recreational facilities at all. It was explained to them that these things had been planned but that "production shortages" had unfortunately delayed the development of the community. Etc., etc., etc.

What they bitched about more than anything else, many of them being young married couples, was the lack of beds. They hated sleeping on the floor. Arnold figured out that we could collaborate on making bootleg beds. I would weld together a rudimentary frame and he would make ornaments in the forge.

So we entered into a partnership. I had to give up lunch breaks and spoonmaking for a while, but we could finish a bed in a week and we each got about two kilos of bread for one, or occasionally a piece of cooked meat or some oil or a couple of rubles to be hoarded against the need for something larger that might arise.

We never questioned the drivers as to how they got the beds out past the search, but I am pretty sure the guards searched only for escapees going out and contraband like guns or knives coming in. Bread and beds were not interesting to our guards.

One day a driver told me that they liked the bed a lot even if the springs (only interlaced wires) were a bit hard. He admired the workmanship, he said, and his wife wondered if I could also make her a flatiron?

Irons became the hot item. It took longer to make an iron than a bed because I had to use several different kinds of steel. I cut a boat shape from a thick slab. This had to be polished smooth on the bottom and sides and I could do it only by hand and that took days and days of stolen periods here and there, out of sight of the brigadier or roaming guards or stool pigeons.

I built a fire box on top, with a little grid and ventilation holes to put charcoal in to heat the iron. I knew that they would have to look pretty to satisfy women who cared enough about appearances to want to iron clothes in Dzhezkazgan, so I took a lot of care in finishing them. They became very much in demand and for a while I could get three kilos of bread for one iron. That made me feel like a rich man, so well-off in fact that I was able to be generous to my friends, especially to Zyuzin, who had protected me so carefully, and so things went along very well for a while. Although I was never strong, I was surprisingly healthy despite mild bouts of scurvy and the occasional round of diarrhea and mild fever.

I lived every day surrounded by the coarsest forms of inhumanity. To the men who guarded me I was a number, СЯ265, and they used the number to control and to humiliate. There was always a guard with a piece of plywood and a pencil to write down your number if you were late out of bed, if you failed to take off your cap when passing in the street, if you stepped out of line in any way. You were nameless: just a numbered object to be thrown in the cooler if you failed to conform and thrown in the death wagon with your number wired to your big toe if you failed to survive.

The death rate in that camp was at least two or three per day, or nearly one in a thousand. It may have been much higher.

Cursing and brutality and insensitivity were blatant and normal. Many prisoners became as brutal and dehumanized as the guards. I shunned such people. Often in their desperation to survive they turned stool pigeon. Even the knowledge of what had happened to other stool pigeons did not seem to deter them. But once they were discovered they usually were killed or, if they were harmless, ignored to the point where they became useless to the MGB who employed them.

The food was scarce unless you were ingenious, and even then it lacked vitamins. Vitamin-deficiency diseases like scurvy and pellagra were common and sometimes fatal. In the winter the cold was intense and the hard, drifting snow was painful as we marched to the work site and back with our hands behind our backs. In the summer and fall the heat cracked our lips and our skin. If we worked outside without gloves we could get blisters from handling the roasted stones or sheets of steel. Heat prostration knocked down a lot of prisoners and few of them ever got up again. The dust was everywhere and blew all day and almost every day. The bedbugs were part of the environment and I never got used to them psychologically, although my body developed an immunity and the swellings around each bite stopped forming.

Men went crazy all around me and for my own survival I had to learn not to care.

There was never enough time to sleep.

And yet my morale was good. I had maneuvered myself up to a plateau on which I knew I could survive. I liked my work. The buzz and clang and general clamor of the welding yard, the blue electric flashes all around, the company of competent people, the smell of ozone: these were pleasant to me, I suppose because I was becoming genuinely skilled and came very close to reaching the real norms set for me. I also learned to handle my own *tufta*. If a job called for steel five millimeters thick I would use three-millimeter stock because I found that no one checked and I could cut faster with the lighter steel. I would make plain single seams, which were fast and easy, and then write up figure eights or doubles because I was "paid" for the total length of seam applied in a day, paid in points toward fulfilling my norm, and yet the only check that was made was on the total number of units turned out: stoves, staircase sections, safes, and so on.

I could claim overproduction and get extra rations, but I still found the carrying too much for me. I still staggered under a sheet of steel as though the wind were blowing me around. So I persuaded Zyuzin that I could increase the real output by quite a lot if he got me an assistant, and to my delight he somehow got my friend from quarantine, Edik L., assigned him personally to me, and moved him into our barracks and onto the bunk next to mine.

So now, although the evenings were lonely and sad when the work was not filling all my time, I had Edik to talk with, and Zyuzin's guitar to listen to, and I began to think of studying the guitar seriously myself because I could see how absorbing it was, and I believed that it would help me survive even though it might be hard on my neighbors because I was clearly not a born musician.

Despite my competence at welding I still had a talent for blunders. My blunders always had a certain class to them, like sending the chisel out through the same hole in the blacksmith's window every time. My time in the welding yard was no exception. Shortly after Edik joined me we finished up the staircase assignment and were given a pattern for big office safes made out of quite thick material. We had to cut the sides and top and bottom and the door, make the hinges, weld the hinges to the door, and then the hinges to the frame. I had to drill for the lock fittings. The locks came from somewhere else.

Edik and I got the patterns and had a good look at them before chalking them out on the sheet metal. The constructions were simple enough but the norm was impossible because of the cutting required: three finished safes every two days. We decided that if we cheated on the thickness of the stock and just put a few spots on the inside corners instead of the full seam called for, we could make up the norm and maybe even beat it. We got started. Both of us cut, one with the new acetylene equipment, which had just arrived and was very fast, and the other with the arc welder, which was very slow. Edik, who was in good physical shape, did all the heavy lifting. He held the sheets in place while I welded them together. The first one was a bit awkward and we had to cut apart one seam and reweld it because it was crooked, but by the time we got the doorframe in place and the hinges welded onto the door, we were getting the hang of the job and moving at high speed. Too high, as it turned out. Edik stood inside to hold the door in position while I welded the hinges to the doorframe. He had to hold it very precisely so that it would swing without binding after it was welded in place, and he braced his back against the back of the safe and put his fingers through the cutouts for the lock fittings and his toes on the bottom, and told me to hurry because it took all his strength to maintain the position.

I hurried. I slapped the seams on one after the other. They had to be as specified because they were visible, so I could not leave anything out. Soon the last seam was going on and Edik was complaining about the heat inside the safe. I finished and said, "That's it!" We had finished our first safe and it was still early afternoon, and I was sure that if we applied my locksmith shop mass-production techniques we could, with appropriate cheating, make a lot of extra rations on this job, so I immediately ran to the stockpile to start chalking out a large number of bottoms, sides, doors, and so on.

Amid all the clatter I became aware of Edik's voice calling, with a hollow sound. He was still in the safe.

"Come on out! Let's get going," I yelled, running to the safe.

"I can't!" he yelled back.

I had welded the door on backward! The hinges would only bend inward and the door was bigger than the inner lip of the doorframe; so Edik was welded inside like Montresor's victim in "The Cask of Amontillado." I ran for the torch. Edik screamed that he was roasting as I started to cut the hinges. There was no other way. I cut as fast as I could, but by the time I got him out he was unconscious from the smoke and the heat and it was some time before we got back on friendly terms.

I was not the only prospector in the DOZ. Tools, chunks of steel, aluminum wire, all kinds of things disappeared into prisoners' padded jackets or hiding places, or went out with the civilian drivers during the day or with the MVD guards at the end of the day. I had already created a shortage of grounding cable. Other prospectors brought it down to the vanishing point. The common solution to the shortage was to clamp a short length of cable from the transformer to a piece of sheet steel or a rod on the ground, then lay the sheet or rod out in the general direction of your work, which might be ten meters or more away in the yard, then lay a piece of sheet steel on that, then a girder that happened to be lying around, and so on until you had made a rough connection to your own work. One day in the spring I failed to notice that some of these connections I had made from the transformer, which stood under an overhang near the enclosed part of the shop, were lying in pools where the snow had melted. I sent Edik to the supply shop for some electrodes and told him to turn on the machine on his way back. For a long time I had had to manufacture my own electrodes by coating thin steel rods with a glaze of some silicon nonconductor that controlled the burning rate. I was not patient enough for this and my electrodes were often quite inconsistent in quality. But now we had some decent machine-made ones which speeded up the work. I saw Edik come out of the building with a package of electrodes. I saw him turn on my welding machine. I saw him step into a pool of water.

I thought he had gone crazy. He began a strange dance, in slow rhythmic gyrations with bended knees, but with his arms and upper body flapping about as if he were in convulsions. I had no idea what was happening. I called, "Stop fooling around. We've got a norm to meet!" But he paid no attention. His legs bent more and more, and he slipped to the ground and lay there twitching.

Edik liked a practical joke, but I thought he might really have taken sick. I put my welding gun down on some gloves and started across the yard just as the door opened and three MVD officers, two colonels and a general, came into the yard. They were on an inspection tour, like the one that had interrupted my colonic irrigation. The results were equally gratifying, although I still had not caught on. The three officers in their neat uniforms and long greatcoats went into a similar gyrating, storklike dance, with their arms flapping and their heads jerking back and forth. Their mouths were open and their eyes were popping but no sound came out. I started to run. I must have stepped in a puddle. I felt the surging voltage take over my whole body. I was terrified and yet I had a strange urge to laugh at the same time. I began to spin around, my arms flapping like wings and my head jerking. Before long we were all on the ground. Fortunately a welder came out through the door, understood what had happened, and turned off the transformer.

The officers were furious. The general's coat was soaked and covered with filings and rust. They were sure it had been an assassination attempt. The whole DOZ came to a halt for the rest of the day as guards swarmed in and a commission of inquiry got under way right away. Edik and I were exonerated because we were victims as well. In the end they could pin it on nobody. Zyuzin and the other brigadiers did a good job of shouting and screaming at the officers for entering a danger area without an escort, and such is their response to authority, even the authority of prisoners who in this case seemed to know what they were talking about, that they finally accepted the incident as an accident.

But such was my reputation from the other camp as the Man Who Shit on the Organs, and as the American Spy (everyone in camp was sure that the incident with the bodyguards on Khrushchev's estate was part of a mission I had been on), that a lot of people believed that I had arranged the whole thing, and my reputation went up another notch.

CHAPTER

20

IT WAS THE SPRING OF 1952. SOON I WOULD BE TWENTY-SIX YEARS OLD. Memories of the freezing dungeon at Lefortovo and the horrors of Sukhanovka had somewhat faded, although my jaw still ached where Ryumin had broken it and I still had and have scars from Sidorov's kicks and Ryumin's rubber club.

Spring on the desert steppe is the only time when there seems to be any life on it. For a very brief period, measured in days, the melting snows leave behind enough of a water table for wild red tulips to blaze out across the otherwise dead land and wild garlic to grow in profusion. If we were on an outside job, or able to sit or lie on the ground outside the work site gates during the count, we picked the wild garlic and took it home for its vitamin C content.

For a brief period during this sudden bloom, the death rate would fall off. Sometimes more than a day would pass without a death in our little town of several thousand slaves. Fantasies of the American invasion, presaged by airlifts to drop arms to us, bloomed along with the desert flowers, and my spirits were as high as anyone's, although I did not really share that particular fantasy. Some people kept themselves alive with hatred. I saw this particularly among former high party officials who had been purged and who now nourished themselves on political rage. They were bitter men who tended to stick together. I never spent time with them because I found them unpleasant, and yet I understood how their anger helped them survive and I was sympathetic from a distance. Some, of course, turned religious, and prayer manifestly saved many lives.

My own belief in God, which is real, is more like a given than an active faith. Although I routinely went to Mass as a child, I was never a church person, or a ritual person. I believed it was up to me to make the best of what God had given me, and what kept me alive always was a determination to do just that. To survive at least, and at best to survive and find some pleasure.

I saw many cases of people who lost hope or let go of their convictions and then, without any apparent cause, died. For some reason this seemed to happen more often with people from the Baltic states, I don't know why. It was especially strange, since they more than anyone else in camp seemed to be the recipients of food parcels from home, and often it was the arrival of a food parcel that seemed to bring on an attack of despair that would turn a man's eyes into a haunted stare so that he became a kind of walking ghost who never spoke. Then one morning, often around three o'clock, we would hear the sigh that comes at the end.

No physical cause.

Suicide was common. There was a man of twenty-six or twenty-seven who worked at the DOZ. His name was Vilunskas. I did not know him well, although he did live in our barracks. One spring day, before the bloom, I was walking with a friend to the mail room. The friend had been told there was a food parcel for him and he wanted company so that there would be a witness if the guards stole from his parcel when they searched it and so that he would have protection in case any of the semicoloreds in camp tried to steal it from him on his way back to the barracks. Vilunskas was coming out of the mail room as we went in. He was reading a letter and his faced looked as though he had been struck: horrified and stunned at the same time.

When we came out he was sitting on the steps of the building. The letter was still in his hand but he was slumped over and his right hand was hidden inside his jacket. I bent over to ask him if he was all right, and he just slumped down and fell off the steps onto the ground, unconscious. I yelled for help. Several prisoners came over and helped carry Vilunskas to the hospital. I could not help it, I had to see what was in that deadly letter, which had fallen to the ground. It was from his wife, telling him she had divorced him. I was swept with a wave of grief for this guy I hardly knew, almost my age. I thought of Mary, and even though I knew she had to be released from her promise to me I felt sadder still. My eyes were blurry. I wiped them and stared at the ground, hoping no one would see how I felt. Something bright on the ground caught my eye and I bent over and picked it up. It was a tiny handmade knife, a folding knife like a pen knife, but only about one inch long in the blade. The end of the blade was red with fresh blood.

I said to myself, The damn fool! He shouldn't try to kill himself over this woman in the first place, and in the second place if he really wants to do it he should choose a weapon that will do the trick. This thing couldn't penetrate anything. I ran to the hospital to show the doctors what I had found. I met Adarich. He said, "That young man is dead."

I said, "That's impossible," and showed Adarich the hopeless little weapon. "Well," he said, "he's dead, and I don't know why. The wound is almost invisible."

Later he told me that he had done an autopsy; the tiny blade had cut the pericardium, penetrated a ventricle, and the heart had bled into the chest until he died.

Vilunskas was from Kaunas in Latvia. He had been a member of a Baltic underground guerrilla group called the Forest Brothers. There were many of them in camp. They were a gloomy, brooding lot, and there were many suicides among them.

There was a Latvian blacksmith named Zelensh in our barracks. I had first met him when I worked with Arnold breaking chisels. Zelensh worked hard and seemed all right at the DOZ, but at night he almost never spoke. He seemed to be in another world. One Sunday when we were allowed to stay in camp, and work was shut down for a day, Zelensh seemed to brood worse than ever. In midmorning they came to take the bedding out for boiling, to get rid of the bedbugs. We sat around on the bare floor just talking or smoking or making tea on the little stoves at each end of the barracks. In the afternoon Major Gusak, the camp commandant, came personally with some guards and a couple of officers and ordered everyone out of our barracks so the guards could go in for a search. This was one of Gusak's entertainments: spoiling our rare Sunday off with this kind of harassment. They would confiscate books of poetry or religion, take down numbers for subsequent punishment in the hard punishment cells or by loss of rations, and keep us standing outside for an hour or more just to amuse themselves. Gusak would swagger about and swear a great deal and parade his authority. He loved to insult former high-ranking army officers, or distinguished professors, or anyone else who had fallen from glory, over whom he could smirk and strut and enjoy the reversal of rank.

Most of us bitched and made jokes under our breath during this ritual. On this day Zelensh simply stood silent, staring ahead, not speaking to anyone.

When it was all over we went back in and sat on the bare bunks and someone put on a pot of tea. Zelensh lay down on his bunk, with his head on his hands, staring at the ceiling. Someone brought him a cup of tea after a while, but Zelensh did not respond. His eyes were still wide open but his neighbor peered closely and said quietly, *"Otdal kontsy"*—he's given up the ghost.

A lot of his mates came and tried to shake him awake, because he looked fine and had been healthy; he had worked well and had good rations. But he was dead all the same. He was about thirty-five years old.

Many of the prisoners spent their entire free time talking politics and cursing the Soviet system. I occasionally got caught up in this, but I really had no taste for such negativism. I kept pleading with Zyuzin to show me more chords on the guitar, and finally, to stop me from bothering him, he somehow found me a beat-up old guitar which I could buy for a couple of loaves of bread. Now when the singing started in the evenings I would try to accompany the singers with my few dog waltz chords, and I began to learn a little bit more about the instrument by closely watching Zyuzin's graceful fingers, and asking him and another friend, Volodya Stepanov, who specialized in Russian songs, to show me how to play each chord they used.

Somewhere Volodya (it is a nickname for Vladimir) got hold of a song about our camp, and the whole barracks would join in, once they learned the words, singing in a soft, mournful voice.

> *Dzhezkazgan, Dzhezkazgan*
> *Across your steppes that never end*
> *No one rides with you as friend*
> *But storms of dust and sand.*
>
> *Winter blizzards blanket you with white,*
> *Wailing through your vastness day and night.*
> *I am alone in this land of fear.*
> *My song laments in a cruel year.*

Not all the songs were so mournful. We had a Russian version of "The Great Ship Titanic," full of ironies, and all kinds of gay tunes from different regions of the Union. But the song that brought everyone together in an agony of yearning was Volodya's "Song of Dzhezkazgan."

I started a notebook showing the fingering of the chords, and I tried to memorize all the sequences. But at the same time what I really aspired to was learning to play notes and classical compositions, just like Zyuzin. He had transcribed music for himself from some accordion music he found in camp, and I became infatuated with the supple movement of his fingers over the strings, and the intricate liquid flow of the soft notes that were so much more beautiful than simple strumming.

I resolved that I would have to have a classical Russian guitar, which has seven strings instead of six, and after a while I found an old woodworker at the DOZ who said he could make one. I watched him make it over a period of months, and in the meantime asked all my friends to think of ways to find me some real guitar music. Zyuzin was very enthusiastic about this: he wanted some new music as well. When my guitar was finished Pavel Voronkin painted an elegant figure of a mythical faun among the trees on the back. And some music turned up. Just one piece, but it was real guitar music: Rachmaninov's "Italian Polka," transcribed for the Russian guitar. Zyuzin started to teach me how to read it.

It was a painstaking business. I still cannot imagine how the rest of the men in the barracks were so patient with my fumbling attempts and the endless repetition of a single bar or two as I figured out the polka note by note and finger by finger. Marching to work I kept my fingers inside my jacket whenever I could get away with it, and practiced trilling thirty-second notes against my chest. I found it immensely difficult, but totally absorbing, which was what I needed. I practiced every night until it was time for bed, seldom even interrupting for tea or to chat with Edik or the others. I became almost obsessed for a while with my beautiful seven-stringed instrument and Rachmaninov's beautiful polka, and after what must have been weeks or maybe months on that single piece, I reached the point where I could haltingly play it through from start to finish, following the printed music, even though my thirty-second notes left something to be desired.

Then someone got me some Chopin waltzes, and that was the next challenge. Working away at that intricate music I could forget the howling winds outside on winter nights, ignore the bedbugs for a while, encapsulate myself from the smell of death. Music was a world of its own, beautifully structured, demanding the most intense concentration from me. I would turn to my guitar after witnessing a terrible death or an act of brutal violence and wipe the intolerable scenes from my mind. Struggling home at night through snowdrifts or choking dust, I would fix in my mind the image of the gleaming white pine sounding board of my beloved instrument, and slip my hand inside my jacket and play and play all the way home, so that the march became shorter and the curses of the guards and the barking of their dogs were quite remote to me.

I bought the guitar with money. Sometimes I would trade extra bread or oil to a prisoner who had managed to hold on to a few rubles, and sometimes the free workers who bought my hardware manufacture would pay in money. Using the same free workers as contraband runners, I could bring in a few simple luxuries after a while. One of the most important was tea: I found that real tea gave me an energy boost in the morning, and once I found I could have it brought in I was never without it as long as I was able to afford it.

I missed coffee. Sometimes I could actually *smell* it, I wanted it so much. One day Pavel Voronkin came up to me in the street outside the barracks and said, "I think there are changes coming. I think things are going to get better. They have brought us real coffee!"

I could hardly believe it. "How do we get it?"

"It's in sacks by the boiler room," Pavel said. "And the funny thing is, no one seems to be picking it up!"

I grabbed a pillowcase and ran to the boiler room. He had been telling the truth. There were three or four sacks of coffee beans. The smell was so good my stomach began to churn. Out of the three thousand people in camp there were not a hundred who knew what real coffee was, so the coffee enthusiasts like Pavel Voronkin and myself were able to stuff our mattresses and pillows with a supply of beans that lasted for months. We smuggled some flat stones back from the DOZ to grind it with, and for a while had fresher coffee than you get in most American homes. God knows how real coffee had ended up in Dzhezkazgan, but it was another contact with reality, with my American roots, and I got a lot more out of it than just a good morning jolt of caffeine. Pavel explained the arrival of the coffee by saying that they were so used to ersatz burnt-grain coffee coming in for the MVD, that when sacks came marked coffee, and turned out to contain brown beans with a funny smell, the administration assumed it was some inferior product meant for the prisoners, and just dumped it out for us to make what we could of it. He was probably right. The Baltics and the intellectuals and a few others scrambled for it and it went quickly enough, but into a relatively small number of hands.

I suppose one of the reasons that the music was so important to me at this period in my life was that, although I knew a lot of people and was on good terms with many of them, I had not formed any deep friendship like that with Arvid Atsinch, who was, if he was still alive, far away in another camp in the area. Edik was a good pal and we had common political views and a very amiable companionship. Pavel Voronkin was bright and sensitive, and we liked each other and I think trusted each other. Zyuzin was kind and protective and a good music teacher, but not close. I did not have anyone with whom I was really close, and so I buried myself in pages of Chopin and Rachmaninov and in the constant exercising and training of my fingers, which were brutalized each day by heavy steel and welders' gloves and were not as trainable as I wanted them to be.

Walking to work and drumming thirty-second notes against my chest, or staring at the beautiful pine grain of my guitar while I rested my hands, I would daydream escape plans. I wanted desperately to escape, but the more I heard about the failure rate the less I believed in the possibility. Almost nobody ever came to me with a credible plan. And while attempts were made every few weeks, they almost all failed.

That very winter of 1952, when the snow was blowing so hard the MVD had to string ropes from the barracks to the mess hall and from the mess hall to the toilets so that we would not wander in circles and freeze to death, a Georgian army officer named Georghadze somehow retrieved his uniform from the storeroom where they kept our personal property, made up some insignia to replace what had been ripped off, and one blinding night when nobody in his right mind would be outside he simply climbed up the barbed wire in the fire zone and went over the wall. They found him when the spring thaw came and the drift he had frozen to death in melted away and revealed his body. The soldiers brought him back and slung the body over some wire outside the gates and left it there for two weeks until it was thoroughly rotten.

I had a friend named Vasya who had worked in the automotive works in Moscow with my father. That was the only real basis for our friendship, but often in the evenings before the mess hall finally shut up and the barracks were then closed, I would go over to his barracks and chat for a while. He told me about a fourteen-year-old boy he had met who had tried two escapes. This boy had been in a band of Ukrainian guerrillas and at the age of ten had been trained as an assassin. Because he was so small and so young, he could easily escape detection, and he had been sent into the village when there was a visiting MGB or other Soviet official the guerrillas wanted to eliminate; he had managed to "execute" ten men and escape without detection before he was caught. He had been assigned to Vasya's motor repair unit, in which there were several junior brigades of free workers, teen-agers who came in every day to work in the unit and take mechanical training. This juvenile terrorist, Vasya told me, got his civilian clothing from the storeroom and wore it under his black prison garb to the work site one day. Then he slipped into a toilet or a tool shed and got rid of his outer clothes with the numbers on it, and simply walked out the gate. The guards knew there were free young kids around and assumed he was one of them.

Later, one of these same young kids saw him walking into town and reported him. The MVD found him watching a movie and eating ice cream in the town of Dzhezkazgan.

The same kid tried it again, concealed in a shipment of stone on a railway car, wearing girl's clothes. He had been put in the ZUR camp for escapees and hardened criminals, and sent to extreme hard labor in the quarries. I guess he knew that would kill him. He was very slight and frail. He was probably not terribly bright either, because they spotted him the next morning sitting on top of a pile of rocks as the train went through Kingir about twenty-seven kilometers north, still wearing his dress and looking quite unconcerned, and they threw him in the cooler.

Two Estonian kids tried a bold plan that did not work. They went to the toilets, climbed though the holes, and buried themselves to the nose in the filth beneath. It was a futile try. They had expected that the guards would leave the watchtowers as usual once a search of the mine zone where they worked had failed to turn them up; then they would just climb the wire in the night and walk away. In fact, as long as prisoners are missing in the head count at the work site, the watchtowers are left manned, even if it takes a week. The boys were found hours later. They weren't even beaten up, just washed with cold-water hoses and given twenty-five years, including three months in the BUR, the hard punishment barracks.

Two brilliant escapes caused a tremendous amount of excitement. Another Georgian named Grigori Ashvili became a legend in Dzhezkazgan. He worked in the rail depot, unloading coal, and, like all the workers on that site, came into the camp at night blackened from head to foot, nothing but a pair of eyes staring out of his mask of a face. There were several free workers handling clerical and dispatching jobs at the coal depot, and Ashvili went to work on one young woman with the total and unwavering objective of making her fall in love with him. He succeeded. She was dying for him to be free, to live with her, and was persuaded to take any risk. Over a period of weeks and months (and obviously much of this was pieced together later by inference) he trained her with diagrams and so on to know the layout of the camp and of his barracks as well he as knew them himself. Then one day she brought him civilian clothes and they slipped away somewhere and she put on his prison uniform and blacked her face and cut her hair. She was similar in height and build to him—he had chosen her for that reason. Free workers were not counted at night. She took his place for the head count. Since she must have had some collaboration from other prisoners, it was a wonder that no stool pigeon spotted her and gave her away. She marched back to the barracks with the column. Since the head count came out all right all the guards left the site with the column, and Grigori Ashvili just climbed under a coal train and rode out with it.

The woman seems to have stayed with his brigade for several days, and then changed back into her own clothes at the work site and washed up and walked out in a normal way. So far as I know they were never caught, and this exploit was the talk of Dzhezkazgan for years afterward.

So was the long, sad story of Sasha the Terrorist. Sasha was a kid from Moscow whose father had died in the war and whose mother had taken him with her to a kolkhoz, a collective farm, where she had to work to support herself and her young son. She was a good-looking woman. The chairman of the kolkhoz took a fancy to her and tried to seduce her. She resisted. The seduction turned to rape. In the midst of it, Sasha came home to the dreary little village house, surprised the director, and chased him away.

Sasha brooded over this for some time and then decided to kill the chairman. He had a pistol—perhaps he found it, perhaps it had been his father's. He followed the chairman and his wife one evening when they went by sleigh into the forest for firewood. Sasha was not a practiced shot. His first bullet only grazed the chairman's arm. His second exploded the barrel of the rusty old pistol and injured Sasha's hand. The chairman grabbed his ax, leaped from the sled, and nearly split Sasha's skull.

A kolkhoz chairman is an official. Trying to kill him, therefore, is an attempted political assassination, never mind what he did to your mother. When Sasha recovered from his terrible head wound he was tried and convicted and, of course, given twenty-five, five, and five.

He was sent to Dzhezkazgan and assigned to the same railroad project where I had once unloaded freight cars. There he became involved in an escape plan with a man named Litvinenko, and it is from Litvinenko that I got the story.

Guards came to the hospital late one evening and told me that there was a man unconscious in the detention cell at the BUR. I called Adarich and the two of us were taken in convoy to see this man. Litvinenko was lying unconscious on the cold concrete floor. His body was covered with bruises from boots, fists, and clubs. Both his hands were broken. Adarich made as complete an examination as he could under the circumstances and told the BUR commandant that the man would die of internal injuries if he was not hospitalized, so he was sent back with us like a loose sack of raw meat and we went to work on him.

Litvinenko was a strong young man of twenty-six. He must have had tremendous inner resources to recover at all. For days he hung between life and death. Then he turned the corner and began to recover gradually but definitely, each day stronger and more alert, and by and by we began to talk and he told me what had happened to him and to his friend Sasha the Terrorist.

Sasha's nickname had nothing to do with his attempt on the life of the chairman. The prisoners called him the Terrorist because he was the most lovable, easygoing person in camp and yet had 58.8: political terrorism. He was only sixteen. Ivan Litvinenko began by taking Sasha under his wing as a protective gesture, but they became very good and close friends and often talked together in a wistful way about their homes and families, and about the possibilities of escape.

Somehow they fell in with an older man I'll call the Principal, a prisoner clerk at the railway project, who had already worked out an escape plan in his mind and was looking for some strong, young, reliable accomplices. The Principal had observed that the prisoners assigned to unload cement cars got covered in cement dust and their numbers and faces were obliterated. It was a bit like the story of Grigori Ashvili in the beginning. The Principal concluded that it would be easy for someone like him to join such a work party without being noticed. He proposed to Sasha and Ivan Litvinenko that they carefully gather boards from which they could construct a false inner wall for one of these cement cars, complete with false rivet ends and so on, measured to the millimeter and provided with precise notches and pegs so that they could be assembled in seconds. Because the prisoners used boards as a sort of stretcher to carry cement bags out of the train, they believed they could smuggle the boards onto the car easily, and because everyone hated staying behind to clean the car in the choking dust, they would volunteer to do the cleanup and thus be the last ones in the car.

They built up their false wall components. Sasha and Ivan rehearsed the action of assembling them while they helped clean out cement cars. They went over every detail with the Principal. The Principal had access to the timetables showing what commodities were arriving when at the depot. He told them one day to start bringing bits of bread and sugar to make a cache at the station, and suggested that once they had several weeks' supply of these tiny smuggled fragments they would be ready to go. But before they had more than a few dozen bits of sugar set aside, the Principal came to them in immense excitement one morning and announced that a cement train would be arriving that day and that he could not stand waiting any longer. They were young and confident and incautious. They immediately agreed. The Principal then proposed another ingenious idea: that he spend the day, while they were unloading, finding two more partners. If five were missing, he argued, the guards might just possibly think they had miscounted a whole rank in the column and not notice the escape. Often the guards would miscount one whole rank; it was a common event. Some semiliterate counting off ranks of five would sing out something like this: "Twenty . . . eight!" (Pencil mark on the plywood sheet.) "Twenty . . . nine!" (Pencil mark again.) "Twenty . . . ten!" (Pencil mark. He's really at thirty but with the pauses while he checks to see that there are really five men in each rank he's getting confused.) "Thirty!" (Pencil mark.)

He's calling it thirty but there are really thirty-one. When he reaches the end he will be short one rank. He will recount as many as eight or ten times until he gets his real number. Curses and groans and people falling down with exhaustion and hunger may propel him to hurry the count. Maybe, argued the Principal, *maybe he'll miscount once the wrong way and get a correct count!* And the moment there is a correct count they march the convoy home and lock up the work site for the night.

Sasha and Ivan Litvinenko hastily agree. The train is coming and they have to get busy. They start unloading, smuggling their boards on the car and hiding them at the end under heaps of loose dust and full bags. The Principal hastily rounds up two more confederates I will call the Accountant and the Professional. Toward the end of the day, Ivan Litvinenko brings them a bag of cement. They slip into a shed and smear themselves. They join the work party on the platform. So far so good.

Sasha tells the rest of his brigade that he and Ivan will organize the cleanup. Cries of "Good old Sasha the Terrorist!" "Always count on Sasha!" The grateful brigade goes off to grab a little rest somewhere. Sasha and the other four grab their boards, smear them with cement, place the Accountant and the Professional up against the end wall and, with well-rehearsed movements, begin to close them in. A small board is left off at the bottom and Sasha is the only one still outside. He slips through the opening and they pull the last piece invisibly into place just as the brigadier's assistant looks in to see how the cleanup is coming.

"Good old Sasha the Terrorist indeed!" this man is heard shouting. The boards barely muffle his voice. "Here, you out there! Sasha has gone off to sneak a bit of a sleep somewhere, that dirty little rat. Get in here and finish the cleanup!"

Bad moments while shovels scrape against the false wall. Then the cursing, coughing, resentful cleanup crew is gone and the five escape artists brace themselves stiffly in their sixteen-inch blackness and wait for the next hurdle.

Very soon they hear a soldier climb aboard. They can tell by the hard boots. It lasts thirty seconds; the soldier of course sees only an empty car, more or less satisfactorily cleaned out, and clambers off again.

Then a marvelous moment as the first shudder of the train pulling itself together reaches them, and the even more marvelous slow click-click as they begin to roll smoothly out of the depot, out of the fenced-in zone, and, they hope, soon out of Dzhezkazgan.

At the gates that evening the guards begin the count. There is the usual mixture of grumbles, curses, and jokes as the first count goes wrong. Rising anger when it is wrong the same way the second time. An officer angrily takes over the count boards. Wrong the third time. One whole rank of five is missing. They must have miscounted when the convoy left camp in the morning. Phone calls to camp. The search begins in the work site as darkness falls. The prisoners shiver for hours on the ground outside the gates. It is finally clear that it will be a long search. Some of the guard remain in the watchtowers. The convoy is marched away but not returned to camp. There are nearly two thousand workers on that site, from several camps. They are kept outside all night, huddling together. In the morning the files on all two thousand are produced, each person is individually checked, and it is discovered that five men have gone, and who they are.

On the third day some of the free civilian administrative personnel who work on the project are arrested and "intensive interrogation" is begun, nonstop. Within twenty-four hours more than a dozen of them have begged for mercy and confessed—one how he smuggled them out in a truck, another how he brought civilian clothes in for them, another who brought passports, and so on. All fabrications, of course, and none tally, and the MGB investigators are going out of their minds.

By the end of that same third day, the five in the boxcar are near the end of their endurance. They are weak from hunger because they had only begun to store food for three of them. The air is so thick with exhalation and the smell of urine and feces that they all have headaches. The train has made several stops, but they have collectively agreed that until now they have not covered enough ground.

Now they cautiously take out the last plate in their wall and Sasha breathes clean air for the first time. He sees that it is dark night and scampers to the boxcar door and pushes it back a few centimeters and sees that they are in a big rail yard on the outskirts of a city. The rest of them come out and look around.

The Principal was the first to volunteer and the Accountant was the second, and so those two slipped away—ostensibly to reconnoiter, but they never came back. After a couple of hours the Professional's nerves began to get pretty ragged. He said he would go and look for the others. He recognized the city as Sverdlovsk and said he knew his way around and would be back soon. He never came back. Finally Sasha and Ivan Litvinenko agreed that it would be suicide to be found in the city after the sun came up. They headed for the country, and had good luck, and by keeping away from towns and major roads they managed to walk right across the Ural Mountains in a matter of weeks. They ate berries. They raided a railway section man's little house for civilian clothes and food. They stuck nettles in their swollen feet to bring the swelling down. They kept to the woods in the hill country and to rough country and swamps in the open, and finally, after an incredible two-thousand-kilometer trek past Kuibyshev, past Stalingrad, they stopped in a small village almost in the foothills of the Caucasus, on the banks of the Kuban between Kropotkin and Krasnodar. There they found shelter with some sympathetic villagers and rested. Ivan Litvinenko stayed with a woman, a young schoolteacher who asked him to marry her and promised to get false papers for him. He agreed, but he was not sincere. Both he and Sasha, who were now the closest of blood brothers, knew that to stay any time in strange territory would mean capture. They meant to push on west now, toward Odessa. They thought if they could find Ivan's relatives in Moldavia they could hide in safety while they built up their strength and put together what they needed for an escape through the port of Odessa.

Long before this the Principal and the Accountant were arrested in Sverdlovsk. They both confessed. Their stories were not believed. They were terribly beaten, confronted with each other, and still stuck to what the MGB were convinced was a prearranged fabrication.

Then the Professional was given away by an informer and he told the same story. The MGB decided to look for the railway car. They were beginning to fear that the story was true.

One night Ivan slipped away from his schoolteacher while she slept, and together with Sasha headed further west. They were able to take the train part of the way. At Odessa they parted. Ivan would go to his home village in the Moldavian Republic, to get money from his parents. He told Sasha to walk every Friday by the famous statue of Cardinal Richelieu in Odessa, and when Ivan had money and food and a plan he would meet him there. He never did. On his second day at home his own brother gave him away to the MGB. The MGB treated him all right, but then he was brought back to Dzhezkazgan. His guards had been humiliated and harassed and kept up all night because of his audacity. Now they took delight in beating him savagely until somebody interfered and Adarich and I were called.

That is, in a way, Ivan Litvinenko's story, because he told it. But I think of it as Sasha the Terrorist's story because, as far as I knew, he was still free.

But any normal escape was doomed. There was no place to hide. The open desert gave you up to the little search planes, and if you did not die of exposure you were beaten up or shot and then, no matter how great the distance, you were brought back for hard punishment or grisly display. I was determined to try no plan that was not foolproof, and so far I had no such plan.

So all through the spring and into the early summer of 1952 I worked away at welding during the day and music during the night and while I dreamed of freedom and prayed for it, I was really resigned to the fact that for the time being at least I was a slave in a slave labor camp and there was no point pretending otherwise. Then in the middle of that overwhelmingly hot summer there was another development that looked bad at first but that soon changed my life radically for the better.

CHAPTER

21

MY SCROTAL HERNIA BEGAN TO STRANGULATE. ADARICH, THE SURGEON, HAD said to try to live with it until I was stronger, but I had let it go on too long. After a while the aches and discomfort it caused me diminished somewhat. It was a bit awkward to walk around with a bagful of fists between my legs, but you can get used to a lot of strange things, and I never went back to Adarich about it because it did not hurt too much and, I suppose, because I was afraid of having surgery in that delicate area. I had some pretty morbid notions of what it might amount to.

But it hurt a lot when I lifted heavy steel at the DOZ. I spent several very bad nights trying to tell myself that the pain would go away, but it did not. I finally had to face the fact that the whole area was badly inflamed and getting worse.

Adarich and Shkarin were shocked that I had waited so long. They said that I would have to have surgery within hours or else I would face the risk of serious peritonitis. "You'll have a bellyful of gangrene, my boy," said Adarich, and took me right off to his little operating room. By now I had a dull, powerful pain throughout the lower abdomen. Adarich did his best to relax me, joking in a very casual way with easygoing remarks about the relationship of the size of my scrotum to my sexual abilities and so on. He sat me on the operating table with my head between my knees, made one injection under the skin at the base of the spine, and then moments later gave me a spinal. He was extremely deft. I felt very little discomfort. Moments later I was on my back and Adarich was pricking the soles of my feet and waiting for sensation to disappear. He had a new assistant physician named Mikhail Kublanov and a big former army feldsher named Leonid assisting him. They put up a sort of screen so that I could see their faces but not my belly or their hands. I could see the instruments being prepared and I was terrified. I said, "Couldn't I have a general anesthetic? I'm frightened."

Adarich said, "Listen, with your heart we'd never wake you up again. This is going to be an easy operation because your abdominal wall is so thin I'll be through it in one cut. There!" I realized that he meant it. I could feel a painless kind of tugging and I could see from their eyes that they were getting into it. Into me. Adarich chatted and joked without stopping. He hurt me quite a bit moving my intestines around. I complained and he told me, "Stop complaining, my boy, you are about to see a sight that no living man has ever seen before: your own balls!"

He told Leonid to hold up my head and he showed me two small round pink objects. I don't know what they were; I was too terrified to look closely. I don't even remember whether I believed him or not.

Adarich was fantastically quick. He explained every step, how he was using some underlying tissue to reinforce the damaged inguinal ring and prevent any further hernia, how he was suturing this layer of muscle and that layer. Kublanov said nothing, just handed instruments and held clamps and hemostats and so on. Then within minutes it was over and he had called Vanya, a powerful young orderly, to carry me in his arms to a bed.

I felt quite triumphant, despite some deep pain from the disturbed bowels, because I had remained conscious through the whole thing. That seemed some kind of accomplishment. Adarich warned me that it would hurt a lot when the spinal wore off, and said he would come and see me in a couple of hours.

It was bad, but I had known a lot worse and I was not upset about it. When Adarich came back, he helped take my mind off the pain by telling me that it now looked as though he would be able to justify the need for another feldsher in the hospital and that since I obviously could not go back to physical work for some time, it would make sense for me to resume training. If I was interested. I jumped at it.

Adarich said, "The medical administrator is an MVD captain named Lavrenov. He's a drunk but not a bad guy in some ways. You'll have to get on his good side. He's agreed to meet you, and I'm afraid I've given him some quite high expectations, my boy, so I hope he doesn't ask you anything we haven't covered."

I said, "What's his specialty?"

"Oh, he's not a physician. He's an army feldsher. I think I can brief you on the kind of stuff he'll want mostly. Injections, a bit of anatomy, nothing you can't handle. But the important thing is, you've got to give him a present."

"A bribe?"

Adarich winced. "You'd better be very sure it doesn't look like a bribe. You have to find something he would like to have and give it to him in a way that looks completely innocent. You've got a few days. I'll have you in here for quite a while, you know. But you'd better start thinking about it."

I had a Parker 51 pen and a Ronson lighter in my little sack in the storeroom, along with my civilian clothes. If it had not been for Valentin Intellighent's befriending me, they would have been gone long ago, but miraculously I still had them. I told Adarich about them and he agreed that they would be ideal.

By now he could see from my face that the post-operative pain was getting very lively. "I'll get you some morphine," he said, and got up to go for it.

I said, "No, Dr. Adarich. I don't want to become addicted to that stuff!" I was quite indignant. He just laughed. He said, "Have it your own way, my boy. But I'm going to get you on your feet in the morning whether you're howling with pain all night or not!"

I was shocked at that thought.

He added, "By the way, my name is Yevgeni Petrovich. You might as well begin to use it. I think we shall be seeing a great deal of each other."

Adarich was one of the jolliest men I ever met in camp. He was stocky and bald with great Ukrainian moustaches that hung right down to the line of his jaw. Although he had been in camp since 1934, eighteen years now, for expressing sympathy for Trotsky, he had suffered relatively little, even in some of the hideous Siberian camps he had been in, because his skill as a physician was so much in demand. He was a powerful man, and in the morning when he came to get me up and I protested, he just lifted me out of bed, gently but irresistibly, and set me on my feet. I was doubled up with the pain of it. "Alexander Mikhailovich, we have to keep you moving so your thick American blood won't clot, my boy, and end up blocking your famous pulmonary artery. So pick the right one up, my boy, and put the left one down, and let's get moving!"

He made me walk all the way to the end of the hall and back. Several times a day he came and bodily pulled me to my feet. Pretty soon I learned there was no point resisting. Although my belly was protesting with sharp hot pains, I began to get up on my own and start walking before he got to me. "That's better, my boy," Adarich said, smiling broadly.

At the end of six days he took out the sutures and warned me to walk carefully but to keep on walking. On the twelfth day he let me go out of the hospital, and I walked stiffly and carefully, expecting something to unzip at any moment, to the storeroom to claim my pen and my lighter. That afternoon we spent going over all the material that Adarich expected Lavrenov to quiz me on, and so by the end of the second week I felt confident enough to meet the administrator.

I had seen Lavrenov two or three times already, and once he had looked in on me in the ward and asked in a friendly way how I was getting along. One night I overheard him arguing with Adarich about some pure alcohol. Lavrenov always issued more alcohol for operations than was really needed and then would come around at night to claim the unused portion for his private use. That night he was drunk already and pretty abusive to Adarich, who was trying to jolly him out of taking the spirits because alcohol was always in short supply and Lavrenov was very far gone already. But Lavrenov just cursed Adarich and grabbed the little flask and stormed out.

But when I met Lavrenov walking in the Zone a few days later he was easygoing and almost friendly. I walked right up to him in a very straightforward way. "*Grazhdanin Nachalnik*," I said, meaning Citizen Chief, "could I have a word with you?"

"What is it, *zeklyuchyonny* [prisoner]?"

I said, "I have found it very interesting to be a patient in your hospital. It seems very well supplied and managed compared to the hospital I worked at in the previous camp."

He accepted the compliment noncommittally. Adarich had made it clear that I should not come right out and ask for the job, just indicate my background and get a conversation going. Lavrenov began to ask details of Atsinch's facilities and I told him, with some exaggeration, the kind of work I had been doing there, and while praising Atsinch managed to suggest that the administration under Lavrenov was better than under Atsinch's MVD boss. Which was true enough. I gave him the impression that I was a person of some prominence in Moscow, but of course I did not mention the U.S. Embassy or my connection with it. In any case, he was interested only in my experiences with Atsinch, and asked a lot of questions to explore my understanding of routines, of basic hygiene, surgical procedures, post-operative care, and so on. I felt I was doing pretty well. Then I said, "Citizen Chief, I want to ask you a small favor."

His face darkened a little.

I said, "I brought with me from Moscow a couple of cherished items that I am afraid are going to be stolen if I try to keep them here. I would be sorry to see them go, but I would rather give them to someone who knows how to appreciate them than have them stolen. I wonder if you would accept them rather than have them just disappear. I feel sure you would appreciate them."

I told him what they were.

He was very good about it. He looked around carefully to make sure nobody was watching, because it would have been a very serious offense for him to accept a gift from a prisoner, and then he said he would be glad to have them, took the pen and the lighter, and pocketed them quickly, and said that he appreciated the gesture very much. He was very polite. His manner was that of one professional to another.

In three days he turned up in the hospital and told me to come to the operating room. There he quizzed me in detail about injections, sterilizing instruments, the uses of intravenous glucose, and so on. Fortunately most of the questions Adarich had anticipated, and many of them touched on procedures I had experienced as a patient. Then he called in the patients due for injections that morning and made me demonstrate.

I felt quite confident. I had developed a knack for working very fast, never deliberating or probing. A split second after I had sterilized the area with alcohol I had the needle in fast, and the patient hardly felt a thing. I would rub very hard with the alcohol, which numbed the area a little, and then bang! jam in the needle, joking all the time with the patient to distract him. Lavrenov nodded with approval as I worked.

Then he took me to the morgue. This was harder. A patient had died of TB and he told me to begin the autopsy. Now, I had never done one on my own, but I had watched both Atsinch and Adarich and had had some instruction from my English-speaking friend Kask. I was very nervous but I put on the best show I could and acted as if I did this sort of thing all the time. I thanked God that I had at least been trained in incisions by Atsinch. I grasped the scalpel in the proper way and made the first incision from the neck to the pubis. I had some trouble opening the chest, but I managed to make it seem that it was because of the pain from my own belly. I managed to extract the lungs, the heart, the liver, and so on, and even remembered some of Atsinch's remarks about what he would look for in the way of pathological indications. I kept moving as quickly as I could. I was determined not to show any hesitation.

It went well. I peeled the scalp forward and called an orderly we referred to as *nye Russki chyort*, "the non-Russian devil," because of his fierce Cherkess nationalism and denial of all things Russian. He was a serious Christian. He spoke poor broken Russian and always said, "I'm not a Russian devil!" So that is how he got his name. Nye Russki's duty in autopsies was to wield the skull saw. He started to saw away, but Lavrenov said, "Never mind. I'm satisfied."

And that was it. I was a feldsher! I had a real *pridurki* job and I was going to learn some real medicine.

At first I was assigned to Vasya Kargin to learn the routines of the duty shift. Then after a few days I took my first full assignment, which was, for reasons I never understood, a twenty-four-hour shift. I took one day, 8 A.M. to 8 A.M., Vasya took the next. We could usually grab a little sleep in the afternoon, but we were on duty for the full period. From midnight until 4 A.M. it was usually quiet. Adarich and Kask and the others slept in the hospital and I could call them if there was an emergency. If there was nothing doing I would practice my guitar for a while, and then systematically read through every medical text in the place. Every half hour a quick inspection of the ward, particularly to see that the mental patients were quiet. Sometimes there would be sulfa to administer every two or three hours.

At four thirty I went over to the small adjoining outpatient clinic to meet the first hopefuls looking for rest, for a chance to malinger, or for more serious help. Sympathy and the chance to spend a few days in bed were the biggest draws. There was an outer room where I, as the feldsher, was trained to put iodine on scrapes and cuts, bandage light wounds, hand out aspirins and stomach powders. If it was something more interesting than that, I had to refer the patient to the doctor, who usually arrived at about 5:30. I wore a white lab coat and all the prisoners called me "Doctor" automatically, unless they were my friends. My friends praised my cunning at getting such an easy job and expressed either envy or good wishes or both.

By 8 A.M. we had seen the outpatients, supervised breakfast, made rounds, and sometimes even started in the operating room. Then my replacement would come in, and I would go for a walk in the Zone to get some air, if it was not too hot, and then back to my old barracks, where I had been reinstalled, to sleep or do pretty much what I wanted until eight the next morning. Once the work brigades were counted out in the morning and the Zone locked up again, whoever was legitimately left behind was free to wander around the Zone as he pleased, as long as he kept well away from the fire zone.

On the second or third day that I was on my own in the outpatient clinic, a patient walked in as soon as I had opened the place. He was a hard-looking man with strange eyes and a grim expression. There were tattoos on almost every centimeter of exposed skin. A professional.

"Doctor," he said grimly, "I have a terrible stomachache."

"Where?" I said, sympathetically.

He motioned me to come close. "Here!" he whispered fiercely, pulling back his shirt. His right hand was inside his shirt, holding a wicked curved knife like a miniature scimitar. "I want opium. I am always treated very well here. You're new. You might as well know that if I don't get my opium, you get the knife."

We used tincture of opium for extreme diarrhea. I had often had it. Five or six drops in a glass of water—very bitter.

I was in a quandary because I knew if I refused him, he would try to kill me and probably succeed, and if I gave him what he wanted, I would never get rid of him and he would have a certain amount of power over me. I was thinking furiously. I got out a cone-shaped beaker and told him to show me how much he usually took. He indicated a little over a centimeter. I quickly reached in and grabbed an iron solution we used, tincture *ferri pomati*, and threw in a few drops of bitters that we kept for appetite, and then stirred in some water and gave it to the addict. I moved as quickly as I could so that it would seem as though I was very sure of myself. I moved to put the table between me and him as he drank it, and felt behind me for a scalpel in case he should pull his knife.

But he just tossed the mixture back and said, "Very nice, Doctor, thank you very much," with a big mischievous grin that transformed his grim features, and went out.

I thought, I'll see him again. So I made up a bottle of my spurious mixture and put a *Tincture of Opium* label on it, and shoved it to the back of the case where no one would use it by mistake. I told Leonid, the other feldsher, about it. He knew the addict. The same man came back the next time I was on duty and told me that after the last dose he had felt great all day. I poured him another out of the fake bottle. He looked a little puzzled when he drank it. I still remember the lilies and snakes and hearts and diamonds all over his arm and the name VANYA on one hand. The next time I saw him he complained that he wasn't getting much of a lift from opium anymore. He looked at the label closely and then asked for a triple dose. After I poured it he walked around the dispensary for several minutes looking disconsolate. I let him alone. Finally he heaved a big sigh and said, "Well, I don't know . . ."

Then he went out. I never saw him again.

Much later I had a visit from a guard named Zavyalov. He was a terror to the prisoners, a brutal man who enjoyed violence. He walked in and demanded ether. "What for?" I asked him.

"I drink it," he said, with a happy smile.

I said, "You'll blow up. That stuff is the most volatile liquid there is!"

"No, I won't," he said. "I keep my whole esophagus open. Give me some and I'll show you."

I thought it was crazy but I did not want any trouble. I gave him 10 cc. in a little medicine glass.

He threw his head back like a sword swallower. Then he threw the ether straight down with a sudden motion. There was a kind of deep rumble from within as the ether boiled up from the heat of his gullet and stomach. Then a terrific rush of vapor as it came back up again. The whole dispensary stank of it.

The guard got up from his chair. His grin was even broader, but his eyes looked very strange. He said, "Thank you! Thank you, Doctor!" in a very loud voice. I saw him head for the door with strange, unsteady steps as if his legs were mounted on universal joints. He missed the first few steps and crashed down into the yard on his face. He never came to me again for ether and the next time I saw Zavyalov, years later, he was a much changed man.

Those mornings in the outpatient clinic when the camp was coming to life were like an old movie in slow motion: the lights still on in the Zone at four thirty and the shadows just beginning to gray out at the edges. People began to emerge from the barracks, silent, slow-moving, making their way to the toilets; the brigade bread men making their way to the bakery, heads down, rubbing sleep out of their eyes, caked with dust, moving like sleep-walkers. The wind had not started up yet and at first the silence was broken only by faint noises of doors opening around the barracks and the muffled calls of guards rousting out the persistent sleepers. Pretty soon though, the pace picked up. The line began to form outside the outpatient clinic. Sleepy, grumbling, still pretty subdued.

Most of them were trying a dodge. The physician had to discriminate carefully between those who really needed help and those who were faking. When someone was caught out, he usually just grinned sheepishly and said, "Maybe I'll make it next time!" The commonest dodge was an artful raising of the temperature, and we had to check carefully to see whether the pulse rate had also gone up its necessary twelve beats per minutes for each degree of fever. Normal pulse rate, you threw the guy out.

There was a Lithuanian quarry worker who always complained about his stomach and had a reputation of being a dogged malingerer. One night they brought him in on stretchers screaming his head off and, as usual, clutching his belly. I was all set to dismiss him again, but I did a routine examination first and to my surprise found that his abdominal muscles were drawn tense in a boardlike hardness. This means that something serious is going on. I put him to bed and took a blood sample to Kask. The white blood count was a whopping high one, so we knew something was wrong.

Adarich diagnosed a perforated stomach ulcer, and that is what it proved to be. I assisted Adarich in the operation to close it up and had my first experience at extensive cleaning of the abdominal cavity and the subsequent suturing, much of which I did myself under Adarich's cheerful direction.

In that case I had been perfectly certain that the man, even though he had such a long history of faking illness, was in bad shape. Often it was more difficult.

Whenever we had more legitimate sick than we could accommodate, Lavrenov had to make the hard decision.

It took a lot to get you into bed. Later in the winter when we cut off a lot of toes for frostbite, we would send the man back to his barracks right after the amputation unless there were extensive complications from infection.

I did a lot of practicing on toes and fingers in the morgue, making lateral incisions in a wedge shape so that there would be skin to close over the end of the stump, then cutting neatly through the joint itself, imagining which tissue would be healthy and which destroyed by the frostbite, and then closing up with the skin flaps. Soon I was quite adept at this, and often helped Adarich with these minor amputations, either cutting or suturing or cleaning away diseased tissue and bad skin. Eventually, during the depths of the winter, this became almost a commonplace procedure and Adarich asked me to do it by myself. At first he stayed with me to help me over the anxiety of being responsible for a living patient, but soon he was satisfied and after that I did a couple entirely on my own. Normally these amputations were done quickly in the evenings when the returning convoys came in with their inevitable cuts, scrapes, bone fractures, and other accidental results of the day at work.

One evening two men came out of the shadows helping a third they supported between them. He was Borodin, a one-legged former navy captain who had a bad reputation as a stool pigeon. Borodin limped along on his peg leg and whimpered softly as he came in. There was a trickle of blood oozing from a dark spot on his forehead. When I looked closely I was terrified. There was a triangular hole straight through the skull and clear fluid and bits of brain tissue were oozing out. There were fragments of bone around the wound but it was a clear, perfectly formed triangle. Amazingly, Borodin was conscious. He kept whimpering, "Help me, please help me." I sent for Adarich. Adarich sent for Lavrenov.

It was clear to everyone that this was a Council of Justice attempted killing, or at least a private vengeance against a stool pigeon. Borodin claimed he did not know who had done it, but that there were two people. The two who brought him in said they had just found him lying behind a shed at the work site.

Adarich was all set to hospitalize him and prepare for major surgery, but Lavrenov forbade him to do that. "Just dress the wound, just dress the wound!" he insisted, and ran off to the headquarters building.

Lavrenov was sure that Borodin would be murdered if he was hospitalized, and while he couldn't have cared less about Borodin, he definitely did not want the bother of an official inquiry into a murder in his hospital. That was the kind of thing that could cost a man his job. Within half an hour he was back with transfer papers and Borodin was shipped out.

We heard later, months later, that he was eventually taken to the Toishet camp in Siberia and that while he was taking his compulsory shower at the time of admission a young man, tipped off by the peg leg maybe, but in any case warned about the stool pigeon by the prison telegraph, knifed him under the shower. He was dead within an hour of arrival at that camp. That's how effective the prison telegraph was.

All corpses came to the hospital morgue, whether they died in the hospital, were murdered by prisoners' justice committees, shot by guards, or died from despair or exhaustion. We usually had between six and twelve corpses in the morgue at one time, and then if they had all been autopsied Nye Russki would call the corpse wagon and load it himself, and off they would go to have their heads bashed in and then be buried in shallow graves in the desert. In winter, for some reason, instead of an axe in the head the corpses got a red-hot iron pushed into the chest. They were usually frozen in winter because the morgue was unheated.

The morgue was Nye Russki's domain. He had to keep it clean, wash down the slab, carry corpses in and out. Guards never went in there, partly because of superstition and partly because the hospital staff spread the story that all corpses were highly infectious. Nye Russki told me that there was a cache of forbidden books and other contraband under the autopsy table, perfectly safe, and that if I wanted to conceal any small articles so that the periodic searches would not put them into the hands of the MVD, I should put them in the morgue. We could easily have hidden weapons there if we had had any. If I had ever been lucky or dumb enough to have a gun in camp I would have stashed it in the morgue.

Autopsies were never performed less than twenty-four hours after a death, by standing orders. Anyone dying in the hospital had a very thorough pathological examination. Anyone shot by a guard was examined only around the wound, and a report was written on the path of the dumdum bullet from the guard's automatic, point of entry, exit point, description of damage caused internally. Lavrenov attended all such autopsies himself and had to make a report to the local MGB commandant, who was known in camp as the *kum*, or godfather.

As far as we could tell, the *kum* was chiefly occupied with creating internal conflict in camp, setting the Ukrainians against the Russians (which was not hard) by spreading rumors and so on, on the divide-and-rule principle. But he had to be notified whenever there was a shooting. If a couple of guards got trigger happy and shot someone on a bet or because they thought they could get away with it or because he stepped out of line in the column or actually did enter the fire zone, the *kum* would come and photograph the corpse, but not before it was thrown into the fire zone to create a legitimate reason for the killing.

The morgue was usually well populated, one way or another.

One morning Nye Russki came to me and said, "How many corpses are we supposed to have?"

I checked the book. "Nine," I said. "Why?"

"Oh, it's all right. Thank you." He went away.

The next day after the camp was counted and locked up, but before the corpse wagon had come, Nye Russki asked me again. There had been no deaths in the night. I said we still had nine and pressed him to know what the trouble was.

"I'm either having eye trouble or trouble with my head," he said unhappily. "I know you are right about the nine, but two days in a row I count ten. Please." He motioned me to go with him.

We went to the morgue. Nine corpses. I counted nine, stretched out in their underclothes on the packed earth floor. Nye Russki counted nine.

"Okay now?" I asked him.

"No. I counted ten a few minutes ago. I *know* I did. What the hell is going on here!"

The next day he came to me looking terrible. "I need some medicine," he said in a panicky way. "We have twelve corpses!"

"Eleven," I said.

"That's just it. There should be eleven, but I'm counting twelve. Please come with me again!"

I went. We counted. Eleven corpses.

Poor Nye Russki felt terrible. He was really a bit superstitious himself, I think, despite the bluff and cheerful manner and the daily embraces with the dead. And I think he was really worried about his mind as well.

The next day he came to me looking very much relieved.

"Please," he said with a big smile. "I know where our extra corpse comes from. Come! Come! I want to show you!"

He took me outside. We had a ladder leading to the roof of the hospital for snow removal in the winter. He motioned me to follow him up the ladder. The morgue roof was lower than the hospital roof and had a small skylight. We looked through. There was an extra corpse, all right. It was sitting up reading one of our contraband books!

Something clicked. I knew that there had been a search on for several days for an *otkazchik*, one of a group of conscientious objectors who would not work on their Sabbath and were always being beaten up for it. The search had been a bit confused because, although no one could ever find this guy, the head count was perfectly all right so that officially nobody was missing.

I said to Nye Russki, "You watch the outside door of the morgue. I'll go and talk to the corpse."

I had recognized him. His name was Valka; I had treated him in the hospital, and had seen him often in the Zone. When I unlocked the door he was lying among the corpses trying to look like one. I went into the morgue humming a little tune. I walked right over and stood staring down at him. I stopped humming and just stared. I did not make a sound for almost a minute. He could not stand the suspense, I guess. He opened his eyes after a bit and grinned at me sheepishly. "Hello, Doc," he said.

"Tell me about it," I said.

He had made himself a wire lock-pick and slipped into the morgue on Saturday, his Sabbath, to avoid going to work. He took off his clothes and hid them under a corpse, and when the guards came to count from the door, because they never would come inside, he was just another corpse. There was no alarm then, when the columns went out, because the total camp count was all right. But his brigadier missed him at the work site and nobody could account for his whereabouts. Once the camp was locked up for the day the kid slipped out and came back in again the next morning to hide until the head count was over.

For two or three days after we discovered Valka, he managed to hide somewhere else in the Zone. Then one morning there was a terrible commotion outside the hospital. He had been found. Gusak himself, the camp commandant, was screaming at the terrified *otkazchik* right in front of the hospital door, which was crowded with staring patients. The commandant screamed curses and started slapping the kid around; then he grabbed him and threw him to the ground and began kicking him. He twisted his arms behind him and slapped on a pair of handcuffs of a particularly vicious kind that tighten up with every movement until you are in agony. They have a sort of ratchet that slips only one way, and unless you are perfectly still, which is usually not possible, they keep on squeezing you more and more.

The patients watching from the hospital door were enraged at this brutality. Gusak had only one guard with him. In front of the hospital they were out of sight of the nearest watchtower, and no guard would have shot anyway with Gusak in a crowd. The patients stormed out and surrounded Gusak and the guard, grabbed the kid, and took him into the hospital. Gusak and the guard were intimidated and could not identify any of this mob because they were in their prison underwear without any numbers. The patients got the boy's handcuffs off and slipped him back into the Zone and told him to be damn sure to rejoin his work brigade the next day.

Within half an hour a guard came to the hospital and demanded the handcuffs. All the patients pretended ignorance. "We don't know anything about any handcuffs! What do you mean?" The guard went away and later an officer came and was very stern. One prisoner said, as if confessing, "I'm sorry, they were thrown down the toilet. You'll have to dig for them." The officer was furious. "How am I going to account for state property!" he shouted, and stalked out. The incident was dropped.

Later that night when everything had settled down, I went to see the man who had "confessed." I said, "I'd like to see those handcuffs, just out of curiosity."

"Doctor, you know I threw them down the toilet."

Now this was a very devious guy, Konstantin the Sailor, a semicolored who had spent a long time at sea and not only had a ship in full sail rippling across his back but the sum where the tattoo artist had worked out the price in German marks, as

$$
\begin{array}{rr}
\text{Tattoo} & 97 \\
\text{Ink} & 13 \\
\hline
110 & \text{marks}
\end{array}
$$

or something like that.

He was in the hospital because he had fallen sixty feet in the copper mine; he had landed on piles of rubber hose which saved his life despite a lot of internal injuries. I always had trouble with him, but I admired his spirit. I said, "Look, Kostya, I know they went down the toilet, but I'd like to see them anyway. I've always heard about these things and I'd like to examine them in case I ever have to deal with them!"

We were sitting in the darkened ward, on his bed. He finally winked at me and produced the handcuffs, with their key, from under the mattress. "Bring them back!" he said.

I slipped into the examining room to look at them in the light. I put the key in the lock and then put the handcuffs on my own wrists and closed them. I would be able to bend my fingers back and turn the key, I thought.

The design was cunning and fiendish. With the slightest movement of my hands the ratchet slipped and the cuffs tightened up. I twisted my hand to get the key. The cuffs tightened harder. I could just reach the key with my fingertips. I panicked. The pain was quite severe and my fingers were swelling and turning blue. I tugged too hard. The key broke off!

I was embarrassed as hell. I could imagine someone walking into the room any minute and seeing what I had done. I had to find a way out. I strode up and down and tried to think of it, but the pain was too much for me. I flipped my lab coat over my hands in a poor attempt to conceal my incredible blunder, then I went back to the ward. Konstantin the Sailor was sleeping.

"Kostya," I whispered, almost choking, "wake up!"

"What is it?" he said, still half asleep.

"I've broken the key and I can't get the cuffs off!"

He started to laugh. He couldn't stop. Soon the whole ward was awake and Konstantin was telling everyone.

"Kostya, please, for God's sake!" I said. But he just rolled about with laughter.

Finally he said, "Go and get a hypo or some other needle."

"What for?"

"Oh, never mind. I always carry one in my heel. You should, too, you know. Even a doctor can end up in handcuffs!"

He pulled out his shoes, pulled a concealed needle out of the heel, slipped it into the ratchet, and I was free.

"Take a hint, Doctor," said Konstantin the Sailor. "If they ever throw these things at you they'll slap your wrists down on their knees to tighten them. Then they'll throw you in the cell for half an hour. By that time you'll be screaming your head off and your hands won't be any good for six months. So keep a needle in your heel. As soon as you're in the cell start yelling. Get the needle out. Loosen the cuffs and keep still so they won't tighten again, and then yell harder and harder until they come to take them off again. Got it?" And then he started laughing all over again. I was blushing when I left the ward; the patients all applauded merrily.

You would assume that in a prison where most of the population was too exhausted to think about sex, and all of the population was male anyway, that venereal disease would be uncommon, and so it was—among the prisoners. But quite frequently a guard would come to me with gonorrhea because he was afraid to face the punishment Soviet soldiers got in those days if they reported their VD to their own clinic. We had sulfa drugs at first, and later on penicillin. I treated many guards, and they usually became at least moderately friendly as a result. Anyway, one morning one such friendly guard, quite a nice guy, which was very unusual, came to the hospital and asked me to come quickly, there was a wounded man at the BUR and we should bring stretchers. Adarich was away somewhere, so I went myself with Vanya and Nye Russki.

The BUR was really a prison within a prison. It was surrounded by its own stone wall on three sides. On the fourth side was the outside wall of the prison, with the fire zone. As we walked over there, the guard told me what had happened. A group of informers held in the BUR on protective detention were being taken for their morning walk. One young man who had been terribly depressed for days broke from the group as they passed beneath the watchtower and began to climb the barbed wire of the fire zone. The man in the tower could have shot immediately. Instead he yelled down one warning. But the poor kid, who by now was moaning and whimpering at the cuts he was getting from the barbed wire, just screamed, "Yes! Please shoot me! I don't want to live anymore!"

The guard took careful aim and shot him in the leg.

We found him in the wire, about six feet up, entangled and motionless. His leg was at a strange angle and bleeding profusely. One of the guards had wire cutters and was already trying to free the body when we got there, and in a minute or two we had him out, ran him to the hospital, and had a look at that leg.

It was shattered below the knee by the dumdum bullet. Only a shred of skin and tendons still held. There was no question of saving it; I knew that much. But Adarich was away. Shkarin was helping out at a work site somewhere. Kask was really only a laboratory scientist and had not touched a scalpel since medical school. Kublanov was terrified of surgery of any kind.

I had to face it: I was the only one who could do it.

I had seen a couple of leg amputations, but I had paid little attention to detail. This was a lot more than a toe or a finger. I *had* to have more information than was in my head. I gave the boy a morphine shot to knock him out and applied a tourniquet above the knee. I cut away the remains of the leg, by just making a clean cut through the bits of skin and tendon that still held on. Then I packed a sterile dressing all around the shattered stump, left the tourniquet in place, and ran to the examination room for Adarich's textbook on surgery.

The diagrams were very clear. I grabbed the book up and ran to the morgue with the amputation knives. I had to practice first.

I did not stop to wash or do any other preparation. There was a cadaver still on the autopsy table. I laid the book down on its stitched-up belly and made the first incision: straight on one side, a wedge on the other to provide a flap. I peeled back the skin. I had no idea how to cut the muscles, but I just followed the pictures. It went remarkably well. I was trembling a lot but I forced myself to keep going, looking carefully for blood vessels I would have to tie, and seeing how the muscles all lay. I knew that I could suture the flap all right: that would not be so different from the toes I had done. I did not saw the bone on the cadaver. Once I got the muscles all cut, I went over the diagrams and the cadaver several times to make sure that everything was clear in my mind. Part of me was praying that Adarich would show up. Another part was beginning to say, All right: you can do it, now *do it!* I went back to the O.R.

I insisted that Kublanov come to help me, to hold instruments and hemostats. I sent Vanya to find Nye Russki; I was not able to face cutting the bone and I thought that Nye Russki, having sawed open all those skulls during autopsies, would probably not mind if I turned that part of it over to him.

Finally it was time to begin. I released the tourniquet and let the blood flow for a few seconds. I picked up the scalpel and took a deep breath. I looked around the room at the eyes of the others. The tension was thick in that operating room and all eyes were on me except those of the unconscious boy. Yet something about his face bothered me, and I covered it with a cloth. Nye Russki stood opposite me. There was a warmth in his good, compassionate eyes that gave me strength. I looked again at the book which Vanya held for me. My hands were still trembling when I made the first incision.

After that it went well. I peeled back the skin and the underlying fascia. I tied off the larger blood vessels. Then I lifted everything away to reveal about two centimeters of bone above the shattered end, and nodded at Nye Russki. He nodded back reassuringly, and then I looked away while he applied the saw. It was a neat, straight cut, and the bone was sound and healthy above the cut. I folded a flap of muscle over the bone to make a cushion and then sutured the whole thing up. We kept saline and glucose dripping into him, and Nye Russki volunteered to stay with him when he came to, and call me or Kublanov if he needed painkillers. Then I simply had to go and lie down. I felt completely exhausted. I went to sleep on

Adarich's bed, and when I woke up Adarich was sitting beside me. He smiled warmly.

"That was a fine job, Alexander Mikhailovich, my boy," he said. "I'm thinking of retiring, actually, now that you can take over."

That boy recovered well. There was some superficial infection for a while. Adarich reopened a couple of centimeters of stitching and put in a drain until it cleared up, and after that there was no more trouble. He was eventually moved into a barracks largely occupied by fellow Ukrainians, and some of them made a peg leg for him. He learned to walk reasonably well, and was made caretaker of the barracks, so that he never had to go out to work again. His brief stint as an informer was forgiven and forgotten, as far as I know. In any case, nobody tried to kill him and I was sorry when he was moved again and I lost track of him, because I naturally felt that in a sense he was a child of my own.

Throughout my stay in the hospital my own health improved and my strength began to come back very well. I supplemented my diet with daily injections of glucose, which I administered at night when the hospital was quiet. I had access to all the vitamins I wanted, especially B and C, and niacin; so there was no more scurvy and no risk of pellagra. A friendly guard got me some brewer's yeast tablets from the military pharmacy, and I took several grams daily, which led to another interesting development in hospital life.

There was a Ukrainian orderly named Musichka who always kept a little bread aside and put it in a jug of water to ferment for a few days to make a very light *kvass*, a sort of beer with little kick to it but a pleasant flavor. Musichka passed this out to patients and staff alike every day, and even though the alcoholic content was almost invisible, the faint beery taste was good for everybody's morale. I used to dissolve my sugar allotment in it, and one day I got the idea that this would be a more palatable way to take the terrible-tasting brewer's yeast.

I had just stirred the sugar and yeast into the *kvass* when a convoy brought in three miners who had been caught when an ore bucket accidentally dumped. Two were dead on arrival and the third one horribly injured, and I had to go and help Adarich in the operating room. I remember cleaning up a badly crushed skull while the man kept reciting prayers without really regaining consciousness. Then Adarich gingerly picked out pieces of skull and tried to patch him up again. He kept reciting prayers until he died. It was about two hours before I remembered my little beverage and went back to the room where I had left it on the windowsill.

The drink was almost boiling. Fermentation was going ahead at a very lively rate. I took a few drops across to the lab and put them under Kask's microscope and watched the little organisms budding and seething in the brew. I thought this might be pretty good when it settled down a bit. I washed out a bunch of lab bottles. I found some wire to clamp their glass stoppers on with, because while I really was totally innocent in the craft of brewing, I knew that there would be some pressure build-up and I would have to hold the stoppers in. Late at night, when the bubbling seemed to have settled down pretty well, I poured the brew into my little bottles and wired on the glass stoppers and put them in a cabinet in the examining room. The next night, of course, when I was off duty, they exploded and nearly scared the life out of an orderly named Yanyev. We had a terrific fist fight over it, but later several of us settled down to a regular production, in small bottles, so we had a brew coming off about every three weeks once we learned how to do it properly. Later in the winter I got some friends in the DOZ to make me a small barrel so we could get into mass brewing, hiding the vat in the morgue, under the autopsy table. But when the first barrel came off, our new feldsher Vasya Kargin got drunk and went around the camp at night embracing lampposts and shouting "Long live President Truman!" The MVD threw Kargin in the cooler. We decided that the brewing was getting a bit dangerous and cut it out for the time being. Soon after, the barrel was confiscated, so that was that.

CHAPTER

22

BEFORE I FINISHED MY DAYS IN THE HOSPITAL I HAD DONE, IN ADDITION TO amputated toes and the amputated leg, three practice appendectomies on cadavers and one on a live patient. I had former patients all over the camps, and many of them stayed friends for the rest of my imprisonment. There were several guards who, having been cured of gonorrhea by me, would do little favors, look the other way if I bent the rules a little, and so on. My confidence in my medical ability was growing, and with it my morale. I developed a strenuous program of exercise once my general health was in top shape again. I had done some minor acrobatics when I was a kid, and now I began to walk on my hands again, usually practicing up and down the hospital corridor, which was about twenty meters long. One night as I was grunting along on the return trip, trying to accomplish the full forty meters on my hands—which I had never made yet—I was interrupted by a scream from the end of the hall. I jumped to my feet and saw an old Polish professor we were treating for hepatitis reeling around the corridor with his hands to his head, yelling what sounded like prayers in Polish. I could not imagine what was wrong. As I ran to him he tripped on the coal box, fell, bumped his head, and went out cold on the floor. I dragged him to the operating room as quietly as I could and began to treat the scratch on his head. I was afraid he might have a concussion, although it did not seem that bad a bump. In a few moments his eyes flickered and opened. He looked quite panicky. "I am going to die, Doctor. Please tell my family. The address is Krakowskie Przedmiescie, 655. Oh, God have mercy on my soul, God have mercy!" And on and on so fast I could hardly understand him at all.

I kept trying to interrupt him. Finally I seized him firmly by the shoulders and gave him a sharp shake. "Stop all this!" I said firmly. "Tell me what the trouble is!"

"I am going to die. I am dying of liver dystrophy. I know the symptoms are hallucinations. I got up to go to the bathroom, and oh, Doctor! When I came into the corridor I saw you walking on the ceiling!"

He was appalled when I burst into laughter. But when I told him what it was about he was greatly relieved and finally got some reassurance when I did a blood pressure and heartbeat and took a blood sample and all the rest, and in the end he was able to laugh a bit weakly over the joke, finish his trip to the toilet, and go back to bed.

Memory brings all these things quickly to the surface. They were the things that created life in the midst of death and humanity in the midst of a constant and diabolical oppression. Incidents like these comic ones, moments of success in the operating room or in the illicit commerce of spoons and beds and flatirons, these are the pleasures that come to mind when people say, "What was it like in camp?" But these were rare moments— small bright spots almost obliterated by the gloom and terror out of which each day was built.

Years later, sitting around with the Trade Union, which was how former inmates referred to themselves to save embarrassment in the presence of the uninitiated, we would drink a sad toast to "all those still at sea," and then talk about the good aspects of those terrible days. We would remember the long and fascinating conversations with men of character and intellect whom we had had the good fortune of knowing through the misfortune of camp. We would remember every joke, every bottle of home brew, every funny song and every odd character: that was easy. To recall the horrors was work, and we usually avoided it. Working now over these pages, I avoid it until I cannot anymore, because that is the real fabric of my story. I take a holiday page after page to recall the funny things, and then remember that I must go back to work.

As healthy and productive as the hospital was, in terms of my physical recuperation and my growth as a human being, in skill and in the maturity that comes from responsibility for the lives of other human beings and from intimate association with a dedicated, warm professional like Yevgeni Petrovich Adarich or the marvelous humanity of a simple man like Nye Russki—who sat, night after night when he should have been off duty, gently massaging the foreheads of men in pain, comforting and carrying the paraplegics to the toilet and trying to share the burdens of their despair—despite all this, when I force my memory to be balanced and accurate and fair, it reminds me that my life was surrounded by death. Unnecessary, cruel, lonely death. It reminds me of grief. I had become hardened in some ways, to protect myself. But grief sometimes broke through any barriers I had built around me, and that was hard.

All the men who would never go back to their families, who died in tears of loneliness. Ultimate, cosmic loneliness showed on their faces.

The fourth ward held the cardiac patients. We had little special treatment for them. The death rate was high. Every few days someone was moved into the bed of someone who had died, and the anguish and fear that came with that bed was terrible to see. It hastened death.

The cancer patients suffered terribly and, since our morphine was limited and had to be reserved for the almost daily influx of the walking wounded in extremes of pain, we simply had to make do with aspirin or mild sedatives, and so the cancer ward was a space filled with pain. I began to hoard a private supply of morphine ampoules. I did not even tell Adarich. When a cancer patient seemed near the end and the pain was unbearable, I would take an ampoule or two from my private supply, and inject it quietly into the poor agonized soul. I would sit by his bed in the night and caress his hand, and say, "There. The pain will be going soon. Soon you will feel much better," hour after hour.

I became familiar with the feeling of a hand that crosses from life into death. A hand in my hand.

And while I sat with one of these dying men trying to give him a little comfort, I knew that all over Dzhezkazgan men were dying alone, falling in their tracks in convoy to die as their fellow slaves stumbled over their bodies, dying without any human contact or comfort in punishment cells, on barbed wire with bullets in their chests, dying in bunks a hundred yards away because there was no room for them here in the little hospital. I knew that most of these men, almost all of them, would have lived out some kind of life with other human beings, raised children, loved wives, done some work they could take satisfaction in, made some choices about the direction of their lives, might have done all this, except that a state that wanted their slave labor had created an elaborate machinery for the creation of guilt where no guilt existed. Almost no one I knew who died, or lived, in Dzhezkazgan, had committed an offense that would be recognized by the law of any country with a democratic parliament and a tradition of loyal dissent. They were innocent men. I took their deaths to be murder, whether they died of bullets or fever or cancer or despair.

There was a boy named Arkadi. Arkadi was a poet from Moscow. He had been in the underground movement and was considered to be dangerous. He had a boisterous sense of humor and an irrepressible talent for embarrassing his captors. As a result he was constantly persecuted in camp and had spent days in a freezing solitary cell in the BUR.

I felt a strong affinity for Arkadi. I call him a boy, although he was a year or two older than I, say twenty-seven or twenty-eight, because he was boyish in his enthusiasm and his humor until the day he died.

He was one of those young dissidents of the late forties who got into trouble with his eyes wide open. He wrote savagely satirical poems about the regime and about the Leader and circulated them privately. To anyone else that would seem like folly or suicide. To Arkadi it was the only honorable thing he knew how to do, to fight the injustice and the waste and the inhumanity he believed were built into his world. He loved Russia, but not what was happening to her.

When they brought him from the BUR he had bilateral pneumonia. We had no procedures for surgical treatment when the lung abscessed, and we had no antibiotics except sulfa. He was going down every day, and yet he was always gay, always making new poems, love poems, poems about the people in the ward, poems about a bright future.

Arkadi had freckles, which is rare for a Russian. He was a tall, lanky guy who liked to stride around the ward in his prison underwear with his bony knees poking through the cloth, reciting poems and telling funny stories. At night we sat together for hours. I would bring cool cloths for his forehead. He had a constant high fever and he coughed a great deal and brought up enormous quantities of fetid green matter from his chest. There was always a heavy smell of decay on his breath. Yet I loved this boy. We sat close together and talked about how the world could be if all nations put their faith in parliamentary democracy. He believed it could work in the Soviet Union, although it would take a long time and a lot of education. I scrounged some fine white paper for Arkadi and had it bound in book form, and he filled the book with poetry, some his own, some he knew by heart from Russian poets he loved, like Gumilyov. I loved Gumilyov's poem "The Captains," about the freebooters, the captains at sea who lived on their courage and their skill, and Arkadi loved to read it to me, aloud, between spasms.

He wrote out poems in French, and then translated them for me. And I remember a romantic poem by Ilya Selvinsky about a Roman woman who had slaves brought up to her as lovers and then had them killed and kept their heads as mementos. This was all decadent poetry, of course, by modern Soviet standards. Gumilyov had been shot in 1921.

Adarich told me that Arkadi could never survive. I suppose that Arkadi himself knew that, privately; he never showed it. In another camp not far away there was a Spanish chest surgeon named Fuster who could have done the surgery, and one of the few things I have to hate Lavrenov for is that he refused to transfer Arkadi to that camp. For four months he went down steadily while we watched, and we could do nothing. Four months of nights by his bedside taking away the little pan of stinking sputum, and trying to cool him down, and watching the laughing mouth catch every few minutes with another spasm.

Once he said wistfully, "How I would love to eat some onions!"

In four years I had never seen an onion. But somehow, through a friendly guard, through friends of Arkadi around the camp (he was widely known), we found some bright green spring onions. He was delighted.

He was very weak. I gave him extra ampoules of glucose and alcohol intravenously whenever I could; they cooled him and gave him a little more strength to breathe, but the abscess in his lung was suffocating him, and we both knew it. One night I was sitting on the edge of the bed beside him. We were not talking; he was too choked, too short of breath.

He managed to say, "Could you lift me up, please? I can't breathe."

I bent over and put his arms around my shoulders and gently lifted him into a sitting position. He motioned toward the little kidney basin. I held it under his mouth and he coughed into it. The cough brought up nearly a hundred cc. of foul stuff. I said, "Here, let me put you down and then I'll go and empty this." He just nodded. I gently put him down again.

When I came back he was quiet. I sat down and said, "Well, Arkadi, you want to sleep now, don't you? Shall I leave you now, and come back in an hour to see how you are?"

He did not answer. I bent over him to draw the blanket up under his chin. Suddenly I became aware that there was no foul smell from his breath. I felt his chest. It was still. I opened his eyelid; the pupil was very large. I pressed it from beneath the lower lid. It formed the oval cat's eye. Arkadi was dead.

I said, "This is a hero's death, but I have no way to honor him."

He died because he believed in something fine and refused to hide it or to compromise it. I could think of nothing finer.

I went outside behind the morgue. There was a friendly guard on duty around the hospital, and he made no objection if we wanted a little walk at night as long as we stayed close by. Behind the morgue was shadow where the floodlights from the walls could not reach. I could be alone with my thoughts there. I could see the stars. I had learned about Sirius from someone in camp, and took it as my personal star. I looked up and said good-by to Arkadi, somewhere in the stars. I thought of the star traveling westward through the night, toward America. I tried to recall Mary's face. It was too far away. I tried to recall my own state of mind of four years back. Was that all? I was maturing too fast. I had seen too much death. Where was the carefree American kid I used to be? I felt a sadness that was like a deep burning in my gut. I wished that I could have some peace in which to feel this sadness; I did not want the sadness to go: it was the right thing to feel at the time. I just wanted to be quiet and peaceful with it, but I could feel no peace because a hundred meters away was a man in a tower with an automatic loaded with seventy-two dumdum bullets in its underslung drum, and I could not feel peace that close to so much power for death.

I yearned for living people to love. One I loved had just died, another was so far away her face was fading from me.

I went back in.

The next day Adarich asked me to help him with Arkadi's autopsy. I just shook my head and went quickly out of the room.

And a strange thing that memory does: for twenty years I never spoke Arkadi's name and never thought of him. When the image of that brave young spirit came suddenly out of nowhere, as I worked to recall the days and nights in that hospital in Dzhezkazgan, it was long after I had reconstructed the whole story and remembered the poetry and the nights on the ward and the details of his dying before I could recall his name at all. That is what terrible pain can do to the memory.

One morning a man in the line-up of hopefuls had such a bad cough and high fever that I knew when I looked out the door that he would have to be hospitalized. So although there was space for only three admissions that day, I mentally filled one of them before I even began my examinations, even though this fellow was almost at the end of the line.

He clearly had a raging pneumonia in one lung. His fever was just a hair below 40°C. His cheeks were flushed and his eyes drooping at the corners. Clearly a sick, sick man. And yet looking at him made me want to laugh. He was tall, with a very round bald head and slumped narrow shoulders. His face was a clown's face and his body was a clown's body. He seemed to have a spirit to match. Despite the illness he smiled and joked while I examined him. He was Ukrainian. He came from the KTR, the extreme hard labor camp. His name was Marusich.

I told Marusich I was going to hospitalize him and made him wait in the examining room while I saw the last two or three in the line-up. Then I took him along to the ward to show him his bed. The minute we entered the ward, a loud voice boomed from the back of the room, "Well, for heaven's sake! Whom do I see? It is his worship, the governor of Zhitomir!"

Marusich stared for a moment, then said, "Look at that! The governor of Odessa!"

The two men embraced each other warmly. I took it for a joke, of course, but I soon found out that both men had indeed been the equivalent of mayor in those considerable cities, and because they had stayed in their posts running their cities during the Nazi occupation, they had been convicted of collaboration and treason and sentenced to twenty years. I made friends with Marusich and discovered that he was still in politics: in camp he was one of the key figures in the Western Ukrainian "community," and a sort of underground leader who wielded a good deal of power. He was very grateful for the careful attention I gave him and told me that if I ever needed a little muscle to help me over a trouble spot here or there, just to call on him. I did not really expect to see him again, because he was in the KTR camp, but it was always possible that we would turn up on the same work assignment when the sad day came for me to leave the hospital, as I was sure it would; so I was glad of this offer and told him warmly and sincerely that I hoped we would meet again. He was a strong man. His lung healed quickly and I was sorry to see him go, because he was a source of cheer in the gloomy ward. As it happened, I would see him again, and soon, and his generosity would prove to be very helpful to me.

There was a crazy Kazakh named Shargai in our camp. Shargai always sang in a very loud voice, day and night, and he seldom slept. Although he kept his barracks-mates awake most of the night, there was nothing they could do about it. If they asked him to stop he looked at them in a way that indicated blank incomprehension. If they tried to shut him up by physical force they got hurt, because although Shargai was good-tempered he could not stand being manhandled, and he was huge and powerfully built. So the prisoners all complained to the administration, and the administration decided Shargai was insane and had to be hospitalized. That made him our problem.

We discovered that he had two passions: smoking crude, strong Kazakh tobacco, and helping other prisoners, especially those in trouble. He hated the administration and the Organs terribly, and assumed that any of their victims was deserving of a great deal of sympathy. But Shargai could not understand that to stop singing might be considered a way of helping: after all, he had a beautiful voice and knew all kinds of soulful Kazakh songs, and a lot of Chinese songs as well, having served briefly with the Kuomintang army.

I did two things. I canvassed all the Kazakhs I knew in camp, explained that we had one of their brothers in dire circumstances in the hospital, and said that the one thing they could do to help the poor fellow was to make sure that he had lots of tobacco. They responded like true brothers and, although the hospital began to take on a heavy smell from this tenacious smoke, we had periods of quiet.

I then discovered that one way Shargai liked to help was to carry things. If Nye Russki had a very heavy corpse, or there was firewood to be carried, or anything where great strength was needed, Shargai volunteered and was silently happy as long as his muscles were straining to lift and balance his load.

I decided to make him the water boy. We had no running water in the hospital. All the water had to be carried by hand from the central reservoir. So I explained to Shargai that there was a serious need for fresh water all the time, that we were always short and the patients were too weak and the staff too busy to carry it. He was delighted. With water he would save all the lives in the hospital. If one pail of water would help a little, one hundred pails would help one hundred times as much. His eyes gleamed with the excitement of saving all those lives by carrying water. Ten hours a day he carried water and at night collapsed exhausted and slept like a dead man. We had far too much water and had to detail ambulatory patients to carry it back. But nobody minded that because Shargai was silent all night, and although he sang in short, panting breaths as he ran back and forth with his pails, it was not very loud and he was never in one place long enough to bother anyone.

Shargai had a vision, a premonition about Stalin. Although there had been a few rumors of ill health in the Kremlin, there was no indication of anything seriously wrong with Stalin and few prisoners wasted energy worrying or hoping he would die. There had been one strange occurrence a few months earlier, in the fall of 1952. From time to time there were political indoctrination meetings held by the MVD, and into one of these meetings one evening burst the strange old fellow who ran the so-called boiler room, where you went to pick up hot water for your tea. He had a package under his arm. He shouted out, "The Soviet Power is overthrown. Stand at attention, you!" This was how he shouted at the captain in charge of the meeting, in a very commanding, peremptory, confident way. "I am in charge now. Take this parcel immediately to the Comrade Leader Iosif Stalin. From now on I am in command!"

Because of the presence of this strange old man, who had been a senior member of the Duma years and years ago, the captain for a moment was so confused and so conditioned to obey authority that he actually sprang to his feet and saluted and took the parcel that was to go to the Leader. Then he soon realized that he was dealing with a madman, and restored order and got the old man back to his boiler room. But there was something that struck everyone there and spread through the camp, about the phrase *the Soviet Power is overthrown.* People took it as some sort of omen.

The case of Shargai was much more arresting. Adarich and the other doctors often met in the evenings for political discussions. Needless to say, they were not much like the session that our boiler room man burst in upon. These talks were carried on at a frank and pretty intellectual level. The other two feldshers, who had virtually no education, and the orderlies, who were nearly illiterate, did not attend. But Shargai heard of these meetings and begged to be allowed to sit in. It was explained to him that he must not sing or the doctors would not be able to hear each other clearly. Shargai had a great respect for the doctors. You could say that he loved them, or us, for anyone with a white coat was included in his worship of the magic of medicine. He loved everyone in the hospital. He exuded love. But for the doctors it was nearly adoration. Because we were fond of him we let him attend the meetings. We did not know then that he had a huge brain tumor, but we did know that his mental condition was weakening. For long periods he was blank and uncomprehending. He was physically still powerful, however, and as winter came on I added coal and extra firewood to his burden-carrying. The extra demand pleased him, but we could see the blanks and the memory lapses increasing in frequency, and the joyousness of the man beginning to slip away.

In the meetings he was usually silent. Sometimes, however, he would deferentially ask leave to speak, and then make an observation usually based on his experience in China with the Kuomintang. His comments were often not very relevant but it was clear that stored away in that disorganized and gradually disintegrating brain there was a great deal of experience and a great many shrewd observations about the ways of men.

In the middle of February Shargai came around to each member of the discussion group in turn, very politely, to say that he had an important announcement to make and to ask, please, and very, very deferentially, if he might be allowed to make it at the next assembly. Everyone was very fond of poor Shargai by now, and nobody would think of refusing him, even though we were all quite certain it would be a strange and probably incomprehensible announcement.

We were very, very wrong.

About nine thirty at night he came to the little gathering. He sat down and looked around at each face very gravely.

"My dear, dear friends," he said. "I am so grateful that you have allowed me to come and make this important statement. It is a very important statement."

Shkarin said, just a trifle impatiently, "Well, that's all right, Shargai, just get on with it now."

We all immediately felt embarrassed, because Shargai said, "I know that I am going to die very shortly. Very, very soon. A few days at the most."

His manner was quite lucid. He went on.

"But that is not my announcement. My statement is that soon after my death the lives of all you prisoners will change radically, drastically, for the better. In fact, before many years after my death, all of you will be free men. But as soon as I am dead, things will begin to change for you."

We all humored him. "Well, Shargai, that's wonderful, tell us more about it. What will cause the change?"

Shargai said, "There will be a single occurrence in the Soviet Union of the greatest importance. It will take place soon after my death."

"Well, Shargai, what occurrence? Is it connected with your death?"

For a long time he would not tell us. Then he said, "Well, my dear friends, you have been so kind to me and I love you all so well, and I shall be so sorry to leave you all . . ." Tears formed and ran down his long, bony nose and dripped onto his huge moustache, and he had to cough and wipe his nose and collect himself before he could go on.

"The event is this. Almost as soon as I am gone, you will learn that the Leader is dead!"

Even though it was preposterous, there was something very powerful in the way Shargai told us this fantasy, and no one knew quite what to say. I do not recall who broke the silence, but I do know that we spent the rest of the evening humoring the poor man because we knew he was right about his own death anyway. Any serious political discussion was forgotten for the evening.

A few days later Shargai started to rave and to complain, when he was lucid, of terrible pains in his head. His eyes protruded and he looked wild and terrifying. But even in his delirium, that deep love of his fellow man and need for their love in return would show itself in the way his iron hand would grasp my arm when I tried to comfort him with pills or an injection.

A day or two later he lapsed into a coma. We kept him alive more than forty-eight hours after that. His lungs were bad from a lifetime of that terrible tobacco. His breathing became stertorous and he brought up a lot of foam. At ten thirty at night on the second day, during my duty, he died. I was with him for the last few hours. I was relieved to see him out of his pain.

We were supposed to wait at least three hours before sending a body to the morgue. I had checked Shargai's eyes by pressing them to see the cat's eye that shows death has come. The body was soon cold. About one o'clock, Vanya came and said he wanted to go to sleep, and couldn't he wake up Nye Russki and take Shargai to the morgue? I said, "Well, it's half an hour early, but he's stone cold now. Sure, go ahead."

They carried him out of the warm hospital into the freezing morgue. It was a bitter cold night. They took him by the outside route and I could hear their boots squeak on the snow.

I heard the morgue door open. It was a very silent night. Suddenly screams came from the morgue. The two men came running by the window and burst in on me almost speechless with fright. "He's come back to life. He's breathing! He has a strong pulse!"

I knew that could not be so. And yet there was always something spooky about Shargai; despite the fact that I had satisfied myself that he was dead and cold, I felt very strange. I ran to the morgue. Shargai's eyes were half-open and froth and vapor were coming regularly from his mouth. I fell on him and grabbed his hand. Dead cold. No pulse.

Of course, what had happened was that changing from the heat of the room where the poor man died to the subzero morgue had caused constrictions to force air and fluid from his chest. Vanya, who knew no medicine, had felt for a pulse with his thumb and found his own wildly beating heart.

I went back to the warmth of the hospital relieved, nearly relieved enough to laugh, and yet somehow moved to sadness for Shargai, and thinking how he had said so fervently that things would soon change for us.

Shargai died on February 28. Three days later, on March 3, there were cries and yells of celebration throughout the camp; news had come in from somewhere that Stalin was dead. Two days later, March 5, we got the official announcement.

Shargai had prophesied. The Leader was dead. And within a very short time things indeed began to change very much for us.

CHAPTER

23

LAVRENOV CAME INTO THE HOSPITAL AT MIDNIGHT. HE HAD NEVER DONE THAT before. He was highly agitated. He said, "What are you prisoners trying to accomplish?"

I said, "What do you mean?"

"Well, there must be a plot or an uprising or something. There is a whole unit of MVD surrounding the camp with machine guns!"

It came out later that there was a rumor among the MVD that Lavrenti Beria, who actually did try to take over the reins of Soviet power, had arranged to make some sort of special signal to all camp inmates to rise up simultaneously. It was as crazy a bit of speculation as you could imagine.

Rumor spread wildly in camp. It is amazing how much of it was more or less accurate. We heard about Marshal Zhukov coming into Moscow and surrounding the Kremlin with tanks and subduing the MVD forces. We heard tales of Malenkov being imprisoned by Beria. We heard all kinds of speculation about the causes of Stalin's death.

The armed forces around our camp were withdrawn soon, but there were rumors of mutinies in camps all over the Gulag Archipelago, which is the name ironically given to the entire network of Soviet prisons and labor camps: islands in a sea of oppression. The only immediately discernible result was a sense of anxiety among all the custodial personnel. In some cases this was shown by an unbelievable demonstration of friendliness toward the prisoners. After all, we might soon be freed, in masses, and it would be very unhealthy to be remembered by seventeen million ex-prisoners as a tyrant and a sadist.

There was an MGB commandant in Camp Number Three, not far from ours. Even before Stalin died, when the first rumors began to seep through the walls that he might be sick, this man, Tsukerashvili, astonished the prisoners who had known only the hardest treatment from him by going around shaking hands with them, calling them comrade, offering to get tobacco for them from town if they ran short, reminding them to put in a good word for him if he were ever accused of bad behavior.

Tsukerashvili was MGB, not MVD, but he was camp commandant because the number three camp was reserved for escapees and people with particularly notorious reputations. The MVD officials who heard of Tsukerashvili's strange behavior decided to get rid of him and reported to Moscow that he had gone crazy. He was called to Moscow to be examined. En route to Moscow he heard of Stalin's death. When he arrived he was kept in detention until the transfer of power was completed and the MGB under control. Then he was courteously examined, declared sane, and returned to his post.

One morning in April or May, while I was giving injections and stitching up minor wounds in the examining room, in walked a colonel of the MGB with his purple-striped trousers and the scrambled eggs on his cap. He picked up a doctor's gown and threw it over his shoulders, then came to me with a friendly smile and said, "Good morning, dear Comrade, I am Colonel Tsukerashvili."

I shook hands in amazement. I had heard the stories, but to see it in the flesh was something different.

"I have come to see your dear colleague, Dr. Adarich," he said. "Is he busy at the moment?"

I said, "I don't believe so. You'll probably find him in the ward. It's through that door to your left."

The man made no move to go. He looked around the examining room, clucking his tongue quietly at the instruments and cases of medicine. He watched the procedure I was doing, and made approving noises, little hmm-hmm's.

He looked out at the line of prisoners waiting for treatment and said good morning to them. When I finished the last injection, he complimented me on the efficiency of our clinic. I was beginning to think he thought *I* was MVD or something, despite what I had heard of him, but he soon made that clear. He pulled up a chair and sat on it backwards, leaning his arms on the back; he offered me a cigarette and lit one for himself and said, "Of course, in your position you must think that the life of an officer is very fine and so on, but you have no idea how badly those bastard colleagues of mine have behaved. Here I've spent my life trying to do my honorable best in a tough service, and look after the interests of you poor prisoners as well as I can, and those bastards start writing reports on me as if I am crazy. Sent me to Moscow! Can you believe that!

"Well, they're straightened out now, all right, but I can tell you, you're not the only ones who have a little trouble in life, not in the least, dear Comrade, *not in the least!*"

He was quite irritated. He kept rubbing his hands together and sucking his breath in between his teeth. Before he had finished his cigarette he stubbed it out and went off to see Adarich, to borrow some medical supplies for his own camp, as it turned out.

Not the only ones who have a little trouble in life!

Lavrenov had almost always been pretty easy to get along with and now he was even easier. He still drank too much, maybe worse than ever, but he was in the hospital a great deal more, trying to be helpful, and as he was a well-trained feldsher and a conscientious man, he was in fact helpful.

After a few weeks he took me aside one day and explained that I had already overstayed the regulation period for the assignment of an uncertified medical person to a hospital job. Almost all *pridurki* assignments were allowed to continue only for a short period—I think it was six months in most cases. I had been almost a year at the hospital, and compared to the lives of almost everyone I knew it had been a "wonderful" year.

"You're a first-class feldsher. I've seldom seen anyone learn so fast," Lavrenov said. "I'm going to recommend that you be sent out as a feldsher. They'll put you in a tough job, you know, maybe even the mines, but if you go as a feldsher you'll be okay."

My buttocks were back to Medical Category One size. The doctors had conferred over my heart every month or two and had declared their amazement that the original 4½-cm. enlargement had spontaneously reduced itself to less than 2 cm. I was healthy again.

Lavrenov said, "Whatever happens, if they want you in the mines it won't be in fifty-one for a while. It's closed down. They had a terrible accident. Elevator cable broke."

I said I had heard that everyone was afraid to ride in the elevators in Mine 51 because they were so prone to mechanical failure.

"This one was the worst in a long time," Lavrenov told me. "Twenty-seven people aboard. Only one survived, you know. He was hanging on to the bars of the roof. He had a lot of broken bones, but he'll be okay, they think.

"By the way," Lavrenov went on ironically, "there was a feldsher killed on that elevator, so you better be careful if they send you there."

"I will," I promised.

"Yeah," Lavrenov said. "This guy—no, he wasn't a feldsher. They lost their feldsher and borrowed a doctor somewhere. I'll think of his name in a moment. His insides were wrecked. They brought him back to his own hospital and he begged his colleagues not to operate on him, can you imagine that? Knew he was going to die, so he said, Don't operate on me, boys, I'm going anyway."

There was only one other hospital I could think of in the area. I had a chilling premonition. I said, "Try to think of his name, Citizen Chief."

"A Latvian doctor," Lavrenov said.

I felt sick. "Atsinch," I said.

"That's it," Lavrenov said. "Of course! I forgot. You were trained by him, weren't you?"

In the space of a few weeks two of the people I had come to care for with an extraordinary intensity were dead, Arkadi and Arvid Atsinch. It made me feel hard. I felt hatred. Lavrenov was trying to be nice and could not possibly have understood the grimness in my face.

It got grimmer. Within a few days the camp *naryadchik* sent for me. The *naryadchik* is a prisoner, a trusty who makes work assignments and reports to the *kum*, the godfather, so he is presumed to be a stool pigeon whether he is or not. Since that is clear from the beginning nobody tells him anything and thus his life is never in jeopardy for informing.

This man called me into the administration office and got out my file. "You're leaving the hospital," he said curtly.

"Where will I be working?"

"Mine fifty-one. But take it easy, brother, you're lucky. You're to go as feldsher."

"But listen!" I said hotly. "That mine is supposed to be closed. The elevator crashed. A friend of mine was killed in it!"

"Catch them closing that mine?" He snorted. "Anyway, the elevator is fixed again. It should last a week at least!"

So that was it.

The summer had come. Walking to the mine with my little satchel of supplies was the hardest part of the day, even though the mine was so close to the camp I could see the watchtowers and the mountains of crushed rock from the camp gates; it was often 110° in the shade, and there was no shade. The hot sun turned my face and neck a dark copper color in a few days and my hair bleached almost to the color of wheat. I was well equipped. In my satchel I carried syringes, bandages, disinfectants, a couple of morphine ampoules, some cardiac medications like digitalis, smelling salts, and a lot of aspirin. And a rubber tourniquet. There was a scalpel and some sutures and clamps too, so that I could deal with deep cuts right on the spot. The mine was a big producer of accidents and had a high mortality rate. I expected to be busy.

It was a relief to go down the mine at first because it was cold at the 240-meter level, and I later carried my padded jacket to wear down there. I had a little niche next to the machine shop near the elevator, and I painted a big red cross on the little table and bench they gave me, and felt as though I was putting out my shingle.

Between shifts there were civilian explosives experts who came in and charged the holes drilled by the previous shift and set off the blasts. Then the first of the new shift went in with air pressure hoses to blow away the fumes and another crew strung work lights. Then the miners came in to dig away the copper ore until later in the day when the next round of drilling began, to prepare blasting holes for the following shift. The mine worked twenty-four hours a day. Outside there were huge man-made mountains of the tailings, a green rock that tumbled out of huge buckets coming up on a sort of chain, around a great wheel to dump their loads.

Silicosis had been the scourge of the mines before I came there, because of the dust that never settled from the air. But after Stalin's death they introduced wet mining. A hose attached to the drilling machine sprayed throughout the drilling, so the dust settled out of the air and the incidence of lung diseases went way down. All the digging used to be by hand. Thousands and thousands of lives were lost to exhaustion. Now they had brought in huge, electrically powered scrapers that vastly increased production and cut down on deaths.

The chambers were connected by tunnels, and little electric trains with trolleys to a cable in the ceiling carried the ore from the chambers, sometimes a mile back to the elevator. A favorite trick was to hang some thin wires down from the trolley to give a newcomer a good electric shock. It was played on me. I felt I had been knocked down by a sledge hammer. The kind of privileged status I had enjoyed in the hospital, where everyone called me doctor and looked up to me, had vanished now. I was just another new joe to be kidded and treated like everyone else.

Most of my work was on crushed fingers. At home in America you would be hospitalized for a crushed finger. But all I could do was put a dressing on the mangled digit and give the poor slave a handful of aspirin. He had to go back to work. If a whole arm or leg was crushed the man would be excused from work, but unless I yelled and screamed that he was bleeding to death he would have to wait at the mine until the end of the shift and then go back to the Zone with everyone else.

Almost every evening I played guitar with Zyuzin, and my music was advancing well. My morale was excellent. I had no hard physical labor to do and I was continuing to learn medicine. I managed to borrow some medical books from Adarich and read pharmacy and physical medicine and even obstetrics and gynecology. The atmosphere in the camp grew easier every day. There were no drastic sudden changes, just a little easing of attitudes. Rations were still terrible. The less skillful at the craft of survival still died quickly, but fewer died, because survival took a little less skill.

As part of the "thaw," the hours of work were shortened from twelve to ten and so, because people had more rest, the poor rations were more nearly adequate. And there was more time in the evenings for rest and recreation. *Tufta* was practiced extensively in the mine, including a system whereby three prisoners would put their output into the quota of a single free worker, of which there were a fair number who had been lured to work in the mines by promises of high wages. With three prisoners helping him, a free worker could in fact produce super-Stakhanovite amounts of ore every day and get an immense wage. The prisoners got only a starvation wage, but that was all right with them because their free friend bought good food outside for them and they ate better than many *pridurki*.

My summer in the copper mine was not a summer of unusual events or memorable encounters. Edik L. was in the mine at that time, but I saw him seldom, and although I found some satisfaction in the steady work of healing and arguing with the MVD on behalf of my first-aid patients, I found the work repetitious and really lived primarily for the evenings of music and talk in the barracks.

With the fall and the sudden drop in temperature, the mine became very uncomfortable. Sometime in late October or November 1953 there was a series of power failures while we were below ground. The elevator was electrically powered. This meant a climb by ladder, 240 meters down in the morning and 240 meters up at night with no light but the meager carbide lamps in our helmets. The rungs of the ladder caught the drip from the walls of the shaft, and where the cold air swept down from outside it froze quickly so that the climb was a terrifying, exhausting nightmare in which you might lose your grip or your footing on the icy ladder at any moment, and the bottom of the shaft was a thousand feet below ground. There were several screaming, gyrating falls to the bottom, and even the guards found the whole experience unnerving.

Sometime in November I was notified once again that the *naryadchik*, the work-assignment clerk, wanted to see me. There was a rumor that he had a friend in another camp who was a feldsher and had been eyeing my job for some time. When I went to see him I was expecting the worst, and I got it.

"You have been assigned to Zheldor Poselok," he told me indifferently, as if he had had nothing at all to do with it. "Your brigadier's name is

Ivanov. You'll be on construction. Hard labor. Extreme hard labor, in fact."

Zheldor Poselok was a huge railway construction project and a notorious man-killer. The *naryadchik* seemed to take pleasure in pronouncing the sentence. I was sure now that he was a tool of the administration. I said, "I'll look forward to meeting you outside someday."

He just stared at me coolly.

I said, "I've never heard of a brigadier named Ivanov. Are you sure such a man exists?"

"Didn't I tell you extreme hard labor? Didn't that mean something to you? Go pack your stuff and meet the convoy here in half an hour. You're being moved to KTR!"

Extreme hard labor was the phrase for people who lived in Camp Number One, the KTR. I felt a real chill. The death rate from exhaustion was spectacular in the KTR. And no wonder I had never heard of Ivanov. I knew almost nobody from the KTR.

Leaving my old barracks was a blow, too.

No more musical evenings with Zyuzin. No more long chats with Adarich. Strange new faces and new routines to learn. Oh well, I thought, it's been a lot worse.

I rolled up my blanket and emptied the wood shavings out of my pillowcase and mattress case. It was time for a new filling anyway. I said good-by to the crippled old man who looked after our empty barracks during the day, and went over to the storeroom to collect my personal belongings, which meant only my navy shirt and trousers. Everything else had gone, now, to Valentin, to Lavrenov. These were the only physical reminders of my American reality, and even though they were stained and torn I vowed never to let them go. I slung my sack over my shoulder and picked up my guitar, took a last look around, and went off to the gates to meet the convoy.

It was still early in the afternoon when I moved over to the KTR, which was adjacent to my old camp. I slung my sacks on the floor and waited for the work brigades to come back from Zheldor Poselok so that I could find Ivanov and be assigned a bed. When the convoys returned I was struck by the fatigue etched in the faces of most of the men. They just came in quickly and flung themselves on their bunks. There was little talk, except among small groups here and there who were obviously working a good deal of *tufta* and getting enough to eat and not too much work.

Ivanov was a bad-tempered, surly, black-haired man in his early forties. He just scowled when I introduced myself and told me he would find a bunk for me when he was good and ready. I sat at the table and waited. Suddenly I heard a loud familiar voice call out, "Well, look at that! It's his honor the doctor!" I looked around and saw a pug nose and two merry eyes in a clown's face on a clown's body. Marusich! We ran and embraced each other.

"My dear Doctor!" he exclaimed. "What good fortune brings us together again?"

"I'm not sure it's all good fortune, Marusich," I said a bit glumly. "I've lost my medical status. I'm here on extreme hard labor for some reason. I'm assigned to Zheldor Poselok."

"And so am I! And so am I! Cheer up! Cheer up! We old hands know how to manage these things, don't we?" He winked a huge wink and grinned and slapped me encouragingly on the arm. "Come! Come!" he said. "You will be my bunkmate. I will ask someone to move down immediately."

This was unheard of. Only brigadiers assigned bunks, and Marusich was not even in the same brigade as I. There were five brigades in the barracks and five brigadiers. But the man Marusich spoke to immediately agreed and showed great respect to Marusich, so I thought maybe things weren't going to be so bad after all. Then I discovered that Marusich had been assigned as day cook, which meant he had sacks of coarse-ground grain to make porridge with and to give to his friends and to bribe the brigadiers. "Just come over to my brigade at noon," he said. "I'll see you get all you need to eat. What a great pleasure to see you, dear Doctor! What a delight!"

Marusich loved to sing and had a marvelous voice. Evenings I would get out the guitar and strum for him, and he brought tears to the eyes of his people with his sentimental Ukrainian songs. But as it turned out I did not spend as much time with Marusich as both of us would have liked. He was in constant demand. The barracks was full of Western Ukrainians, and Marusich was sought out as a sort of magistrate to settle disputes, and as the leader in whatever kind of plots against the Russians or discussions of anti-administration strategies were going on at any given moment. I was not fluent in Ukrainian, although I understood a good deal by now since there was such a large Ukrainian population in camp. I missed a lot of the whispered conversations that flowed around my new protector's bed, but it was clear that he was a man of some substance in the brigade and in the barracks.

I never even saw Ivanov again that evening.

In the morning, when we got to the project, Ivanov started handing out assignments. He was flanked by two real toughs, his assistants. I just walked off and found a place to hide for a while, in a tool shed. At noon I went out and found Marusich's little field stove and had two bowls of thick, nourishing porridge, and then went back to my hiding place for a nap. When I got to the door of the shed, one of Ivanov's toughs was waiting for me, a wiry, arrogant little man.

"That's it!" he shouted. "You're coming to work!"

"Go to hell," I said quietly.

He picked up a short stick and came toward me holding it like a club. There was a half meter of concrete-reinforcing iron bar on the ground and I grabbed it up. I said, "That's fine! If you want it, come and get it!" I danced around him on the balls of my feet like a boxer. I was in good shape, fresh out of the hospital, fast and trim and alert and agile. He looked a bit scared and backed off. I spent the day roaming around the work site, watching men lay bricks and mix cement and carry lumber. I tried to look as though I were on my way from one job to another and to keep out of sight of Ivanov and his thugs.

I did not see him again until we were back in the KTR. I came out of the toilet to find him and the two heavies waiting for me. The position did not look very good. Ivanov said, "Are you going to work?"

"When I feel like it. Not before. I may never feel like it."

He looked thunderstruck. The three of them advanced on me. I just smiled. I said, "Before you do anything, I think you'd better listen to me for a minute. I have something confidential to tell you. Call off your thugs and step over here."

I was very cool. I could see that my manner was getting to them. Ivanov waved the two tough guys back and stepped aside with me. "If you're trying to buy me it better be something pretty good," he said, very menacing.

I smiled at him. I was enjoying the show a lot, and it was playing out my way very well. I said, "Listen, you're in trouble, don't you know that? If anything happens to me, *anything*, if these trained dogs of yours beat me up or you report me to the *kum*, or *anything*, do you think your head will stay on your shoulders very long? I have very influential friends, you know!"

He was taken aback. Even if it had been a bluff it might have worked because I was putting on a real performance. But it was no bluff. I said, "I suggest you talk it over with Marusich. So long, Ivanov." And I just put my hands in my pockets and walked away.

Ivanov did not make a move to follow.

I told Marusich about it in the barracks. He laughed and slapped me on the back. "Good work, my dear Doctor. Good work! Your healing powers are quite magnificent. You can heal a wound before it is made. I am impressed. Now leave the rest to me, my dear friend, and I will look after it."

"How?" I said.

Marusich laughed a merry laugh. "None of your business! None of your business! Leave it to me. Leave it to me!" He went off singing loudly in Ukrainian about love and roses and broken hearts.

So that was that. Ivanov was a Russian. The Russians in our barracks were outnumbered ten to one by Marusich's Ukrainians. I felt that, for a while at least, I could do what I wanted. Marusich said, "If the godfather catches you, dear Doctor, you are on your own. In the meantime, please do not worry about a thing!"

The second day, roaming about the vast area of Zheldor Poselok, I stopped to help some guys who were struggling to lift a huge beam. When we got it up on the wagon they thanked me and offered me a cigarette and we sat down under the wagon, because it was snowing, and had a smoke. These guys were from Moscow. When I told them I used to work at the United States Embassy one of them said, "Then you've got a friend, brother. There's a guy named Aksyonov here who used to work at the embassy too. I'll tell him how to find you."

I could not believe it. I remembered Aksyonov only vaguely—a young Soviet employee. I remembered that he had been born in London and spoke excellent English, but I was not even sure what his work had been at the embassy. Translator, probably. But there was something about the name that felt bad, and I soon remembered it. One of the protocols that Sidorov had shown me at the end of my first interrogation was signed by Artur Aksyonov. A very bad protocol. He claimed that he knew me intimately and that we had long political discussions in which I had spoken violently against the Soviet Union. I remembered that when I read that lying protocol I vowed to kill the man who wrote it. Now I thought, It's not worth it. I'll just beat him up and take some satisfaction. I did not wait for the Muscovite to send Aksyonov to me; I looked him up. He was a patient in the small clinic in the KTR. He had a bad case of scurvy. I went to the clinic in the evening and told the feldsher I had official business with this Artur Aksyonov and dropped a few medical terms and so on; so the feldsher assumed I was legitimate and went inside, and a few minutes later out came Aksyonov in his hospital underclothes. He recognized me right away. He said hello in a friendly way, but he looked a bit guilty.

I said, "Well, what do you have to say now?"

There was a long pause.

"I'm sorry," he said in a low voice. He could not look at me. "I was in Lefortovo. They nearly killed me. I had to sign it. I couldn't stand the beatings. I'm sorry, Mr. Dolgun. I'm really sorry."

It was a long time since I had heard myself addressed like that in English, and deferentially. My violent intentions simmered down somewhat. I thought, Yes, you poor little bastard, I can believe you signed under pressure. I did too, but nothing that could ever hurt another soul.

I slapped him twice.

He did not react, just stared at the ground. I walked away without looking back. Later we became friends, but not close friends. I knew I could never get into his soul, and although it was a treat to speak English and he was eager for my friendship, I never spent that much time with him. He was an unhappy little man. He was almost on his knees to me for attention and that put me off. I got over hating him for what he had done to me, but I had no interest in getting to know him intimately.

I was getting harder and more cynical about life. The loss of Atsinch, even though I might never have seen him again anyway, had scarred my outlook. I was still optimistic about my survival and eventual release, but I was much more sour on the world. Arkadi's death had had the same effect. I was dedicated now to doing everything I could, exploiting every decent opportunity I could find, such as Marusich's friendship, to deny my labor to the inhuman, diabolical system that had taken the lives of my friends.

The fourth day at Zheldor Poselok I found an unfinished boiler room in the basement of a building at the project. It seemed to me from the way material was stacked around and covered with dust that work had been suspended in it and that no one ever went there. It would be a restful place to spend the day, I thought. There was a barrel of cleaning rags, still clean, to make a bed with, and enough boards and stone to build a sort of shield so that even if anyone did come into the basement I would not be seen. I set about fixing the place up to suit me, and by the end of the day had it quite comfortable. Now all I needed was companionship. I roamed around and found the Muscovites and chatted with them until I felt that one of them might be interested in taking some chances, and I took him aside and asked him if he'd like to spend his days in a relaxed way. He refused absolutely—he had nobody like Marusich to look after him with the brigadier. It took me a long time to find anyone who would be able to disappear just like that, but I finally found a couple of guys and they helped me fix up the place so that it was practically invisible, and for several days we slept and smoked and gossiped and got pretty bored.

At noon I would go over to Marusich's stove. I could hear him singing long before I got to him. People would say, "There goes the nightingale again." I would eat my porridge and talk with Marusich a while and then drift back to my companions in the boiler room.

One day we heard footsteps on the floor above, and then voices and the sounds of people coming down the ladder. Before we could douse our cigarettes the boards over our hideaway were flung aside and two colonels —one MVD, one MGB—had swept into the room. The MGB was Voloshin, the godfather of this camp. He was steely cold and furious. "What are you prisoners doing in here!"

But I had had a marvelous inspiration even as the boards were coming

off, and instead of skulking and looking guilty I leapt to my feet with my
cigarette and held it up in the air as if I were tracing in smoke the air
currents in the room.

I said, "Citizen Colonel, you have made me lose track of my engineering calculations here, I'm afraid. You see, we're evaluating the proper
alignment of transfer girdles to equilibrate the oxygenometric status, and
the calculations are quite delicate. If you can wait one minute until I get
this stretch done I will be glad to go over our engineering conclusions with
you."

It was pure doubletalk, of course. My health and my morale were so
good at that time that I was able to carry something like that off with real
panache, just as I had confronted Ivanov on my refusal to work. I knew the
MGB and the army were impressed with scientific language, and that
pseudo-scientific would do just as well as the real thing. I counted on their
being much too proud to challenge me because they could never risk losing
face by appearing not to understand. It worked. Voloshin said respectfully,
"No, no, we won't interrupt. Please get on with your important work. We
are just making a general inspection."

They left. I noticed with relief that nobody had written down our
numbers. I knew that the MVD colonel would make some inquiries later
on, in an oblique way, and eventually discover that in fact he did not have
any engineers working in that subterranean boiler room. Our hiding place
had lost its usefulness, but it had been very pleasant while it lasted. Now I
had to find something else to do or somewhere else to hide, and I began
again to prowl the length and breadth of Zheldor Poselok to see what I
could find.

At one end of the project there were half a dozen two- and three-story
apartment buildings going up. Construction and engineering shacks were
scattered around the area. I walked among them, peering in windows and
moving in and out of buildings. I had no particular objective. Just snoop-
ing. Suddenly I came around the corner of a building and bumped right
into a tall man who was walking very fast. The blow nearly knocked me
over. I was about to yell "Why don't you watch where you're going!"
when I realized who it was: Victor S.! My friend from the first six months
in Dzhezkazgan. We just stood there gaping at each other for a moment
and then both started shouting at once.

"What are you doing here! My God, isn't this marvelous!" And so
on.

Victor told me his story. After I left him in that first camp when I was
taken back to Moscow for interrogation by Ryumin, Victor had got himself a *pridurki* job in the administration office. But at the end of six months,
when he found out that he would be sent off to hard labor again, he heard

of an ingenious form of *mastyrka* and decided to try it as a way of getting out of hard labor. It was a little-known technique for faking silicosis.

In his sack of personal belongings in the storeroom, Victor had a small silver ring. Following the instructions he had heard about, and never knowing whether it would make him seriously ill or not, he filed a small quantity of silver dust from the ring and mixed it with tobacco into a number of cigarettes. He smoked the cigarettes, inhaling as deeply as he could. The theory was that a microscopic film of silver dust would build up in the lungs in a way that would show a strong shadow in an X-ray without seriously impairing the lungs. Victor smoked the cigarettes wondering all the time whether he was committing suicide, but there was absolutely no noticeable physical result. Then he went to the hospital coughing in the way he had seen silicosis victims cough, and demanded an X-ray. Sure enough, there was a terrible shadow on the lungs, and he was disqualified from hard labor. He was sent to Spassk, the camp for incurables. That is how serious his "silicosis" looked on the plates. Then, not long before I ran into him, as part of the post-Stalin thaw, the government granted amnesty to all incurables, and Victor was freed. These invalids, who were written off the records as political prisoners and released, were all expected to die soon and were not given travel rights, so they all stayed on in Dzhezkazgan, and Victor applied for an engineering job at Zheldor Poselok. They took him on in the planning and design office. It was a soft job with modest but adequate pay. Victor was sure he could get me assigned to it. He had a lot of friends among the engineers, he said, and the engineers worked closely with the camp administration on the labor assignments, so it would be no trick to have me reassigned.

It seemed too good to be true, but Victor was as good as his word, and within a few days I was reassigned. They gave me pots of paint and stacks of brushes and told me I was the project safety and propaganda artist. I protested that I could not even draw a house with two windows and a door and smoke curling out of the chimney. They said that did not matter; I was simply to print up big posters that said, ONLY THROUGH HARD LABOR CAN YOU BECOME FREE. Or WEAR PROTECTIVE HEADGEAR ON THIS PROJECT. I was no good at it at all. I would start a line with letters twelve centimeters high and end up squeezing together letters eight centimeters high and very skinny so they would not run off the end of the poster. Victor was my supervisor and he didn't care. The engineers were not interested at all. The guards were mostly illiterate and all they had to do was ensure that the prisoners at least seemed to be working, so my days were relaxed and the company was very agreeable. Victor and I had plenty of time to talk politics and sports and speculate about the future together. After a few weeks of hopeless sign painting, somebody from the godfather's office complained about the lousy posters, so Victor had me moved into the office with him as a blueprint planner, which was pure *tufta* and meant nothing at all except that we were able to spend most of the day together, and I was officially designated an engineer.

Curiously, with the relaxation in regulations and hours of work and the softening of the harshness between guards and prisoners, I became less disciplined about keeping track of time and maintaining any kind of regimen to my life. It was a confused period anyway. A number of amnesties were granted. I think the first one was freedom for children under the age of fourteen. There were only about six in the whole area and even though the mere presence of six juveniles in such a dreadful prison is a monstrous indictment of the system itself, their going did not change things for the rest of us, except to cheer us up somewhat because it was a sign of change. Similarly, all prisoners with sentences of five years were released and pardoned. That accounted for maybe three men out of three thousand, but it was another sign.

There were two army generals, former members of Zhukov's general staff, in the KTR at that time. In the convoy to Zheldor Poselok the guards used to find every opportunity to lord it over these two old men and humiliate them. They would call them out of line for imaginary offenses, and swear at them and spit on them, using the title *general* in mocking tones all the time. One convoy leader used to make one of the generals lead the convoy in a position of mock eminence. He would say, "My sergeant will lead the general, and the general will lead the whole convoy!"

Now, one day the two generals were excused from work and the story went around that a tailor had come to measure them. Not long after that they were brought new uniforms with full regalia, told they had been pardoned and fully rehabilitated, and put on the train to Moscow. According to the prison grapevine, Belyakov, the camp commandant, went with them to the train and offered to shake hands with them before they went on board. They both spat in his face.

The barracks in KTR had prison status when I first went there, and we were locked in after the evening meal. Now this prison status was removed and the locks were taken off the doors. We had a celebration and tore all the bars out of the windows and threw them on the ground.

The gates between the KTR and the adjoining camp were opened, and while the perimeter wall was still guarded with machine guns and the gates locked at night, the inmates were free to move between the camps and visit each other until lights out. It was rumored that reliable prisoners were to be given passes to come and go between camp and their work assignment without having to march in convoy: no barking dogs and cursing guards for them. Everyone dreamed of having a pass. Soon a list was posted of the numbers of those prisoners who would be issued passes, and every day we saw a few new smiles on the faces of those men who had this thrilling experience of imitation freedom.

The numbers were finally taken away. I came out into the Zone one morning to find hundreds of prisoners yelling and laughing and ripping the linen patches off their sleeves and breasts and backs and caps and trouser legs. The air was filled with a snowstorm of number patches. No official order had been received in camp, but the prison telegraph had brought the news that it was about to happen and so we all just went ahead without the order, and Belyakov, the commandant, let it happen without any reprisals or even threats of reprisals. The next day the official order was promulgated. This seems like a small matter, but for all the prisoners of Dzhezkazgan the number was the prime symbol of our slavery, of our demotion from human being to object. Its disappearance was like the beginning of a fresh new day.

There were rumors of labor camp mutinies in Siberia, and guards and administration and even the godfather became noticeably more friendly, in a sickening way, every day.

A "culture brigade" was formed to give camp entertainments. I signed up as a musician. I found my old bunkmate Volodya Stepanov, the guitar player, and worked out a couple of duets under his guidance. I also practiced and repracticed my Rachmaninov and my Chopin, for solo numbers. The brigade was allowed to assemble in the mess hall in the evening and practice. We hung blankets in the windows so the other prisoners would not be able to see us until the night of the performance, and we worked hard until lights out. Sundays were now work-free days all the time, and the culture brigade practiced all day.

One of the acts was an acrobat named Grigori Levko. I showed off for his benefit one night and walked the length of the mess hall and back on my hands. He suggested that I do a partner act with him, and began to train me to hold him up on my hands while he stood on his own, and a number of other routines. There was a fine, trained Ukrainian baritone, and an accordion and a mandolin, and we rehearsed an orchestral number together. There was a sort of announcer and comedian who acted as master of ceremonies.

After several weeks of practice we staged our first concert on a Sunday afternoon. The mess hall was packed. There was only room for about five hundred out of the total population, in the two adjoining camps, of over four thousand; so we gave the same performance every week for several weeks. It was probably pretty ragged stuff, but we thought we were just fine, and so did the starved audience. The applause was deafening and the calls for encores so insistent that we usually ended up playing the whole concert all over again.

Then a wonderful thing happened: a movie projector was brought in and Saturday night, once a month, we had a movie. They were terrible propaganda movies about heroic tractor drivers, but we loved them. Two brothers named Boyko, who were professional electronics technicians, were put in charge of the operation and maintenance of the projector and its sound system, and they requisitioned tubes and other parts and began to build radios. The godfather found out about this, but instead of punishing anyone he brought over his own radio for repairs. Soon other radios came in for repairs, and the Boyko brothers were able to requisition extra parts and to copy circuits. They built some excellent radios which they tied into a sound system with a loudspeaker in each barracks so that the whole camp could have music. There were often fights at night. "Turn that goddamn thing off!" "No, damn you, leave it on; that's my favorite symphony."

It was the early spring of 1954. The weather was beginning to moderate, but the ground was still covered with deep snowdrifts. The ache in my jaw where Ryumin had kicked my teeth out had been a minor chronic annoyance that was usually negligible but sometimes flared up. Finally I decided it was time to do something about it and persuaded the dentist at the KTR clinic to have a look. He found some root fragments and proceeded to remove them immediately, with a local anesthetic. In the process he damaged a blood vessel and nothing would stop the bleeding. Finally he packed some cotton in the pit in my gum and told me to clamp down hard on it for as long as I could. I went back to the barracks, full of painkillers, and determined to keep the pressure on all night if I had to. Of course, with all the drugs the dentist had given me, I went off to sleep early and slept all night, probably with my mouth open. When I woke up in the morning there was a huge clot on the bed beside me: I must have bled all night. I felt terrible. The bleeding had stopped but I had lost almost a quart of blood. I was feverish and light-headed. I stumbled to the clinic through the snowdrifts and got a clearance to stay in camp for the day, so I went back to bed and slept for a few hours. When I woke up I felt better but still light-headed. I ate a little bread I had stored under my pillow, and then went for a slow walk around camp. There was a bulletin board on the wall of the administration office. I seldom read it because almost everything posted on it had been heard through the *parasha* before it got into print. But it was a lazy day and, like everyone who has nothing to do, I was loafing around and looking at things I would never have bothered to look at before. I stopped to read all the old news on the bulletin board. In the lazy frame of mind I was in, I would have read the back of a cereal box.

Your eye can pass over a great mass of words without really seeing them but a word with a strong psychological impact for you will leap off the page. The strongest is your own name. Suddenly my name hit me in the eye from the middle of a long list I had not even absorbed the sense of.

I looked at the top of the list. "Prisoners Eligible for Passes: Apply at Administration Office."

I forgot about the pain in my jaw and the fever and the faintness. I ran to the office, certain that I would be told it was a mistake. It was no mistake. I was expected to go out of camp with the culture brigade to perform for other camps, and as a result a pass had been issued that would allow me to move about without convoy. This might have seemed an invitation to escape, but of course there was no way to cross the desert without being spotted by the little plane or dying of exposure, and the issuing of these passes had generated very few escape attempts. Security at the railway station and on the roads had been kept up and maybe even increased.

My pass was issued in the guardroom in the wall by the gates. The guard on duty pulled out my file and checked my photograph and my prayer and issued the pass. It seemed a maddeningly long process although it was probably less than one minute. I kept expecting the door to open at any moment and the *kum* to come in and yell, Cancel that pass! This man is dangerous! But nothing happened. The guard opened the door leading from the guardroom to the outside of the gates and suddenly there I was, for the first time in five and a half years, standing in the open air without a wall around me, with no guard standing over me, with no dogs barking! It was pure euphoria. I had an urge to run and roll in the snowbanks and laugh and cry and sing and yell. I knew that I had to be back inside the camp by eight o'clock that night, but it did not matter a damn. For the moment I was as good as a free man and I did not allow the slightest sense of reality to interfere with my savoring of the feeling.

I could have climbed a tree if there had been trees or swum in a river if there had been a river.

Instead I walked to Zheldor Poselok to see Victor. He congratulated me warmly on my pass. I asked him if he could leave work for a while and go for a walk but he was involved in something complicated and would not leave it.

So I decided to go and see the town of Zheldor itself, which is almost attached to Zheldor Poselok, just a short walk. Zheldor is not what you would call a tourist attraction, just a few drab apartment buildings for the free workers, a few drab shops, a bit of a marketplace. But the idea of walking in a street where I could *go into a shop*, any shop, however drab, and buy a pack of machine-made cigarettes, or even just look at them without buying, was a seduction I could not resist.

I had hardly walked into the little town before I was accosted by a former patient, a young man who had been treated for hepatitis; he had completed a ten-year sentence and was now working out his five years of exile as a free worker. He hailed me in a very friendly way, assuming I had been freed. When I told him, no, I just had a pass, he thought that was just about as good, considering that he couldn't leave the area either till his five years were up, and in any case it called for a celebration, didn't it? I was in no mood to refuse. We went to his apartment building. There were several other people living there but they were away at work.

My friend somehow found two bottles of vodka. We drank the first bottle very quickly, thinking up toasts to every conceivable meritorious person: toasts to Adarich and Kask, toasts to the late Shargai, toasts to Victor, toasts to my host's friends, and so on. When we ran out of good guys to toast we toasted the bad guys ironically, wishing them all kinds of miserable accidents. We toasted the *kum* and the camp commandant. We toasted the MVD and the MGB—or KGB, as it was now known. And pretty soon the bottle was empty and I was feeling indomitable. Nothing bad could ever happen to me again, I told my friend. This was the beginning of a new era. I was at the silly stage. I told my friend that the future would have been impossible without him and so on and so on. And soon we were started on the second bottle.

The inside of that apartment was all I saw of Zheldor, and before long I was having trouble seeing that. Somehow I became aware that the time was approaching when the convoys would be leaving the work sites and heading back to camp. I had a sudden feeling of panic. I had forgotten completely how I came to be where I was, and how to find my way home. My friend was not in much better shape, although he had been getting into condition for a few months or a year; I had not had a serious drink for more than five years. I persuaded him to take me to the beginning of the road back to camp and point the way. Neither one of us could walk straight. Somehow he got me onto the road and pointed off in the right general direction and embraced me and gave me a push to get me started. I fell flat in a snowbank. He helped me up again. I embraced him and told him he was truly one of the world's great men. Then I started to walk back into Zheldor and he went off toward camp. He realized before I did what was happening. He ran back and spun me around and started me off again. I cursed myself fiercely under my breath and set to work to keep my eyes ahead and try to see only one set of telegraph poles instead of two, since I was sure there only was one, and started to trudge stoutly back to camp. The trouble was, no matter how determinedly I set one foot before another I kept weaving back and forth across the road in a sinusoid pattern, and what would have been a trip of three kilometers must have ended up as more like five or six. It took a long time. I passed or was passed by many columns of prisoners marching back to our camp and other camps. They laughed and hooted to see a drunk passing along, caroming from snowbank to snowbank. Sometimes I was recognized and then the hoots really got derisive!

"Working on the hospital supplies, eh, Doc?"

"I thought you'd lost that barrel, Doc!"

Long before I got to the gates I realized that there was a little knot of men waiting under the lights and I was afraid they were waiting for me. It took a terribly long time to go the last quarter mile. I kept stumbling, and each time I fell down it was harder to get up. I just wanted to drift off to sleep in the comfortable snowbanks. As I got closer I realized that the welcoming party consisted of Voloshin, the godfather who had caught me goofing off in the boiler room, and Belyakov, the camp commandant. There were a couple of guards standing with them.

I finally made it to the gates in front of a cheering column of two or three hundred prisoners who were standing for the search and count. I slowed down to the most dignified pace I could manage and drew myself up very tall in front of Belyakov and Voloshin. I gave them each a snappy military salute. Then I fell down in the snow again.

A guard drew me roughly to my feet. Voloshin spoke to me like a Dutch uncle.

"Prisoner Doldzhin! Aren't you ashamed of yourself! An educated man like yourself! A man of qualities! An engineer and an intellectual! To bring yourself to such a swinish, brutish state. What a terrible loss of dignity!" He was very stern, very earnest. But his words were almost drowned out by Belyakov, who began to scream at me.

"Death to you, you bastard! You'll rot in jail for this! You whore and son of a whore and father of whores! I will personally see that you are ruined!"

He told three soldiers to take me immediately to the hard punishment cell in the third camp. I do not remember how we got there. I only remember waking up with a violent headache and the shivers. The cell was unheated. Fortunately they had left me all my clothes, including my padded jacket. Once I had drunk some water and walked up and down a bit I began to feel better. Then I wanted a smoke, but when I felt in my pockets I found that they had taken everything out of them. When the guard brought my breakfast, just a lump of sour black bread and some hot water, I asked him to bring my cigarettes back because I had to have a smoke.

"*Nye polozhna.*"

But I was prepared. Somewhere along the line of development from a scared innocent, bewildered and sure that my arrest was just a mistake from which I would soon be rescued, to my present status as a sophisticated and competent prison survivor, I had learned always to substitute a bit of tobacco for the rolled cotton pads in the padded jacket, in case of exactly this sort of eventuality. You reached a finger into the little slit above your tobacco and got out enough for one cigarette. You had a few slips of newspaper, or you kept the brown paper squares they issued you in prison, because they were certainly no good for toilet paper unless you were so dried up you were producing nothing but goat droppings. You rolled your crude cigarette. I had also learned how to make fire from the padding of that same jacket. It works best if you have soaked some of the padding first in potassium permanganate and let it dry out before stuffing it back in the jacket. Then you pull out a small wad of your chemically impregnated cotton. Plain cotton will do, but it is slower. You roll up a very tight stick of cotton, about two inches long and perhaps an eighth or a quarter of an inch thick. Then just before it is closed, you slip the edge of another flake of cotton under the last edge of the rolled-up stick and begin to roll it the other way. Soon you have a tight, hard stick of cotton, the core of which is rolled one way and the outside the opposite way.

Now you need something hard and smooth to use as a roller. The sole of a hard leather boot will do. I used the lid of my bucket. You press it down on the cotton stick on the concrete floor and roll back and forth very fast. It takes a good deal of energy. You have practiced before, so you have an idea of how long it takes. About one minute or perhaps two. Then you quickly unroll the outer layer of your cotton stick and you will find that where the two layers meet it is black and hot, and if you blow gently you can start a spark that will spread—quite quickly if you have the chemical cotton—and you can light your cigarette.

I played a marvelous game with the guard. He knew I had been searched and relieved of my tobacco. I would smoke a whole cigarette quickly between visits, and then when he came and looked in the peephole the cell would be full of smoke.

He would be in there in two seconds. "Smoking is *nye polozhna!* You know that!"

"How could I smoke!" I gave him a broad shrug of the shoulders. "You took away all my tobacco! I'm dying for a smoke. How could I smoke!"

The guard was baffled. He went away. I knew he would peek frequently for a few minutes. I would wait until the frequency of peeking died down and then repeat the performance. Once again he would burst in and the smoke would be thicker than ever.

"I don't know where it's coming from," I would say plaintively. "I wish I could get my hands on some of that tobacco. Must be something wrong with the ventilation system!"

He never found out. I ran out of tobacco on the fifth or sixth day. But until I did, playing that game on the guards helped a lot to get through the time.

They kept me there ten days. I was expecting three months, which I knew would be hard. I had started a calendar, begun lecturing myself again, repeating a number of procedures I had used in Lefortovo and

Sukhanovka. I sang at the top of my voice and they never bothered me. I knew I could get through three months of solitary, even though it would be terribly lonely. When they let me out at the end of ten days it seemed like nothing, although I was terribly hungry and weak from the minimum rations.

Fortunately I still had my soft job with Victor, although of course they took away my pass and told me I would never get another. So although I had starved and shivered for ten days, I was not long getting back into shape. Now, with the gates unlocked between the camps, I was able to wander back and forth in the evenings, and I visited Adarich and Kask regularly, and they bootlegged a few cc. of glucose into me when I came back from hard punishment, to help me back into A-one condition. Physically, then, I was fine. But I was never really cut out for a useless life. I had no interest in getting myself stuck with mining or even arc welding again, but the almost complete pointlessness of my *tufta* in the blueprint shop was beginning to get me down.

I heard that there were plans for the construction of a new village. It was to be built from scratch, new streets, new apartments, new shops, new everything, and the *parasha* said that there would be jobs for technical specialists like electricians and bricklayers and so on, that these jobs would be filled from the prisoner population, and that if you were lucky enough to get such a job you would have a permanent pass and would live at the project virtually as a free man. Nothing ventured, nothing gained. I went to the *naryadchik* and put my name down for the project. He told me it was called Nikolsky Project, and that the work of clearing the site had already begun. He gave me a form on which to register my specialties. I put down arc welder, of course, and then plumber, although I had never touched a pipe. I thought that the pleasures of living in freedom were well worth the physical effort of a welding job or a plumbing job. But all the time I knew that, because of my behavior over the first pass, the chances of getting a second one were next to zero, so I was not cheerful about the prospects.

I usually kept my worries and my pessimism to myself. But one night I let down my guard and complained to Adarich. "I really don't know what to do, Yevgeni Petrovich," I said. "I'm healthier than I ever was since I came here. I have a soft job in an office with a good friend. But I'm bored all the time."

Adarich looked at me with a mischievous twinkle in his eyes. "Remember Shargai's prophecy?" he said.

"Sure, sure," I said testily. "Things were going to get better for everyone. All right, things have got better. I'm glad they pulled the gates down between the camps. I'm glad they got rid of the numbers and all that, I'm glad the guards don't harass us all the time the way they used to. That's great, but I look at myself at the end of each day and I ask, Are you any farther ahead than you were when you got up this morning? Have you learned anything? Is the world any better on account of you? And all the answers come back, No."

"Why don't you ask those engineers to train you, teach you stresses and materials and mathematics and all the disciplines they know?"

"Because those guys are totally absorbed in *tufta*. They don't *have* to do *tufta*, because they get adequate pay, you know, and they practically set their own norms. But *all* they want out of life is to cheat the system. That's vital when you're in the mine. You know that. But it's not enough to build your life around. Anyway, what are you grinning at?"

Adarich looked very coy. He said, "Now *I* am going to prophesy. I am not supposed to tell you anything about this, but by this time next week your life will have changed radically for the better because of a single drastic event in the Soviet Union."

Shargai's words. I was not ready for jokes and riddles. I said, "Stop it, Yevgeni Petrovich, I don't know what you . . ." And then I got it. I said, "You mean I'm coming back?"

He just grinned. "I never said anything about that," he said, pretending to be indignant.

That was a Wednesday or a Thursday. On Monday morning I was told by a guard, "You are ordered to stay in the Zone today. Report to the *naryadchik* at nine o'clock."

Different *naryadchik*. He doesn't know me. Seems a decent guy. He has to fumble around a long time to find my file. Finally brings it out. I can hardly contain myself. "Oh, yeah. Here it is. There has been a request for you in Camp Number Two. You move over there today. Collect your stuff and meet the convoy—no, sorry, you can just go over yourself. Barracks number five. Brigadier Zyuzin."

Zyuzin! My spirits went right down again. That meant back to the DOZ, probably, unless his floating brigade had been moved again. I said bleakly, "What is the work assignment?"

The *naryadchik* said, "Oh, you're not working with Zyuzin. Just living there. Didn't you know? You've been specially requested in the hospital as senior feldsher. I thought you knew all about it."

CHAPTER

24

IT WAS AN UNEASY THAW. MOST OF US WERE OPTIMISTIC. I KNOW I WAS. BUT even though there were plenty of indications of change for the better and some substantial changes had already been made, there was also a sense of lack of equilibrium, as if the changes could swing around and blow the other way. The camp personnel were manifestly anxious all the time and wiser heads among us, like Adarich, said that anxious men do not react well in critical situations and that, with so much change going on around us all the time, there could be a crisis, a totally unpredicted and unpredictable crisis, at any time. I argued against this point of view. I said that it was normal for people to feel anxiety in times of change. I said that the rumors of mutinies in some of the worst camps in Siberia had generated positive change for us, and that it was likely to keep on getting better. But Adarich, who was usually so optimistic and jolly, worried a lot about the instability of things.

Certainly things were much better in the hospital. Shkarin was gone, released, and Adarich was fully in charge. The mortality rate was way down as a result of reduced working hours and increased rations, as well as a more humane attitude (real or created for the occasion) on the part of the guards. Hope had a lot to do with it. Hopeful men do not die so easily and many with twenty-five-year sentences began to believe that they would never have to serve the whole time. I was one of them. I became sure that my innocence would be recognized eventually and that among other amnesties would be one for the innocent. Perhaps I was being romantic. If so, I was not alone. Where there had once been at least one death a week that could be attributed only to despair, to a complete loss of hope, now the few corpses that appeared in our morgue were there because old bodies had given out, old diseases had left their mark and robbed a man of life after years of malnutrition and exhaustion. Virus fevers still took off the weak. Accidents at the work sites were less common but they still happened and men died of them. But where we used to have anywhere from eight to twelve corpses any normal day in the morgue, now it was two or three. The hideous ritual of axing skulls, if it still went on, was done out of sight of anyone, and perhaps it had been discontinued, though the corpses were still loaded onto wagons naked with a tag tied to their toes.

The hospital was much better equipped and the supply of drugs was increased. There was plenty of penicillin now, and the incidence of fatal bronchial diseases was sharply down.

We had new X-ray equipment, and we had a physiotherapy unit with heat lamps and other equipment presided over by a skeletally thin scientist named Carl Riwe.

Riwe was a physicist. We called him Doctor, which he was, although he was not a physician. Kask and Adarich had taken a liking to him and pity on him when he was admitted in a state of terrible emaciation and total exhaustion not long after I went to Mine 51. They decided to try to find a position for him in the hospital, and when the electronic equipment arrived unexpectedly, they were able to argue convincingly that Riwe was the only man around who could be trusted to handle the expensive machines with understanding.

Riwe was a German. He and his family had been kidnapped and Riwe himself put in a *sharashka*, a soft prison for technical experts. But he refused to do experiments or develop processes or equipment for his captors, even when he was told that his family would be arrested. He was given twenty-five years then, and sent to Dzhezkazgan, where he would have died if Kask and Adarich had not taken him over. He still had not heard the fate of his family.

Riwe was as bald as a bottle. Kask wanted him as a guinea pig. He had been working for years on a lotion to grow hair on bald people, and Riwe was the most spectacularly bald case he had ever come across. "What a challenge," he used to say wistfully. But Riwe kept refusing. He said he had been bald since he was twenty-five (he was in his fifties now) so it was not likely to do any good, and besides he was used to being bald and would feel strange if he ever got hair.

But Kask would not let him alone. He argued that his "Pink Lotion" would bring happiness to millions around the world if it could be tested and proven. He put it to Riwe not as an opportunity but a duty. He said the lotion was his lifework and ambition and he could not bear to lose such a spectacular chance to experiment. He said that if it worked and if Riwe was still convinced he would be happier without hair, he could always shave his head and that he, Kask, would help him do it. He said that a man with hair could shave himself bald but a bald man could never shave himself hairy, and on and on and on and on until poor Riwe gave in just to get some peace.

The funny thing is, it worked! It did not grow hair in the strict sense of the word: Riwe developed a thin coating of fuzz, like a newly hatched chick. You could only really see it when the light was behind him. It never needed cutting and it never got longer or thicker. Kask was ecstatic. It proved he was on the right track, he said, and Riwe, who really was compassionate and patient, underwent test after test and examination after examination while Kask tried to figure out what had gone wrong and what had gone right.

The uneasiness that Adarich felt and worried about was widespread in the camp, although optimism was in the ascendant. The old hostilities between national groups, particularly Russians and Ukrainians, were very much alive and some of us believed that the *kum* was increasing his efforts to promote such quarrels as a way of heading off the mutinies that all camp commandants and godfathers doubtless had nightmares about all the time. Marusich and I had agreed that the energies of the national organizations would be put to better use if they were pooled to fight the KGB and the commandant in subtle ways, but it was hard for the two groups to get together.

Now, back in the hospital with lighter case loads and a great deal of freedom to move around the camp, I began to go among these groups to see what I could do to get them working together instead of against each other. Curiously, because I was American the two groups considered me neutral, and used me to carry messages of negotiation between their leaders. One way in which I was helpful to both sides was to arrange to hospitalize a member of their organization if the prison telegraph reported that this person was likely to be arrested or transferred by the KGB. Sometimes a week or two in the hospital was enough of a delay to cancel the plan entirely, and the man could stay on and continue to work with his group. The part I played was very small, but during this period there began to be a greater spirit of cooperation among the various groups and, as we learned later in a very dramatic way, this cooperation was growing in other camps in the area as well.

During this period of rising hopes, more and more prisoners entered formal appeals against their verdicts and sentences. It had been generally accepted that although most prisoners were innocent of anything more subversive than casual talk, and many not even guilty of that, there was simply no point in appealing your sentence because once the Organs had said you were guilty then you were indeed guilty and that was that. But now the appeals were entered thick and fast. One elderly Jew from Smolensk wrote an appeal every week, always to the same address. After twelve weeks he had received no reply. So, having a little money saved, he asked and got permission to send a cablegram to Moscow. The cable consisted of one word: NU?

The replies to appeals, when they did come, were often baffling. One man had written a careful description of his case, telling the prosecutor's office that he had been convicted of spying and terrorist activities in Leningrad in 1940 and 1941, but that he had a certificate showing that he was serving in the army in the Ukraine during that period and had many witnesses to attest to this, so could he please expect a review of his case? In reply, after many weeks, a letter came saying that, regarding his request, inquiries had been made and it was confirmed that his wristwatch had been legally confiscated. Irrational incidents like this were not uncommon. We never knew whether it was bureaucratic stupidity or a deliberate device to so discourage the appellant that he would discontinue bothering the government.

The real effect was to harden the resolve of many of us to find ways to harass our captors, and to accelerate the process of freeing us by making it less and less useful to have us around as slaves.

In the meantime the camp administration tried to be nice to us, and we were easily seduced because it had been a long time since there had been any pleasure in most of our lives.

The culture brigade was still touring the camps. I had been suspended for a while after I came home drunk from town, but I soon got back into it, and we were busy practicing and increasing our repertoire two nights a week when we got the news that we were to be combined with a similar brigade from a women's camp in the Dzhezkazgan area, and that in fact some women performers would be invited to come and work with us at the next rehearsal. This was tremendously exciting. All the men were scrubbed shiny when the night arrived. There were only about ten of us, and, when they came, two women. We were taken outside the camp itself to the administration building opposite the gates, and there we met in a large upstairs hall. There was a female guard with the two women. Both the women were singers. One was a radio operator from Minsk who had worked in a jamming station. Her whole shift was arrested the night the clock was five minutes slow and they failed to jam the first five minutes of a broadcast from Franco's Spain. She got fifteen years. Her name was Zoya Tumilovich. The other girl was an Armenian named Nadya, but I never got to know her very well because something snapped when I met Zoya, and all those years of repression and deprivation, of the total absence of a woman from my life, threw up an enormous, irresistible need to be close to this woman. It was not a matter of falling in love: I just had to be close to her, hold her hand when I could, flirt with her, look in her eyes, do what I could to be near her.

The guards were very easygoing when we first got together. They allowed us several minutes of informal ice-breaking before we had to begin our rehearsals; so the men all strolled over to the women, both sexes terribly shy, and there was a round of solemn embraces as there might have been meeting a group of old friends of the same sex. But when it was my turn I could not resist putting my lips to Zoya's cheek and pressing my hand hard in the small of her back. She looked in my eyes and blushed but she did not pull away. I stuck to her like a burr in those first few minutes and made it as clear as I could that I was terribly interested, and she responded very warmly. By the second or third rehearsal we were exchanging very frank gazes and sneaking touches under the noses of the guards. It was immensely arousing and frustrating at the same time because there was no conceivable way of being alone together.

The concert we were to do jointly was just a few weeks away. I was confident that during the traveling between camps and the excitement of performances Zoya and I would find some way to be alone. But suddenly that confidence got a bad blow. The rehearsals were canceled indefinitely. There were rumors of a terrible rebellion at the camp near Kingir, about twenty-seven kilometers from ours, and suddenly everything became as harsh and tight and terrible as it had been when I first arrived in Dzhezkazgan.

The story I pieced together from a number of sources. At first it was just confused rumors. Guards in a Kingir convoy had come to work drunk and shot a man for fun and the whole camp had gone on a protest strike. Or the guards had shot a whole work column and the camp was rioting. Or variations on those basic events. Later on Victor turned up at the hospital. He had been in Kingir at the time and was able to describe a good part of what happened. None of our guards would tell us anything. Lavrenov was absolutely tight-mouthed about it, and nervous as a cat. But finally we put together a story that looked like this:

The convoys had been getting pretty lax. You used to have to march silently with your hands behind your back, but in the thaw many convoys had stopped being rigid about this. One day a Kingir convoy leader started shouting at his column that the prisoners were not obeying regulations and they better get their hands back and shut up. It was very tense and there was a lot of muttered ugly talk from the prisoners. One guard was drunk; just one. He got carried away, or perhaps he was frightened by the mutinous appearance of the prisoners, or perhaps his convoy commander egged him on. No one knew. But what was known was that he opened fire with his submachine gun, his *avtomat*. By the time he had emptied the drum of its seventy-two dumdum bullets there were nine men lying dead and more than thirty wounded, some of them very seriously.

The Kingir camps were well organized. There were two or three women's camps there and a continual stream of love affairs between men and women who never saw each other. They were assigned to alternate shifts at the work sites, where they would leave notes and drawings for each other and develop elaborate and serious relationships. Once in a while a male column going to the work site would pass a female column returning, and they would call out, "Is Ivan Stepanovich there?" or "Which of you is Tanya L.? Is Tanya there?" In this way they sometimes got glimpses of each other and years later I found out that many of these couples married after their release. At this time the relationships were part of the fabric of closeness that allowed the whole Kingir complex, men and women, to communicate through a very rapid *parasha* and arrive at an area-wide decision overnight. They came to the work site the next morning and simply sat down, with a universal refusal to work until that guard had been punished and a special commission from Moscow had been sent to the camps to investigate conditions there.

The authorities announced that the guard had been apprehended and imprisoned. Things quieted down for a couple of weeks. Then word came from another camp in another area, via the prison telegraph, that the guard in question had turned up there looking quite tanned and healthy as if he had been on a vacation somewhere, sporting a new medal and back at work. There was no way to corroborate this, of course, and it may have been a provocative fiction. But fiction or not, it was believed and it was provocative.

The KGB had unsubtly shipped in a huge *etap* of professional criminals. They expected the *urki* to carry on as usual and intimidate the politicals, but things had changed among the professionals by now. I had seen it coming as far back as early 1951 when I left Sukhanovka the second time. Now the *urki* knew a great deal of what was going on and had stopped calling the political prisoners fascists and even included them sometimes as part of The People, the *lyudi*, if their record of resistance against the authorities was a good one. Besides, these professionals heard there were a lot of women in the area and they were not going to risk losing the favor of these women, if they ever met, by harassing the men with whom the women were said to be on good terms.

The Kingir camp came to a full stop this time, according to the story that was passed on to me. A commission of army generals from Moscow appeared, but this backfired as well because some of the prisoners recognized these so-called generals from Moscow as local KGB. Guards began to get trigger happy again, and there was a lot more shooting. The prisoners broke down the walls between the camps. There were never armed guards inside the camps, so they could get away with this by keeping a good distance from the watchtowers and using other buildings as barricades. Now the guards fled the camps entirely. The prisoners dug trenches and took over the food supply center. It became a state of siege. The prisoners were organized under a former colonel of the army named, I think, Kuznetsov, and they declared themselves a local soviet, loyal to the Moscow government, and demanding only that wanton killing stop and that a genuine commission come from Moscow to see things as they really were. They conducted themselves with great discipline. There was a move to kill all the known informers in camp, but Kuznetsov managed to persuade the prisoners that their best interest lay in conducting themselves with the greatest of restraint and dignity. He was a romantic too.

A whole division of the MVD was entrenched around the camp. Inside, the prisoners managed to build a radio transmitter to let the civilians outside know what was going on. They also built a huge kite and sent it thousands of feet into the air carrying leaflets which were then released over the town of Kingir, explaining the prisoners' determination to behave in a civilized way and repeating their demand for an investigative commission.

The MVD cut off the water supply; the prisoners dug a deep well. The military pulled down the gates with tractors and called to the prisoners who wished to come out, saying that they would be given safe conduct; this was a move to lure out the informers, who were presumed to be terrified for their lives. Some informers fled, but the prisoners built up barricades inside the open gates, and declared the barricades to be a line no one could cross with impunity unless approved by the camp soviet.

They held political lectures and gave safe passage to KGB officers from outside to come in and see how responsible people were conducting themselves. They kept sending out the same message in every way they could devise: the radio transmitter, the kite, the lectures with invited official guests. The message was: We are not mutineers. We are simply political prisoners trying to defend our rights as Soviet citizens.

Finally a genuine commission came from Moscow. For three days they held hearings on a red-covered table inside the gates. Then they left and a division of crack tank troops called the Black Cats moved in with dozens of tanks armed with blank cannon shells. They stuck the cannons inside barracks windows and blazed away. Hundreds of prisoners had concussions. Thousands panicked and fled into the streets and many were run down and crushed by the tanks tearing insanely through the whole area. The streets were wet with blood and littered with crushed limbs and intestines. All resistance was totally broken, and later on bulldozers came in and scooped up a mountain of corpses for a mass burial. This happened on the fortieth day, and on that day we found that our own camp was surrounded by tanks too. The gates were opened so we could see them and see the cannons pointed straight into the camp. We did not know only blanks had been fired at Kingir. No one was taken to work that day and nothing was said. The wordless message was allowed to sink in. We were completely stunned and subdued by it all.

I assumed, as soon as the full story of Kingir began to be revealed, that I would never see Zoya again and that all these notions of bringing men and women together would be called off after what had happened a few kilometers away. But I was wrong. Perhaps the MVD assumed that the show of force had been sufficient, and perhaps they were right. Those tanks certainly put an end to any dreaming that might have been going on about the softening of fundamental concepts of who held power and what it was used for and how it was used when the chips were down. Once the smoke had rolled away the administration seemed as though it wanted to pick up life where it had stopped briefly for Kingir. The culture brigade rehearsals were resumed. At first they were a bit subdued, but gradually we got back into the spirit that had begun them. There was no point sulking. We had been prisoners for years, nearly six years for me, twenty for others; this was a chance to bring some music and some warmth and some humanity to our fellow sailors, all lonely and oppressed on those Gulag waters. So we got on with it.

The first mixed concert was held in our own mess hall. I stole fifty grams—about two ounces—of hospital alcohol, pure alcohol, to fortify me before going on. I really do not remember much about that concert, except that it was received with wave after wave of applause from a house so full that people were sitting on each other. I remember that Zoya sang beautifully and that I was swept by desire for her. I think I probably played acceptably; my Seventh Waltz of Chopin was applauded as though it were Arthur Fiedler and the Boston Pops. Our acrobatic display went off without a hitch, despite my pre-concert double shot of hospital alcohol. There was a short humorous sketch that got laughs before the first line was spoken. We had pulled together five tables to make a stage, and rigged a makeshift curtain which, like all makeshift curtains in all amateur theatricals, did not work very well. The make-up room was the kitchen, and to get to the stage we had to stumble across the legs of the audience at one end of the front row. The center of the front row was reserved for the commandants and the godfathers of our own and the adjoining camps, and the women's camps, and they led the applause and were to all intents and purposes as enthusiastic as the prisoners. Backstage between the acts there was the kind of first-night jitters and excitement that I believe is common in any theatrical performance. The performers helped each other tidy up their borrowed civilian clothes and for luck embraced each participant as he or she went out to begin a number. The good mood and excitement caught even the guards, who made rude but not unpleasant peasant jokes and hung around and watched us backstage with considerable curiosity. We all began to feel that Kingir was just an aberration, a disruption in the smooth flow of gradual improvements in our lot. Zoya and I exchanged unambiguous glances all that Sunday afternoon. We still had no way of finding some privacy but I felt sure a way would come. Zoya told me she had found out that there would be another concert the following week at a different camp, and we would see each other again soon.

The next morning I was called to the prison photographer, a prisoner named Epstein, where I had to borrow a civilian jacket and have a formal photograph taken. Epstein did not know what it was for. "Probably the KGB want to see you again," he said gloomily. "Maybe for a confrontation. It happens."

I asked him to make me a copy of the photograph for my own use and he agreed, and I tried to shut the possibilities of what it all meant out of my mind.

The best way was to practice my music and my acrobatic routines with Grigori Levko. Levko taught me a solo number called the Crocodile, in which I would lie on the floor, lock my elbows against my sides and lift myself straight off the floor with my hands only, my feet straight out behind me not touching the floor, and then gradually remove one hand from the floor so my whole body was suspended horizontally above one hand. Then I worked on being able to pick up a flat handkerchief with my lips while walking on my hands. I could get a standing matchbox, but the extra inch-and-a-half descent to get the handkerchief kept eluding me. I made it an all-or-nothing objective to get that handkerchief. Little obsessions like these, plus the concentrated guitar practice, kept my mind off the possibility of another encounter with the interrogators.

The second concert was an even greater success than the first, although that may be just in my memory because I was confident enough not to need a dip into the hospital's pure alcohol supply beforehand. Zoya and I spent every second we could together backstage. Several times the guard came over and interfered.

He would say, "Cut out the monkey business now! You'll get in trouble."

I would say, "What monkey business? We're just talking."

"You know what monkey business. Move apart now."

But every touch from Zoya inflamed me, and I could not believe it would be long before we would really be together. We even managed a real, deliriously marvelous kiss just before parting, with no one watching.

The next morning I could sleep in. It was my twenty-four hours off at the hospital. I was half asleep in the midmorning, daydreaming of Zoya's soft lips for the two-hundredth time, when I felt a hand on my shoulder. I opened my eyes. It was a guard who had been fairly friendly because I had treated him for VD.

He said quietly, "Wake up, Doc. Prepare yourself for *etap*."

I was out of the bed in an instant. It was like a kick in the shins. I could not believe it. I had wiped all of that out of my mind. My heart began beating wildly. I felt faint and terrified. I said, "Listen, Citizen. What is it all about, do you know?"

"No, I don't, Doc. All I know is you're supposed to go see the *naryadchik*."

That sounded funny. The *naryadchik* was usually just concerned with labor assignments, not *etap*. On the other hand, he was probably hand in glove with the godfather. I was shaking when I went to the administration office. My file was already on the desk. I could see the photograph

Epstein had taken. It seemed to be fastened to some kind of card with official red stamps on it. I must have looked terrified when I said to the *naryadchik* in a hollow voice, *"Etap* for where?"

He said, "Don't look so gloomy, for God's sake. It's not a real *etap*. You signed up for a plumber, didn't you?"

I looked blank. I'd forgotten about that.

"Nikolsky Project," he said. "Here's your pass. Here's your work assignment. You meet the convoy at the gates at two o'clock. There's four hundred going from this camp so try to get there early."

It was the strangest sensation. Half an hour before I had been indulging in lascivious dreams about Zoya. Now I might never see her again, and yet I felt happy because a moment ago I had imagined my life in ruins. The worst possibility was another trip to Moscow for horrors I refused even to think about, and now the horrors had dissolved like a bad dream. I was to be almost free! I would live in an area I had never seen before and once again have to tackle work I had absolutely no knowledge of. It was a scenario I seemed to have read before. Suddenly I felt terribly excited. I was sad to be losing Zoya and sorry there was no way to communicate with her, but that was a feeling that got lost somewhere in a jumble of vibrant new hopes for the future.

By twelve noon I had claimed some bread from the kitchen. I stood eagerly at the gates as my new fellow workers began to appear from all directions, making each other's acquaintance, gossiping underneath the shadow of those terrible watchtowers we were about to leave, perhaps forever, speculating with shining eyes and irrepressible excitement about the possibilities of the new life that lay just ahead. What a resilient thing the human spirit is! No pay, no freedom to travel at our own choice, rations a North American worker would throw to the pigs, no evidence that more disaster was not right around the corner, and yet, if you had asked any one of those four hundred ragged souls gathering for muster at the same gates where corpse wagons used to pause for the ax, they would have said, "The future? Looks pretty good to me!"

That is what I felt, anyway.

CHAPTER

25

ONE BY ONE WE WERE LED THROUGH THE CORRIDOR IN THE WALL THAT passes the guardroom. There was an arrangement at the guardroom window like a bank teller's cage: a window with a slit. There all the necessary papers were passed out and checked against your prayer. Trucks were waiting outside. There was a mood of elation in the whole group.

As the day wore on and we waited and waited without moving, uncertainty and doubt began to grow in the group. Prisoners are conditioned to lies and disappointment in the Gulag Archipelago. Before long there were dozens who had begun the most morbid speculations: We were really being taken out to be shot; we were going to Siberia; we were going to an even worse Asian camp than Dzhezkazgan.

Cooler heads reminded each other of the photographs and the passes and the certain word on the *parasha* that Nikolsky Project was under way and would be employing thousands of prisoners. I was irritated at the wait but not anxious. It was a plumber named Margolinshch who had told me about the proposed new project, weeks before when he was briefly in the hospital. Now he was sitting right here in the truck with me. I counted on his showing me something about his trade before I was trapped into revealing my inexperience. Anyway, the fact that he was here somehow confirmed in my mind that we were really going to Nikolsky and that all was well.

Finally the trucks were all loaded. Two guards mounted the standing platform between us and the cab. *They had no submachine guns!* This was a marvelous symbol of good fortune. The trucks moved out. Some of the Ukrainians began to sing lively country songs. I moved over beside Margolinshch and told him I was counting on him.

"Don't worry about a thing, Doc," he said cheerfully. "I'll show you everything I know. And if they give us any choice of partners, why don't we just say we've always worked together? That way you'll never have any problems." Margolinshch was a skinny, good-humored guy; I thought it would be fine to work with him and I said yes to his proposal right away.

In about half an hour we arrived at the town of Nikolsky. It was a jumble of half-constructed buildings. Piles of stone and brick and lumber, and wagons of cement bags, and lines of workers straggling back and forth. We passed a sewage or water trench and suddenly cheers went up from hundreds of workers digging it with shovels and pickaxes. They were all women! Soon we realized that most of the workers already on the project were women. A terrific buzz began to run through the truck. Soon we stopped outside a high barbed-wire fence with four watchtowers and no solid walls. Inside the fence there was a grouping of several two-story apartment buildings. These would eventually be part of the normal town that we had come to build, and as it turned out the buildings we were to work on were basically the same as the ones we were assigned to live in. But the apartments inside the barbed-wire fence were not for us. To our surprise we were sent across the road to another group of similar buildings that had no enclosure at all. I asked one of the guards what the barbed wire was for. He gave me a leer. "Women's camp," he said. "Women work with men here. But we wouldn't let them loose at night with bastards like you around. They have to stay in there at night."

That little piece of news went through our group like an electric charge, and within seconds private and shared plans were being developed for digging under the wire, climbing over it, finding legal ways to walk inside it and get out again intact. The prospect of working side by side with women was enough to set all those thin, drawn, normally impassive faces grinning and chattering like children. I was just the same: I had already had a taste of it and it tasted pretty good.

In the meantime we were all assigned, four to a room, to completed apartment buildings. We had brought our own mattress bags and pillow-cases, and the apartments had steel beds. Things were looking better all the time. I stuck with Margolinshch and we were put into a build-ing with all the other plumbers, a whole brigade of plumbers, probably half of them somewhere near my level of skill. There were eight apart-ments in each two-story building. In the morning we were given our assignments. Two plumbers were to install cold-water plumbing for the eight apartments of one building in seven days. It meant nothing to me, but Margolinshch was shocked. "How they expect us to do such a thing?" he wanted to know in a thick Latvian accent.

But there was clearly no time to sit around and grouse. We either had to get our norm fulfilled or work some pretty smart *tufta*, and for the moment we just got to work, measuring the run of the pipes, bending them on a crude hand-operated pipe bender set up on our outside workbench, hacksawing off the proper lengths, threading them, putting on the connec-tors with lead paint and caulking fibers, and so on.

At the end of the first day we had scarcely begun the first apartment and we were totally worn out. We got up at the first light on our own. We were convinced that the only way to hold on to these "free" jobs was to meet our norms or come pretty close. We had breakfast while it was still cold out. Margolinshch made tea you could float a nail in. He drank so much of it that by the time we left for work he was quite high and terribly cheerful.

"Wait till you're catching on to it! Wait till you're catching on to it! We never make eight apartments in one week, but we come damn close."

But at the end of the first week we had completed only two apartments out of the eight in our first building, and we were beginning to feel too tired to go on. There was to be no day of rest, obviously. I began to wonder if we could apply some American production techniques to the job, as I had on the locks. I had no access to extra glucose and the ration was still the normal camp ration, so I could see a situation developing again where I would just blow around with the wind, as I had in the arc-welding yard, if we could not invent some way to be more efficient. I suggested to Margolinshch that we measure up five buildings at once—forty apartments —then cut all the pieces and mark them, and finally do all the assembly at once. I was sure we could increase our output considerably that way, and although it seemed pretty outlandish to Margolinshch, he simply poured himself another cup of opaque tea and said, "Let's go then."

We never came damn close or even a little bit close to a rate that would produce a full building in one week—neither did anyone else in the whole plumbing brigade. But we pulled well ahead of our first week's miserable 25 per cent of the norm. We were so tired our original excitement over the presence of women virtually evaporated. Margolinshch talked a lot about women in the first few days. He would say, "Just wait! Just wait till a few days off come. We get ahead of norm a bit. Just wait!" But soon he stopped talking about all the wonderful things he was going to do to all the wonderful women he would find. I often thought of Zoya and I missed very much the sense of affection that had grown up between us, but at this stage I was so tired all the time that I knew if we were to meet somehow and somehow find ourselves a bed to get into together I would go right to sleep.

Gradually we arrived, Margolinshch and I, at an understanding that we could work only so much. We knew we were doing better than the other teams, because of our system, even though they would come in and report at night that they had completed so many apartments and we had none to report because we were spending all our days cutting and bending, getting ready for a blitz of assembly when we had our five buildings all ready to service. We began to take life a little bit easier then, for the sake of survival.

One day I found that there was a set of measurements that made no sense. Margolinshch said, "All right, Al, you made them, you better go back and measure again." This was frustrating because we were beginning to swing along very fast in our routine of cutting and bending and even preassembling. But it was also a relief from physical work, so I was glad to go.

When I came to the building, the tired, thin women lugging plaster in through the door in a wheelbarrow refused to let me in. I would get in the way of their work, they said. I protested and yelled that their building would certainly not be much use if we could not get the plumbing done. One of the women pointed at the construction shack. "Go and see the brigadier," she said. "If you get permission, then we can't stop you."

I went over to the shack. I heard a tough, high-pitched voice inside giving orders to the women workers in a very no-nonsense way. It sounded like a man with a very high voice. I looked in. Here was a strong, broad-cheeked, fair-haired woman of thirty-five, handing out assignments as if she had been doing it all her life.

"Well, what do you want?" she asked brusquely when I came in. She was leaning way back in her chair. The chair was tilted back on two legs. She had her feet up on the desk. This looked particularly strange because all the women, this brigadier included, wore short skirts over long trousers, and this woman's skirt was up around her waist.

I said, "I'm the plumber and I need to get into your building to measure it."

She said, "Well, you're not going in now!"

She had a strong, brassy voice that was very appealing.

I said, "Why not?" But I said it less angrily than I might have. I found the spectacle of this interesting-looking woman very appealing—not in a sexual way, just as an interesting, vital person. I was in no hurry to end the conversation.

Neither was she, as it turned out. She answered, "Because it's lunchtime. Go and get your lunch and sit here and eat it with me and tell me where you come from."

We had a great talk. Her name was Galya Zaslavskaya. When the Soviet army was advancing into the Nazi-occupied Ukraine, where her home was, she was forcibly evacuated to Vienna, along with a lot of other Ukrainian young people. There she was forced to work in factories serving the Nazi war machine. During this period she became fluent in German and made many good friends among her Austrian fellow workers. After the war she stayed on in Vienna with her friends. She had a good job and was comfortable there, but she was homesick too. In 1948 she began to correspond with her mother in the Ukraine. The mother begged her to return. She told Galya that she had asked the authorities and had been assured that there was nothing to fear about coming home. Galya returned. She was arrested and charged with treason. The evidence? She had allowed herself to be forcibly taken to Austria by the Nazis. She got twenty-five years.

She was fascinated that I was an American. "I hear there is a girl somewhere in Nikolsky who is in love with an American prisoner. Do you know anything about that?" she asked.

Once before I had heard rumors of an American colonel captured in Korea who was supposed to be somewhere in Dzhezkazgan but I had never been able to find him. "Do you know any details?" I asked.

Galya said, "No. I'll see if I can find out. But by God, I just remembered! We have an American girl here, too. She speaks Russian so well I completely forget sometimes that she's American!"

Galya leaped up from her chair. I was so flabbergasted by this news I could hardly move. For a wild minute I wondered if it could be my sister

Stella, even though I knew she was safely away in England. Galya Zaslavskaya said, "Come! Come! Come and meet her! She's from New York City, same as you!"

I rushed outside after Galya. We picked our way through piles of lumber and broken rock and all the usual junk that litters a construction site and finally came to a group of women sitting around smoking by a pile of cement bags.

Galya called out, "Hey, you! Meet your fellow countryman!"

A thin, dark-haired girl got up carefully and came over to me and held out her hand. She spoke perfect English. She said, "Hello; my name is Norma Schickman. I'm from Brooklyn, New York."

It was a strange feeling. Oddly, although I had expected to be instantly attracted to and fascinated by any American woman, I felt nothing special for Norma Schickman, except that it was a pleasure to talk about home with someone who knew it. She had been teaching English in Moscow when she was arrested for espionage. Her story was similar to mine: a father who was a technical expert brought to Moscow on contract and then drafted into the army. Norma and I became good friends and saw a good deal of each other then and later in Moscow, but nothing more came of it than that. I asked her if she knew anything about another American who was supposed to be somewhere in the area, with a girl here in Nikolsky, but she had nothing to offer on that subject. I shook hands with her as if she were a man and went out to measure my building. I was sure we would meet again. She said she would keep her eyes and ears open for news of another American in camp.

After a few weeks it became clear to everyone that the approach we were making to our plumbing task was more efficient. There was talk of making Margolinshch a plumbing brigadier and imposing our system on all the plumbing teams. I began to relax a little about our norms. I began to feel a little easier about taking a noon break and spending a little time walking about Nikolsky to see what I could see and whom I could meet. Once in a while I took my bread with me and had lunch with Galya Zaslavskaya. One day she said, "You know, Al, you have quite a reputation around here. There is a lady poet in our library who is dying to meet you."

"Are you joking? I didn't even know there was a library."

"Well, there is. Her name is Ruth ———."

So a few days later, when some plumbing trouble developed in the women's camp and I was given a pass to go inside the fence and fix the pipes, I put a good pair of pants on under my work clothes, and took my lunch with me, and once I had the leaky pipe fixed I asked where the library was and went directly to the building that was pointed out.

I found Ruth inside, in a wing of the building that had been set aside as a tiny library. She was very gracious. She said she had heard that I was well read and had interesting things to say about America. I was very flattered and did not even think to ask her where she had heard these things. I assumed it was from Galya Zaslavskaya. Ruth said, "Will you do me the honor of taking lunch with me?"

Very formal. I said, "Of course. I would be honored."

We went into her quarters, attached to the library. It was cramped in the small room, but she had a small hot plate and started to boil water for tea. I felt very mischievous, for some reason. I said, "Do you mind if I take off my pants?" and started undoing the buttons. Poor Ruth. I was sorry the minute I said it because she went very pale and her lip started to tremble. She told me later she thought she was about to be violated. I was almost spastic trying not to laugh, and yet chagrined at the same time. I said, "I mean, I just want to take them off so I'll be more comfortable." This made things worse. I decided just to go ahead. Her eyes were horrified as I started to drop my work pants. Then she saw the clean pants underneath. For a while we were both helpless with laughter. I apologized for the joke. She said, "Well, you know so many violent things go on around here. I'm not sure it was good to mix the men and the women. Some of those men are like beasts."

I said, "I don't see how anyone has any energy for anything like that."

She said, "Well, you look healthy enough!" And then immediately blushed and trembled again at the lips. "I didn't mean . . ." she said, flatteringly, and she did not. She was terribly lonely, it came out finally, for an American colonel named Walters whom she had been seeing in Moscow for some months before she was arrested and on whose account she had been arrested. Later I found out that the KGB, during her interrogation, humiliated her physically while forcing her to describe in intimate detail all the sexual encounters she had had with this Colonel Walters, whom I had met briefly. It was because of him that she had wanted to meet me—because of the American connection. There was nothing flirtatious between us. Our relationship was then, and continued to be, platonic, with much discussion of her beloved colonel. We became good friends. She urged me to come back often for books, when I had the energy and attention to read again. Later, years later, when we met again in Moscow at gatherings of the Trade Union, Ruth and I would make the room shake with laughter when we recounted the time I took my pants off in her room at Nikolsky.

When Margolinshch and I began to install our preshaped plumbing units we ran into an electrical crew at the second building. I always enjoy watching skilled hands at work, and I was fascinated to see one woman, whose figure was lithe and graceful, wield the wire and the cutters and the pliers with immense speed and deftness. There was a wisp of pale blond hair hanging out of her cap. She stopped for a moment and took off her electrician's glove to wipe the sweat from her forehead. I was shocked to see that the backs of her hands were badly scarred from what I took to be electrical burns. She must have sensed me watching from behind because she turned around for a brief moment, and in that brief moment I saw a wonderful face: cool, aloof, frankly appraising. Dark eyes that I first thought were brown, because the surprising eyebrows above them were incongruously dark brown under the honey hair. Later I found those eyes were dark, dark blue—almost black. I never saw eyes like hers anywhere else. She stared back at me for a moment, raised her eyebrows in a kind of dismissing shrug, and went back to work.

I was hooked. I had to get to know this woman. I thought she could not be more than twenty-one or twenty-two years old. She had a full, sensuous mouth and a dimple in the middle of her chin. I am usually very forward and direct, but this time I felt I had to go around a bit first. I went to find Galya Zaslavskaya.

Galya laughed. "You're hardly the first one to ask. She is a Latvian girl named Gertrude. Half the men in camp are in love with her without having spoken to her. But you might as well forget it, my friend. They haven't spoken to her because she won't let them near her. She's called the Touch-Me-Not and she's cold as ice."

I could not believe that. I purposely extended my work in that building. I found ways to pass by where she was working or to install pipe where she was wiring. I tried to work hard and efficiently when she was in the same room, and I never offered to speak with her. One day while I was standing on a box trying to attach a connector above my head and using two pipe wrenches at the same time, one of the wrenches slipped out of my hand. I was standing on one foot, reaching for the pipe, and if I had had to come down for the wrench I would have dropped everything. I was balancing on my one foot trying to decide what to do when Gertrude dropped her work and ran to hand me my wrench. I thanked her in a very matter-of-fact way, and went on with my work.

At the lunch break we sat on the floor together and ate our bread silently. I tried not to gaze at her, not to look at her at all, although the picture of those dark eyes was making me dizzy with the effort of avoiding them.

Suddenly she said in a clear, soft voice, "Where are you from?"

I was so relieved I said, "Moscow," without thinking.

She said, "No, I've heard you talking with your partner. You have a very slight English accent, isn't that so?"

I told her I was an American from New York City. She looked wistful. She said she had always dreamed of living in a country where you could determine your own future. Not necessarily in America, she said—in fact, she had really thought of her homeland the way it was supposed to have been before the Soviet takeover. Or France or England. We immediately fell into a political discussion. Gertrude was, indeed, very cool. I could tell that if we were to have any friendship it would have to be, for the present, at the level of discussion we had started with. She was passionate about leaving the Soviet Union. Her parents had been arrested for being dissenters of some kind, and Gertrude, who was only fourteen at the time, had routinely been arrested with them. She told me she was only eighteen now. I was amazed. She took off her jacket for a while during lunch; it was quite warm in the little room. I saw that she had an exquisite figure. I was falling in love without reservation, and yet I had to be reserved.

"You must understand that I am very cynical about people," she said with a kind of cool sadness. "Many men have tried to make friends with me and I have trusted them until I found out all they wanted was to sleep with me. I have had the same experience with women. I know everyone says I am very cold; well, it's true. I have been hurt a great deal in my life and I am going to be very careful from now on."

And yet, as the time went by, when I did not seek her out as a lunch companion, she sought me out. We began to talk, in an oblique way, about a future in which we were both out of the Soviet Union, both in some land where you could build a life of your own. There were just the faintest shades of suggestion from both of us that this might be a future we could make together. But it was perfectly clear that our relationship in camp was to be one of the spirit only. It became very strong. And yet I had an exquisite dilemma. As I became stronger and less exhausted, the sexual pressures within my own twenty-eight-year-old body, in the presence of a number of sympathetic and attractive women, were becoming very acute. And yet I really wanted nobody but Gertrude.

For a day or two I was distracted from my dilemma by another fortunate turn of events. When I got back to my room one night Lavrenov was waiting for me.

"How is it going?" he asked.

"Pretty well, Citizen Chief. How about you?"

"Well, we have some problems. That's what I came to see you about. You don't have anything to drink here, do you?"

"Unfortunately, Citizen Chief, we're dry."

"Well, no matter. What I came to tell you is that there are so many little accidents and colds and infections and so on here at Nikolsky that we are using up too much transport to bring those people over to the hospital. The women's camp at Kingir has sent a physician over to handle the women's enclosure. Now I want to assign you to look after the men. Will you do it?"

Would I! It meant less fatigue, more interesting work, much more freedom to move around. Besides, I had come to love medicine and, frankly, to enjoy my role as "the Doctor."

Lavrenov made all the arrangements. For a couple of days I was busy setting up and stocking a little clinic right in the apartment block. On the third day I took a break and went off to find Gertrude and tell her of my good fortune. Nobody seemed to know where she was. As it happened, I had a pass to the women's enclosure that day, so I took my bread with me and went to the library.

Ruth invited me into her little room and put on the teakettle. She had a very mischievous look in her eyes. She produced two fresh boiled potatoes, a fresh tomato, and a green onion. Some book lover had brought them to her, she explained with a grin as she made us a real treat of a lunch from these simple ingredients. Finally I asked what she was grinning about.

"I thought you would never ask," she said, almost coquettishly. "You see, I've found out who the other American prisoner is, and who the girl is that's in love with him."

I almost spilled my tea. "Who!" I shouted.

"The American prisoner is a former employee of the United States Embassy in Moscow!" she said triumphantly.

"Ruth, for God's sake, who is he? Stop tormenting me. How did you find all this out?"

"I found it out from the girl who is in love with him. She has not seen him since the last concert of the culture brigade. Her name is Zoya Tumilovich!" And she burst into laughter.

Zoya! I knew that if I could find Zoya and find some way to get together my dilemma would be solved. Gertrude might be my future, but my present needs were urgent. Ruth told me where Zoya worked and I immediately went in search of her. Finally I met her in the street. It was impossible to be very demonstrative there, but Zoya knew how to show what she felt through her eyes. We had only a moment together with everyone looking on. But in that moment promises were silently exchanged, and now it was only a matter of finding privacy.

When I got back to my clinic Lavrenov was waiting. Six beds had been moved in to create a little infirmary, and Lavrenov was checking over my supplies. I had a good supply of simple drugs and some cardiac medications, plenty of syringes, splints and bandages, aspirin and iodine, glucose for intravenous feeding. Lavrenov arranged that I would move my own bed into the examining room so that whenever I had in-patients, I would always be near them. He also had brought me an orderly who was busy cleaning things up.

"I think you had better meet the physician from the women's enclosure," Lavrenov said. "If you have an emergency that is too urgent to wait for Adarich or someone else from the Zone, you can call on her. She's just a few minutes away. I told her to come over and see you this afternoon. Watch out for her. She is tough. She worked for the Germans during the war. I don't know whether it's true or not, but they say she did some experiments for them on prisoners. Very hard. Be careful." I promised I would.

About three in the afternoon the door opened and a striking, dark-haired woman with bright red lips and sparkling eyes walked into my little clinic. "My name is Dr. Irene Kopylova," she said. "Since we are to be colleagues, I thought we had better get to know each other. Can you make tea?"

I had to apologize. I had a burner but nothing else.

"It doesn't matter," she said. She reached in her satchel and produced a small bottle of pure alcohol, some white bread, and little pots of butter and jam. She spread butter on the bread. Then she mixed a spoonful of the jam with a little water and added a generous slug of the alcohol.

"There!" she said, pouring the pink mixture into two medicine glasses. "We can always manage when we really want to, can't we!"

We drank to each other's health. Irene motioned me to sit down while she walked up and down in the clinic, never taking her eyes off me.

"I hear you're an American," she said.

"That's true."

"Well."

A long silence. She picked up a chair and brought it very close to mine and sat down with her knees touching mine.

She said, "I think we shall become very good colleagues, Alex. I look forward to our—ah—*working* very closely together."

I was not sure what to say. I lifted my glass and saluted her and drank it off. She filled it again immediately. She said, "Because of my position, I am able to arrange passes for people to enter the women's enclosure. I have quite—ah—private facilities over there. Perhaps you would like to come and return the visit sometime?"

I said I would like that very much indeed. The woman made me nervous as hell, but I also found her obvious sexual intentions very arousing.

I also thought that a pass into the women's enclosure would solve my problem of getting to see Zoya; that was worth taking my chances with Dr. Irene Kopylova. For several days I managed to use the pass, which arrived later that same afternoon, without having to account for myself to the tigerish lady doctor. I managed to get into Zoya's building on the pretext of looking for a patient. I was in my lab coat, with my stethoscope. There was tremendous excitement. Every other woman I saw would exclaim, "Oh, Doctor. Is there any chance you could listen to my chest?"

And so on. Zoya came in and we caught a few precious moments together and embraced fiercely and kissed each other so hard we nearly burst. "My dearest Alexander!" she said breathlessly. "I am working on getting the confidence of one of my roommates. Be patient a few days, my handsome one! We will find a way!"

Then I had to slip away.

Margolinshch came to see me. He was officially brigadier of all the plumbers now, but he had other news that was more important, he declared.

"Well?" I said.

"Not here! Not here!" We were in the infirmary among the three or four patients I already had in bed with fevers or intestinal problems. Margolinshch waved me toward the examining room. We went in and shut the door.

"I have a woman!" He announced it like the next world war, very fierce.

I dutifully congratulated him and asked who it was.

"Woman orderly for your woman doctor friend!" he said, continuing in the voice of apocalypse. It seemed that the combination of moving into the inner sanctum of the medical profession and the possibility of sexual fulfillment all at once had turned his usual tea jag into a cosmic experience.

"Woman doctor invites us all to party!" he boomed, ignoring the fact that the door he had so judiciously closed was made of thin plywood. "Tomorrow noon! She gives me pass for doing plumbing in her building! Doctor! Doctor! It will be heaven! I know! I know! I told you just wait!! Just wait!"

And he danced out of the clinic.

A note came from Irene that afternoon, confirming the party.

We all assembled in her clinic at noon sharp. Margolinshch had somewhere found a dark striped suitjacket two sizes too small for him, which he insisted on keeping buttoned so that it made tight creases across his belly. The orderly was as tall as Margolinshch and much broader. She was very pink and wore a solemn, shy smile, and said almost nothing. Margolinshch's moustaches were twisted tight and pointed straight as pencils.

Irene was very commanding. She told us all where to sit, and when she buttered bread and put sliced smoked sausage on it, she instructed us to eat it in a voice that meant business. She poured four glasses full of pink alcohol and jam and water, although I doubt that there was much water in mine. She was breathing quite hard each time she was near me, and always bumped against me or let her arm stroke across mine or pressed her breast against my hand when she bent over to refill my glass, which she did a great deal. I had come with the idea of braving it out, and getting away with nothing more than perhaps some heavy flirting. But somehow all this provocation and the repeated big slugs of pink stuff she poured in my glass overcame this resolve. I remember that after a very hurried lunch, during which Margolinshch wolfed his bread and sausage and kept squeezing his arm around the waist of the blushing, hulking woman orderly, Irene suddenly commanded the orderly to take Margolinshch into the outer room and make sure that all patients understood the clinic was closed until further notice. The moment the door was locked behind them we embraced each other eagerly. It had been almost seven years for me; I have no idea how long for her. Any discretion or sense of personal nicety was forgotten in a rush of quite uncomplicated physical urgency. She did not wait for undressing; our mouths were all over each other's, and her hands groped and found and opened my clothes. In a moment she had pushed me onto a chair and leaped on me. It was over in minutes. Meaningless but necessary, I thought, in a mixture of shame and contentment. After a few moments for subsiding, Irene got up from her position astride me on the chair, cleaned herself quickly, pushed her hair into place, checked her face in the mirror, gave me a sort of approving smile as if I had obeyed a minor but essential order quite correctly, checked to see that my clothes were in order, and opened the door. She took me with her into the outer room and motioned Margolinshch and the big orderly inside. Margolinshch's eyes were shining and wet, and his grin as broad as his moustache. The door closed. There were groaning sounds and much scuffling and bumping from inside. Then there was a long silence. Then there were low voices, hers a bit petulant I thought, his a bit apologetic. But we could not make out the words.

Time passed. Irene began to fidget. She found some tobacco in a drawer and ordered me to roll cigarettes. We both drew in long lungfuls and let them out again in long slow breaths and waited.

A woman came to the outer door and said, "Dr. Kopylova, I have a problem with—"

"Shut the door. The clinic is closed for another half hour!" Irene said sharply. The woman went away.

Finally the inner door opened. Margolinshch and his friend came out looking miserable. Neither looked at each other or at Irene and me. Margolinshch quickly picked up his plumber's tools and his overalls, made a funny little bow to his friend, and dashed out. Irene and I exchanged knowing professional looks. The big orderly burst into tears and fled back into the examing room.

I put my stethoscope around my neck, shook hands with Irene, thanked her tipsily, and made my way with as much dignity as I could back to my own examining room, where I told the orderly to keep the door shut as I had an experiment to perform. Then I stretched out on my little cot and had a solid two hours of sleep.

Margolinshch was in the clinic half an hour after evening outpatients' hours began. I was surprised it took him so long.

"Doctor, Doctor! It was not heaven. It was hell. I think I am going to commit suicide unless you can help me. What can I ever do!"

I smiled at him. It was an old problem by now, and I had read as much as I could and talked it over with Adarich on many occasions. A sort of delayed honeymoon impotence. So many prisoners had complained of it, when they were first released and had their first experience with a woman, that, frankly, I had been afraid about my own performance and quite possibly was rescued by Dr. Irene's liberal pink-jam-and-CH_3·CH_2·OH prescriptions. When Victor had been living as a free man for a few months, he met and married a lady that he had become very much in love with. Their first night was a disaster. Victor had been suicidal and had come to me much as Margolinshch did now. I gave Margolinshch the same treatment. Six drops of tincture of strychnine in a glass of water, with orders to come back for more before he next anticipated a sexual encounter. The more important part of the therapy was a large dose of reassurance, an explanation of how heightened anticipation and anxiety can ruin everything the first time out, an absolute preachment that being a prisoner for so long was more than enough excuse and the experience did not mean that his manhood was gone forever.

Margolinshch came back for more strychnine in a couple of days. He never needed it again, and every time I saw him after that he was grinning and humming away at some Latvian tune. I saw the pink orderly a few times and she looked very satisfied as well. My relationship with Dr. Irene Kopylova was, after that first encounter, purely professional and somewhat aloof, though not unpleasant. She found herself a former Russian army sergeant who liked obeying orders, and I went back to working out an arrangement that would allow me to spend a lot of time with the eager Zoya.

CHAPTER

26

IN THE END IT WAS EASY AND UNCOMPLICATED. ZOYA, WHO WAS SUCH A friendly and generous soul, had no trouble persuading two of her roommates to keep watch while we made love in their apartment. Probably most of the women in the block knew of it, but nobody bothered us about it. Zoya's bed squeaked and we had to throw the mattress on the floor, but that did not matter at all. We both knew what was happening. It was not a case of falling in love at all; it was just that we recognized in each other a strong physical appetite and a kind of harmony in our willingness to share the enjoyment of that appetite. It was not complicated or soulful. No great sighs of anything but physical gratification and joy in the exploration of tenderness. There had been precious little tenderness in our lives for so long. Soon Zoya made friends with a woman guard. I brought over some hospital supplies of alcohol when I could keep some from Lavrenov, who now, as my supervisor, had two bases to raid. I gave little medicine bottles to Zoya every few days and she gave them to the guard and the guard turned a blind eye when Zoya wanted to leave the enclosure at night. For a while it was most nights. We would move well away from the apartment buildings and find a heap of sacks in a tool shed, or bring our coats and throw them down somewhere. Once or twice we boldly walked a couple of kilometers out into the stark desert and made love under the incredible stars.

I felt a little uneasy about Gertrude. Yet I was young and romantic enough to make a complete distinction between the highly spiritual involvement I had with her and the easy, giving, physical, and uncomplicated meetings with Zoya. Zoya and I were honest with each other. We knew what we wanted each other for, and we found it perfectly acceptable. We rejoiced in each other's body and made no pretense of any future together. We could never have lived together and we knew that perfectly well.

Gertrude and I, however, began to talk more and more about finding a way to be together "after." I explored endless fantasies about bringing her to America, about seeing the Great Lakes with her, and Niagara Falls, and the Grand Canyon, and of course exploring the streets of New York City that now seemed so far away. In none of this fantasy was there any sex. Gertrude to me had a purity of person that somehow stood outside of sex. I knew that when, one day, we escaped together and made a new life in a free land we would marry and have children, but that had nothing of Zoya in it; it was on another plane. We talked with growing intensity every time we met. Gertrude became animated and warm with me, but we never so much as held hands.

There was a seminar for women physicians at Kingir, and Dr. Irene Kopylova was invited to attend. Lavrenov came and told me that I would have to take over the women's clinic for a few days. The women were so anxious for the touch of a man that attendance at the clinic tripled while I was there. Many of them wanted me to listen to their chests. I had never treated women before and I was pretty shy about it, but I never dismissed them or made fun of them even when it was clear that there was nothing wrong but lack of attention. God knows that was real enough and wrong enough. I prescribed a few bitter drops of some kind, or some aspirin, or valerian, which is very soothing, and told them to come back the next time. It is interesting that in this state of really exaggerated sexual tension and appetite I never felt any inclination to take advantage of these poor women, and I never did.

The worst embarrassment was when Galya Zaslavskaya turned up. She had a kidney infection and had to receive penicillin injections. Irene had left her record for me to examine. Galya came into the clinic and refused to take her trousers off for her injection, and I had to coax and cajole and finally shout at her and order her to at least pull down the edge of her waist band so that I could inject into her upper hip. She had to have these injections every three or four hours, and every time she fussed over undoing her trousers. This was another thing we often got laughs with, years later in Moscow, when Galya Zaslavskaya and her husband were very much a part of our trusted circle of Trade Union members.

Whenever Lavrenov came to see me he was either drunk or at the very least had had something to drink. We were on good enough terms by now, but communication became less and less frequent. When he did not come there was no message from him, and he never seemed to have received messages I sent. When he did come, he was often not very clear about our conversations afterwards, and particularly forgetful about special needs I had for medical supplies.

From my training under Adarich and Atsinch I had come to rely very heavily upon the therapeutic value of injections of various kinds. But syringes were in short supply and although I was very careful there was always a certain rate of loss through breakage or theft. Lavrenov never could seem to remember that I needed syringes.

One day I decided, since I was free, to go to the town of Dzhezkazgan myself and see if I could buy syringes at the pharmacy there. I had some rubles of my own and not much to spend them on, so I thought I would procure my own supply and keep it locked away very carefully. I raised this with Lavrenov on his next visit and he breathed pure alcohol over me and gave me his permission. I found out that an ambulance would be making the round trip that day, going from our area into the town, on to other camps, and back past Nikolsky after dark. I asked for a ride into town and the driver was agreeable. He dropped me off in the market-place and we agreed to meet there again that night at five o'clock.

The marketplace in Dzhezkazgan was like a big yard surrounded by dusty yellow two-story stone buildings. In the center of the yard were several rows of market tables with the goods laid out on them and sunshades held above them on poles. The Kazakh women picked their way among the stalls and pawed over the chunks of raw lamb and dried meat and pancakes. When they wanted to urinate they just squatted in the street, and there was a strong smell of human urine in the streets of the town. I spotted the drugstore across the square and headed for it. It was late morning. The temperature was about 90°F and there were few people around. Just as I came up to the drugstore I met three men I knew: Felix Zaporozhets,* George Zhorin, and another I had treated back in the Zone but whose name I never did know. They hailed me very warmly. They were released now, sentences complete except for the exile they were serving in Dzhezkazgan, working in various projects as free workers.

"Hi, Doc, where are you going?"

I said, "The pharmacy. I've got to buy some syringes."

"Ah, the hell with syringes, let's go get a drink and celebrate. Long time!" Etc., etc., etc.

Well, it was a long time, even though these guys were not particularly close friends. But here I was walking around free again and the idea of a drink sounded awfully good. Something inside me said, *Remember the last time!* but I was sure I could keep control of myself, so I said, "Sure. Let's go get a drink."

"To the pharmacy then!" Zhorin said.

I didn't get it. I said, "No—I agreed. Let's get a drink instead."

"That's right," Zhorin said. "There's no vodka in town so we have to drink perfume."

The thought made my stomach heave in that stifling heat. I remembered men coming back from perfume drunks and going to the latrine and when they came out the whole building smelled hideously of perfumed feces. I said, "Not for me, thanks!"

But Felix Zaporozhets said, "Come on, Doc. We'll take it home and mix it with something so you can't smell the perfume. Be a good fellow, hey? Come along."

Fortunately the pharmacist was all out of perfume, because of the vodka shortage. I was relieved when we came out. I held on to my rubles in case we could find some vodka somewhere, and just then Zhorin said, "Say! Look who's back in business!"

It was a Georgian *mors*-vendor, and my friends seemed to be his favorites, from the way he welcomed them. *Mors* is sweetened cranberry juice. The boys said, "*Mors!*" and went dashing across the square to the little stand. The Georgian had black bushy eyebrows and a hooked

* Felix Zaporozhets' father, Ivan, had been deputy chief of the Leningrad secret police (NKVD) and had been implicated in the assassination of the Leningrad party chief, Sergei Kirov, in 1934. Zaporozhets Sr. and his wife were later shot. Felix being a juvenile, his life was spared and he was sent to the labor camps.

nose that nearly reached his chin. He was very jolly. He poured out big glasses of *mors* and then said, "Now, brothers, do you want the number-one drink? I have the finest *mors* in the world, of course, but if you want to reinforce it a little, I also have some very fine *cha-cha*." *Cha-cha* is Georgian moonshine. I had never had it. We all said yes to *cha-cha*. The Georgian ducked under the counter and came up with a bottle of almost clear milky-yellow stuff. He poured a big slug into each *mors* glass. It tasted awful. I was nearly sick.

"Not the best *cha-cha* in the world," the Georgian said. He wiped his hands on his white apron. "But definitely the best you can find anywhere. Have some more."

We had some more. I began to get control of my stomach. The Georgian looked furtively up and down the street every time he poured the booze, but we were never bothered. By and by Zhorin asked the Georgian just to give us a couple of bottles we could take home with us to his apartment. The Georgian made a terrible fuss—how dangerous it would be for him to sell us a whole bottle of *cha-cha*; he would get run in, etc., etc. We were willing suckers. In the end we paid him about three times the going price for a bottle of illicit booze. We went to George Zhorin's apartment and got happily, stupendously drunk.

I suddenly remembered five o'clock. The boys helped me find my way to the marketplace. I was quite cockeyed and fell down in the street in front of the ambulance. Fortunately it had good brakes. I pulled myself up and said to the driver, "Going back?" He had a funny expression on his face; I guessed I looked pretty potted. But he said, "Sure. Hop in."

The minute I shut the back door of the ambulance, which was empty except for the driver, he took off at a tremendous speed. I hung onto the stretcher for dear life. We banged and rocked over the lousy roads. The curtains were closed and I could not see out. I was sure I would be sick. I could not understand why it was taking so long. After what seemed an hour but must have been less than forty minutes we stopped and the driver called, "Destination. Everybody out."

I practically rolled out the back door and was sick in the dust. I heard the ambulance drive off. Then I realized it was not dust I was sick on: it was a paved road. I could not remember any paved roads in Nikolsky, only dust. I wandered around for some time gaping at the buildings and street signs: the Workers Club, Proletariat Street, Communist Labor Street. All paved. Nice town. Finally I saw a sign: City Market. Son of a bitch brought me back to the same place. I go along to the market. Not the same market. Different place altogether.

Sobering thought. Where the hell am I? Man walking by.

"Excuse me, Comrade, can you tell me where I am?"

"Right here," he said brusquely, and kept walking.

I followed after. "What city is this?"

"The same city." I could see he was disgusted with me.

Well, I finally found out I was in Kingir. Dzhezkazgan was 27 kilometers away, and Nikolsky somewhere in between.

It was getting dark. At nine there would be a roll call. I would be counted missing and that would be the end of my pass.

Out on the road, humping along as fast as I can. Walk all night if I have to and try to be innocently asleep in the morning. Maybe I can get away with it.

Convoy of trucks comes along. Dazzling headlights. Flag a ride. Truck stops. Voice says, "Hop in."

I hop in.

Then a look at the man. Suddenly feel quite sober. MVD colonel. I could see his insignia in the light from the instrument panel. The driver put the truck in gear and the convoy lurched along. The colonel said, "Where are you from?" in a friendly way.

I made a fatal mistake. Of course I should have addressed him as *comrade* but I was too conditioned by my years in camp.

I said, "Citizen Colonel, I live right here in Kingir. I'm going to Dzhezkazgan to visit friends."

The colonel just pursed his lips and gave me a very funny look. Then he rapped on the roof of the cab. A soldier riding outside stuck his head in the window and the colonel said something to him and then something to the driver. I couldn't hear. In a few minutes the truck stopped by a tall gate with watchtowers.

"You're a prisoner," the colonel said. "I can always tell." He told the guards to throw me in a cell and he would see me in the morning.

They kept me all the next day. I was dying with anxiety. My stomach was knotted up.

Finally the colonel sent for me. It turned out that he was security chief for the whole Karaganda Region, including Dzhezkazgan and Kingir and a lot more. I had picked a real winner!

I said, "Yes, I'm a prisoner. I'm a doctor at Nikolsky Project. I could not get syringes from the supply room. I hitchhiked to Dzhezkazgan. I was going to buy syringes with my own money. I met some old fellow prisoners. They gave me some bad stuff to drink. I never would have touched it if I had known. It made me very sick. I never drink like that. I feel terribly ashamed. And I am so worried about my patients."

And a lot more pious stuff like that. Maybe it worked a little bit. The colonel told me that he had been sure I was planning an escape, as Kingir is a major rail depot. But now he would just charge me with drunkenness, which would mean the end of my pass. He pulled my pass out of the little dossier they had made on me. I said, "Please don't cross it off!"

He said, "Yes. I am going to."

He made two big black crosses in India ink across my photograph and everything. He wrote on the back "To Be Deprived of All Passes Forever."

It was like a death warrant.

At first, when I got back to camp, I was able to bamboozle the guard who had missed me at roll call. I told him Lavrenov had given me permission to leave the area, that I was treating a guy in another camp, and so on. Astonishingly, I got away with it. But I knew if they ever asked for that pass and saw what was on it I would be in deep trouble, so next day I burned it.

A search had been started for me, I found out later, and there were questions asked, but Lavrenov, who probably was not sure what it was he had authorized, went to bat for me. And so if it had not been for the October Revolution anniversary celebrations I probably would have been all right, because all the time I had been at Nikolsky no one had ever asked for that pass.

There was some anxiety among the administration about the possibility of the October celebrations setting off a riot or a mutiny, and for the week before and after the celebrations we were all shipped back to the Zone and had to stay in overcrowded barracks. Of course when it was time to go back to Nikolsky I had no pass to show. I had thought it would be easy to get away with it. But Voloshin, the godfather who had caught me the last time I got drunk, interrogated me personally and in detail. He was sure I had sold the pass or given it to some unauthorized person.

They knew I had been missing for two days and that Lavrenov had suppressed the information. Voloshin said, "You know, we have an open charge against you. We can always charge you with attempted escape. The only way you can protect yourself is to be truthful."

I had my own ideas about how those bastards regarded the truth. And about how they treated people whom they had persuaded to confess. But I could see no other route. I told him about the *cha-cha*, without naming names. I said, "Look, I did not spend the whole time roaming around. I was in your own prison in Kingir. Check the records."

He checked it out. He was ready to go easy on me then, except that I still could not produce the pass. I never told him it had been canceled by the chief of security, and I hoped he would never find out. But he simply said anyway, "Prisoner, there will be no more pass."

And I never went back to Nikolsky again.

The worst part was not seeing Gertrude and not making love to Zoya. I wrote them both every chance I got. I sent off the letters with truck drivers, and Zoya wrote back frequently—warm, affectionate letters, memories of nights under the stars, how much she missed me, and so on. Gertrude wrote sad letters about how long it seemed to be before she would ever see freedom, and how committed she was to finding a way to leave the country. Occasionally there would be oblique references to a future in which I appeared. I was enormously gratified by those few words.

When I wrote to Zoya I opened with "My dear love Zoya." To Gertrude it was always, "My very, very dear Gertrude."

They put me back in the DOZ. I was much more competent and careful now, and I soon was running a five-speed lathe, making machine parts of some precision. The work was not so bad, but once again I had to march in a forced convoy with guards and dogs, and I had to work hard mentally to keep reminding myself that I had some optimism about the future.

A pay system had been introduced by then. It was the fall of 1954. We had a little money. If you saved carefully, a couple of rubles a month, you could treat yourself to some candy or packaged cigarettes or toothpaste and other small but, to us, rare luxuries like that. We could get margarine and other foods from outside, and for the most part my health was excellent.

A Lithuanian friend who had a pass had made friends with three schoolteachers in Dzhezkazgan, one of whom taught English. He encouraged me to start writing to her to help her English and my morale. So now I was corresponding with three different women. My Lithuanian friend had won their good will by taking them firewood; every day he had tied up scraps of wood with steel wire and left the bundle hanging on the door of their apartment, and after a while they got over their fear of talking to a prisoner and became quite friendly with him. My letters to the teacher of English, whose name was Yelena, were half in Russian and half in simple schoolbook English, which was all she could manage. But simple as they were, they added to my stock of devices for getting through the time which I hoped and prayed was getting shorter now.

There were so many indications of change. Prisoners were paying attention to dress. Men cut wedges out of the bottoms of their trouser legs and inserted gussets, and so, fifteen years before it was a big thing back home in America, we were cheering ourselves up in Dzhezkazgan with flared pants. Fancy boots were becoming a big thing. Prisoners had time and energy now to make things for themselves, and elaborate high felt boots with rubber soles and colored patterns up the sides began to appear all over camp.

After a while Lavrenov asked for me back in the hospital, and although Voloshin had not cooled off enough to give me a pass outside the camp, I went back to my old job as a feldsher. It was pleasant in the hospital again. Now the incidence of severe infections and other illnesses related to extreme fatigue and malnutrition was way down, and so was the mortality rate. We still had plenty of cardiac patients, and the agony of their deaths was, somehow, harder than ever for me to watch. In a way I was becoming more impatient, more cynical, and more selfish. I heard that a transaction called *zachyoty* was to be instituted. Under this system, for every day of hard labor you put in, two days were deducted from your sentence. And if you had the nerve to go to the copper mines, you got three days off for every day you worked. I was beginning to be obsessive about getting out. For some reason I was sure that Gertrude would get out before me, and that if I were long behind her I would never see her again. I thought it over for a long time, and then put in an application to work in the copper mines. Adarich said I was crazy, but I knew that if anyone could devise a *tufta* that would produce tolerable days in the mines, it was me; I had seen it all, I thought. And even if I could not, I wanted out so badly I was prepared to tackle real hard labor this time. It was not a memorable period. I drugged myself with work. I just shut my eyes and bulldozed my way through it. I was assigned to an assembly group, putting together the electric dragging machines. Part of the work was on the surface and part down below. On the surface we uncrated the parts and checked them. Then we loaded them onto the elevator. Down in the mine we had to unload them again and start to put them together. I found the work tolerable until one day my two partners were crushed by falling rock. One died and the other lost both his legs. That left me with a deep fear of being underground that I had never had before. I was close to those boys when it happened, and I remember how the whole area of crushed rock was dark red with their blood. I decided then that I had better find a way to goof off again as soon as I could, and that if I could not I would ask Lavrenov to get me back in the hospital, and just forget about the remission of extra days.

A lot of women began turning up in Dzhezkazgan. Some were looking for their husbands. Sometimes in convoy we would pass a few women in the streets at Zheldor Poselok, or even outside the mines. They would look us all over very anxiously, and we stared at them with great curiosity. Once in a rare while there would be a yell: "Alexei! Alexei!" Someone had recognized her husband. And then people arranged to send notes, and if the man was working in a slack place like Zheldor Poselok, ex-prisoners would help her to go there and find a place to hide and they would meet and begin to plan for the future that we were all sure was coming now. It was rumored that a special commission would be coming from Moscow to review all our cases, and that perhaps many of us would be released.

Now another amnesty was announced. The thousands and thousands of prisoners of war, Russians who had been captured by the Germans and then imprisoned for treason when they returned home, were released and forgiven. Presumably my friend Dr. Irene went out with this group. The camps began to look distinctly underpopulated. I was afraid that Gertrude had somehow been let out with this group, because her letters suddenly stopped coming. But friends reported that she had gone into a depression and was speaking to nobody, and this was why she didn't write.

Parasha, the usually reliable prison telegraph, brought news that the long-awaited commission from Moscow had begun its work. No one could yet say when the commission would get to Dzhezkazgan, but the news was this: thousands of prisoners were being released every day. Since there were about seventeen million political prisoners in the Soviet Union in the early fifties, it would take some time before the wave of releases would get to us, we assumed, but that was not the bad part. The bad part was that the only ones who were not released were those who had not had a trial but had been sentenced by committee or tribunal or special procedure. Gertrude had been sentenced by committee; she had not had a trial. Now, friends reported, she assumed she was going to be in camp for the rest of her twenty-five-year sentence. That was why she was so depressed. I tried writing her to cheer her up. But I had a hard time knowing what to say. I had been sentenced by special procedure myself.

CHAPTER

27

FROM THE BEGINNING I HAD BEEN FORBIDDEN TO SEND OR RECEIVE MAIL. Suddenly, without explanation, on August 20, 1955, I got a letter from my mother. It was very simple. Her handwriting was weak and irregular, which made me think she must be sick. But she said that she was all right, that the MVD had given her my address, and that she wanted news of my state of health. That was about all. I quickly got hold of Epstein the photographer and got another copy of my pass photograph and sent it off to Mother with a short note that could not possibly excite the censor, saying that my health was good, that I was thrilled to hear from her, and that if there was any chance of a food parcel, I would enjoy a few treats. Like any other boy in camp.

Before long a parcel came. Obviously Stella must have sent it from America, and my mother forwarded it to me. It contained Maxwell House coffee! In a vacuum-packed tin. I had tasted no real coffee since the bonanza we'd found outside the barracks several years back and this flavor and aroma were nostalgic and intoxicating. There were canned butter and canned bacon, also real treats, because fats were still hard to come by. And there was a whole carton of Chesterfield cigarettes. I lost most of those to the guard who inspected the parcel for contraband and I came close to losing everything else because I got into such a fight with him over the cigarettes, but I cooled off in time and realized that everything has its price. He let me keep two packs out of the ten.

I shared the cigarettes with Pavel Voronkin, who had moved into my barracks and was becoming a very close friend. During one of the mixed culture brigade concerts I had briefly met an attractive young woman from Harbin, where Pavel had lived as a child. She was the child of Russian specialists in China, as Pavel was. They started to correspond through my introduction, and without ever setting eyes on each other fell in love. Then, after a few months, they managed to meet each other and found that a real and tangible affection had grown. They agreed to marry if they ever got out alive. Pavel was to see Yulya only twice before she was released in an early amnesty. But they kept up a vigorous correspondence. Yulya stayed in the area and vowed to wait for him. Her letters were long and warm and frequent. Many of them were brought to Pavel bootleg by free workers at Zheldor Poselok. They really kept Pavel alive at this period, because he had begun to feel, like my beloved Gertrude, that he might never be released. Pavel too had been sentenced by committee.

I managed to get myself transferred again to Zheldor Poselok. The work assignment was ostensibly hard labor, so the two days' *zachyoty* was allowed. In fact I found it easy to set up the same kind of totally *tufta* life I had arranged before, and because there were so many exciting rumors of freedom I found the idleness tolerable.

I had convinced myself that the refusal to release those sentenced by committee made no sense at all and would soon be corrected. Although, of course, there was a deep fear, which I suppressed as well as I could, that I might be wrong.

The fall and early winter of 1955 were dull and routine, except for some spectacular ice storms and very heavy snow. We were able to arrange a small Christmas celebration for the first time. Voloshin, although he still refused to relent and give me a pass, was civil and even friendly in a greasy sort of way when I met him in the Zone. He went through the Zone often now, trying to rehabilitate his image with the prisoners.

There were many stories of suicide among the camp administrators all over the Soviet Union, and particularly among KGB officers. The hard, cynical exterior they had always shown us during interrogation could not really have shielded them from some awareness that their lives were made of daily obscene outrages against their fellow men and women. Now the prospect of millions of these violated bodies roaming the streets of the Soviet Union brought home to them some sense of the reality of all this. Probably most killed themselves out of fear. But I hope and I think I believe that there were some who did it out of self-loathing.

There was a rash of suicides in our area in January of 1956: the commission—*the* commission—had arrived in Kingir. Within twenty-four hours we heard that they reviewed a case every two or three minutes in an almost purely pro forma way, and that more than one hundred releases were declared the first day.

Now we understood what the construction of Nikolsky Project had been all about. For many of the released there was no home to go back to. Their wives or husbands, children, parents had died in prison or been shot or disappeared. Many of the released still had terms of exile to serve. There was an acute need to keep the mines of Dzhezkazgan functioning, and the work force would largely be made up of ex-prisoners. Nikolsky was to be their home.

Soon details began to run through the *parasha* telling us how the commission operated in Kingir. There were four members. One was a representative of the Central Committee of the Communist Party; one was an official of the Office of the Chief Prosecutor, General Rudenko, who had signed my arrest order in the first place; one was a top-level KGB; and one was a representative of the political prisoners.

Every day the spectacular news came that hundreds more had been released from Kingir. The excitement in our camp was almost unbearable. Discipline became very lax, even in the mines. Even the dumbest, coarsest, toughest guards started trying to behave like human beings. Many of them could not manage it without seeming childish and silly; they had never learned adult ways of being decent. By late February the air was electric. First one camp and then another in Kingir had been emptied and declared closed. The few prisoners not released from a camp would be moved to a neighboring camp while the commission went on with its work. Then the really dramatic news was released: the commission would arrive in Dzhezkazgan on March 1.

The lists were posted. On the first day the agitated, anxious faces lining up to be taken to the administration building were surrounded by almost all the rest of camp, some joking, some wishing their friends luck, some staring silent.

The stories came back within the hour as the first free men returned to camp. A man would go up the steps to the room where the commission met. The door would close. Within minutes he would be back out, stumbling like a drunk, grinning, maybe jumping up and down, maybe just pale and stunned.

Some lay on their bunks. Some sat in a trance. A few got busy in a practical methodical way, packed up their stuff, went around and shook hands with their friends, and then marched to the gates and were free, just like that. The first groups of free men had to wait several days before their passports, train tickets, and release certificates were arranged.

By the third day it was clear that many of them had no sense at all of how to manage on the outside. There were many deaths from drunkenness, and from accidents arising out of drunkenness, or because people just stepped in front of trucks, without seeming to see them, when they had not been drinking at all. Careful warnings were made to all the men walking out free, but many of them were totally unable to hear anything at all.

It was the suddenness of it, combined with the anxiety. One moment you were a prisoner. The next moment you might be free but you dared not count on it because life had dealt so many blows you were conditioned by disappointment. Then, when you walked in and they asked your prayer and asked if there were any special circumstances and the prosecutor's man said no there were not, and you were told you were free and pardoned, you were absolutely unprepared. You hadn't had to lie or argue in your own behalf, or do anything but stand there and hear a ritual which by now was reduced to less than a minute if there were no special circumstances. It was too much to absorb.

The committee would work for fifty minutes and then go out for a stretch and a smoke, and then get back at it. They took an hour for lunch, and then went on. One day they released a record three hundred prisoners.

The first camp was emptied and closed; a hundred or so who had not been interviewed were moved from the KTR next door, and the gates between, which had been open for over a year now, were sealed shut again.

Pavel Voronkin's name came up very early. V is the third letter in the Russian alphabet, and is printed exactly the same as the English B. Voronkin came out looking shattered. He had known it might be so, but we all had encouraged him to think optimistically, and he wept openly and brokenly and told us that because he had been sentenced by special committee, he was to have his case reviewed again at some unstated future date. My stomach knotted at the news. I was almost sure I was in for the same thing. And I was right. I went to the administration building. I stood in front of the commission with my heart beating so loud it would break windows. The four men looked very tired. One of them was in full uniform. His name was General Todorov and he represented the political prisoners. He had served eleven years and been completely rehabilitated.

Todorov said in a tired voice, when he heard my prayer, "We can't review your case, Doldzhin. We have nothing but a slip of paper with your charges. We have to send to Moscow for your full file from the KGB. It will take between one and two months, and we will call you back. That's all. You have to go now. Bring in the next case."

That was it.

In a few weeks they moved away to do the women of Dzhezkazgan. I consoled myself somehow, I don't remember how. I think there was a lot of music at night. Pavel and I played a lot of chess and wandered about the half-empty camp, looking at the names and dates and verses and pictures scrawled or scratched or painted on the walls of empty barracks, and picking up the odd spoon or notepaper or books or other things left behind by the thousands who had simply rushed to leave as soon as their release was granted. We had to go back to work. I saw a number of old and familiar faces at Zheldor Poselok, only now they were free men and women. I got a short warm note from Zoya: "Good-by. I will think of you. I embrace you. Zoya." Well, that was all right. I felt good for her. There was no news from Gertrude.

Adarich was gone, gone on the first day. Kask was gone and the dear, great-hearted non-Russian devil, Nye Russki, who came to me simply and openly and embraced me without a word and then straightened his moustache and his back and walked out of the gates with his sack over his shoulder, tall and quick and happy.

Zyuzin was gone, with his fine guitar and his practical good sense. Epstein was gone, no more photographs. Kublanov and Feldman. Kuznetsov, who worried about spoons. Dear Edik, who would never again be welded into a safe. Aksyonov, whose face I had slapped.

Grigori the acrobat was gone, and so was Stepanov the musician. All the old friends were gone but Pavel Voronkin, and we became closer and closer and vowed we would be friends the rest of our lives. Letters came often for Pavel from Yulya. Often I brought them home with me from Zheldor Poselok.

I got another letter from my mother. Her handwriting was so shaky it was hard to read, and the sentences did not all make sense.

For a while some prisoners were kept in camp until they had arranged new accommodations. The administration moved to head off more accidental deaths by imposing some order on the newly released. But by and by everyone was placed in work and accommodations in Dzhezkazgan or Nikolsky, or put on a train back to his home, and soon there were only a few hundred prisoners left, all in our camp. We heard that the towns of Nikolsky and Dzhezkazgan were overrun with professional criminals taking advantage of the horde of unworldly and innocent new arrivals who knew so little of the world. I wondered if any of my old *urki* acquaintances or other members of Valentin Intellighent's tribe from Kuibyshev were plying their trade there.

The old KTR camp next to us, Camp Number One, which had been sealed off, was opened up again. A whole trainload of Komsomol kids were brought in and established there. We heard they were volunteers of Khrushchev's new campaign to develop new areas of virgin soil. They were coming to build the new city of Nikolsky. Which we had built. We could hear their voices singing drunkenly every night. They would yell and carry on till the small hours of the morning. Soon in *Dzhezkazgan Pravda*, the local newspaper, there were glowing stories about how special, dedicated Komsomol brigades were building the new city of Dzhezkazgan, building it from the "virgin soil" where nothing had stood before, and so on. We laughed bitterly at that.

Pavel could not laugh. He had begun to believe that the commission had been lying to him, putting him off with a story, when they told him his case would be reviewed again. As the weeks went by with no word of any kind, even the warm letters from Yulya were not enough to keep the chill from his heart. He lost his appetite and got very thin and weak. He seldom spoke to me. I tried as hard as I could to get him to discuss the future. He and Yulya had decided to live in Tashkent, and once in a while I could strike a bit of a spark by asking him to tell me more about the kind of life they were planning there. But usually he was morose and silent.

One day I came back from work and found him standing in the middle of the Zone looking very strange. I was afraid he had suddenly gone mad. He was shaking his head and waving at me and opening and closing his mouth, apparently trying to make words, but nothing would come out.

I ran to him as quickly as I could. "What's the matter, Pavel? Are you sick? Do you need some medicine? Shall we go to the clinic?"

He just shook his head and tried to say a word. Finally, although there was no voice, not even a whisper, I detected the word *cable* forming drily in his mouth. I said, "What cable?"

He managed to croak an answer this time. "Cable from Moscow."

"What did it say?"

"It's a cable from Moscow!" He looked quite disoriented. I peered at his pupils. They were a little dilated but not much. He shook his head in amazement and fell against me and embraced me so violently I could hardly breathe. Then he found his voice again. It was very husky. He said, "Oh, Alex, it is so marvelous I don't know what to say to you. I've been completely rehabilitated. No record, no nothing. I'm a free man. A free man! The decision was made even before the commission came here. There was a screw-up in the bureaucracy somewhere. I've been a free man for three months only nobody remembered to tell *me*!" We stared at each other. I felt my mouth stretched in a grin. Suddenly we began to laugh. Pavel Voronkin laughed and skipped about like a child. His thin face was red and shining, after weeks of deathly pallor. We ran to the barracks. I helped him pack his stuff. "Yulya is somewhere in Dzhezkazgan!" he said. "I'll be with her tonight, Alex! Do you know what that means?"

I nodded. I was trying not to show what it meant to me that my last friend in camp was going. But Pavel saw my thoughts. "You'll be next, Alex! You'll see. You'll be next, and then we'll all be free. They can't keep you much longer."

Pavel Voronkin skipped out the gates of Dzhezkazgan and I went slowly back to a dwindling barracks community that now contained not one human being that I knew well or really cared about.

Soon the sixty or seventy of us left in the old camp were loaded into trucks and taken across the hill to another camp.

When I climbed down off the back of the truck Lavrenov was waiting for me. He looked well, but there was alcohol on his breath and it was only ten o'clock in the morning. Lavrenov told me he was now working in another camp near Dzhezkazgan. Krestyovy. He said that I was the only medically trained person left in this area, and that he wanted me to accept the assignment as chief of the hospital. I was too gloomy in those days to be, in any real sense, delighted with the assignment. But I knew that it was just what I needed to help me survive however much longer it was going to be in this lonely existence. The new camp was full of the leftovers from all the other Dzhezkazgan camps. At first there were nearly twelve thousand in the camp, but they were being freed in large numbers, and my work was not very heavy after a week or two.

One day a man whom I recognized from Nikolsky but hardly knew came into the hospital to see me. I did not have many beds occupied. The camp had shrunk again to a few hundred. I was just sitting there looking disgustedly over the littered and empty yard. The man seemed nervous but not sick. I said, "What do you need?" He was embarrassed. He looked at the ground for a while.

Finally he said, "They asked me to come and see you."

I said, "Who asked?"

"At the women's enclosure. Nikolsky. They said you're a close friend of Gertrude's, maybe her only close friend."

I felt an instantaneous cold panic. I wanted to throw the man out and shout at him, "I don't want to hear what you came to tell me!" Instead I just stared at him.

He licked his lips a while before speaking. He said finally, "She was very depressed, you know. She drove herself hard at work. Well . . ."

I think I pleaded with my eyes to have it finished.

He said, "Well, yesterday she was up on the high-tension line, connecting the main service. She just took off her gloves. They saw her—she very calmly and deliberately reached inside the box and took hold of the two terminals."

I just stared. My eyes were dry. My life was dry.

He said, "It was six thousand volts, you know. It was over right away. She wouldn't have felt anything."

He waited for a while. I think he must have been a very decent man. When he saw I could not possibly speak he got up quietly and went to the door. He said, "I'm sorry, Doctor."

And when he was gone I sat and stared at the empty copper sky. It got darker and I still stared. There was no one in the room, no one in the camp, no one outside the camp, no one in the Soviet Union, no one in the whole world. I knew the feeling of being utterly, totally alone. And in the morning I saw the dawn come up and I knew that nothing had grown or been born in that night.

CHAPTER

28

IT WAS JULY BUT I WAS SCARCELY AWARE OF THE HEAT. I HAVE LITTLE recollection of the days as days. They were not defined by contact with people. They were empty and forgettable days. I was disgusted. I knew now I would never be released. I knew that somehow some day I would pull myself together and work out a way of living out the remaining years in camp, but for now I was prepared to wallow in disgust and self-pity.

I slept most of my free time. I heard that the commission was back again. Every day there were fewer and fewer prisoners around. One morning I was roughly shaken awake by a guard I only knew a little. He said, very angrily, "Are you Doldzhin, you son of a bitch?"

"Yeah," I said, in a very sour voice, "I'm Dole-gin. What the hell do you want?"

"I'll want your balls if you don't smarten up. You're still a prisoner, don't forget that. Get up!"

I was about to tell him I certainly had not forgotten I was a prisoner, but he was still talking.

"We've been trying to find you for three days. Don't you ever look at the bulletin board, you son of a bitch? Things are so screwed up here nobody knows where anybody is. They've been calling for you at the commission. Get dressed and get the hell over there on the double!"

I did not rush. I knew the kind of delay after delay that they were going to throw at me. I washed and went to the toilet and had some breakfast and went out to see for sure that my name was on the board. It was. I heard a voice call out, "Say, Doc!" It was Vasya Kargin. I had assumed he was freed long ago. But he had a special committee sentence like me, though I had not known that. He was not optimistic but he looked in better shape than I.

I asked him where he was living.

"Right here in this Zone, Doc. How about you?"

I had been moping so much I had not even known there was one of the old gang around I could have spent some time with.

There were about a hundred men waiting outside the administration building. Everyone agreed that there was an absolutely regular pattern to these reviews. The interview lasted about five minutes. If they were going to free you, they said so directly at the end of the interview. If not, they told you to please step outside while they considered, and then they would send a guard out a few minutes later to tell you that you had not yet been released. I guess they were not so hard-boiled, this commission, and could not stand anymore the terrible picture of desolation when they had to tell a person face to face that they were not going to issue a release.

I was appropriately cynical and sour. I knew the bastards still considered me an American spy despite the total lack of evidence and the completely fabricated protocols that Chichurin had concocted. There had been no evidence of any attempt by my own government to get me out. I had been completely abandoned and knew that I would be so for the rest of my life.

When they finally called me in, my face was set in the grim look I think of as my prison mask. I said my prayer in a tired way. I scarcely looked up. A voice said, "Do you consider yourself guilty of the charges of espionage and anti-Soviet propaganda that have been made against you?"

I snapped my head up and curled my lips back. I was really angry at this charade. I snapped out, "For Christ's sake, would you believe a prisoner and a well-known enemy of the people before you'd believe the MGB who wrote out the protocols? What are you asking me for? Of course I am guilty!"

It was patently a crazy way to behave and I was in a real sense crazy, although I certainly had my faculties even if I did not have my wits.

They saw that I was agitated. Somebody said, not unkindly, "Doldzhin, you go outside and have a cigarette and calm down."

"Sure, sure," I said sourly. It was just what I had anticipated. They can't stand telling it to your face. No guts. I just walked out without a word and nodded to the guard who had brought me over from the camp. "Come on, kid, let's go," I said.

The old prison hand, going back to his only real home. Hard. Cynical. Tired. But he'll make it, somehow. Even get away with calling a guard "kid." They know an Old Con when they see one. Don't fool around with an Old Con. I'll soon be the Hermit of Dzhezkazgan. Everyone gone but me.

We had walked about two hundred meters when I heard someone calling my name. I looked around. The vice-chairman of that commission was limping across toward me waving and calling. He had a wooden leg and was pretty slow, but he was hopping as fast as he could and waving in a very agitated way.

"Come back, come back!" the man shouted.

I shrugged at the guard. "What kind of crap are they going to pull now?" I asked him. The guard shrugged back.

The vice-chairman said, "We told you to have a smoke and come back. Have you calmed down a bit now?"

I stared at him suspiciously. There was a moment when I felt my heart begin to beat a bit hard and I knew some hope was sneaking in. I suppressed it. I said in my Old Con voice, "Yeah, yeah, I'm calmed down."

I went in front of the commission, very stiff.

The chairman said, "Tell me, where would you like to go?"

I was quite puzzled. I said, "What do you mean, where would I like to go? What are you people talking about?"

He said easily, "I mean where would you like to live? Do you have any relatives?"

I said, still not allowing myself to believe what was happening, "Well, my mother lives in Moscow."

"Would you like to go to Moscow?"

I just looked at them for a long time. Then I said in a choked way, "Would you let me go to Moscow?" I felt quite subdued and very cooperative all of a sudden. The Old Con voice was forgotten.

The chairman said, "Yes, we will release you to Moscow, but it is a conditional release. We are required to read you this document. And you must sign it."

It was a fairly long statement. It declared that during my years in camp I had been naturalized (without consulting me, let it be clear!) as a Soviet citizen. That if I went to Moscow I must undertake never to try to contact the American Embassy. That if I did try to make that contact or try in any way to leave the Soviet Union I would immediately be put in a closed prison, not a camp, for life. No trial, no privilege of review. That I would be under constant surveillance by the KGB.

Was that fully understood?

I said yes, it was fully understood. I signed.

The chairman said, "Yes—well, you can go now."

The vice-chairman limped outside and told the guard I was free. That was it.

It was July 13, 1956. I had been kidnapped on December 13, 1948. The passport they gave me later was stamped July 12, so the whole hearing had been no more than a formality.

I was in shock. I stood waiting for the guard to take me back to camp. He said, "What do you want?"

I said, "To go back to camp and get my things."

He said, "Go ahead . . . *kid*. I'm waiting here to see if there's anyone they don't let out."

I stepped to the side of the building and sat down on the hot earth. No one paid any attention. They were used to it by now. My mind was racing crazily. I remember that I smoked cigarette after cigarette.

A voice brought me back. Vasya Kargin.

"Say! Doc! I'm free! You, too?"

I nodded at him dumbly.

"Well, what the hell!" he said. "What the hell! Let's . . . well, let's just *go* then!"

We went off arm in arm. By and by we began to giggle. We headed toward Dzhezkazgan, toward the town. We began to sing different songs. I don't know what Vasya sang. I bellowed out

> *Give me land lots of land under starry skies above!*
> *Don't fence me in!*

I translated it for Vasya.

We dug in our pockets for money and found that we each had a few rubles.

"Let's buy a bottle of vodka!"

"Let's buy *two* bottles of vodka!"

Hard drinkers in camp used to boast about downing a whole bottle of vodka in one swig. We dared each other to try it, and accepted the dares.

We bought two bottles. The only other thing they had in the shop was expensive sardines. We said to hell with that.

We found an isolated spot behind a construction site, picked up an old jar, washed it at a public faucet somewhere, and sat down with the vodka between us. We used the washed-out jar as a glass.

First Vasya poured and drank and poured and drank until his half liter was gone.

I did the same.

I felt nothing at all.

I said, "Let's get another bottle."

Vasya said, "Good. I don't feel a thing yet."

We went back to the shop and got another bottle and drank it down.

Vasya got up and said, "Well, Doc, that's disappointing. I just feel the same sort of shocked, stunned feeling I had when they told me. How about you?"

"Same thing," I said.

Later that night Vasya found himself suddenly drunk, climbed through the window of an unfinished building, fell through the uncovered floor into a trench, lay there all night, and had to be pulled out with a rope in the morning.

I went back to camp in a state of stupor, with no sensation of being drunk.

I stayed in camp for the week it took to arrange transportation. I slept most of the week. I was allowed to cable my mother the date of my arrival in Moscow. Finally I assembled my guitar and a huge medical kit of syringes and drugs and medical books. It was July 20. The train was ready.

The guy who supervised our truck ride to the station was the ether drinker, Zavyalov. Most of the guards had submachine guns, automatics. Now they seemed distant and unreal to me. I asked Zavyalov why the guns, and he said, "To keep you together so you won't run into a truck and get killed. It's terrible, Doc, how many we've had to draw up accidental death reports on. A real lousy job, you know. We don't want any more of that stuff!"

"No heavier burden than a sense of responsibility, eh, Zavyalov?" I said. He took me quite seriously.

My prison release certificate showed that I had served from December 13, 1948, to July 13, 1956, at corrective labor. Released with no record, Ukase number so-and-so. On the back it said, Destination: Moscow.

We got on the train. I recognized a lot of former patients. Many of them had a fair amount of money to buy food. I had very little—14 rubles—but they shared the food with me. We rolled across the desert and looked out the windows at the red sun going down and then the stars coming out.

Nobody slept. The songs began soon. I got out my guitar. Someone had a balalaika, someone an accordion, someone else a crude homemade fiddle.

Dzhezkazgan, Dzhezkazgan,
Across your steppes that never end
No one rides with you as friend
But storms of dust and sand.

I watched the stars ride with us over the jagged horizon. I thought, *A journey into the unknown.* It seemed an important thought somehow. It stayed with me.

Winter blizzards blanket you with white
Wailing through your vastness day and night.

The train wheels clacked and hammered a rhythm ten times as fast as the song. I sang and played chords for the slow, sad melody but my mind raced. The song was corny and sentimental but I was deeply moved by it. Here I was on a train full of strangers whom I knew better perhaps than anyone on earth, with whom I had shared a nightmare experience that no one could ever know who had not spent years in an unreal camp like ours. If you share someone's nightmare, you know that person well. We had all shared each other's nightmares.

I am alone in this land of fear.
My song laments in a cruel year.

Not so alone, now.

Three young men had taken me under their wing. All three had been patients, although I had not gotten to know them well. Two were from the Baltic area: Estonia and Lithuania. The other was a Ukrainian. They were all changing trains in Moscow and heading on home. They kept me well fed and we stuck together throughout the ride. The time came when we should have arrived in Moscow, as I had cabled my mother. We were still far out in the country. I began to be very anxious about her waiting for me to show up, and no train.

Night fell. The lights of Moscow showed up in the distance as we came around a curve. But the train was going very slowly now. There were many stops as we came into the outskirts. The sky was beginning to pale again as we came nearer to the center of the city. In the end we were seventeen hours late. I got off the train with my three young friends. We were all heavily laden. I had my sack and my medical kit and my books. I was bent nearly double trying to carry them all. I wore my patched, thin, and threadbare navy surplus shirt and my equally worn navy surplus gabardine trousers: the remains of the clothes I had on when they picked me up. I wore them proudly.

I looked all around the milling platform for my mother, although I scarcely expected her to be there after all that delay. I thought I would just get a bus to her apartment.

Suddenly I felt a hand on my sleeve. I craned my neck around my bundles. There was a drawn, terribly old face, too old, a face that I had kissed and thought of so often. My mother had tears in her eyes but she was not crying. She said, "My poor Alex. They have crippled you terribly!"

I dropped my things and stood up. We just stared at each other a moment and then she was in my arms, laughing and crying at the same time. "Why, you're not crippled at all! You're fine, aren't you, my poor poor Alex, my poor poor Alex!"

My mother was only fifty-seven. She looked seventy-five. There was another old woman with her. I was introduced to her. She was a practicing physician and they shared an apartment on Kirov Street, just a short walk from the station. The doctor carried my guitar and I could walk upright with my other two bags.

At the apartment my mother shamed me. She said, "Alex, you got off the train with three boys. Where are they?"

I had forgotten my benefactors. I told her about them and she insisted that I go and find them. It took me an hour to track them down. I was exhausted by the time we got back to the apartment, but my mother had prepared an immense meal for us all. She seemed nervous and forgetful and a little strange. I wanted to be rid of my friends, as much as I was grateful for their help, because I knew there was something wrong with my mother and I was anxious to hear about it as soon as possible. Finally the boys had to leave to arrange for their next train. My mother's friend discreetly left the room and went for a walk, and we were alone.

I said, "Mom, what happened?"

She began to clench and unclench her fists. Her eyes were quite strange. Suddenly something caught my eye: her fingernails were terribly distorted and crooked. I grabbed her hands. I made a terrible surmise. I said, "You've been in prison! They've tortured you!"

She nodded. She could hardly speak. I realized now that there were scars on her temples and forehead and that she had been beaten. I began to feel sick. As her story came out, slowly, haltingly, confused, I had to hold myself under control to keep from vomiting.

They had arrested her in 1950. For months she had pestered the MGB (it was still MGB then) for news of me. At first they told her I had been shot as a spy. She had a breakdown. Shortly after she recovered she got my triangle letter from Kuibyshev, in which I asked whether the American Embassy had given her my personal belongings. She went to the embassy to demand help. At the gates the MGB arrested her. She was still emotionally very fragile. They beat her with rubber truncheons, trying to get her to incriminate me. They pushed needles under her fingernails. Now her nails would never be straight again. After a very short period of this she went quite insane and, without sentencing her, they put her in a prison insane asylum in Ryazan.

I just sat there shaking my head in horror as this story came out.

Then she said, with fear in her own voice, "And Alex, I'm not completely all right in the head even now."

I begged her to go on. I hardly dared ask about my father. So I just said, "Tell me everything that happened." I remember that my voice was very hoarse but I did not cry.

They let her out early in 1954 and she came back to Moscow without a kopek. "I had a terrible time when I came back here. They had taken my apartment. The MGB man who had interrogated me was living in it. He had all my furniture. They said I was an enemy of the people and I did not deserve to have anything."

Soon the tears were pouring down my cheeks but I did not sob. She told me she had gone to the police over and over again to claim her belongings. Her certificate of release did not mention any political charges and so the police dismissed it as meaningless. If she had been charged and then released they would have been responsible for finding her a place to live, but she had never been charged and they just said, What the hell? and turned her into the streets.

She actually slept under the bridges of Moscow! She was completely alone. Now she told me about my father. Two days after she was picked up they took him. He came back to Moscow in 1955. By now she had been granted a tiny room. The court had agreed that under normal circumstances she should have gotten her own apartment back, but since her son and her husband were convicted enemies of the people she could not possibly be given a larger room. They gave her a room that was ten feet square, but they told her to go to her old apartment and claim her own furniture. When she got there the apartment was empty. The MGB man had heard of the court's decision and sold everything except a kitchen table that my father had made by hand. The court interrogated the neighbors and concluded that we had American furniture and books and other goods worth an estimated 11,000 rubles. Under Soviet law they were obliged to make restitution to her, but only of 10 per cent. So she got 1100 old rubles, or about $50, and on that she was able to live for a while. When my father showed up and expected to move in with her she was nearly hysterical, she said. She raged at him for having brought us all into this hell, and told him to get out and never come back. My father decided to kill himself. But a man he had known when he ran the transport service for the chief prosecutor's office—a writer named Lev Sheinin, who once was chief criminal investigator for the USSR but had the misfortune to be a Jew and so spent some time in camp himself—talked my father out of suicide and helped him get a job in Istra, a town about fifty-five kilometers from Moscow. My mother and father never saw each other now. They were completely alienated.

I was exhausted from traveling night and day and by the emotional extremes my mother was putting me through. Suddenly my body reflexes took over to rescue me. I began to yawn uncontrollably. We made up beds in the little apartment. The doctor came back. I stood looking out of the window for a while before I fell into bed. I thought, Somehow I have to get out of this terrible place!

It would not be easy. I looked up my father. He was bitter and lonely, but very glad to see me. I had assumed that he had suffered on my account, as my mother had, and so I felt guilty about him, too. The guilt was quite painful. But my father had been arrested under 58.10. Two witnesses testified that he had been heard to say twice that Soviet cars were inferior to American cars. Since American cars were at a premium right after the war in all the high levels of the Soviet bureaucracy, this would seem to have been a reasonable observation, but it earned my father a ten-year sentence to a labor camp in Mordovia.

My mother and I could not continue to impose on her elderly friend. We moved to her tiny room. Although it was clear from the first few days that living so close to her would be difficult because of her precarious mental condition, I wanted to stay with her until I could be assigned a room of my own, and that would take months and maybe years. I could not even apply for my own place until I had a job, and job hunting would have to be the first order of business as soon as I was registered as an occupant in mother's building. Everything you do in the Soviet Union has to be officially registered.

I went to the local passport office; an officious, insolent little junior cop was in charge of our block.

I wrote out a housing application and signed it and submitted it, along with my passport and my certificate of release from camp. The policeman glanced over the papers. Then he looked at the building management office records on my mother's room. Then he just shook his head and pushed my papers back at me.

"Sorry," he said.

"What do you mean! I've just come from camp. I've got nowhere to live. She is my mother. This is my only home."

"It's too small for two people. The law demands nine square meters for each person. She has only eleven square meters. You're out of luck."

I was purple with anger. "Well, just what the hell do you expect me to do? Sleep in the street?"

"Not my problem; that's the law. You'll have to leave Moscow."

Before I could start yelling again he told me brusquely that if I wanted to complain I had the right to appeal to the Chief Passport Director of the Moscow Police. Number 22, Leningrad Prospekt.

I went all the way across Moscow on foot. To my surprise, the police major who interviewed me at 22 Leningrad Prospekt was very sympathetic. I let down my usual guard and told him everything about my case, from the beginning.

He heard it all with growing amazement. At the end he shook his head, and then suddenly pounded his fist on the desk and stood up. "You've had one hell of a time, Comrade, one hell of a time. Wait here. I'll be right back."

He went quickly out of the office. In less than five minutes he was back. He gave me a reassuring sideways jerk of the head and said, "Chief wants to see you." Sideways jerk of the head again to indicate where. "Come on."

The chief wore a general's stars on his shoulder boards. He shook hands warmly and offered me a cigarette. "You know, those local bastards are just damned irresponsible and thick-skinned. I want you to know, Comrade, that we have given them formal instructions *twice—twice*, mind you—that they are to do everything they can to help unfortunate comrades like you re-establish yourselves in a normal life. I don't know what the matter is!"

He picked up the phone and called the officious little jerk who had turned me down. In two minutes it was settled, with an impressive show of firm authority. No rage, no fireworks; just a no-nonsense order. I could live in my mother's room.

Walk back across Moscow to my mother's block. Sign another form. Get the official okay.

"But just for one month!" the little twerp warned. "Then if you don't have a job, you leave Moscow for good."

He had to have the last word, of course.

Moscow was launched on a very big building boom. I was sure, with all my experience in construction, that finding a job would be a cinch. But I was wrong. The daily trip downtown to scan the bulletin boards was frustrating because all there appeared to be was plain manual labor and, while I was quite prepared to do that if I had to, I was sure that with my various skills I could earn much more so that my poor mother could have a little comfort and we would not be so oppressed in our stark little cubby-hole.

I held out. A couple of arc-welding jobs appeared on the notices but by the time I applied for them they were already filled. September came and went and I was thirty years old. Most of my early adult years had been spent in prisons and camps. I felt a sense of waste and an urgency to establish myself and begin to live a decent life while I still had the energy to enjoy what was left of my youth. I wanted to marry and have children.

I wanted all those things a normal young American wants. Few of them would be available to me in Moscow, I knew, but I felt that once I had stabilized my life a little I could get to work on a plan of some sort for getting my mother and me back to the United States.

In mid-October a notice appeared on the bulletin boards that looked promising.

MINISTRY OF HEALTH PUBLISHING HOUSE

Typist with working knowledge of English
Must be able to use English typewriter.

There was simply no such thing as a male typist in Russia. But I did not know that. The personnel chief at the publishing house of the Ministry of Health was amused when I submitted my application. I told her I had to support my mother. She said, "Look—first of all it pays only 78 rubles a month [about $75] and that's not enough. Second, this is a woman's job. Third, you are much too well qualified. Let me go over your documents again."

She looked at my certificate of release from prison. She read my character reference from Lavrenov. He had been generous. He said I was highly efficient and reliable and that I was quite qualified to operate an independent medical station and had substituted for qualified surgeons on a number of occasions.

She asked me about my English. I told her I had been born in New York City. I did not tell about working at the U.S. Embassy, because I believed that I would never even be considered for a job if they knew that.

She was obviously very much impressed by everything I showed her and told her. She said that they were organizing a new branch dealing with foreign language medical publications and had not been able to find anyone who could handle the English division, and that I was perfectly qualified.

"Look," she said. "Why don't you take this typing job for one month. In the meantime, we'll draw up an application for the position of senior editor in the publications branch. This is a highly paid job, Comrade, and they will not process the application quickly. That's why I suggest you take the typing job for the present."

I said, "What about the fact I've been a political prisoner? Won't that be an obstacle here? To a senior position like that?"

She laughed in a sardonic way. "You must be really naïve," she said. "There are so many highly skilled former political prisoners in Moscow that we couldn't fill half our key jobs if we kept them out."

I suppressed the urge to ask her why the hell they'd all been put away in the first place. Not her fault.

She said, "However, I will need to indicate how it was you came to be born in the United States, and I need to know where you were working before you went to camp."

I had to think fast and I had to make a tough decision. I decided to lie. I said, "Well, you know there were many Soviet specialists in America in the twenties. My father was a trade attaché there for a couple of years. We came back when I was two."

She wrote the lie down. "And your job before you went to camp?"

"I was with . . ." I thought fast and lied again. "The Ministry of Foreign Affairs."

I did not say *whose* foreign affairs.

She looked impressed. She wrote some more words and then she said, "That's it, then. Just bring me a letter from the ministry confirming you worked there, and I can assure you you've as good as got the job."

She flashed me a friendly smile. I smiled back but I felt terrible inside. There was no conceivable way short of forgery to get that letter. I dimly heard her telling me where to report for the typist's job on Monday. I went out gloomily and walked all the way home, trying to figure something out.

I thought my position through very carefully. I wanted that job badly and I knew they needed me badly. I finally decided on a bold step. I wrote a detailed letter describing my case fully and accurately, except for one detail. I did not admit in the letter that I had lied to the personnel chief. I simply stated that the Ministry of Health required a certificate indicating where I had worked prior to my arrest, and that I was forbidden under the terms of my release to go to the embassy.

I also wrote that I would like very much to reclaim my personal belongings from the embassy and, since I could not go there myself, I wondered if the foreign ministry through its regular contacts could request the return of my clothes, and pass them on to me. This was a move designed to let American officials know that I was alive and in Moscow. It was the first step in my repatriation. The clothes and books and other things were secondary. The essential need was to make that contact and let my country know it still had a living, breathing citizen named Alex Dolgun.

In the letter I was honest and straightforward about my birth and the circumstances of my coming to Moscow. I read it all over several times. Then I put it in an envelope and addressed it to the personal attention of V. M. Molotov, the foreign minister. I posted it and crossed my fingers.

Then I reported to the publishing house of the Ministry of Health and started my work as the Only Male Typist in the USSR. At the end of the first day I was given a job certificate to prove I was employed and a notice requiring me to report to the appropriate militia office and register for my military ticket, which meant selective service.

The job certificate from the personnel department gave my name as A. M. Dovgun-Doldzhin, perpetuating the inexplicable MGB spelling mistake from years back. It declared that I was employed as a typist with a knowledge of English and a salary of 78 new rubles.

Doldzhin, unlike Ivanov/Ivanova and other Russian names, gives no indication of the sex of the person. The building management chief, a tall, fat woman in her fifties, looked at the certificate and said in a whiskey voice, "Well, why didn't this typist come herself?"

I said, "She did come."

"Then where the hell is she?"

I laughed and said, "Right here. It's me."

The woman was quite upset. She looked at the certificate, peered around the table and looked at my trousers, blushed, and stammered, "Please forgive me; my mistake; I didn't realize you were an 'it'!"

The selective service registration worried me a bit. Not that I thought it likely with my blood pressure and enlarged heart and history of hernia that I could be obliged to serve in anyone's army. But I knew from my work in the consular section of the embassy that under American law anyone who actually serves willingly might be considered to have renounced his American citizenship. I just did not want to take any chances. I reported, told the officer in charge of the local office that I was a very sick person with high blood pressure and a weak heart, and requested a medical examination with a view to being exempted. This was promised and I was told not to worry. In the meantime I would have to carry the military ticket, but at the next annual review of status I would be thoroughly examined and if what I said was true, I was told, then I would certainly be exempted.

The next few weeks of typing English language documents for use in foreign publications of the Ministry of Health were quiet and uneventful. This period would have been quite settling for me because of its regularity and simplicity, except for an event at home.

One night I woke up well after midnight with a sudden sense of imminent danger. When I rolled over on the little bed in our room I saw my mother in the half light, approaching me stealthily with a hammer raised up as if to strike. Her face was fearful, but determined.

I leaped out of bed and grabbed the hammer. She did not struggle at all. I said, "You're having a bad dream!"

She shook her head no, with perfect certainty. "It's no dream, Alex. I heard them talking in the hall. I've suspected since you came back that you were really in the KGB, and when I heard them just now whispering at the door I knew it. They want you to poison my food, don't they?"

I said, "Mother!" I turned on a light. "Wake up, Mother. This is just a nightmare." I opened the door of the room and showed her the empty hall. "Look, dear. There's no one there. You've been dreaming."

"No, Alex," she said solemnly. "You can't keep it from me now. I know you are with them now."

Then she went back to bed, and I lay awake for the rest of the night, torn between grief for her poor mind and fear of what she might try to do.

In the morning she was perfectly lucid, as indeed she had been during her strange attack in the night, but she looked at me differently, and over the next few weeks I came to the sad understanding that she did quite honestly believe I was in the KGB, and that she heard voices more often than she let on to me.

At the end of three weeks I received a letter from one of Molotov's deputies telling me to bring my passport and other documents to the Ministry of Foreign Affairs, to room number so-and-so, to meet with a man named Petrov.

There were no other instructions.

I went there the next day. The reception guard had a pass for me and showed me how to find Petrov's office. I knocked and went in and introduced myself.

Petrov said, "Ah, yes. I have something for you. One moment."

He went out of the room and came back shortly.

"Here is your document," he said. "Please read it over to see that it is accurate."

Now, the astonishing thing about this document is that it corroborated my lie. Why the foreign ministry decided to do this, whether they had asked for my application form from the Ministry of Health—whatever their motive was I will never know. But the document Petrov gave me stated simply that from 1942 to 1948 I was employed by the Diplomatic Corps Division of the ministry as a *referent*. The word meant nothing to me. The closest I could come to a translation into English was "reference man," and that means nothing either.

When I took the document to the personnel chief in the publishing house at the Ministry of Health she glanced at it and then looked at me with a big smile. "Comrade Doldzhin!" she said. "You should have told me! You *are* a very modest man! Why did you not say that you were one of us!"

I had no idea what she meant. I just looked at the floor and shrugged and said, "Well . . ."

She said, "Tell me. How much extra were you paid for your MGB security work?"

I was dumfounded. Somehow I managed to put her off. I said it was confidential or some such thing. To this day I do not know whether she was fishing, or whether the word *referent* was some sort of code word used accidentally by the foreign ministry, or whether the foreign ministry itself had somehow gotten the mad notion that I had MGB connections. Maybe my mother was not the only deluded person in Moscow, I thought. God knows crazier things had happened in official Russia. I later learned that some services of the foreign ministry are virtually indistinguishable from the secret police, but what led this woman to think of me as one of "them" is still only a guess. I let on that my work had been so secret I preferred not to talk about it, and that settled it. And, as she had promised, the editorial job was waiting for me. I started the next day in the periodicals division, on Petrovka Street.

In 1956 the Soviet Ministry of Health was already circulating more than forty medical journals around the world. They had an insufficient budget to publish these journals in various language editions, so they appended foreign-language summaries to the major articles, in English for the English-language countries. My job was to find translators for all the English-language summaries, make contracts with these translators, edit their work, and verify the medical accuracy of the translations. In the meantime I was to begin organizing all this work as a new branch of the publishing house.

The work was interesting. The pay was nearly twice what I had been making as a typist. For a while I was sufficiently busy and excited not to be too distracted by my mother's dark fears and the voices she continued to "hear" in the hallway or coming through the floors and walls. Perhaps she caught something of my enthusiasm for the new job. For a while things were easier in the little room. I stood in line for several hours to buy us a new refrigerator so that she could have some iced tea and we could keep milk fresh in the room. When I got into the store I discovered that the line-up was really just to put your name down for the type of refrigerator you wanted (either the high price or the low; I optimistically chose the high-priced one) and then leave a postcard that would be mailed to you when your number came up. I was warned it might be a wait of more than a year.

Now I took steps to try to get my clothes and books and radio and camera back from the U.S. Embassy. The letter I had received from Molotov's deputy, in addition to sending me to Petrov for my employment certificate, had instructed me to contact the Foreign Legal Collegium about my belongings. This is a state agency that deals with foreign embassies on questions of inheritance and other legal matters.

When I could take some time away from the job, with permission from the director of the publishing house, I met with a representative of the Collegium, who listened sympathetically to my story. He said, "You know, the state would normally charge you a service fee: twenty-five per cent of the value of whatever you retrieve. But I'm going to recommend that it be reduced to ten per cent; you have suffered enough, Comrade, and I believe the state should not demand too much of you now!"

In a week I was called to the Collegium for an official interview. I met in an office with the chairman and with a sharp-faced, pleasant younger man who was introduced as Comrade Aleksandrov, the attorney for the Collegium. I spotted him as KGB. The Collegium had to be crawling with them. But I decided to play their game for the moment and act as though Aleksandrov was indeed their attorney and nothing more. The chairman said, "We have talked with the Embassy of the United States. They have money for you and they will be glad to see you. All you have to do is go there in person and they will turn it over to you. Our attorney"—nodding toward Aleksandrov—"will go with you to see that everything is correct."

I felt very playful and decided to force Aleksandrov to show his hand. So I said, "Well, I can't go to the U.S. Embassy, you know. The terms of my release forbid it. There is always a KGB operative watching the gates and as soon as they see me it's back to prison and I'm sure you understand that I won't run *that* risk."

The chairman said, "Look, Comrade Doldzhin, take my word for it, as long as you are with our attorney it will be perfectly all right. We've done this work. We want you to collect the money so we can close the file. You can't possibly get into any trouble if you are with Comrade Aleksandrov."

I was enjoying this. I knew that what he said was perfectly true, of course, but I wanted them to be made to prove it. I said to Aleksandrov, "I'm sorry. I just can't go there with you."

There was a tense pause in the room.

I said, "The only possible person I could go with is an officer of the KGB."

The chairman was exasperated. He said, "That's not necessary at all! We are official state representatives. You are in perfect safety. You . . ."

But I just kept shaking my head, no.

The chairman ran out of patience. He said, "Oh, all right, Aleksandrov. Show him your card."

Aleksandrov showed me a card like the one that had been shown me on Gorky Street eight years before. Red and blue. *Aleksandrov, M.I., Major. Operative. KGB.*

I pretended astonishment. I said, "Why didn't you tell me! Of course! That's fine!"

The chairman said, "Just one thing. The Americans are very hostile toward us over the Suez crisis just now. We just request that you stay very close to him during your visit. Since you are a former American" (*former?* I thought) "this will give Aleksandrov some protection."

What an irony, I thought. And then I realized it was just a pretext to keep me from getting loose. I wasn't taking any chances just then, anyway.

The KGB-disguised-as-a-cop at the gates refused to let us in until Aleksandrov persuaded him to make a phone call to okay my visit. Then we went inside. My feelings were very odd. This place which should have been my place of employment. These people who had done nothing for me all these years. . . . I felt strangely cool and aloof. The consul came. He acted very cool too. He said, "Mr. Dolgun, we have a thousand dollars due to you. Would you like it deposited to your account in New York, or in cash here?" Nothing about how are you, or would you like us to act on your behalf, or anything like that. Just, how do you want your dough?

I said, without thinking, "I just got out of camp. I've got a job but they haven't paid me yet. I'll take it in rubles."

So that was that. I signed a chit for the receipt of my accumulated retirement savings. No mention of back pay for eight years or danger pay or any kind of acknowledgment of what I had gone through trying not to compromise my country while Sidorov and Kozhukhov beat me to a pulp.

I felt pretty let down. I said, "What about my personal stuff?"

He said, "Oh. Well, we have made a complete inventory, you know. Those things are in one of our warehouses, but we have thousands of crates to look through. We'll let you know."

Years later I found out that in fact my sister Stella had authorized them long ago to give my things to the Soviet Red Cross. I never did find out if the consul was lying or whether their records were so messed up they really did not know. But all the time *I* was running the consular file section, the records were in excellent shape.

Outside, Aleksandrov, who seemed to be quite a decent guy considering he was KGB, said, "You should have taken dollars, you know. You can buy a lot in Moscow with hard currency, without waiting. Cheaper too."

I just shrugged.

From then on I threw myself into my work. I was determined to find a way to leave the country sooner or later, but my need for the moment was a normal life and enough money for me and my mother to live decently. Hard work was a sort of drug for me. A tranquilizer. The number of journals we serviced increased from forty to sixty, many of them involving special material for the World Health Organization. I had a tough time trying to find enough contract translators who could deal with the medical articles. I put in a lot of extra time. To augment my income I free-lanced my services to other publishing houses and translated books on a number of subjects, including medicine and sports. I began to save to buy a car. I made sure Mother had good food. I brought her flowers and did my best to make her comfortable. Every so often she would become obsessed with her conviction that I was KGB and involved in a plot to have her imprisoned again, and at least twice more she attacked me physically. I knew she should be hospitalized, but I couldn't bring myself to send her to an institution.

I traveled the sixty kilometers to Istra regularly to see my father. He worked as an auto mechanic and his salary was very small. I left a little money with him on every visit. He was a warm and lovable man, and we were on the best of terms; the alienation between him and my mother saddened me tremendously.

With the pressure of work in my branch, I was soon in a position to look for extra staff. I got myself a free-lance contract to translate a book on obstetrics and gynecology. It meant a killing load of extra work but the royalties promised would likely make my dream of a car of my own realizable, so I plunged into it.

One day in the street I ran into my old pal and workmate Edik L. We started hugging each other like mad in the middle of the passers-by and burst into laughter all over again about the episode of the safe. Then Edik said, "Guess who is here! Felix!"

I said, "That bastard! He got me so drunk on *cha-cha* I nearly spent the rest of my life in Dzhezkazgan. He's a nice guy. Let's get together."

"That's not all," Edik said. "Felix married Galya Zaslavskaya. Remember her?"

Of course I remembered her. That weekend we had a grand party and drank a lot of wine and talked over old times. I brought a girl from the office with me. Nothing serious, though. I wanted to marry, and yet I had decided to reject the idea for the time being. Partly because memories of Gertrude haunted me, and partly because I knew that if I did devise an escape plan it would be better to be on my own.

At the party Felix said, "Alex, someone is coming tonight I really want you to meet. One of the greats of the Trade Union. Did you ever hear of George Tenno?"

Everybody laughed at that. George Tenno was a legend in the camps. No one else we knew of had survived more than one escape attempt. Tenno had tried two spectacular escapes and was still alive to tell of them. I had the sharpest laugh of anyone. I told the party how I had been beaten half to death because of my alleged association with Tenno.

"Well, well!" Felix said. "So now we will make an honest man of you and introduce you to George Tenno. He's coming here tonight!"

George Tenno was lean and handsome, with a long aristocratic nose and strong intelligent eyes that looked at you with remarkable calm and assurance. I liked him on sight. He shook hands firmly and said, "Well, of course I recognize you! I was made to study photographs of you. Extensively and painfully. That was in Lefortovo in forty-eight and forty-nine."

George Tenno and I became close friends very soon. George had been a commander in the navy, assigned as intelligence liaison officer with the

British during the war, and often traveling on convoys bringing supplies in through Archangel and Murmansk. On his last return trip he became very friendly with the captain of the British cruiser he was assigned to. This man was promoted to vice-admiral after the war. In 1948, recalling George's fondness for a certain brand of British pipe tobacco, the vice-admiral had sent a Christmas card to Moscow, with a pouch of the tobacco. At this time George was undergoing special training. His English was excellent and he was going to be sent to the United States as a spy.

But the MGB decided that this Christmas message from a British vice-admiral smacked of conspiracy. They arrested both George and his wife, Natalie. For two years he was interrogated and had a very bad time. Finally he was sent to Dzhezkazgan, and Natalie to a camp in the far north, both with twenty-five years for high treason.

And then, once he was rehabilitated after the Khrushchev amnesties for senior military officers, he was immediately called upon by his former trainers, the GRU—the military intelligence service.

They knew his qualities and they wanted him back. But George wanted none of them. He wanted out of Russia by now. He was in no mood to fool around with espionage on anyone's behalf. And so, to avoid being returned both to party membership and the intelligence service, he feigned mental illness. He requested an examination at the psychiatric clinic. He told the examining psychiatrist, "You know, I've suffered a lot in prison. I've been tortured. Of course I am a loyal Soviet citizen, but somehow, whenever I see one of these fat faces of party officials now, I just want to kick him in the ass. It's terrible. I know it's wrong but it just comes over me. Something snaps in my head and I . . . Oh, excuse me!"

At this point he would drop his matches. George twirled two matches nervously throughout the interview. Every minute or so he would drop them. Then he would break off in mid-sentence and say very politely, "Excuse me. Of course you understand that I have to pick them up?"

He would drop to the floor, grab his matches, and start again.

It must have been an impressive performance. After a lot of tests, Tenno was certified Unfit for Military Service and taken off the rolls. Then he went to work as an editor for the Research Institute for Physical Culture.

Having such a good and trusted friend as George Tenno became increasingly necessary in the early months of 1957 as the strain of my mother's unpredictable behavior became worse and worse. I looked to him as the source of stability in my life. I counted on him absolutely and he never let me down. My mother was not suffering. I was able to make her physically very comfortable, even though our quarters were so meager. She was lucid most of the time in her conversation and able to look after herself fairly well. But every so often the terrible fear she had of being taken again by the KGB, and her sad, bitter delusion that I was involved in the conspiracy to take her, would boil up and sometimes become violent. It was all I could do to hold on to my own sanity.

Finally, mercifully, the issue was resolved for me. One afternoon she fell asleep with the teakettle on the gas burner. The kettle boiled dry. Mother awoke to the smell of burning: the bottom of the kettle had melted. She became possessed with the idea that this was part of a plot against her, and that somehow it showed that the neighbors in our building were implicated. She stormed through the building creating scandal. She accused them all. One woman we knew was married to a policeman. She got hold of her husband. They all knew of my mother's history of confinement in a mental institution. The policeman called the appropriate authorities. My mother was taken away for examination and she never came back. She was permanently hospitalized as a paranoid schizophrenic. And although I was miserable for days about this, and angrier than I had been for a long time at the viciousness and insanity of the system that had brought her to such a condition, I was able to comfort myself with the knowledge that she was safer and more comfortable now, and that for both of us life would be more tolerable than it had been.

I was able to visit Mother twice a week and take her food (without which she would have starved, by the way; that's the way it works in Russia). The staff of the hospital soon became very fond of her and gave her the keys to the linen room, which was a responsibility that she loved; and I think, in a way, it kept her alive. She was very pleasant with me whenever I visited, but she told me that she was not fooled at all, that she knew perfectly well the so-called hospital was a KGB institution, and that I was of course a KGB myself, and no amount of protesting from me could shake her from this terribly ironic delusion. Despite this I found my visits with her a source of emotional strength. We talked about New York, and how wonderful it would be to go home, and about her dear sister Tessie in New Jersey, and all my cousins, and so, despite the madness, there grew a bond of warmth and affection that sustained both of us.

One day I was asked to speak to the head psychiatrist of that hospital department. This woman sat me down and very gravely explained to me that my mother was a raving paranoid with monumental and impenetrable delusions. I said I knew she had some misapprehensions about things, but I did not feel they were quite so terrible as all that.

"Oh, very, very serious, Comrade! She has told me the most vivid stories about living in New York City, can you believe that? She describes the streets and the buildings with such clarity that I find myself almost believing her. I have seldom seen such an advanced case. I am sorry to have to tell you that she is very, very far gone into a world of her own making."

I sat and listened to this recital for some minutes without giving the doctor any sign. When she had finished what she thought was a dramatic and convincing account of my mother's terrible state, I paused for a minute and then told her the truth about my background, and the reasons why Mother was the way she was. I was annoyed enough to enjoy her discomfort. However, doctors don't apologize, especially when they're caught out by laymen. The psychiatrist showed me the door, in real confusion, and kept on making noises about how I would have to understand that my mother needed close supervision and the best of care and it was necessary that I visit regularly and so on. As if I needed to be told that.

I was lonely in my little room. I occupied myself with work and with conversations with George Tenno on the subject of escape. At work my chief was impressed with my diligence, and the political bosses were more impressed than I would have wished. One day I had a visit from the Communist Party secretary of the publishing house, a man named Kudryashov. After chatting for a while about how well I seemed to be getting along with the development of my new branch, he came to the point of his visit.

"It is time, Comrade, that you undertook some public service work, and I have a volunteer assignment for you that I believe you will be very effective in."

I had been afraid this would come sooner or later. Everybody in the country is expected to do a certain amount of "volunteer" community work. Some of it is political, some not. My assignment was very political. Kudryashov wanted me to become an agitator! This meant that at election time I would have to canvass apartment buildings in my area, remind people that they had to get out and vote, take down everybody's name, put up election posters, and generally assist the whole process of getting out the compulsory vote.

I said, "Look, Comrade Secretary, I would like very much to oblige you in this but my health is really very poor, you know. I had a bad heart and blood pressure irregularities and a number of other problems from my prison experiences. It is all I can do to get through a day's work here. I don't see how I could take on any extra responsibilities."

Kudryashov was very frank. He said, "I don't think you understand, Comrade. While this assignment is, of course, purely voluntary, there is no way you can back out of it. It has been decided for you by the *treugolnik*."

The *treugolnik*, or "triangle," is the ruling political triumvirate in every Soviet agency and bureaucratic establishment, factory, shop, hospital, and so on. It consists of the head of the agency (or factory manager), the local head of the union, and the party secretary. This trio had virtually absolute political authority within the publishing house, and I knew that unless I was prepared to jeopardize my position I would have to go along with it. At least elections occurred only once a year.

So when the spring elections came, there I was, out in the streets with my notebook, signing up voters! I hated it. I particularly hated the election day itself. The streets were blaring with loudspeakers set up at every polling station, in schools and in libraries. I had to get up early and harass all the people on my list to get to the polls before noon. This was allegedly to ensure an early report to the nation on the results of the vote. But since the vote was ensured anyway (there were only two candidates and you had to vote for both of them), the real reason for the early vote was to let the bureaucrats get away for some fun in what remained of their weekend. At the polling station there were long lines of tables with cards hung over them showing big letters, from A to Я. You lined up at your initial, signed for your numbered ballot, and filled it out in front of the official. Constitutionally in the Soviet Union you are allowed to indicate on the ballot that you reject the candidate, and there is even a curtained-off booth where you can go if you wish to exercise your right to the secret ballot. Hardly anybody dares to take either option; the subsequent harassment is simply too unpleasant.

The day after the election I began to worry a lot about having participated in it. Under American law, as I recalled it from my consular days, an American national who voted in a foreign election risked losing his U.S. citizenship. I could argue that my participation had been forced, but it bothered me anyway. I discussed it with George Tenno.

"Al, Al! What were you thinking of, voting for those bastards!" George exploded. "Why the hell didn't you do what I do? Just sign out of town for election day and tell them you're going to vote in Zagorsk or Istra where you're visiting your father or wherever you want to go!"

"But I happen to know you spent the weekend in town."

"Sure." George laughed at me. "Sure I did, but I signed out first. I said I was going to visit my relatives in Tallin. Then I stayed right here. They never check!"

And so that is what I ultimately did, although I did have to work as an agitator for two years before that obligation was discharged.

One night a few months after my mother had been hospitalized I was working late on my translation of the gynecology and obstetrics book when there was a knock on the door of my room. I had few visitors and I assumed it must be a neighbor needing some kind of help. I opened the door and stood there dumfounded to see a familiar face from camp, complete with MVD uniform: Lavrenov, the hospital supervisor.

I was not very glad to see him, but he threw his arms wide and stepped into the room before I could say a word. He overwhelmed me with a huge embrace. "Dear old buddy!" he exclaimed over and over again. "How marvelous to find you at last! I've been searching and searching for you. You have no idea how marvelous it is to see you. I don't suppose you have anything to drink in the house?"

As it happened, I had been saving a bottle of wine for the next meeting of the Trade Union. But I thought perhaps I could use it to placate Lavrenov and get rid of him. The bastard was sorry it wasn't vodka, but he accepted a glassful anyway and glared disappointedly when I filled my own glass. He sat back in his chair and loosened his tie and drank his wine and offered his glass again. I refilled it. He drank half of it off. Then he sighed and wiped his mouth with the back of his hand. A long sigh.

"Well, well," he said sadly.

I said, "What's the matter?"

He said, "Dear old friend, you would not believe the injustices the world is capable of."

I just stared at him levelly about *that* one. He was altogether unaware of the irony of what he said. "Listen," he went on, "listen to the terrible thing that has happened to me. After all my years of service, they've kicked me out of the MVD!"

"No!" I said, trying to sound shocked and sympathetic. I just hoped he'd finish off the wine and stagger out. I poured my glass into his. He took it absently and drank it off.

"Not only that, but they took away my party membership, isn't that terrible? They said it's because I drink too much. I don't drink too much. I like to drink. Who doesn't? But that's no reason to punish a man like this. Know why I think they really did it?" He held out his glass for more. The bottle was empty. Lavrenov crinkled his brow in disappointment. "That all you got?" he asked.

I nodded. I said, "Why did they fire you?"

"Well, I'll tell you the truth, because you'll understand it. Nobody else believes me! It's because I always did so much to help the political prisoners. That's why! They thought I was too soft on you guys. The bastards. You don't have any vodka in the house, ha?"

I had a little but I was damned if Lavrenov was going to have it. Anyway he was the kind of drunk who gets well away on a half bottle of wine and he had already finished most of a whole bottle, so I got up to show him the door. He made no move.

"It's back home to Byelorussia for me, you know. I'll work as a common feldsher, that's all I can do. I leave tomorrow. Nowhere else to go. Lost my room, lost everything."

He was getting maudlin. He looked morosely around the room. I just stood there. "Listen, dear old friend," he said after a while. "I've nowhere to sleep. You've got an extra cot here. Please let me spend the night? I'll be gone in the morning."

I thought, Oh well, then I'll be rid of him, and after all he was decent to me in camp and gave me a break. I said, "Sure."

He took off his boots. He threw his jacket over himself like a short blanket and was snoring in five minutes. I was awake half the night with the snoring, and in the morning I had little resistance when he asked for 600 rubles to help him get to Byelorussia. He promised to send it back when he got his first pay, but of course I knew I would never see the money, or Lavrenov, again. And I never did.

I did get another call from Aleksandrov of the KGB, however. He told me that the U.S. Embassy had another sum of money for me, and we arranged to go there together to pick it up. Aleksandrov's manner was quite affable, and after we came away from the embassy with the additional $270, in dollars as he had suggested, he took me to a special hard currency shop where you could buy all kinds of manufactured goods— export models, so you knew the quality would be good—at very low prices. Together we looked over the refrigerators, and I chose a huge automatic model which was available right away and for which I paid $140 U.S.

I explained to Aleksandrov that I had my name in for a standard model refrigerator. He said, "Well, you won't need it now. If your card ever comes, would you consider giving me a call? I could certainly use a refrigerator." It seemed terribly strange to be doing anything helpful for an officer of the KGB, and yet I liked Aleksandrov; I could not help it. I agreed that I would turn over my refrigerator card to him when it came.

In 1958 the periodicals division was moved from Petrovka Street to the huge Ministry of Health building on Rakhmanovsky Lane, and not long after we had settled in there Kudryashov came to see me again. I wondered what the hell it would be this time. He wanted me to join the party!

In the eyes of a dedicated Soviet, of course, the invitation would be a great honor. To me it was an obscene insult, but I could hardly say that. I wondered how I could refuse without courting harassment.

I said, "Comrade Secretary, you forget I have served eight years as an enemy of the people. I have not been rehabilitated. I am out on conditional release. It is inconceivable that such a great honor would be given to someone like me!"

"Nonsense, nonsense, dear Comrade!" Kudryashov boomed. "Utter nonsense. That is no deterrent at all. There were many serious errors made during the Stalin era. Many innocents have been wrongly imprisoned. You must not give it a thought. I will gladly sponsor you for membership. I will gladly find the second sponsor, and believe me, we know your worth, dear Comrade. I won't have any trouble finding a sponsor. You can be sure of that. Now, what do you say? Aren't you pleased to be invited?"

"I am flabbergasted," I told him truthfully. "It comes as a complete surprise, Comrade Secretary. I am sure that you will understand that I need a few days to think it over."

"Of course! Of course!" he said jovially. "I'll come back and see you early next week."

When he came back I put a sorrowful look on my face and told him, "Look. I have been studying the literature to prepare myself for this great honor. And I have come to the conclusion that I am really not yet politically mature enough to join the prestigious ranks of the Communist Party. So with great reluctance I will have to decline your invitation."

There was nothing he could say to that.

Everything in the Soviet Union seems to be part of a campaign. Soon there was a campaign to recruit police assistants, or *druzhinniki*, to do "voluntary" street patrol three evenings a month. The inducement was three days' extra leave with pay, but I said the hell with it. I got a certificate from the mental hospital saying that my mother was mentally ill and I was her only support, and that let me off the hook for the *druzhinniki*. I spent my evenings with my mother twice a week, with my friends, or working on my translations.

With the promise of the fee for the gynecology book, against which I was able to borrow a considerable sum, and with the money I was saving from other free-lance work, I soon had the equivalent of the roughly $4,000 necessary to buy a used Opel Olympia, which had 56,000 kilometers on the odometer. Gas was only about thirty cents a gallon, and I was able to drive to Istra on weekends and get my father to help keep the car in shape. Unfortunately I had to sell the car again because the loan was called before the fee for the book came through, but later I got a very good used Pobeda for about $5,500, and for the rest of my life in Moscow I was never without a car.

A car, I thought, would be a useful escape tool. I knew that security was rigid, but to get anywhere near a sea coast or a border, with appropriate survival kits and whatever else would be needed to get across that border, a car seemed an essential. Escape was the first order of conversation between George Tenno and me most of the time.

From time to time when we met with other members of the Trade Union there were always two mandatory toasts. The first was to "those still at sea"—an old sailors' toast—referring now to those still in prisons and camps. The second, dedicated to the Soviet rulers, was "May they die a dog's death." We would talk solemnly sometimes, recalling friends who had not made it. But the mind needs relief from such memories, and mostly we tried to deal in the funny and successful episodes of camp life. It was a sad fact that for some survivors there was really no other topic of conversation. What had been the worst time in their lives was transformed by an ironic alchemy into the best time, the most meaningful time. The future for them had been killed; they could look only to the past for meaning; that was when the best in them had been demanded by the most terrible challenge to survive, and now they were exhausted. Throughout the Soviet Union there are thousands, and maybe millions, for whom work and days are just spaces between those times when you gather to reminisce with the old gang from Taishet or Kingir or Kolyma or Dzhezkazgan or any one of thousands of Stalin's slave camps. George Tenno and I found the spectacle of such people discouraging. We were determined not to fall into that trap. We had compassion for those people, but for us the business of life lay in the future, and the future meant getting out of Russia.

We took leaves together and drove extensively, looking for routes that would bring us closest to the border with the minimum of harassment from border guards, whose job is to prevent the willing departure of Soviet citizens. At one point we even bought scuba gear and fixed up a compressor with a special valve working off my car engine. We thought we might take a scuba holiday near a Black Sea port such as Novorossisk, put on the tanks, swim out at night, intercept an outbound Western ship, climb aboard and claim asylum. We had to give that idea up when a navy friend of George's told him that there were elaborate detection devices installed in all such areas to defeat precisely our kind of plan. So I guess we were not all that original, or all that unique in wanting out.

One of George's perfectly legitimate trips to Estonia triggered off a series of events that for a while looked like the end of my escape plans and indeed the end of my freedom. I got a call from the chief investigative officer of the MVD. I was required for a little talk at their central office in Moscow. I had no illusions about any such "little talk." I said to myself, *Well, it's happening again, isn't it*. I tried to recapture the Old Con emotional posture. I bought a dozen packs of cigarettes and lots of matches and stuffed my pockets with them. I called all the Trade Union friends I could reach and warned them that this might be the start of a new campaign against former political prisoners. The past was dotted with such campaigns, and in camp I had met all kinds of *povtorniki*, "repeaters," the victims of such campaigns.

At nine o'clock in the morning, grim-faced and angry, I turned up at the central office. Immediately they began asking me about George Tenno, where we had gone together, what we were plotting, why we traveled by car. It looked pretty bad. I wondered if we had been bugged somehow. I kept my cool, told only the truth (though not of course the whole truth).

George had gone to an athletic meet in Tallin, on the Gulf of Finland, in October. When they asked me if I knew anything about his going to Tallin recently, I confused the dates in my mind somehow, and said, "Sure. Mid-September. An athletic meet."

The effect on the room was instant and electric. The interrogators began to whisper excitedly among themselves. I asked to be taken to the toilet. They seemed to have lost interest in me for the moment.

On the way back from the toilet the guard opened the door to the wrong interrogation room. I caught a glimpse inside. Natalie Tenno was sitting inside looking haggard.

At the end of two days they let me out, without, of course, indicating any reason for my having been there. It was almost a week before I saw George again. This was the story:

There had been a spectacular bank robbery in Tallin in mid-September. Three men had driven up to the bank at noon, shot the guard and every other witness they could see, and taken off with more than 2,000,000 new rubles.

One of the robbers was caught. He figured, apparently, that as long as the others were free he would be kept alive, and so he fabricated a very clever story. Having been in camp with George Tenno, and knowing his reputation, he told the police that Tenno was the brains behind the robbery and the ringleader, and so the following night, when George and Natalie returned home from the theater, six armed men were waiting for them in the darkened apartment. They flew George up to Tallin to confront the robber, then back to Moscow for interrogation. But George's alibis were ironclad. His trip had been in October, not September as I had wrongly said (Natalie had made a similar slip, by the way), and all his fellow workers swore he had been at work the day of the robbery and for the whole month leading up to it. In the end the cops apologized to George, though not to Natalie or me.

Throughout this period I was often aware of being followed in the streets. Later, when I got my phone, it was bugged; you could hear the interference. I had a lot of health problems stemming from Sukhanovka and from camp; it was not a fiction when I tried to escape extra duties by pleading ill health. I would be stricken with attacks of uncontrollable vomiting due to high blood pressure. There were frequent deep spasms in my belly. My broken jaw often ached terribly. When it seemed as though the surveillance over me was unending, my blood pressure would sometimes peak over 200.

And through all my troubles, George was an unfailing prop, a pillar of moral support.

One day in the early sixties George mentioned that he had recently talked with a friend and former prisoner who had written a novel about camp life. He gave me a *samizdat*—underground—copy of it. His own story was represented in it through a composite character named, in the book, Commander Buinovsky. I had met the other half of the composite, a naval officer named Boris Burkovsky, who now commands the historic revolutionary cruiser *Aurora*, which is a floating museum in Leningrad harbor. During the Yalta Conference, Burkovsky served as a liaison officer and had the misfortune to dance at a reception with Kathleen Harriman, the daughter of the U.S. Ambassador to Moscow. I say "misfortune" because it was for this "offense" that, much later, in 1948, he received a charge of high treason and a sentence of twenty-five years. Burkovsky and I used to play Ping-pong in camp. So I read the novel eagerly and found it very good, and very accurate as a portrayal of camp life.

Then George Tenno told me that the writer wanted to interview me about my prison experiences, for another book he was planning. This was a bit risky, we thought, and so we arranged a code having to do with soccer scores, and eventually George phoned and in a casual-sounding coded sports conversation let me know the time I was to come to his apartment to meet this writer.

I arrived sharp on the agreed time of seven in the evening. I walked upstairs and knocked on the door. George introduced me to a grave, clean-shaven man with brooding eyes, who stood there with an old army leather dispatch case over the shoulder of his old military shirt. George said formally, "Please meet Aleksandr Solzhenitsyn."

We shook hands.

Over two sessions I spent several hours with Solzhenitsyn. Since he had never, in all of his researches, met a sane survivor of Sukhanovka, he was very anxious to hear about my experience there and to try to understand how I had survived. He was also fascinated with my account of psychic cell 111 at Lefortovo, and of my techniques for keeping myself together through the long period of solitary confinement. Much later George was to tell me that Solzhenitsyn was putting together a monumental work on the prison system, a book to be called *The Gulag Archipelago*. The book in which George Tenno's history was combined with the identity of Burkovsky in the person of "Buinovsky" was, of course, *One Day in the Life of Ivan Denisovich*.

Having escaped service in the street patrol *druzhinniki*, I knew that I was a prime target for Kudryashov, and sure enough, one day he turned up and told me I had been assigned the voluntary task of leading a five-man volunteer fire brigade in our office, and that extra leave went with the assignment. I found that quite acceptable. It was totally nonpolitical and susceptible to *tufta*. I wrote elaborate reports about how we stayed late night after night checking fire extinguishers, the safety of stoves and hot plates, escape routes and so on. I wrote up splendid accounts of fire drills that had never taken place, and I conscientiously did a good deal of "agitation" among my fellow workers just to make sure that my reputation as an eager fireman would be remarked upon by the *treugolnik*. I remained fire chief until the end of my days in Moscow, but Kudryashov was eventually caught taking kickbacks from authors and was forcibly "retired."

All this time I still had the question of my military ticket and selective service status hanging over my head. The promise that I would be examined for reclassification or exemption had not been fulfilled, but since I had never heard from the board again, I decided that it would not be prudent to raise the issue myself, and I just let it ride. But sometime in 1962 or 1963, all males were called in to be issued new military tickets, this time in the form of a booklet with several pages in it: more makework for the bureaucrats. I had learned a lesson from George Tenno, and when I went to pick up my new card, and had to fill out a form with some new information to be included in this booklet, I spoke to the major in charge in a sort of suppressed, urgent voice, and told him I had to speak to him privately. He offered me a chair and told me to go ahead and say what I had to say.

I pulled out two matches and began to twirl them violently between my fingers. I said, "Listen, comrade major. I'm very sick. I want to be examined. I have already served—Oh! Excuse me. I'm sure you understand I have to pick them up."

I dropped to my knees on the floor, scrabbled for my matches, resumed my seat with perfect composure, and went on:

"I have already served. Nine years. In the American forces in Korea. Then I spent eight years in the ranks of the—Oh! Excuse me!"

Drop to the floor again. Then back to my chair.

"Where was I? Yes. Eight years in the ranks of the KGB. Furthermore, dear comrade major, *furthermore*! I am a graduate, a licensed graduate of the school of obstetrics and gynecology of the United States Embassy, 1943–48. So you see I could not possibly serve!"

The major looked quite nervous. He said in a soothing voice, "Uh, look. Here's a glass of water. Now relax please. I have to—"

I interrupted him. "Excuse me! You understand I have to pick them up!" I picked them up. "Now, comrade major, you were saying?"

"Uh, yes. I have to see my chief for a moment."

I was taken to the chief. I repeated the whole impossible, crazy story and did the thing with the matches again for his benefit. He looked sympathetic but alarmed.

He said, "Look, comrade, I really don't think you have to worry. I, uh . . . I'm sure at the next examination you will be exempted. Please relax."

They sent me away quickly. A few days later my booklet arrived in the mail, my new military ticket. In the section under "Former Experience" it said that A. M. Dovgun-Doldzhin was "Untrained Soldiers" (sic), and under "Civilian Training" it said, "Completed Obstetrical School, U.S. Embassy, 1943/48."

No mention of my nine years in Korea or eight years with the KGB. But that booklet was a great hit at gatherings of the Trade Union. Whenever we met and there was a new member of the group, someone would say, "Alex, show your military ticket." It always got a good laugh.

Later that year the room I had applied for when I first started work in the publishing house came through. I had only had to wait six years. Now I was officially entitled to two rooms, my mother's, where I was registered, and the new one. By the stratagems available to those who understand the Moscow bureaucracy I was able to exchange these two rooms for a small apartment, about thirteen by sixteen feet, with its own little bath, toilet, and kitchenette. In America we would call it an efficiency apartment. In Moscow it was considered a luxury.

It was in a nine-story concrete-block building in the northeast suburbs, on Sirenevy Bulvar, "Lilac Boulevard," right at the end of the subway line, near Shchelkovskaya station. My apartment looked out over a little garden courtyard, and I could see the street where the head of the Moscow Soviet had planned to plant miles of lilacs before he was caught red-handed taking bribes for getting rooms and apartments for people. I had a two-ring gas stove with a little oven. I was able to squeeze in my big hard-currency refrigerator. With a bath and toilet all my own, I felt very grand indeed.

It was a lengthy drive to my office in downtown Moscow, but I preferred driving to taking the long subway ride, because by now I had learned how to get a completely full tank of gas for one ruble. All kinds of truck drivers used to register more trips than they actually took, because that way they could make much more money. They could adjust the odometers in their trucks by prodding the gears with a matchstick. But then they had to get rid of their extra gas. Millions of gallons were simply siphoned out into the sewers somewhere out in the suburbs of Moscow. It is a wonder the city did not blow up. But many drivers, like myself, arranged to meet truck drivers regularly and buy our tankful for one ruble. That amounted to about seven cents a gallon, so everyone was happy. *Tufta* again.

The biggest risk in keeping a car in Moscow was having your tires stolen. There was a sort of semi-underground "private industry" that sold millions of rubles' worth of protection devices for cars. They made a set of smooth, round-headed wheel nuts that no wrench would fit, except a special eccentric key that fit *inside* an eccentric hole in the end of the bolts and was specially made to fit only your wheel bolts. Thieves countered with big pipe wrenches with hard teeth that would get a grip on the round bolts. Then private industry made a rotating collar that fitted outside the bolt, case hardened, which simply rotated if you applied a pipe wrench to it.

Thieves began to open the central hub cover and take off the axle nut to steal the whole wheel—hub, brake drum, and all. Private industry countered with a plate that covered the whole hub, held in place by bolts with their spinning exterior caps. And so the war went.

One day, years after I moved into that apartment, I got a faded postcard in the mail. It had my own signature on it. It was an eleven-year-old application for a refrigerator. I remembered Aleksandrov. I called him at his office.

"Remember the American guy you took to the U.S. Embassy?"

A short pause, then a warm laugh. "Sure I do! Are you Dovgun-Doldzhin?"

"That's me. Do you still want the refrigerator?"

"What refrigerator? Wait a minute! You mean you finally got your card?"

"That's right!"

"I'll send a messenger right over."

So there was that little debt repaid.

In the publications branch I was now the chief of a considerable establishment. I employed a staff of six full-time editorial assistants—copy editors, proofreaders, and typists. I had twenty-eight free-lance writers under contract. When the work got out of hand I would contract some translation to a friendly but overloaded translator, do it myself, and collect some overtime that way.

I was easily able to integrate myself practically, though not emotionally and spiritually, into the daily life of a Moscow bureaucrat. I discovered that *tufta* is really as much a part of civilian life in the Soviet Union as it is in camp. Without cheating the system nobody could survive; so everyone is engaged in *tufta* all the time. In Russia many people lead a kind of double life in order to be able to live with the extremely controlling and regulated manner in which the government tries to manage its society.

I had to go to political education meetings regularly. Every two or three months someone from my superior's office would come around with the schedule of "Voluntary Political Education" sessions for the next quarter or so, and say, "Now here's your schedule; we know you've volunteered for it." (I had not!) "You will be expected to study these particular sections of Lenin's works or these speeches by Chairman Brezhnev," and so on and so on.

Nobody wanted to go but nobody wanted the harassment that came with refusing. We were supposed to write out ten-page analyses of a chapter or a political idea for each session. This was where *tufta* came in. We all cheated. We made up the reports by simply writing out several pages of Lenin or Brezhnev with enough words changed so that it would seem to be in colloquial Russian instead of the dense, uncommunicative, incomprehensible doctrinaire crap of the original. It hardly mattered. The papers we submitted were never read; they could have been pages from Dostoevski or Peter the Great for all the administration knew. All they wanted was so many pages in your handwriting. When we gathered for "discussion" we had to read aloud certain pages from the work under study and then, if you had a young, gung-ho party leader who really believed in the system, you simply had to put up with an hour of readings and dry analysis and try to keep awake. Fortunately we had a very knowing leader for a couple of years. He would say, "Now, Comrades, today we are going to examine the following fourteen pages. But since I know that you are all very well-read and politically sophisticated and intelligent people, I will just go over the headings with you, and a few representative paragraphs, and then you will be free for advanced reading during the rest of the period."

We would get through the fourteen pages in a few minutes and then he would release us early. There was one stubborn old party member who wanted to read the entire chapter out loud whenever it was her turn. She could not pronounce the words of foreign origin; she was scarcely literate but terribly enthusiastic. Our instructor would admonish her: "Now, Comrade, that is very good, really very good, but you know, we are all very knowledgeable here. These comrades have read these works many times. They almost know them by heart, so I really think we can stop there!"

It was routine. Every official is afraid for his position. If he does not go through the motions, someone will report him. The political supervisor or party secretary has to be able to report that the enrollment in the political indoctrination (volunteer) classes is 100 per cent. This is of course impossible in a volunteer class, yet it is achieved everywhere. *Tufta*. That's it. The whole of life in the system is *tufta*. Back in camp, whenever a prisoner died of typhus or some other disease that had been "eradicated" twenty years earlier in the Soviet Union, we were instructed to indicate heart disease, or any other noncommunicable disease, as the cause of death. Those contagious diseases, which killed so many, had not been officially reported in the Soviet Union for decades. Many physicians and feldshers told me later that this was normal in civilian medical practice too. In those days, if some innocent and truthful physician reported the outbreak of

several cases of cholera, say, he would get hell from the supervising health
unit and an instruction to change the report because Don't you know that
we don't have any such epidemic diseases anymore?

In 1964 I met my wife Irene. We married in 1965 and our son Andrew
was born within the year. George Tenno was with us on all the great
occasions, sad and happy, of our lives. Irene soon came to love and admire
him as much as I. He was still planning spectacular escapes. In the summer
of 1968 he went on a trip to Estonia to pick up two handguns from friends
in the underground there. He never got to Estonia. On the way he became
violently ill. He was flown back to Moscow. Through friends in the
ministry I arranged for him to be seen by top specialists. They made an
exploratory operation. He had scirrhous cancer that had metastasized
wildly. He died in one month. He was fifty-six.

All my best friends died. But at least I now had Irene, and a fine son of
my own. And there was someone else who was to supply the last great
turning point of my life—my sister, Stella. We had been in correspondence
since my release, correspondence of the kind in which you safely say I am
fine how are you, and not much more. What I had not known was that
Stella had been slowly and determinedly badgering everyone she could get
to listen to her, trying to convince them that her brother, a foreign service
employee of the United States government, was alive and well and somehow forcibly detained in Moscow, and that it was time the United States
government did something about that. The time had not come yet, but it
was on its way.

CHAPTER

29

MY SISTER STELLA MARRIED A BRITISH SUBJECT, A MEMBER OF THE ROYAL
Air Force, in Moscow, in 1942. She had met him at the British Military
Mission, where she worked during the war. The wedding reception early in
the afternoon was a lot more cheerful than it would have been if anyone
there had known what the late afternoon would bring. By six thirty Soviet
authorities had put her new husband on a train for Murmansk to meet a boat
for England. In their view, Stella was a Soviet citizen, and marriages
between Soviets and foreigners were just not acceptable.

The reason they looked on Stella as a Soviet was this. When she reached her sixteenth birthday, the only way she could get a ration card was to have a Soviet passport, and the only way to get a Soviet passport was to turn in her American passport. I had avoided this trap by getting a job at the United States Embassy; for Stella the alternative would have been to starve.

In the years following that interrupted wedding party, Stella made five formal applications to leave the Soviet Union in order to join her husband. They were all turned down. Then in 1946, at a Kremlin reception, the British ambassador, Sir Archibald Clarke-Kerr, made a personal appeal to Stalin on her behalf and in a couple of days it was all arranged. That was how things were made to happen in the Soviet Union in those days. It was practically the only way. If similarly high-level appeals had been made on my behalf at the very beginning, it is likely I would have been spared the ordeals of Lefortovo and Sukhanovka, but all that was done for me by the U.S. Embassy then was a couple of letters of protest, one of which Sidorov had shaken maliciously in my face.

When Stella arrived in England in 1946, it was to meet a husband she scarcely knew. Too much time had passed. Nothing was the same anymore. Without rancor they agreed to separate and in November of 1946 Stella left for New York, where she became an interpreter at the fledgling United Nations. At least once a month she wrote me and I always wrote back, usually pretty punctually.

And so when she heard nothing from me at Christmas in 1948 she was puzzled. But at first she was more annoyed than worried. I was a bit harum-scarum, self-centered and forgetful. She assumed that I must have taken a Christmas trip or just neglected to tell her about it. The first person she heard from about what really had happened was Mary Catto.

When I failed to show up for our date to see *Prince Igor* at the Bolshoi, on that Monday night, December 13, 1948, Mary believed at first that she had been stood up. She had no way of knowing that I was pacing up and down in a stuffy box at the Lubyanka, and I guess she hadn't taken seriously my romantic stuff about a mission and would she wait for me and all that. So it was several days before she decided to contact the embassy to find out what was going on. She was told curtly and officially that I had disappeared, and then someone had the kindness to tell her privately that it was feared I had been arrested by the Soviet authorities, but that she should not jump to any conclusions because there was no confirmation. Mary wrote about all this to Stella, who by then had gone to Paris with the U.N. General Assembly. When she got back to New York she set about trying to get the State Department to do something about my case and trying to get some information about my whereabouts and well-being—or otherwise.

State was no help. They admitted they knew little about me. They surmised I was in prison somewhere. They said that relations between the United States and Russia were so touchy just then that if any approach were made on my behalf I might be shot. The State Department's Richard H. Davis, who had known me in Moscow and was back in Washington, even phoned our cousin Marie Jackson and told her in a way that was fraught with frightening implications that on no account should there be any public outcry or any attempts by the family to get publicity. The family were all frightened and of course they shut up, although Stella did not stop trying.

The truth is, relations between the U.S. and the USSR *were* very touchy at that time. The cold war had become a grim reality. The vast majority of Americans were nervous about Communist spies, as Senator Joseph McCarthy and his witch-hunting kindred spirits virtually took over the American political conscience for so many years. In the Soviet Union Stalin had initiated a new wave of terror. Suspicion spread its tentacles into every aspect of relations between the two countries. So although Stella was a tough-minded girl, she was young and she was a bit new at being back in America, and inclined to do what she was told by important officials.

However, she sought advice wherever she could get it. Our cousin Stephanie Hazak worked in Washington as an assistant and private secretary to the Secretary of the Air Force. She arranged numerous interviews for Stella. Few were sympathetic in any practical sense. One exception was old Senator Langer from South Dakota, and when he said that there was really no way he could do anything without making a public stink, Stella burst into tears. The old man hugged her sadly and tried to comfort her, but his hands were tied by this notion that publicity in the case could only harm me. Even my former boss, Bedell Smith, had absolutely nothing helpful to offer.

For nearly three years Stella got nowhere at all and was nearly in despair. Then came news. Incomplete, alarming, and yet news all the same. It came in a strange way.

During those trips by Stolypin car between Moscow and Dzhezkazgan in 1950, at every stop the prisoners exchanged information with other prisoners going in the opposite direction, hoping that sometime a message might make its way to relatives or friends. I never really believed these exchanges would lead to much, but one kind German, whom I do not remember at all but I bless him anyway, managed in 1951 to report to Stella that he had met me en route, and that I was in a forced labor camp in Central Asia. That was all, and it was not very good news, but to Stella it meant that at least I was alive, and it revitalized her determination to do something for me.

But still the people at State, and the people she saw every day at the United Nations—among them Eleanor Roosevelt—told her that the risk of raising an outcry was that I would be shot.

By this time my mother had received my triangle letter from Kuibyshev, had gone to the embassy in Moscow with it, and had been picked up by the MGB. Now Stella's regular letters to our mother received no reply, and after a while the letters themselves, and even the monthly money orders Stella sent, began to come back to New York marked NO LONGER AT THIS ADDRESS. That was all.

If Stella guessed at the reality behind this cryptic notation, she must have suppressed it; when I told her the truth years later she was so shocked she was almost incoherent for several hours.

It was not until 1955 that she would hear from Mother again. Her letter was written in such a shaky handwriting and its composition was so strange that Stella knew something was wrong and assumed that Mother must have been very ill. The letter said only that I was in Central Asia, and that I needed fats, and asked if Stella could send some food. Stella immediately sent off a parcel to Mother. That was the parcel, miraculously forwarded to me in Dzhezkazgan, with butter and bacon and Maxwell House coffee and Chesterfield cigarettes in it.

And then, in 1956, came the first glimmer of good news, and it made Stella's heart leap. It was a letter from the State Department:

Your brother has visited the Embassy in the company of an officer of the KGB. He seemed in excellent health. When asked if he needed help he said that he did not. Embassy officials at his request gave him moneys due to him under the retirement savings plan.

Or words to that effect.

Well, if anyone at the embassy asked me whether I needed help, he must have spoken in a very low voice; I never heard it. In any case, Stella asked the State Department once again what they could do for me, now that I was safely out of prison camp. They told her to wait. They said there was nothing they could do until I made some sort of approach. Stella did not believe this. She guessed accurately that I was in no position to make an approach. By now we were in correspondence. Of course I had to be careful. I would never have tried code and I was even reluctant to make reference to common experiences in order to convey a hidden message. I knew that my mail was given the most intense scrutiny in the "black chambers," and that any attempt to tell her the truth of my situation would be risky. I confined myself to saying that I had a good job as a senior editor, that I saw Mother frequently in the hospital and was able to visit Father from time to time, and that the weather was fine.

Stella had no way of knowing whether I wanted help or not. On the surface it looked as though I might not. She wrote back diligently and waited for a sign.

During this time I was examining the possibilities of escape, of course, and going over plans with George Tenno. I assumed that if I was ever to get out it would be through my own efforts, and so in a sense there was nothing I could talk about. I gave no sign.

Stella remarried. Her new husband was a charming, energetic official of the United Nations. They moved to Vienna. Soon her time and imagination were understandably caught up in the excitement of her own new life. I gave no indication in my letters that anything was amiss with me, and until the middle sixties Stella was able to allow herself to be almost completely occupied with the excitement and turmoil of motherhood. She was raising two brainy boys in a lively city. Occasionally she traveled through the other Western European capitals with her husband, and every two years they spent a few weeks in New York.

She had of course contemplated getting on a train to Moscow with a tourist visa and coming to see me. Just like that. That is Stella's way. But she is careful, too. And when she sought advice about this, from United Nations and American officials, the advice was unanimous: because she had left the Soviet Union with a Soviet passport, she would still be a Soviet citizen in their eyes. If she went, she risked never coming back again. I had seen plenty of cases of just that kind of thing in camp, and I might well have given her the same advice, although I was dying to see her.

I showed all her letters to Mother. Mother would gaze at them and hand them back. "That is not Stella," she would say, pointing at photographs of the family Stella had sent me. "No, these are not Stella's children. This is all a plot of the KGB. You see, I understand it all very clearly now."

To the end of her life, she never accepted Stella's children as a reality, and she never believed I was in communication with my sister. When my Andrew was born, in 1965, I brought him to the hospital, and my mother was enchanted and accepted him completely. She was terribly proud of this grandson she could actually see; she simply did not believe in the existence of my nephews in Vienna.

Stella also believed in my son; it seemed on the surface further evidence that I was settling into a permanent life in Moscow. But in 1966, a cousin of her husband's traveled to Moscow on an official visit and was courageous and kind enough to come and see me and Irene and the baby in the apartment on Lilac Boulevard. I was so excited I was nearly indiscreet. But I turned up the radio full blast, moved close to this first flesh-and-blood envoy, and told him in no uncertain terms that I was counting on Stella. That she had to do something to get us out of the Soviet Union. That if there was any way possible for her to come and visit, please to try as soon as possible. I was very urgent about it. When the cousin went back to Vienna he told Stella that if she did not come to see me I would be broken-hearted, and so she started trying to figure a way to do it safely. But a lot of time was to pass before she made it. Too much time. In the winter of 1967 my mother was taken to the hospital bathhouse in her underclothes, caught a chill, developed pneumonia, and died. We buried her on a cold, cold day. George Tenno stood with us at the ceremony. I felt a deep bereavement; despite the madness of those last years, my mother had been an emotional anchor for me, and my visits had been a vital connection with my past. And something had convinced me that she would see Stella again soon, and that their meeting would be the beginning of the homeward trip somehow. Now that was gone. I did not dare write Stella the full story of the circumstances that had wrecked my mother's life.

Early in 1968 I got a letter that made my hands shake with excitement. Stella was coming to Moscow. Her husband was to make an official visit on United Nations business. She would travel with him, with diplomatic immunity. We would see each other at last. I was too busy at work to get down to Istra to tell Father, but I wrote him immediately and he wrote back that he was thrilled and would come up to Moscow in time for the visit. He never made it. He choked on a piece of meat and suffocated. Stella's visit was planned for August; I buried my father in March.

Stella and her husband arrived in Moscow by train, via Poland, on August 18, 1968, a Sunday. I got a call at the apartment at eleven thirty in the morning. Her voice was steady and cheerful and confident and yet very excited at the same time. "Alex, dear; we are just washing up at the hotel. We'll be over to see you shortly in a taxi."

I could hardly stand the wait. I strode up and down in the apartment until Irene thought she would go crazy. Two steps, a half-step sideways, two steps back. Hands behind my back. The old Sukhanovka habit. I still do it when I am anxious about something.

We kept watching out the window. Finally Irene, standing at the window with Andrew, said, "Here's a taxi!"

Two surprisingly fat people in European clothes got out. I could hardly believe that one of them was my sister, although it looked like Stella. Soon there was a knock on the apartment door. I opened it. It was Stella, very fat. But for a long time I forgot about that because it was hugging and tears and laughter.

Then we sat down. "Tell me everything!" Stella said. I was horrified, and made warning signs with my hands and eyebrows, while saying, "Of course, of course." Then I said, "Stella, dear, you've put on a bit of weight," very shyly. There was a roar of laughter from both of them. They began to undress. Irene was embarrassed for a moment. Then we realized that they were both wearing two sets of American clothes over their own clothes. They brought these suits and dresses as gifts, but officials had warned them that if they were seen coming to the apartment with a suitcase full of clothes, we might be accused of speculating on the black market. The only thing they carried openly was a plastic Lego game for Andrew.

Stella and I could hardly stop grinning at each other. To create a little security I put a pillow over the telephone and turned the radio and television up to full volume. Then I told my sister what had happened over the last twenty years. Twenty years! A lifetime of experience to recount in two days, and most of it a tale of the most appalling events. Stella was bold and strong and had guessed at some of what I had to tell her, but she was not prepared for the full magnitude. The waves of emotion that swept over her were visible, physical waves. And I could not stop until she knew the full outline of those two terrible decades. Stella's fiber did not weaken until I told her how our mother, whom she adored, had been tortured and gone insane. That was too much. In the end it was the story of our mother that filled her mind with nightmare images, she said, to the point where the full impact of what had happened to me was submerged under her grief for Mother.

The most important subject, the immediate future, we saved for a more secure location than the apartment on Lilac Boulevard. We visited Mother's grave. When we were perfectly sure there was no one in sight, Stella said, "All right. Tell me. Do you want to get out?"

"Do I want out!" I said. "Listen, Stella. I would walk out of here naked, backwards, on my hands and knees if that was the only way to do it. I've *got* to get out! But I've got to be careful. I've got to get Irene and Andrew out with me because they'll never be safe if I leave them behind. And it may be possible, the way things are going, for me to get a tourist visa to Yugoslavia and simply not return. The essential thing is to find ways to let each other know what's going on, and that probably means personal visits, and that means it's going to take time. But we can't take any risk of blowing everything up, do you understand?"

"I understand," she said firmly. She hugged me very hard. "I'm not going to let anyone forget you any longer," she said. I knew she meant it, and for the first time I began to believe that I would really see my home again, and soon.

When Stella got back to Vienna she wrote a personal appeal to President Lyndon Johnson. The reply she got from the State Department made her furious.

Mr. Dolgun is one of an unfortunate number of dual nationals [it said] who desire to visit their relatives abroad.

There was not much hope, the letter said flatly.

Stella did not agree. She wrote a registered letter to Averell Harriman describing the case in detail. Harriman had, after all, been ambassador to Moscow and was said to be well liked by the Russians. If Ambassador Clarke-Kerr had been able to get her out in 1946 by personal intervention, maybe Harriman was her best hope to spring me.

Harriman did not reply until November.

Unfortunately your brother's case is similar to that of a number of other dual nationals in the Soviet Union. Since the Soviets continue to regard your brother as a Soviet citizen under their law, any further representations by the U.S. Government on his behalf would probably be no more successful than they have been in the past.

Now Stella was hopping mad. She knew I was no "dual national." I had been born in the States. I was on the foreign service staff when I was kidnapped. And as for those so-called representations on my behalf, she thought bitterly, is that what they call a letter of protest in 1948 and then not one finger lifted since?

She wrote Richard H. Davis, my former colleague at the embassy, who was now ambassador to Rumania. He answered that the whole thing seemed hopeless to him. Stella kept badgering the State Department. She confronted them with the truth about my citizenship and my foreign service status. At first there was no indication at all of help. Now there was a new administration in Washington, however: Richard Nixon had been elected. Once again she wrote a personal appeal to the top man, to this man who had promised so much in the field of international affairs. Her letter was never answered.

In January, after Stella had sent a virtual snowstorm of letters to the State Department, she got a faint glimmer of hope in one reply: a suggestion. Alex should apply for an exit visa and work through normal channels, the official suggested, and added, "It is difficult, of course, to be optimistic in this connection."

Not for Stella. She might get angry, but her optimism was not going to be dampened now. She kept up the paper bombardment to everyone she could think of, and she got my aunt in New Jersey to send me a formal invitation to visit her. The letter came in both Russian and English and contained a signed undertaking to assume all the costs of both my transportation and my living expenses "while in the United States."

Armed with this paper, which would at least demonstrate that I intended to visit a genuine relative and would undercut any arguments based on the regulations, I decided to take the plunge and risk making an application on my own.

The first thing was to get a "character reference" from my bosses at the publishing house. Whenever anyone in the Soviet Union wants to travel outside the country, the state places on the shoulders of his employer a large part of the responsibility for ensuring that the traveler will come back. The employer must send a character reference. This is in reality nothing more than an estimate by the employer as to whether or not the traveler will return. If the employer recommends the applicant for travel abroad, and the traveler subsequently jumps ship, then there will be a very rough time for the employer. So such character references are not given out lightly.

In my case it was not given at all. Rather, they sent the character reference, all right; that was mandatory. But it concluded that I was "not recommended for travel abroad." I guess they knew which way my toes were pointed. In any case, my application was rejected.

So I applied again, this time for permission to visit my sister in Vienna. A trip to Austria would, I reasoned, seem less politically complicated than one to the U. S., and besides I thought that an appeal to visit my full sister would carry more weight than one to visit an aunt.

I waited eight months. In the meantime, at Stella's end, her unceasing efforts with the pen were at least beginning to get some humane replies, and in February of 1969 a letter from the U.S. consul in Vienna indicated that action might have begun. What the nature of that action was the consul did not disclose, but the letter did say that ". . . we hope that with persistence and steady effort the Soviet authorities can be convinced to grant your brother exit permission."

Did that mean persistence on my part? On their part? Did it mean anything? Stella was not sure, but at least for the first time someone in Official America was saying something that had a positive note.

The reply to my request for a visa to Austria was answered by a telephone call from a woman named Ivanova of the visa department.

"In respect to your visa application, Comrade Doldzhin, you are rejected."

"Well," I said, "I would like to know the reason."

"No reason is given."

I said testily, "Under the law you are required to state the reason!"

"Yes. The reason is that you are attempting to visit a distant relative. Only visits to close relatives can be approved."

I barked into the telephone!

"I beg your pardon, Comrade Doldzhin?"

"Did you say 'distant relative'? The application was for a visa to visit my *sister*!"

There was a pause. Then she said, "I see. Please wait a moment. I'll have to check."

It was considerably more than a moment. I was getting madder and madder as I waited. Finally she came back to the phone.

"Well, I have checked, and you are right. But it does not matter. You're still rejected. You will have to wait one year before you can reapply."

Before I could expostulate anymore she hung up.

In September of 1969, Senator Hugh Scott of Pennsylvania, whom Stella had approached through a friend, wrote that State was still claiming I had dual citizenship. If they thought that was going to slow Stella down they had another think coming. She simply increased her badgering efforts.

She sent a Pakistani friend to see me. He was in Moscow on U.N. business, and diplomatically protected. We met in a hotel bar, and of course we were watched. I indicated to him that nothing important should be said in the hotel, and I knew that if we spent much time together outside it would look bad. We sauntered to the front door of the Rossiya like the most casual acquaintances. As we went down the steps I said in a fast whisper, "Let Stella know that I am making applications through proper channels and they're throwing a lot of roadblocks. I'll keep trying. So should she."

He said, "She'd like a formal indication from you if you want her to step up her efforts. She'll send you a tie. If you feel the time is okay to pull out the stops, write that you like the tie. If you think she needs to coast, tell her it doesn't suit." He saluted with his newspaper and walked off into the night. We had not talked for sixty seconds. I was not harassed by the police.

A month later a gaudy tie arrived. I wrote Stella that I loved it.

And now, as Stella's nonstop campaign increased in intensity, there were signs that the long-dead machinery of State was beginning to stir. "We're trying to move this case off dead-center," wrote one official.

"Good," Stella said to herself, and wrote more letters.

Finally, in December 1970, a breakthrough. A letter from State admitted that my case was *unique*, as Stella had maintained from the beginning. No more of this "one of a number of dual nationals" stuff.

But Stella was fed up with the letters going back and forth, and she decided to personally approach some high U.S. official. Ambassador John P. Humes had arrived in Vienna, a Nixon appointee. Since he had a political appointment and was not a career diplomat, Humes probably had fewer fetters than anyone she had approached yet. He gave her a personal interview, listened in awe as she told my story, and said when he had heard it all that he was "outraged." "We'll do something about this," he said. Evidently he meant it. He promised Stella he would pursue the case at the highest levels. He urged her to let him know about any new developments. Within a few weeks he told her that he had arranged to talk with Secretary of State William P. Rogers, and that he would urge Rogers to take the matter up with the top Soviet leaders. He also told Stella to get word to me that I should apply for a permanent exit visa. Ambassador Humes was shrewd and well advised. He knew that to move the Soviets now I would have to appear very serious and very bold.

The *treugolnik* at the publishing house were dumfounded when I told them why I wanted a new character reference. They stalled, of course, in true bureaucratic style. I called every week. They kept stalling. Finally they tried a very strange strategy. I had an interview with the director of the publishing house, Mayevsky.

He said, "Look, none of us can understand why you would want to leave the Soviet Union, but since you seem to be so determined, we will of course give you a character reference. All you have to do is take a medical examination, to show that you are physically fit."

I was so eager to get on with it that I did not even ask what difference it made to my character whether I was healthy or not. Mayevsky offered to send his own car to take me to the doctor. Seemed generous to me. I accepted. The next thing I knew we were pulling up in front of the State Asylum for the Mentally Ill beside the Red Army theater. I thought, That's a funny place to go for a medical examination.

I was right. They kept me for three weeks. All I got in the way of an examination was regular blood pressure readings. The chief psychiatrist, when I asked what the hell was going on, simply said that the *treugolnik* had asked her to keep me under observation for a while. I was able to have my work brought to the hospital. The hospital was mostly filled with dissidents, not madmen: naïve guys who had reported on a corrupt *treugolnik*, for example. I began to guess at the pattern. Discredit by association with an asylum.

Back at work three weeks later I reminded Mayevsky that I had fulfilled his conditions and that he had promised me my character reference. But he was not through with obstruction.

"I will issue the character reference right away," he said. "All you have to do now is bring your wife in for an interview with the *treugolnik*."

"Why?" I demanded. "She doesn't work here. You have nothing to do with her. You have no business demanding anything of her!"

He kept very cool. "Do you want the character reference or not?"

I said, "Do I have your word that you will issue it after the interview?"

"You do."

We came at five the next day. I had briefed Irene carefully. She has a very short fuse. I knew that she was dying to see these bastards and throw their own crap right back at them, so I warned her.

"Everything may depend on this. You must keep yourself in control, Irene. You *must*."

She laughed a hard little laugh she has when she is angry. Her dark lashes and her beautiful gray eyes looked very confident. "Don't worry!" she said.

And she was magnificent.

I was with her during the interview. At first they tried to get me to discuss my reasons for wanting to go to the United States.

"Why ask me? Ask your own foreign ministry—they'll tell you everything you want to know," I answered, knowing they didn't have the authority to make such a call. They gave up on me and turned to Irene.

The triangle members had all their questions prepared on pads of paper. I could tell from the set of Irene's jaw muscles that she was working awfully hard and that the fire was close to the surface, but she gave them no satisfaction. When it got really abusive, as it did, with all kinds of questions implying her lack of stability for wanting to go to such a terrible place as America, and suggestions that her fine Soviet son would end up as a gangster and probably take his own life, she just lowered her head and looked at the floor while she struggled for control.

They told her she was treacherous for not talking me out of going. She answered in monosyllables. They said millions had been spent on her education and now she was virtually stealing all those millions from the USSR by taking off for the United States. She lowered her head again. If I tried to intervene on her behalf they cut me off. They kept it up for three abusive hours, and when we finally made it out to the street, Irene said, "If you don't buy me a bottle of wine right now, I'll go crazy."

We drank two.

And then, within a surprisingly short time, they gave me an excellent character reference. A marvelous character reference! I was an excellent worker, a dedicated fire chief, a first-class translator and editor, a diligent member of my team, a good leader.

And, oh yes. "On numerous occasions he has been hospitalized in mental institutions. This person is not recommended for travel outside the Soviet Union."

This was sent to OVIR, the visa office. I never saw it. But I had good friends in the ministry who did.

I probably should have kept quiet but I could not. I sought out the official I believed responsible for drafting the reference and confronted him. "Why do you lie!" I said. "Why tell them I have been in mental institutions *on numerous occasions.*"

He waved me aside. "Listen, what's it to you whether it's once or several. We put it that way just for safety's sake!"

I applied at the visa office. The refusal was immediate. "There is simply no possibility that the United States will give you permission to go there, so forget it," they said.

By now I was a mixture of frenzy and cool. Sometimes, after another refusal or rejection or piece of highhanded effrontery like the asylum trick, my blood pressure would quite literally go right off the instrument. At other times I was philosophical, resigned to the likelihood that this would all take time, and confident that with Stella's help it would come out all right. Irene and I decided to take a holiday. In August we packed the car, took Andrew with us, and drove to the Black Sea.

September 2, 1971. We came back to the apartment refreshed and good-humored and ready to tackle bureaucracy all over again. And there was a wonderful piece of paper in the mail. A letter from the Embassy of the United States of America, Moscow. They wanted to see me regarding departure from the Soviet Union. They had been informed by the Ministry of Foreign Affairs of the Soviet Union that "appropriate authorities will not impede your visit to the Embassy."

There was a copy in Russian, which I could show to guards at the embassy gates.

Unknown to me, my case had begun to move at a very high level. I would soon get direct word about it in an alarming way. In the meantime, as requested, I phoned the man who had signed the letter, Peter Swiers, the consul, and made an appointment. He said he would meet me at the gates. It was a good thing he did. They did not want to let me in. Three KGB in militia uniforms closed together to block my way. They refused to look at the letter. But the senior man had clearly been given my photograph to study, because he scrutinized my face very carefully. "Where are you from?" he said finally.

I pointed at the embassy. "There," I said. He turned and looked at Swiers standing inside. Swiers nodded. The KGB then nodded at me. "Pass," he said.

It was a marvelous feeling to be inside now, with so much promise in the air. Swiers was the most amiable young man. Before I could say anything he excused himself, wrote on a card, "Do not speak here. Bugged. Safe only in Ambassador's office."

He began the formalities of drawing up a passport. Then, when the routine paperwork was done, we went in for a long friendly talk with Ambassador Beam. When I left, I had a To-Whom-It-May-Concern letter, testifying that the United States was prepared to issue an entry visa to me and my family. It felt like a piece of pure gold.

Soon after that, I got the news that I was being dealt with at The Top. It came in a form that made me sweat. The phone rang. It was Stella, in Vienna! I could feel my blood pressure soar. I knew that my phone was listened to, and now that we seemed so close to success I could not imagine why Stella would take the slightest risk of jeopardizing what seemed to be in motion, even if it was slow motion.

But Stella knew exactly what she was doing. Ambassador Humes had briefed her. She said, very distinctly, pronouncing the Russian words with perfect clarity, "Alex, dear, I want you to know that your case is now being discussed at the highest levels on both sides!"

I nearly dropped the phone. How could she do this to me? I yelled, "Stella! Stella! What are you saying!"

She said calmly, "You have nothing to worry about. Secretary Rogers has had a personal conversation about you with Mr. Gromyko. Do you understand that?"

I could not answer. My mouth hung open. I stared at Irene across the little apartment. I suddenly saw clearly what Stella was doing.

Stella called out, "Alex? Alex?"

"I'm listening, Stella. You bet I'm listening!"

"Well, I'll say it again then. Secretary of State Rogers . . . the Secretary of State . . . of the United States . . ."

"Yes! Yes! I hear you!"

"Has personally discussed your case . . . with Mr. GRO-MY-KO!"

There was a pause.

"He has also had conversations about you with Ambassador Dobrynin. He says that these conversations have given him good reason to think the outcome will be favorable. Is that clear, dear?"

It was wonderfully clear. If there was any doubt in the minds of the KGB who monitored my phone, they would never act now without checking very carefully at the highest level. Stella would never have told me these things if they were not true. When my KGB monitors confirmed it all, they would be very careful about me from then on.

My heart raced wildly. I was dizzy. I could hardly talk to Irene. We took Andrew and went for a long walk, and when I was sure we were far away from any possible tail I told her what I thought was happening. Her eyes were like gray fire.

When I applied for our visa this time, OVIR demanded a 10 per cent deposit from each of us, against the ultimate total cost of 800 new rubles. Within about a week a postcard came advising that the visas were ready; the letter from the U.S. Embassy and the conversations at the top seemed to have done the trick. I gave silent thanks to William P. Rogers that was almost a prayer.

But my harassment was by no means over. It was kept up until the very end.

For example: To qualify for the temporary Soviet passports that we had to have in addition to the visas, we had to turn in all our papers and get a certificate showing they had been submitted. When I went to turn in my military ticket ("Untrained Soldiers. Graduate in Obstetrics and

Gynecology," etc.) I was told that they could not issue the certificate until I showed my passport.

"But I don't get my passport until I show proof I've turned in this ticket!"

"I'm sorry, Comrade. That's the rule."

"Let me see the major."

The major came. I beckoned him, very confidently, to a place in the room where we could talk confidentially. I said, "Major, I'm sure you'll understand. I'm going abroad, to the United States in fact, on uh . . ." I looked furtively to make sure nobody was listening. ". . . On very important—uh—business. I'm sure you understand me?"

The major immediately caught my conspiratorial tone. He loved it. He dropped his voice and said, "Of course, Comrade. What can we do for you?"

I said, "Well, this man told me that he cannot issue the certificate for turning in my military ticket. And I'm just not sure how I could explain to the Ministry of Foreign Affairs that the military are placing obstacles in the way of this mission. It could get very . . . Well, I'm sure you understand the need to keep things very . . . uh . . . You understand?"

The major was marvelous. "Don't you worry about this at all, Comrade. I'll sign for your ticket on my own recognizance."

And he did so forthwith.

When I went to the United States Embassy with the Soviet passports, to confirm officially that we would be able to leave, the "militia" KGB at the gate tried to take me away to lock me in their little holding booth and might have done so if Swiers had not yelled and screamed and pulled at the man's arm. They hate a scene.

In the meantime, in Vienna, totally unknown to me, of course, Stella's impatience was almost running over. She simply could not believe, after the Rogers intervention, that there would be any more delay. She concocted an elaborate plan to "kidnap" me, by coming to Moscow, dressing me and my family in the latest American clothes so we would look like Americans, driving us to the embassy, where she would show her own passport and demand admission. Then, if there was any obstacle, she would have a photographer in the street opposite taking pictures of the scuffle or the capture or whatever happened, and three corresondents from major Western publications standing by with the story ready to blow if we weren't all immediately released. If we were allowed in we would immediately claim asylum. It was a bold, crazy, wonderful, Stella-like plan. But when she warned Ambassador Humes that she was contemplating "independent action," he begged her not "to sabotage what was already under way," and finally persuaded her that the end was very close.

It was. I took my family to the embassy early in December to claim my American passport. In fact the embassy kept it for me until the end, for safekeeping. Peter Swiers took us to the ticket office to buy our Air Austria passage to Vienna, and our Pan Am tickets to New York. The Air Austria flight was chosen because there were too many stories of someone with an exit visa going off on an Aeroflot plane which made an unscheduled stop in Leningrad, and the would-be émigré was never seen again.

December 13 passed, and it was twenty-three years since I had gone for that walk down Gorky Street, with the clock on the telegraph office that will forever in my mind say ten past one. Sleep was almost impossible. Friends were kissed farewell in a whirl of faces and promises. The refrigerator to give away, the books, the letters and photographs for Irene's mother, the old guitar I had not played for so many years. And finally the apartment on Lilac Boulevard was stripped of everything to do with me, and the door was closed for the last time. December 21, 1971. Peter Swiers took us to the airport. And still the tenacious bastards were not through making trouble.

The KGB at passport control looked at our visas.

"No, these are not in order," he said firmly. He pointed to their small airport interrogation room. "You will have to step in here," he said authoritatively. "It's nothing, I'm sure. It will only take five minutes. Don't worry."

Don't worry! I had heard that before. I was almost paralyzed. I looked at Swiers in panic. Swiers knew exactly what to do. He vaulted over the counter like an Olympic athlete and started yelling at the KGB.

"What's the matter with these papers!" Swiers yelled. "I am a representative of the United States Government and I demand to know WHAT YOU THINK IS WRONG WITH THESE PAPERS!"

"Please! Please!" the KGB said in a loud whisper. "Please lower your voice!"

"I WILL NOT LOWER MY VOICE UNTIL YOU EXPLAIN!"

The KGB was red with consternation. "Look, look," he whispered lamely. "Her visa is not the same as his."

"Of course they're different!" Swiers roared, only a little more temperately. "She is a Soviet citizen and he is an American. Of course their papers are different. Read them, man!"

The KGB was utterly cowed. "Of course, of course," he said mildly. "Yes, of course, of course." And he waved us through.

I could hardly see. This seemed, somehow, after all the terrors and so much time, to have been the narrowest escape of all. Everything in a blur now. Blurred images of kind, handsome girls moving around us in the airplane, offering food and drinks and coffee in fluent Russian and English, with German accents. Blurred runway slipping past. Blurred rooftops. Ground falling away.

Roads leading away from Moscow. Roads I had walked so often in the corridors of Lefortovo, in the cell at Sukhanovka, roads to freedom, blurring now, too far down to make out clearly, roads to freedom blending with white snow and black forest lands, and the unfamiliar rumble and whine of jet engines and the kind hands bringing drinks and coffee, and Irene, tears in her eyes, singing softly to herself to keep her courage up lest the plane crash after all.

Schwechat International Airport, Vienna. Stella, her husband. Tears and laughter. A sea of grinning, warm, strange faces. The strong, welcoming hand of John P. Humes. A big grin. A warm welcome.

Christmas in freedom, with my indefatigable sister, in Vienna, the city of music.

The wonderful, inexhaustible kindness of Ambassador Humes, who had even arranged a *per diem* for us throughout our stay in Vienna, and in New York until we got settled, and who personally arranged to have our tourist-class tickets home exchanged for first-class. The one diplomat who would not accept the idea of my being one-of-a-number. The one who made it happen.

And then that brilliant day in January when we climbed aboard a Boeing 707, an American airplane, bearing the big blue Pan Am globe, which I had never seen before.

Painted on the nose of the airplane, the name *Great Hopes*.

An ocean underneath us. The ocean whose floor I walked in my imagination, beating my way home to America, how long ago? Where was it exactly that I left the coast of Spain in my mind and walked into the sea and under the waves and kept on going west? How many more paces today? Fifty-three hundred? How many kilometers? Force yourself to think, Alex! Do the arithmetic. *Pardon me, boy, is that the Chattanooga Choo-Choo?*

Irene gripping my arm suddenly and pointing. Skyline growing out of the clouds, as familiar as all the landscapes in my memory, although it is thirty-eight years since I saw it slip down out of sight behind the stern rail of a ship whose name I can't remember.

John F. Kennedy International Airport. *Everyone is speaking English!* My cousins are all there. My mother's favorite sister, Tessie! I see all their faces in a blur. Before we climb in the car I look back at the sky toward the east. There are faces there, too. Dear faces. If they could have come to share this . . .

George Tenno, most of all.

Mother. Father.

Pavel Voronkin and Victor S. and Galya and Adarich and good Nye Russki. Zoya Tumilovich. Arkadi.

Gertrude.

Arvid Atsinch. Who said when I last saw him, "Whatever you do, write about us. Tell the world about us. People have to know."

I promised I would.

A Note on the Type

The text of this book was set on the Linotype in Janson,
a recutting made direct from type cast from matrices long
thought to have been made by the Dutchman Anton Janson,
who was a practicing type founder in Leipzig during the
years 1668–87. However, it has been conclusively demonstrated
that these types are actually the work of Nicholas
Kis (1650–1702), a Hungarian, who most probably learned
his trade from the master Dutch type founder Dirk Voskens.
The type is an excellent example of the influential and
sturdy Dutch types that prevailed in England up to the
time William Caslon developed his own incomparable designs
from them.

*Composed by Maryland Linotype Composition Co.,
Baltimore, Md. Printed and bound by The
Haddon Craftsmen, Scranton, Pa. Typography
and binding design by Virginia Tan.*